P9-DDX-239

9201   00 285694 01 0   (IC=1)
DRAKE'S INTERNATIONAL COOKBOOK
(1) [1974 0641.59DRAK

q641.59 Drak
Drake's international recipe
cookbook

DATE DUE			11994
APR 0 6 2001			5
APR 2 6 2002			895
OCT 1 7 2008			97
			87
			2000

DISCARD

MAR 7 1975

VESTAL PUBLIC LIBRARY

0 00 10 0109857 1

VESTAL PUBLIC LIBRARY
Vestal, New York 13850

Drake's International Recipe Cookbook

Drake Publishers
New York

Published in 1974 by
Drake Publishers Inc.
381 Park Avenue South
New York, New York 10016

Copyright © 1974 by Meijer Pers B.V., Amsterdam, the Netherlands

Editorial and Production Services by Gadd/Videoaids

ISBN 0-87749-617-X
LCCCN 73-18873

Printed and Bound by
Gráfica Editora Primor S.A.
Rio de Janeiro - GB - Brazil

Paper: Suzano-Feffer Group

CONTENTS

I Hors D'oeuvres and Appetizers

II Soups

III Pasta, Noodles, and Rice

IV Egg and Cheese

V Fish and Seafood

VI Meats

VII Poultry and Game

VIII Vegetables

IX Sauces

X Desserts

Index

HORS D'OEUVRES & APPETIZERS

Scotch eggs

8 servings

- 1 pound sausage meat
- ½ teaspoon sage
- 2 tablespoons finely chopped parsley
- ½ teaspoon thyme
- 8 hard boiled eggs
- ½ cup flour seasoned with
- ½ teaspoon salt
  Freshly ground black pepper
- 2 eggs, lightly beaten
- 1 cup fine breadcrumbs

Combine sausage meat, sage, parsley and thyme. Pat mixture into 8 rounds. Surround each hard boiled egg with a sausage pattie. Roll the eggs in the seasoned flour, then in the beaten eggs and finally in the breadcrumbs. Fry in deep hot fat 10 minutes until the sausage is cooked. Serve hot or cold.

Welsh rarebit (rabbit)

Cheese toasts

2 servings

- 1 cup Cheddar cheese (grated)
- 3 tablespoons milk
- 2 tablespoons butter
- ¼ teaspoon salt
  Freshly ground black pepper
- 1 teaspoon prepared (Dijon type) mustard
- 2 slices toast, freshly made

Place the cheese and milk in a saucepan. Stir over low heat until the cheese melts. Add butter, salt, pepper and mustard. Stir until butter melts. Spoon the mixture on the toast and brown under the broiler for 2 minutes until lightly browned.
Note: Beer can be substituted for the milk in this recipe. The mixture may also be enriched with an egg yolk.

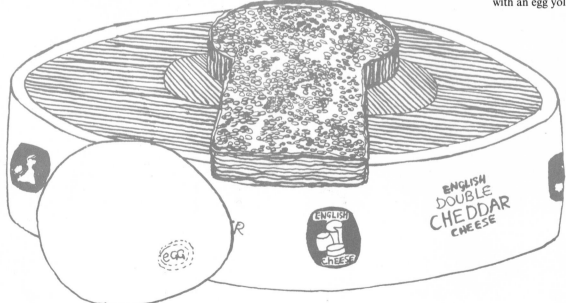

Devils on horseback

Angels on horseback

6 servings

> 12 large dried prunes or 12
>   black plums
> ½ cup red wine
> 1 bay leaf

Stuffing:
> a. *12 anchovy fillets, curled*
>   *round 12 almonds*
> b. *12 teaspoons chutney,*
>   *chopped*
> c. *12 pimiento stuffed olives*
> 6 *thin slices bacon*
>   *Watercress or parsley for*
>   *garnish*

Place prunes or plums in a saucepan. Add wine and bay leaf. Simmer over low heat for 20 minutes until just tender. Cool prunes in the wine and remove pits. Fill each prune with one of the stuffings. Wrap ½ a bacon slice round each prune and secure with a toothpick. Place in a small baking dish. Heat in a 400° oven for 10 minutes until bacon is crisp. Drain on paper towels. Place on a serving dish and garnish with watercress or parsley.

Note: Devils on horseback may be served on small squares of hot buttered toast.

4 servings

> 8 *fresh oysters*
> 4 *thin slices bacon*
> 2 *slices hot buttered toast,*
>   *each cut into 4 squares*

Simmer the oysters in their own liquor over low heat for 4 minutes. Drain and wrap each oyster in half a slice of bacon. Secure bacon with tooth picks. Place under a hot broiler or grill over charcoal until bacon is crisp. Serve on squares of hot buttered toast.

Gefüllte kalte Eier

Gerollte Eierspeise

Böhmer Eierspeise

Filled eggs

4 servings

Aspic:

  1 *(15 ounce) can chicken broth*
  1 *egg white, lightly beaten*
      Shell of 1 egg
  1 *package unflavored gelatin*
  2 *tablespoons water*

  8 *hard boiled eggs*
  2 *gherkins, finely chopped*
½ *cup finely chopped ham*
  2 *teaspoons chopped capers*
½ *teaspoon tomato paste*
½ *teaspoon prepared mustard*
1½ *tablespoons mayonnaise*
      Few drops Worcestershire sauce
¼ *teaspoon salt*
      Freshly ground black pepper
  2 *tablespoons chopped chives*

To prepare the aspic, combine the broth, egg white and egg shell in a saucepan. Beating vigorously with a wire whisk, bring the mixture to a boil. Stop beating, lower the heat and simmer 10 minutes. Carefully strain the broth through several layers of cheesecloth into a bowl. Sprinkle the gelatin over the water to soften. Add the gelatin to the warm broth, stirring to dissolve. Chill the aspic while preparing the eggs. Cut the eggs in half. Remove the yolks and place in a bowl with all the remaining ingredients except the chives. Combine thoroughly and stuff the egg whites with the mixture. Sandwich the egg halves together and arrange on a serving dish. When the aspic is syrupy, spoon a thin layer over the eggs and chill them. When the first layer is set, spoon more aspic over the eggs. Repeat several times more. Sprinkle the chives over the eggs and serve.

Rolled eggs

4 servings

¾ *cup breadcrumbs*
½ *cup milk*
  2 *cups minced chicken or veal*
  1 *cup minced ham*
¾ *teaspoon salt*
      Freshly ground black pepper
  2 *egg yolks, beaten*
  4 *eggs, beaten*
  2 *tablespoons butter*

Soak the breadcrumbs in milk. Stir in the chicken, ham, salt, pepper and egg yolks. Form into a sausage-like roll 2 inches in diameter. Butter a large piece of aluminum foil. Wrap the roll in foil and steam over boiling water for 1½ hours until firm. Beat the eggs with a little salt. Heat 2 tablespoons of butter in a large skillet, pour in the eggs and prepare a flat omelette. Remove from the pan. Roll the omelette around the steamed chicken, cut into 1 inch slices and secure each slice with a toothpick. Serve hot.

Bohemian eggs

6 servings

  6 *eggs*
2½ *cups water*
1½ *tablespoons salt*
      Coarsely ground black pepper
½ *cup shredded onion skins*
  2 *teaspoons caraway seeds*

Boil the eggs gently for about 8 minutes. Rinse under cold running water. Gently tap the shells so they are evenly cracked on all sides. Place the eggs in a pan with the 2½ cups water, salt, pepper, onion skins and caraway seeds. Bring to a simmer and cook 5 minutes. Remove from the heat and let the eggs stand in the seasoned water at least 8 hours. Drain, peel and cut in half lengthwise. Serve on individual plates.

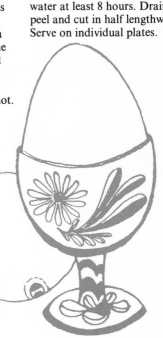

Cheese sandwiches from Solothurn Switzerland's limited agriculture is mainly suited to dairy farming, which means, of course, that Swiss cooking is full of cheese dishes.

Solothurner Käseschnitte

Cheese sandwiches from Solothurn

4 servings

  8 slices day-old white bread, crusts removed
¼ cup dry white wine
  4 tablespoons softened butter
  8 thick slices soft cheese
  1 teaspoon paprika
  1 teaspoon cumin

Brush the slices of bread on one side with wine. Spread the other side with butter. Arrange the slices, buttered side up, on a baking sheet. Place 1 slice of cheese on each piece of bread and sprikle with paprika and cumin. Bake in a 350° oven for about 10 minutes until cheese is melted.

Piquant egg dishes, either hot or cold, are always favorites in Austria. Eggs Tyrolean style.

Filled eggs

Tiroler Eierspeise

Eggs Tyrolean style

4 servings

> 4 large potatoes, cooked, peeled and sliced
> 4 hard boiled eggs, sliced
> 4 anchovies, drained and chopped
> 2 tablespoons finely chopped parsley
> ½ cup heavy cream
> ¼ teaspoon salt
> Freshly ground black pepper
> ½ cup dried breadcrumbs

Butter an ovenproof casserole and arrange ⅓ of the potato slices on the bottom. Cover with a layer of ½ the eggs and anchovies. Repeat the layers and top with the remaining potato slices. Sprinkle with 1 tablespoon parsley. Combine the cream, remaining parsley, salt and pepper and pour over the potatoes. Sprinkle the breadcrumbs on top and bake in a 350° oven for 30 minutes. Serve from the casserole.

Egg roll skins

14 skins

  2 *cups sifted all purpose flour*
½ *teaspoon salt*
  2 *eggs, lightly beaten*
1¾ *cups water*
  2 *tablespoons oil*

Sift the flour and salt into a bowl.
Make a well in the center and
add the eggs. Stir until well
blended. Add the water gradually.
Continue stirring with a
wire whisk until the batter is
smooth. Pour 1 tablespoon oil in
a heavy 8 inch skillet. Heat until
oil is hot. Tip out the excess oil,
leaving a thin film of oil in the
skillet. Pour about 2 tablespoons
of batter into the oiled skillet.
Tilt the pan in all directions to
spread the batter evenly and
thinly over the surface of the
pan. Cook over low heat for 1½
minutes until firm but not
brown. Cook on 1 side only.
Stack the pancakes on a plate
and cover with a damp cloth to
prevent them from drying out.
Brush the skillet with oil before
cooking each pancake. Let
pancakes cool completely before
filling. Egg roll skins can also be
made by the same method as
wonton wrappers (see recipe on
this page). Add only ¼ teaspoon
salt and twice as much ice-cold
water as called for in the wonton
recipe. Cut the dough into 7 to 8
inch squares.

Wonton wrappers

40 to 50 wrappers

  2 *cups all purpose flour*
  1 *teaspoon salt*
  1 *egg, lightly beaten*
  3 *to 4 tablespoons water*
    Cornstarch for dusting

Sift the flour and salt together
into a bowl. Make a well in the
center and add the egg and 2
tablespoons water. Mix until
well blended. Add the remaining
water a little at a time, using
only enough to make the dough
hold together. Knead dough
until smooth. Cover the bowl
with a damp cloth and refrigerate
45 minutes. Dust a board
lightly with cornstarch. Divide
the dough into 2 pieces and roll
out paper thin (not more than
1/16 inch). Cut dough into 3 inch
squares. Cover wrappers with a
damp cloth until you are ready
to use them.

Spring onion brushes

*Scallions (quantity as
indicated in recipe requiring
spring onion brushes)*

Wash the scallions and remove
the roots. Take a thin slice from
the white end of the scallion and
cut off enough of the green so
that you have a 2 to 2½ inch
scallion. Split the scallion in half
lengthwise about ⅓ the way up.
Split again so that you have a
crosswise cut. Spread the cut end
out a little and place scallions
in a bowl of ice water until they
have curled fringes. Drain and
use as directed.

Deep fried wontons

Stuffed mushrooms

Deep fried paper wrapped shrimp

6 to 8 American servings
6 to 8 Chinese servings

> *20 to 24 wonton wrappers*
>
> *1 double recipe wonton filling as for soup wontons*
>
> *1 recipe sweet sour sauce*
>
> *1 egg, lightly beaten*
> *Oil for deep frying*

towels and serve hot with the sweet sour sauce on the side. Wontons may first be boiled, drained, dried thoroughly and then deep fried.

Divide the filling in 20 to 24 equal portions. Place 1 wrapper in front of you with a corner pointing toward you. Put a portion of the filling just a little off center towards you on the wrapper. Brush the edges of the wrapper very lightly with beaten egg. Fold over so the corner that pointed toward you just "misses" the opposite corner by ¼ to ½ inch. Press down on the wrapper around the filling to expel the air and seal the wonton. Brush a little of the beaten egg on the top of the right hand corner and the underside of the left hand corner. Pull both corners toward each other carefully and press them together. Heat the oil for deep frying until quite hot. Add the wontons a few at a time. Reduce the heat a little and deep fry until golden brown. Turn them over once during the frying. Remove with a skimmer or slotted spoon, drain on paper

4 American servings
4 Chinese servings

> *8 large whole, undamaged Chinese dried mushrooms*
> *¾ cup (4 ounces) lean pork, minced*
> *1 whole scallion, finely chopped*
> *¼ teaspoon minced fresh ginger root*
> *1 tablespoon bamboo shoots or water chestnuts, minced*
> *½ tablespoon soy sauce*
> *½ tablespoon sherry*
> *½ teaspoon oil*
> *½ tablespoon finely chopped parsley*

Soak the dried mushrooms in hot water for 30 minutes. Squeeze mushrooms to remove excess water. Cut off mushroom stems. In a bowl, combine pork, scallion, ginger root, bamboo shoots or water chestnuts, soy sauce, sherry and oil. Mix until well blended. Place mushrooms on a flat plate stem side up. Fill mushroom caps with stuffing. Place plate in a steamer with a lid or cover with foil. Steam over simmering water for 30 minutes. Sprinkle with parsley. Serve hot as an appetizer.

4 American servings
4 Chinese servings

> *4 large shrimp*
> *¼ teaspoon salt*
> *¼ teaspoon white pepper*
> *1 clove garlic, crushed*
> *2 teaspoons sherry*
> *4 pieces of waxed paper, 8 inches square*
> *1 tablespoon oil*
> *4 thin strips of red sweet pepper*
> *1 scallion, white part only, quartered lengthwise*
> *4 thin slices fresh ginger root*
> *Oil for deep frying*
> *Shredded lettuce*
>
> *4 tomato wedges*

Shell the shrimp and take out the black vein. Mix the shrimp with salt, pepper, garlic and sherry and leave for at least 15 minutes. Toss occasionally. Drain. Rub one side of the pieces of waxed paper with the oil. Place 1 shrimp on top of each piece of paper diagonally just off center. Line with 1 pepper strip, 1 piece of scallion and 1 slice ginger. Fold the paper as illustrated in the picture. Heat oil for deep frying until hot, but not smoking (about 350 to 360°), and deep fry the shrimp for about 5 minutes. Remove with a slotted spoon and drain. Place the packages, unopened, on shredded lettuce and garnish each with a tomato wedge.

*Juicy barbequed spareribs and
crisp deep fried wontons are a
wonderful way to start a meal.*

Steamed buns

24 buns

> 1 package dry yeast
> 1 tablespoon sugar
> 1¼ cups lukewarm water
> 3½ to 4 cups flour
> 2 tablespoons oil
> 4 scallions, minced
> 1 clove garlic, crushed
> 3 cups minced roast pork
>
> 2 teaspoons sugar
> 2 tablespoons soy sauce
> 1 tablespoon sherry
> 1½ tablespoons cornstarch
>   dissolved in
> 3 tablespoons chicken broth
> 2 teaspoons red food coloring

Sprinkle yeast and sugar over ¼ cup lukewarm water and stir to dissolve. Let stand 10 minutes. Add remaining 1 cup lukewarm water and mix well. Add the flour ½ cup at a time until approximately 3 cups have been added. Turn the dough out onto a floured board and knead the dough, incorporating as much of the additional flour as is necessary to keep it from sticking to the board and your hands. Continue to knead until the dough is smooth and satiny, about 7 minutes. Place the dough in an oiled bowl, cover with a towel and let rise until doubled in bulk (1 to 2 hours depending on the warmth of your kitchen). Meanwhile prepare the filling. Heat the oil in a wok. Stir fry the scallion and garlic for 1 minute. Add the pork and stir fry until heated through. Add the sugar, soy sauce and sherry and stir to blend. Add the dissolved cornstarch and stir until thickened. Set the mixture aside to cool. Punch the dough down and knead on the floured board 3 minutes. Shape into a log about 2 inches in diameter. Cut the dough into 24 equal pieces. Roll each piece into a circle about 3 to 3½ inches in diameter. Divide the filling into 24 portions and place 1 portion in the center of each round of dough. Pull the sides of the dough up around the filling and pinch the edges together. With the palms of your hands, gently shape the buns into neat, round balls. Place on pieces of waxed paper, cover with a cloth and let rise 20 minutes. Place the buns in a steamer on their pieces of waxed paper and steam 20 minutes. or until glossy and smooth. Dip a chopstick in the red food coloring and make a dot on top of each bun. These buns may be made ahead and reheated by steaming again for a few minutes.

Egg rolls

Siu mai pork dumplings

The Chinese are fond of appetizers. They like to start off a meal with them and accordingly have developed a wonderful range of mouth-watering tidbits to be sampled before the real dinner starts. They are also lunch time favorites. Apart from the dishes listed in this book, there are thousands of others, and in China all sorts of dried nuts and seeds are also served at formal dinners. Great attention is paid to the presentation of the appetizers. This category includes a great many steamed and deep fried foods as well as cold dishes and salads. Many of the appetizers are listed under other headings such as the salads, which are to be found among the vegetable dishes; the shrimp balls, which are listed under seafood, and poultry dishes such as drunken chicken. They can be served either as appetizer or luncheon dishes. On the other hand some of them can be served as snacks in between other more elaborate dishes.

14 rolls

1 recipe egg roll skins

½ pound lean pork
¼ pound shrimp
1½ to 2 cups bean sprouts
3 tablespoons lard or oil
8 whole scallions, finely chopped
½ cup bamboo, shredded
8 water chestnuts, cut into
   ⅛ inch slices
3 thin slices ginger root, minced
½ teaspoon salt
½ tablespoon soy sauce
½ tablespoon sherry
1 egg, lightly beaten
   Oil for deep frying

Prepare the egg roll skins according to the recipe. Cut the pork across the grain in ¼ inch thick slices and then into strips. Mince the strips finely. Shell the shrimp. Remove the vein and chop shrimp into very small pieces. Rinse the bean sprouts under cold running water. Heat 2 tablespoons of the lard or oil in a wok or a skillet. Add the pork and stir fry for 1½ to 2 minutes until it turns white and loses any trace of pink. Add shrimp and stir fry for 45 seconds. Remove from the pan and add remaining tablespoon of lard or oil. Heat until hot. Add scallions, bamboo, water chestnuts and ginger root. Stir fry for 1½ minutes. Add bean sprouts and stir fry for 45 seconds. Return pork and shrimp to the pan. Add salt, soy sauce and sherry and heat through. Remove from the heat. Place in a colander to drain and cool completely. Divide the mixture into 16 parts.

Place one part slightly off the center of each skin

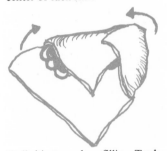

Roll skin to enclose filling. Tuck in sides neatly

Brush opposite side with beaten egg

Continue rolling egg rolls. Place them on a plate with sealed edge down. Fry the egg rolls in deep fat for 3 to 4 minutes. Turn the rolls once to brown evenly on all sides. Drain and serve hot

20 dumplings

Filling:
¾ cup lean ground pork
¼ cup minced fat pork
1 tablespoon minced bamboo
   shoots
1½ tablespoons minced water
   chestnuts
1½ tablespoons chopped
   mushrooms
1 tablespoon sherry
1 teaspoon soy sauce
⅛ teaspoon salt
⅛ teaspoon sugar
   Pinch of white pepper
1 egg white, lightly beaten

½ recipe wonton wrapper dough

Mix all of the ingredients for the filling in a bowl until well combined. Roll out the dough as described on page 20 and cut it into 3 inch rounds. Place a spoonful of the filling on each round. Gather the dough up around the filling, leaving the dough slightly open and the edges flared. Drop each dumpling on the board a few times to flatten the bottom. Place dumplings in a steamer and steam 20 to 25 minutes.

Belgische kalfspaté

Belgian veal pâté

16 servings

   2 *pounds ground veal*
 ½ *pound ground calves' liver*
   1 *small onion, finely chopped*
   1 *egg, lightly beaten*
 ½ *cup sour cream*
   2 *tablespoons finely chopped
       parsley*
   2 *teaspoons salt
       Freshly ground black pepper
       Dash of nutmeg*
   1 *tablespoon Madeira or
       sherry*
 ½ *pound thinly sliced bacon*

Mix together all the ingredients
except the bacon and beat
until thoroughly combined.
Line a pâté mold with bacon
strips and pack the veal mixture
into the mold. Cover with the
remaining bacon. Cover the
mold with aluminum foil, then
a lid. Place the pâté mold in a
larger pan and add boiling
water to come halfway up the
sides of the mold. Bake in a
preheated 350° oven for 1 hour.
When the pâté is done, remove
the lid and place a brick or
other heavy weight on the pâté.
Refrigerate overnight. Unmold
the pâté and remove the bacon.
Serve, sliced very thinly, and
arrange slices on a bed of lettuce
leaves.

Kaasstokjes

Cheese sticks

50 to 60 sticks

 1½ *cups grated Gouda cheese*
 1¾ *sticks butter, softened*
   1 *egg yolk*
 ½ *teaspoon salt*
 1½ *teaspoons Worcestershire
       sauce*
   3 *cups flour*

Combine ¾ cup cheese and all
the remaining ingredients and
mix until well blended. Wrap
the dough in wax paper and
refrigerate for 2 hours. Roll the
dough out to a ¼ inch
thickness and cut into strips
3 inches long and ¼ inch wide.
Coat the sticks with the
remaining grated cheese and
arrange them on a buttered
baking sheet. Bake in a
preheated 400° oven for 15
minutes.

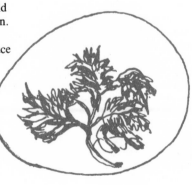

Kaastruffels

Cheese truffles

 1¼ *cups butter, softened*
   1 *cup grated Gouda or Edam
       cheese*
 ½ *teaspoon salt
       Freshly ground black pepper
       Pinch of cayenne pepper*
 ½ *teaspoon Worcestershire
       sauce*
   6 *slices stale dark
       pumpernickel bread, finely
       crumbled*

Blend together the butter, cheese,
salt, pepper, cayenne pepper and
Worcestershire sauce until a
smooth paste is formed. Shape
into balls 1 inch in diameter and
roll the balls in the bread
crumbs. Refrigerate for 1 hour
or until firm. Serve as a snack
with cheese balls and cheese
zebras.

Kaaszebra's

Cheese zebras

4 servings

   6 *tablespoons butter*
   4 *egg yolks from hard boiled
       eggs, sieved*
 ¼ *teaspoon salt
       Freshly ground black pepper
       Few drops Worcestershire
       sauce*
   2 *tablespoons grated
       Parmesan or Gouda cheese*
   4 *thin slices dark
       pumpernickel bread*

Beat the butter until soft. Blend
in the egg yolks, salt, pepper,
Worcestershire sauce and
cheese until the mixture is
smooth. Cover a slice of
pumpernickel bread with a layer
of this paste, exactly as thick
as the slice of pumpernickel
bread. Alternate layers of cheese
paste with pumpernickel bread.
Wrap in aluminum foil and
chill in the refrigerator for at
least 2½ hours. Cut with a sharp
knife into thin slices. Arrange
the "zebra's" on a platter
garnished with lettuce leaves.

Tamara keftedes

Fried tamara rissoles

4 servings

- ½ *pound smoked cod's roe*
- 1 *onion, coarsely chopped*
- 2 *cloves garlic, crushed*
- 1 *slice day old bread, without crust, crumbled*
- ¼ *teaspoon cinnamon*
   Freshly ground black pepper
- 1 *tablespoon chopped fresh mint or*
   1 teaspoon dried mint
- 2 *tablespoons chopped parsley*
- 1 *egg*
- 1 *tablespoon water*
- ¼ *cup flour*
   Oil for deep frying

Combine all the ingredients except the flour and oil. Put through a mincer or chop finely. Set aside in a cool place for 3 hours. Form into small patties, coat with flour and deep fry in preheated 375° oil until nicely browned.

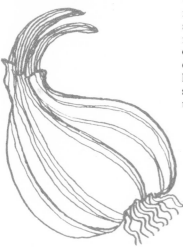

Omeleta me rizi

Rice omelet

4 servings

- 3 *medium sized tomatoes*
- 1 *teaspoon salt*
   Freshly ground black pepper
- ½ *teaspoon sugar*
- ½ *cup dried breadcrumbs*
- ¼ *cup flour*
- 4 *tablespoons butter*
- 1 *onion, thinly sliced*
- 5 *eggs*
- ½ *cup cooked rice*

Peel the tomatoes and cut into thick slices. Season with ½ teaspoon salt, pepper and sugar. Mix the breadcrumbs and flour together and coat the tomato slices. Heat 2 tablespoons of the butter in a large skillet, add the tomatoes and fry for about 3 minutes on each side until nicely browned. Remove from the pan and keep warm. Add the remaining butter and fry the onion until soft and golden brown. Beat the eggs, add the remaining salt and pepper and stir in the cooked rice. Add this mixture to the frying pan and cook over medium heat until the eggs are set. Fold the omelet in half and transfer to a warm serving dish. Place the fried tomatoes on top and serve hot.

Dolmadakia

Stuffed vine leaves

4 servings

- 1 *(16 ounce) jar vine leaves*
- 6 *small onions, finely chopped*
- ¾ *pound ground veal*
- ⅔ *cup rice, soaked for 5 minutes in boiling water and drained*
- 1 *teaspoon crushed dried mint leaves*
- 2 *teaspoons finely chopped parsley or dill weed*
   Pinch of cinnamon
- 1 *teaspoon salt*
   Freshly ground black pepper
- 2 *tablespoons olive oil*
   Chicken broth or water
   Juice of 1 lemon

Carefully unfold the vine leaves and rinse under cold, running water. In a bowl, combine the onions, veal, rice, mint, parsley, cinnamon, salt, pepper and olive oil. Form about 1 tablespoon of the mixture into an oval shape, place on a vine leaf and roll up. Continue until all the stuffing is used. Arrange a layer of leftover leaves on the bottom of a small casserole just large enough to hold all the stuffed leaves. Place a layer of stuffed leaves very close together over the layer of leftover leaves. Make another layer of leftover leaves and continue layering until all the stuffed leaves are tightly packed into the casserole. Pour over enough broth or water to barely cover the vine leaves and sprinkle with lemon juice. Weight the stuffed leaves with a plate. Cover the casserole and

bring to a boil over moderate heat. Reduce the heat and simmer slowly 1 hour. Let the leaves cool in the broth. Drain and serve cold. The vine leaves may also be served hot and the broth enriched with the egg and lemon mixture used in Avgolemono soup.
Served cold, the vine leaves are an excellent cocktail snack.

Fish roe paté

Finely ground fish roe and stuffed vine leaves

Taramasalata

Fish roe paté

4 servings

¼ *pound smoked cod's roe*
3 *slices day old bread, without crusts, crumbled*
4 *tablespoons olive oil*
2 *tablespoons lemon juice*
1 *teaspoon water*
1 *teaspoon grated onion (optional)*
1 *teaspoon chopped parsley
   Black pitted olives*

Mash the fish roe, add the breadcrumbs and gradually stir in the oil and lemon juice, beating until smooth. Beat in the water to make it light and fluffy. Add the onion and parsley. Transfer to a serving bowl and garnish with olives.

Quiche au jambon

Pipérade Basquaise

Quiche au jambon

Ham quiche

6 servings

Pastry:
- 1½ cups sifted all purpose flour
- ½ teaspoon salt
- ½ cup butter, cut into small pieces
- 1 egg yolk
- 3 tablespoons cold water

Filling:
- ½ pound boiled ham, cut into small pieces
- ¼ pound Swiss cheese, grated
- 4 eggs
- 1 tablespoon flour
- 1 cup milk
- ½ cup heavy cream
- ¼ teaspoon salt
  Freshly ground black pepper
- 3 tablespoons butter, melted

Sift the flour with the salt into a bowl. With a pastry blender or the fingertips, blend the butter into the flour. Stir in the egg yolk and water. Form the pastry into a ball. Wrap in wax paper and chill for 30 minutes. Knead the pastry on a lightly floured board for 2 minutes. Roll and fit the pastry into a 9 inch pie plate. Add diced ham and grated cheese to the uncooked pastry shell. Combine eggs, flour, milk, cream, salt and pepper. Pour over the ham and cheese. Add melted butter. Bake in a 400° oven for 30 minutes.

Pipérade Basquaise

Eggs in the style of the Basque country

4 servings

- 2½ tablespoons olive oil or vegetable oil
- 4 scallions, finely chopped
- 2 cloves garlic, crushed
- 2 green peppers, cut into strips
- 3 medium sized tomatoes, peeled, seeded and chopped
- ¼ teaspoon salt
  Freshly ground black pepper
- ¼ teaspoon thyme
- 1 bay leaf
- 3 tablespoons butter
- 4 slices Canadian bacon
- 8 eggs

Heat the oil in a skillet. Sauté scallions and garlic for two minutes. Add peppers and continue cooking for three minutes. Add tomatoes, and season with salt and pepper. Add thyme and bay leaf. Simmer uncovered for 15 minutes stirring occasionally. Fry bacon in one tablespoon butter until lightly browned on both sides. Season eggs with salt and pepper. Scramble eggs in remaining 2 tablespoons butter. Place the eggs on a hot serving plate. Make a trough down the center. Fill trough with vegetables. Arrange bacon round the sides of the dish.

Oeufs au crevettes

Eggs with shrimp

6 servings

- *6 hard boiled eggs*
- *3 tablespoons butter*
- *3 scallions, finely chopped*
- *1 tablespoon parsley, finely chopped*
- *½ teaspoon tarragon*
- *1 cup small shrimp, chopped into small pieces*
- *1 tablespoon mild (Dijon) mustard*
- *½ cup heavy cream*
  Pinch salt
  Freshly ground black pepper
- *3 tablespoons grated Parmesan cheese*
- *1 teaspoon additional butter*

Chop eggs finely. Sauté shallots in hot butter. Add eggs, parsley, tarragon, shrimp, mustard and heavy cream. Season with salt and pepper. Heat mixture for 3 minutes. Place in a buttered baking dish or individual small dishes. Sprinkle with grated cheese, dot with butter and place under a preheated broiler for 3 minutes until bubbling hot and lightly browned. Serve with freshly made toast.

Foie de poulet

Chicken livers flamed in brandy

6 servings

- *2 tablespoons butter*
- *½ yellow onion, finely chopped*
- *1 carrot, finely diced*
- *1 pound chicken livers*
- *3 slices boiled ham, diced*
- *3 mushrooms, sliced thinly or 1 (3 ounce) can mushrooms, drained*
- *2 tablespoons brandy (opt.)*
- *2 tablespoons flour*
- *½ cup white wine and*
- *½ cup beef broth*
- *1 cup seedless green grapes*
- *2 tablespoons finely chopped parsley for garnish*

Heat the butter in a large skillet. Sauté the onion three minutes until transparent. Add carrot and continue cooking for 2 minutes. Add chicken livers and stir over high heat until almost tender. Add ham and mushrooms and cook two minutes. Add brandy and light it with a match immediately. When the flames have died down, stir in the flour and add wine and broth gradually, to form a medium thick sauce. Add grapes and cook just until the grapes have heated through. Garnish with parsley.

Quiche Lorraine

Bacon and egg pie

6 servings

Pastry:
- *1¼ cups sifted all purpose flour*
- *½ teaspoon salt*
- *3 tablespoons butter or margarine, cut into small pieces*
- *3 tablespoons solid shortening*
- *3 tablespoons ice water*

Filling:
- *½ pound bacon*
- *¼ pound (1 cup) Swiss cheese, grated*
- *4 eggs*
- *1 tablespoon flour*
- *1¼ cups milk or half and half or heavy cream*
- *½ teaspoon salt*
  Freshly ground black pepper
- *1 tablespoon butter, melted*

Measure flour and salt into a bowl. Add butter or margarine and shortening. Combine with a pastry blender or fingertips. Add water a little at a time. Stir with a fork and form pastry in a ball. Wrap in wax paper and chill for 20 minutes. Roll on a lightly floured board and fit pastry into a nine inch pie plate.

Filling:
Fry bacon until crisp. Drain and crumble the bacon. Place in the uncooked pastry shell with grated cheese. In a small bowl combine eggs, flour, milk or cream, salt and pepper. Pour over the bacon and cheese. Add melted butter. Bake in a preheated 375° oven for 30 minutes until custard is firm and golden. Serve hot or cold.

Pissaladière

Onion and tomato pie

4 servings

Pastry:
- ½ *package (1¼ teaspoons) dry yeast*
- 2 *tablespoons lukewarm water*
- 1¼ *cups sifted all purpose flour*
- ¼ *teaspoon salt*
- 2 *tablespoons cold butter cut into small pieces*
- 1 *egg*

Filling:
- 3 *tablespoons olive oil or vegetable oil*
- 6 *medium sized onions, cut into thin rings*
- 2 *cloves garlic, crushed*
- 2 *medium sized tomatoes, peeled, seeded and chopped*
- ¼ *teaspoon oregano*
- ¼ *teaspoon salt*
  Freshly ground black pepper
- 1 *(2 ounce) can anchovy fillets*
- 12 *black olives, pitted*

Dissolve yeast in water and allow to stand for 10 minutes. Sift flour into a bowl. Add the salt. Blend the butter into the flour with a pastry blender or fingertips. Add egg and cold water. Stir with a fork and form into a ball. Knead lightly for one minute. Place pastry in a bowl. Cover with a towel and leave for two hours. The dough will rise slightly. Knead dough for two minutes until smooth. Roll out dough on a floured board and fit into an eight inch pie plate, flan ring or quiche pan. In the meantime, heat oil in a skillet. Add onions and garlic. Cover and simmer for 15 minutes, stirring occasionally. Add tomatoes and oregano. Season with salt and pepper and simmer uncovered for 15 more minutes until all the liquid has boiled away. Fill onions and tomatoes into the pie shell. Bake 30 minutes in a 375° oven. Decorate baked pissaladière with anchovies arranged in a criss cross design. Place halved olives in the spaces between anchovies. Serve hot.

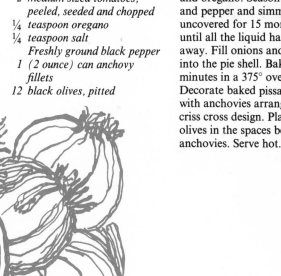

Croustade aux fruits de mer

Salade Niçoise

Croustade aux fruits de mer

Fruits of the sea in pastry

8 servings

   2 *packages frozen individual patty shells or 1 prepared pie shell*
   1 *egg, lightly beaten*

Filling:
   1 *cup dry white wine*
   ½ *cup water*
   ½ *cup clam broth (from canned clams)*
   1 *small yellow onion, cut into thin slices*
   1 *slice lemon*
   1 *pound flounder fillets*
   ½ *pound scallops*
  12 *medium sized shrimp*
     Freshly ground black pepper to taste
   1 *(5 ounce) can whole baby clams*
  ¼ *pound mushrooms, finely chopped*
   1 *tablespoon butter*
   1 *teaspoon lemon juice*

Sauce:
1½ *tablespoons butter*
1½ *tablespoons flour*
   1 *tablespoon parsley, finely chopped*
   2 *egg yolks*
  ¼ *cup heavy cream*

Thaw the patty shells and form into 2 balls. Knead on a floured board for one minute. Roll out two circles of puff pastry, one about 12 inches in diameter and the other about 9 inches. (Cut circles using dinner plates as a guide.) Sprinkle a cookie sheet with water. Place the smaller sheet on top of the larger sheet and brush with beaten egg. Bake pastry in a 400° oven for 20 to 25 minutes until the pastry is puffed and golden, or bake a prepared pie shell and serve this dish as a one crust pie. Place the wine, water, clam broth, onion slices and lemon in a skillet. Add the fish fillets, scallops and shrimp. Bring to simmering point and poach fish for 8 minutes. Remove fish. Strain the poaching liquid into a clean saucepan and boil until 1¼ cups liquid remain. Sauté mushrooms for 5 minutes in 1 tablespoon butter and lemon juice.

To make the sauce:
Melt the butter in a small saucepan. Stir in the flour. Add the reduced poaching liquid gradually. Add parsley. Combine egg yolks and cream and add to the sauce. Remove sauce from heat and stir in mushrooms. If you are making a two crust pie, remove the top crust. Place the flounder, scallops and clams in the pastry shell. Spoon the sauce over the fish. Arrange the shrimp round the edge of the pastry. Cover with the top circle of pastry. Bake in a preheated 400° oven for 5 minutes and serve hot.

Coquilles St. Jacques provençale

Coquilles St. Jacques provençale

Scallops with tomato and garlic

4 servings

1	pound scallops
¼	cup all purpose flour
1½	tablespoons butter
2	medium sized tomatoes, peeled, seeded and chopped
2	cloves garlic, crushed
2	tablespoons finely chopped parsley
¼	teaspoon salt
	Freshly ground black pepper
	Tomato sauce

Dredge the scallops in flour. Heat the butter in a frying pan and brown scallops for three minutes over moderately high heat. Add tomatoes, garlic and parsley. Season with salt and pepper. Stir carefully and simmer over low heat for 10 minutes. Serve very hot on scallop shells or small dishes topped with tomato sauce.

Salade Niçoise

Salad Riviera style

4 servings

8 large lettuce leaves
 (preferably Romaine or
 Boston lettuce)
2 hard boiled eggs, quartered
2 medium sized ripe tomatoes,
 cut into wedges
8 canned anchovy fillets
8 black pitted olives, halved
1 (6 ounce) can tuna,
 flaked into large pieces
1 green pepper, cut in half
 and then into strips
2 teaspoons capers

For the dressing:
1½ tablespoons olive oil
 or vegetable oil
1½ teaspoons tarragon vinegar
½ teaspoon salt
 Freshly ground black
 pepper
1 clove garlic, crushed

Simmer green pepper in
boiling water for 5 minutes and
rinse in cold water. Wash the
lettuce leaves and dry with
paper towels. Place the lettuce
leaves in a salad bowl and
arrange all the remaining
ingredients on top. Combine
olive oil, vinegar, salt, pepper
and garlic. Toss the salad with
the dressing just before serving.

Gougère

Cheese puff

6 servings

1 cup milk
4 tablespoons butter, cut into
 small pieces
½ teaspoon salt
 Freshly ground black pepper
1 cup sifted all purpose flour
4 eggs
1 cup Swiss cheese, grated
2 tablespoons milk

Place the milk, butter, salt and
pepper in a saucepan. Bring
milk to boiling point adjusting
the heat so the butter has
completely melted when
the milk boils.
Remove the pan from the heat
and add the flour all at once.
Stir the flour into the milk
vigorously and place the pan
over a moderate heat. Cook
for two minutes until the dough
can be formed into a ball and
there is a film of flour on the
bottom of the pan. Remove
the pan from the heat and add
the eggs one at a time beating
each egg well into the mixture
before adding the next egg.
Reserve ¼ cup of cheese.
Beat remaining cheese into the
dough. Butter and flour a
cookie sheet. Draw a 9 inch
circle in the flour. With a soup
spoon, place balls of dough
around the circle so that the
balls are just touching each
other. They will run together as
they bake. Brush with milk
and sprinkle with remaining
cheese. Bake in a 375° oven for
40 minutes. Remove from the
oven and cool on a wire rack

before breaking into pieces.
In Burgundy this pastry is
considered the ideal
accompaniment to a glass of
wine. It can also be served with
a salad instead of bread, or the
center may be filled with either
meat, chicken or fish prepared
in a sauce. The Gougère freezes
very successfully.

Tarte à l'oignon

Onion pie

4 servings

Pastry:
1 cup sifted all purpose flour
¼ teaspoon salt
¼ cup butter cut into small
 pieces
1 egg
2 tablespoons cold water

Filling:
3 tablespoons butter or
 margarine
6 medium sized yellow onions,
 cut into thin rings
¼ teaspoon salt
 Freshly ground black pepper
 Dash nutmeg
3 egg yolks
⅔ cup heavy cream

Measure flour into a bowl.
Add salt. Combine butter with
the flour using a pastry blender
or fingertips. Add egg and
water. Stir with a fork, and
form pastry into a ball. Wrap
in wax paper and chill for one
hour. Roll out the pastry and
fit it into an 8 inch pie plate,
flan ring or quiche tin. Fry
onions in hot butter over
moderate heat. Cover skillet
and simmer onions for 30
minutes, stirring occasionally.
Season onions with salt, pepper
and nutmeg. Combine egg
yolks and cream with a fork
and add to the onions. Remove
from the heat and fill into
pastry shell. Bake in a 400°
oven for 30 minutes. Serve hot.

In prehistoric caves discovered in France, ancient fossils of snail shells have been found alongside the fossilized remains of fish bones and oyster shells. Very good circumstantial evidence that the taste for snails must be as old as mankind itself. The ancient Romans had extensive snail farms. The Roman snail farmer Fulvius Hirpinus imported young snails from Africa and the Balkans for Roman gourmets and raised them in large earthenware pots. To enhance their flavor he fed them a steady diet of wheat flour which had been cooked in wine to make a kind of porridge. Roman cooks made a very delicious dish out of the snails with a piquant sauce of olive oil, wine, anchovies, pepper and cumin.

The best and most delicious snails of France come from the vineyards of Burgundy and Alsace. But snails are loved so much both in France and abroad that the French vineyards cannot produce enough of them and the French have to import a large number from Turkey.

After snails are caught they are left to fast for a certain period so that they can get rid of any poisonous foods they may have eaten. They are then cooked in a little ash and water while still in their shells, removed from the shells and cooked again with garlic, onion, and preferably a dash of brandy. The shells are then very carefully washed. If the snails are not used immediately,

they are canned or frozen and the shells are packed separately in bags. Snails can be bought in this way in delicatessens and gourmet food stores all over the world. They need only be heated with butter and herbs. In France, however, people prefer to cook snails fresh, and in the country people still believe that there is no better cough medicine than snail broth.

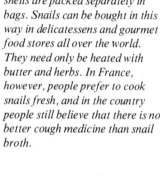

Escargots à la Bourguignonne

Snails in wine

4 servings

- ⅔ cup butter
- 3 anchovy fillets
- 2 scallions, finely chopped
- 2 tablespoons parsley, finely chopped
- 2 cloves garlic, crushed
- 1 tablespoon brandy or Pernod (opt.)
- 1 package (24) snails and shells
- 2 tablespoons fine bread crumbs
- 2 tablespoons white wine

Beat the butter with a wooden spoon until softened. Rinse anchovies in cold water to remove excess salt. Pat anchovies dry on paper towels. Mash anchovies and add to the butter. Add scallions, parsley, garlic and brandy to butter. Chill butter one hour until firm. Place a teaspoon of butter in each shell. Slip a snail into each shell and seal in place with remaining butter. Press breadcrumbs onto the butter. Place snails in snail dishes or muffin tins; or crumble aluminum foil and spread on a cookie sheet. Place shells in depressions in the foil to prevent them from tipping. Sprinkle white wine over shells. Bake in a 375° oven for 8 minutes. (If the snails are prepared in snail dishes but without shells, bake for only 5 minutes). Serve hot.

Artichauts vinaigrette

Artichokes vinaigrette

6 servings

- 6 artichokes
- ½ lemon
- 1 teaspoon salt

Vinaigrette sauce:

- ½ teaspoon salt
  Freshly ground black pepper
- 1 clove garlic, crushed
- ½ teaspoon mild (Dijon) mustard
- 2 tablespoons vinegar
- 6 tablespoons light olive oil or salad oil
- 3 tablespoons parsley, finely chopped
- 3 tablespoons chives, finely chopped
- 1 tablespoon capers
- 1 tablespoon sweet gherkins, finely chopped
- 1 hard boiled egg, finely chopped

Cut off the artichoke stems very close to the bottom. This will enable them to stand without tipping when they are served. Remove any blemished outer leaves. Snip off the point of each leaf with a pair of scissors, cutting about ¼ inch down each leaf. Plunge artichokes into a large pot of simmering salted water. Add lemon half. Cover and simmer 45 minutes or until a leaf will pull away easily. Combine the ingredients for the vinaigrette sauce in the order listed. Serve sauce in individual small containers. Serve artichokes hot or cold.

Antipasto is the Italian appetizer. Give free rein to your imagination in arranging attractive color combinations when you prepare an antipasto plate. It's fun to make up combinations which include the favorite delicacies of each individual. Usually a glass of chilled vermouth is served with the antipasto.

Antipasto

Antipasto plate

Create your own antipasto. Start with a border of lettuce leaves and sliced tomatoes. In the center arrange a variety of thinly sliced meats: prosciutto, a smoky flavored Italian ham; salami, a highly seasoned sausage; salsiccia secca, a peppery, very dry, pork sausage; capocollo, smoked pork. Garnish with quartered hard cooked eggs, anchovy fillets, radishes, green or black olives, carciofini (artichoke hearts), celery, and delicious peperoncini, a small green pepper, pickled in vinegar. Sprinkle olive oil and a little wine-vinegar over all. Pickled beets and sweet red peppers may be added for color.

Pomodori ripieni

Stuffed tomatoes

4 servings

Rice stuffing:
  4 *medium tomatoes*
$^1/_4$ *teaspoon salt*
$^1/_2$ *cup cooked rice*
  2 *tablespoons chopped*
     mushrooms
  1 *teaspoon capers*
  1 *teaspoon parsley flakes*
$^1/_4$ *teaspoon dried oregano*
     Dash black pepper
  1 *tablespoon oil or margarine*

Slice off stem ends of tomatoes; set aside. Scoop out pulp and sprinkle inside with salt; turn upside down and drain. Combine remaining ingredients; mix well. Fill tomatoes and replace tops. Brush tomatoes with oil. Place in shallow baking dish. Bake in a slow oven (325°) 15 minutes or until heated throughout. Serve hot or cold.

Tuna stuffing:
  4 *tomatoes*
$^1/_2$ *cup tunafish, flaked*
2–3 *tablespoons mayonnaise*
  2 *teaspoons lemon juice*
  1 *teaspoon capers*
  1 *teaspoon chopped parsley*

Slice off stem ends of tomatoes; scoop out pulp; turn upside down to drain. Combine tunafish, mayonnaise, lemon juice and capers; mix well. Fill tomatoes. Garnish with mayonnaise, capers, and chopped parsley.

Acciughe con peperoni gialli

Anchovies with peppers

4 servings

2 (1³/₄ ounce) cans anchovy
  fillets
¹/₄ cup milk
1 green or red pepper
4 lettuce leaves
2 teaspoons capers
2 hard cooked eggs,
  finely chopped
2 teaspoons tarragon vinegar
1¹/₂ tablespoons salad oil
1 tablespoon chopped
  parsley

Soak anchovy fillets in milk
about 15 minutes to remove
excess salt. Rinse under running
water; separate and drain on
paper towel. Blanch, peel and
seed pepper; cut into strips.
Place lettuce leaves on plates.
Arrange anchovies and peppers
alternately on lettuce. Sprinkle
with capers; top with chopped
egg. Combine vinegar and oil;
sprinkle over salad. Garnish
with parsley.

Sardine sott'olio alla veneta

Venetian sardines

6 servings

3 (3¹/₄ ounce) cans skinned
  and boned sardines
6 lettuce leaves
1 green pepper
2 tablespoons margarine or
  butter
1 clove garlic, minced
1 cup (8 ounce can) tomato
  sauce
¹/₄ teaspoon dried sage
¹/₄ teaspoon sugar
  Dash black pepper
2 hard cooked eggs, sliced
2 teaspoons capers

Drain sardines. Place lettuce
leaves on serving dish. Arrange
sardines in a radiating circular
desgin on lettuce. Chill. Blanch,
peel and seed pepper; cut into
strips. Melt margarine in small
skillet; sauté garlic. Add
remaining ingredients. Cook
over medium heat, stirring
constantly, about 10–15
minutes. Cool. Spoon sauce
over sardines. Garnish with
pepper strips, egg slices and
capers.

Cipolle al forno

Baked onions

6 servings

6 medium onions, unpeeled
³/₄ cup salad oil
¹/₄ cup lemon juice or vinegar
¹/₂ teaspoon dry mustard
¹/₄ teaspoon salt
¹/₈ teaspoon black pepper
1 green pepper

Slice off tops and bottoms of
onions; place onions in shallow
baking pan. Bake in a moderate
oven (350°) about 25 minutes.
Cool slightly. Remove skins.
Combine remaining ingredients;
blend well. Pour over onions.
Chill. Blanch, peel and seed
pepper. Cut into strips. Garnish
onions with pepper strips before
serving.

Cipolle farcite con purea di tonno

Tuna-stuffed onions

6 servings

1 cup dry white wine or water
1 cup vinegar
1 clove garlic, minced
1 teaspoon salad oil
1 bay leaf
¹/₄ teaspoon dried thyme
6 medium onions, peeled
1 cup (7 ounce can) tunafish
¹/₃ cup chopped green olives
1 tablespoon chopped parsley

Combine wine, vinegar, garlic,
oil, bay leaf and thyme in
saucepan. Add onions. Bring to
a boil; simmer about 20 minutes
or until onions are tender. Cool.
Remove onions. Chill. Cook
liquid mixture over high heat
until mixture is reduced by half.
Strain and cool. Mix together
tunafish and olives. Carefully
remove centers from onions. Fill
onions with tuna mixture.
Spoon sauce over onions.
Garnish with parsley.

Gravad sild

Danish marinated herring

4 servings

  4 *herring or trout, about
     6-ounces each*
  4 *tablespoons dill weed*
  6 *tablespoons vegetable oil*
⅔ *cup vinegar*
  2 *teaspoons salt*
  1 *tablespoon sugar*
½ *teaspoon ground white
     pepper*
  1 *teaspoon dry mustard*

Fillet fish and remove skin.
Place alternate layers of fish and
dill in a non-metallic bowl.
Combine and beat with a fork
oil, vinegar, salt, sugar, pepper
and mustard; pour over fish.
Cover bowl; refrigerate for
several hours or overnight.

Sildgratin

Danish herring au gratin

6 servings

  2 *schmalz or matjes herring
     fillets*
  4 *tablespoons margarine or
     butter*
  1 *tablespoon chopped onion*
  3 *tablespoons flour*
  2 *cups half-and-half*
½ *teaspoon salt*
¼ *teaspoon ground white pepper*
  2 *tablespoons chopped parsley*
  6 *small cooked potatoes,
     peeled and sliced*
  2 *hard cooked eggs, chopped*
  2 *tablespoons grated Parmesan
     cheese*
  1 *tablespoon margarine or
     butter*

Soak fillets in cold water for
24 hours; drain. Cut fillets into
½"strips. Melt margarine
in saucepan, add onion and cook
until transparent. Stir in flour;
remove from heat; gradually
add half-and-half. Cook over
medium heat, stirring constantly,
until mixture comes to a boil
and is thickened. Stir in salt,
pepper and parsley. Butter
6 individual casserole dishes;
arrange 1 sliced potato in
bottom of each, cover with half
the sauce. Divide chopped egg
and herring evenly among the
casseroles, top with remaining
sauce. Sprinkle with Parmesan
cheese; dot with margarine.
Bake in very hot oven (450°)
about 15 minutes, or until
bubbly and top is lightly
browned.

Rosolli

Finnish herring salad

4 to 6 servings

  1 *salted regular or schmalz
     herring (about 1 pound)*
½ *cup whipped cream*
  1 *tablespoon pickled beet juice*
½ *teaspoon sugar*
  1 *teaspoon vinegar*
  2 *cups cold, cooked potatoes,
     coarsely diced*
  2 *cups cold, cooked carrots,
     coarsely diced*
  1 *(1 pound) can beets, drained
     and coarsely diced*
  2 *medium, tart apples, peeled,
     cored and diced*
  1 *large pickle, coarsely diced*
  2 *hard cooked eggs, coarsely
     chopped*
½ *tablespoon finely chopped
     onion
     Parsley or watercress sprigs*

Soak herring in cold water for
24 hours; skin and fillet.
Combine whipped cream, beet
juice, sugar and vinegar; chill.
Cut herring into cubes; combine
with remaining ingredients,
except parsley; mix well. Fold in
whipped cream dressing. Chill.
Serve garnished with parsley or
watercress.

Sillpudding

Herring pudding

4 to 6 servings

  1 *salted regular or schmalz
     herring (about ¾ to 1 pound)*
  2 *tablespoons margarine or
     butter*
1½ *cups thinly sliced onion*
  3 *cups cooked potatoes,
     peeled and sliced*
¼ *teaspoon ground white pepper*
  2 *eggs*
  2 *tablespoons flour*
1¾ *cups milk*

Soak herring in cold water 24
hours; skin and fillet; cut into
½" strips. Melt margarine in
large skillet, add onions and
cook until transparent, stirring
occasionally. Add potatoes;
cook, stirring occasionally,
until heated through, about 10
minutes. Place half the potatoes
and onion mixture in bottom of
greased 9 inch round (2 inches
high) baking pan. Arrange
herring pieces over potatoes,
sprinkle with pepper; cover
with remaining potato mixture.
Combine eggs, flour and milk;
beat until just blended, not
foamy; pour over potatoes.
Place pan in larger baking pan.
Pour boiling water in outside
pan to a depth of 1" on
smaller pan. Bake in a hot oven
(425°) until top is browned and
custard is set, about 30 to 40
minutes. Serve hot.

Joppe's shrimp salad. Denmark's small delicate shrimp have a sweet and salty taste. They are so delicious that no gourmet would ever think of covering them with mayonnaise.

Joppes räksallad

Joppe's shrimp salad

4 servings

> 1 *pound shrimp, cooked and peeled*
> 2½ *cups sliced fresh mushrooms*
> 2 *medium tomatoes, sliced*
> 1 *(8½ ounce) can asparagus spears, drained*
> 2 *tablespoons oil*
> 2 *teaspoons vinegar*
> ½ *teaspoon salt*
> ¼ *teaspoon dill weed*
> 2 *hard cooked eggs, sliced*

Arrange shrimp, mushrooms, tomatoes and asparagus in salad bowl. Combine oil, vinegar, salt and dill; pour over salad mixture. Garnish with egg slices.

Salted herring and sweet beets produce the unique Scandinavian flavor of Danish herring salad.

To bring out its choice and delicate flavor, the Swedes carefully marinate their salmon.

Sildsalat

Danish herring salad

6 servings

  2 salted regular or schmalz
    herring
  3 medium cooked potatoes,
    peeled and diced
  2 small cooked or canned
    beets, diced
  1 large pickle, diced
  2 medium tart apples, peeled,
    cored and diced
½ cup cooked ham, tongue or
    corned beef, diced
  2 tablespoons finely chopped
    onion
  2 tablespoons margarine or
    butter
  2 tablespoons flour
1¼ cups half-and-half
  1 tablespoon vinegar
  1 teaspoon prepared mustard
½ teaspoon salt
    Pinch of sugar

Soak herring overnight in cold water; skin and fillet. Cut herring into ½" pieces. Combine with potatoes, beets, pickle, apple, meat and onion. Chill. Melt margarine in saucepan; stir in flour. Remove from heat; stir in half-and-half, vinegar, mustard, salt and sugar. Cook over medium heat, stirring constantly, until mixture comes to a boil and is thickened. Carefully stir into salad mixture; chill. Serve on lettuce, garnished with additional hard-cooked egg slices, if desired.

Gravad lax

Swedish marinated salmon

6 servings

  2 tablespoons salt
  2 tablespoons sugar
  1 tablespoon peppercorns,
    crushed
  1 pound salmon, cut into
    2 fillets
  1 large bunch fresh dill,
    chopped coarsely

Combine salt, sugar and peppercorns. Place fish on large piece heavy duty foil. Cover fish with dill; sprinkle with salt mixture. Top with second fish fillet. Close foil securely using a drug store wrap; place on dish or tray. Pile several weights or 3 or 4 cans of food on foil packet. Refrigerate at least 48 hours turning packet several times. Be sure to keep weights on packet. Remove fish; scrape off seasonings. Slice thinly and serve with salmon sauce.

Västkustsallad

Swedish Westcoast salad

4 servings

   1 (6½ ounce) can lobster
   1 (10 ounce) can whole
    clams, drained
   1 cup cooked shrimp, peeled
   1 (3 ounce) can sliced
    mushrooms
   ¼ cup mayonnaise
   ¼ cup sour cream
   1 tablespoon lemon juice
 ½–1 teaspoon salt
    Lettuce leaves
   2 tomatoes, quartered

Drain lobster and remove membranes. Combine lobster, clams, shrimp, mushrooms, mayonnaise, sour cream, lemon juice and salt; toss lightly until mixed. Arrange salad on lettuce leaves. Garnish with tomato wedges.

Krabbsallad

Swedish crab salad

4 servings

   1 (6½ ounce) can crabmeat
   2 stalks celery, chopped
   1 teaspoon grated onion
 1–2 tablespoons lemon juice
   ¼ teaspoon dill weed
   ½ cup sour cream
    Freshly ground black pepper
    Lettuce leaves

Drain crabmeat and remove membranes. Combine crabmeat celery, onion, lemon juice, dill, sour cream, and pepper. Toss lightly; arrange salad on lettuce.

Hummersalat

Danish curried lobster salad

4 servings

   1 (6½ ounce) can lobster
   ¼ cup mayonnaise
   ¼ cup sour cream
   1 teaspoon lemon juice
   ½ teaspoon curry powder
   2 stalks celery, chopped
   1 apple, cored and diced
    Lettuce leaves
   2 hard cooked eggs, quartered

Drain lobster and remove membranes. Combine mayonnaise, sour cream, lemon juice and curry; blend until smooth. Add celery, apple and mayonnaise mixture to lobster; toss lightly. Pile salad lightly in lettuce leaves; garnish with egg wedges.

Solöga

Swedish sun's eye

1 serving

   1 egg yolk
   1 tablespoon chopped
    Bermuda or red onion
   6 anchovy fillets, chopped

Place egg yolk in center of a salad plate. Surround with a circle of chopped onion, then a circle of chopped anchovies. To eat: stir all together and spread on toast. (Mixture may also be lightly fried in butter, then spread on toast.)

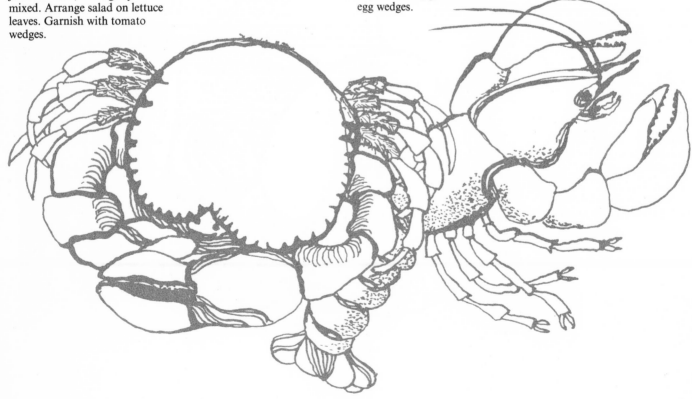

Smörrebröd med köd

Smörrebröd med salat

Smorrebrod with meat

Again the base is important—thin bread or crisp-bread spread with butter well seasoned with mustard, anchovy, parsley; thin-sliced cucumber, apple or onions, finely chopped, parsley or chervil, so thick the bread cannot be seen. Now to build your sandwich . . .

Slices of ham, wedges of apple, stewed prunes.

Rolled sliced ham filled with herb or horseradish mayonnaise and chopped egg.

Ham with sliced pineapple and banana and sweetened mayonnaise.

Ham with scrambled egg and chives.

Ham with chopped egg, topped with chopped chives.

Raw ground beef with fried egg and chopped chives.

Raw ground beef mixed with raw egg yolk and chopped pickles.

Sliced roast beef, tongue, or braised veal or pork roll rolled around asparagus tips with

Italian salad, pickled muchrooms or sliced tomatoes with horseradish mayonnaise.

Sliced liverwurst with sweet and sour pickles, cucumber slices, crisp fried bacon or sliced egg.

Smorrebrod with salad

Thin bread, spread with seasoned butter, then a mound of

Cold lamb salad, sliced cucumbers and parsley.

Chicken salad, sliced egg and a cherry tomato.

Egg salad, topped with rolled, thinly sliced salami.

Lobster salad topped with mayonnaise and sprinkled with chopped pistachio nuts.

Now take a look at your works of art. Is there room for a bit of parsley? A cherry tomato? A cauliflower floweret? A radish or carrot curl, a flourish of chopped chives, parsley, or bacon bits, a sprig of dill, a tomato wedge, strips of green or red pepper, sliced olives, onion rings.

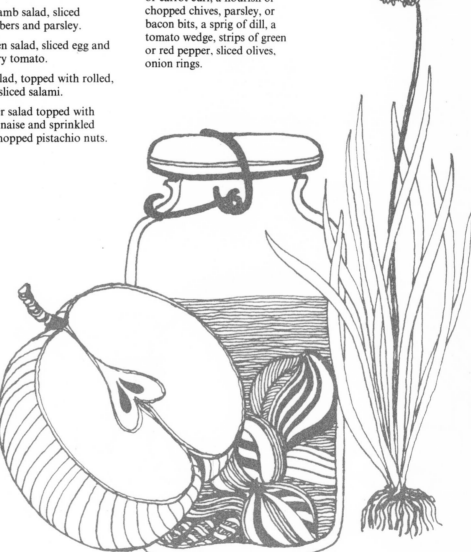

*A wide variety of breads are used
in making open sandwiches.*

Open sandwiches are a Danish
national institution. The Danes
call these sandwiches simply
'smörrebröd', literally, bread and
butter, but anyone who has tried
any of these artfully arranged
sandwiches will know that three
or four pieces of smörrebröd are
more than enough to make an
elaborate and filling meal.
Danish restaurants have menus in
which the diner can choose from
literally hundreds of different
types of smörrebröd. The choice
is often baffling – there are, for
example, over 20 different
possible variations of
'smörrebröd med ryer', simply
open sandwiches with baby
shrimp.
Open sandwiches in a somewhat
simpler form (but no less
fancifully created) are taken to
work at the office for lunch and
children carry them to school in a
small tin lunch box, with 'eat
heartily' often inscribed on the
top. Smörrebröd are also perfect
for picnics.
Danish beer, exported to almost
every country in the world, goes
perfectly with smörrebröd. The
Danes often drink their beer
accompanied by a glass of
'akvavit', a clear, innocent
looking fluid, but a drink to be
treated with respect. Akvavit is
drunk from thimble-sized,
long-stemmed glasses filled to the
brim. First the sweet but strong
akvavit, and then a swallow of
beer – the perfect combination
with smörrebröd!

Smörrebröd

Smorrebrod—breads

There is no more pleasant
experience in eating than
picking-and-choosing from the
fantastic variety of small,
beautiful and marvelously tasty
sandwiches known as
smorrebrod. They turn up as a
first course, as a lunch, or,
as the Danes like, in a full course
meal—first fish, then meat
and/or salad, then cheese.
Both the art and the fun of
making open sandwiches is
variety—variety of color,
flavor, texture. For you don't
really make your sandwich—
you compose it, as an artist
plans a picture. First the base—
and for that you need a variety
of breads—thin-sliced, crust-
trimmed, white, light rye, dark
pumpernickel, Knackebrod or
Rye-krisp, light and dark, too.
Think about taste when you
choose your bread. White for
gentle flavors—fish, chicken,
mild cheese. Light rye for strong
fish or full-flavored meat. Dark
rye for spicy, well-seasoned
mixtures. Spread base lightly
with sweet butter, anchovy
butter, herb butter, parsley
butter. Next a lettuce leaf, or
a thick covering of finely
snipped parsley or chervil;
cucumber slices, paper-thin;
thin-sliced apple— let your fancy
be your guide. Shapes? Squares,
oblongs, fan-shaped, triangles,
circles— any shape you fancy—
and your cutters—dictate.

Smörrebröd med fisk

Smorrebrod with fish

Thin bread, thickly spread with
seasoned butter, lettuce,
thin-sliced cucumber, tomatoes,
potatoes, topped with—

Herring, marinated in wine
sauce, cream sauce, or fried.
Marinated or jellied eel.
Smoked eel with mayonnaise
or horseradish whipped cream.
Thin-sliced smoked salmon
roll, filled with horseradish
whipped cream.
Scrambled eggs topped with
sliced smoked salmon.
Anchovy fillets with sliced
hard-cooked eggs.
Herring tidbits with tomato
and egg slices.
Herring salad with sliced
cucumber rings.
Baby shrimp with a
mayonnaise, served separately.
Cold fried fish with sauce
remoulade or sauce tartare.
Sardines with tomato sauce.
Crab salad topped with sliced
egg and tomatoes.
Crab with sliced egg and
asparagus tips.

A few of the many kinds of artistically prepared open sandwiches.

Leverpostej

Danish liver paté

10 servings

    4 *tablespoons margarine or
        butter*
    ½ *cup flour*
    1 *cup milk*
    1 *pound beef liver*
    ½ *pound salt pork*
    1 *large onion*
    1 *egg*
    1 *teaspoon salt*
    ¼ *teaspoon black pepper*

Melt margarine in small
saucepan; blend in flour.
Gradually add milk, stirring
briskly until smooth. Cook over
medium heat stirring constantly
until thick and bubbly; cool.
Cut liver, pork and onion into
small pieces. Puree in small
amounts in blender at high
speed or put through food
grinder. Stir pureed mixture into
white sauce; blend well. Add
egg, salt and pepper; mix well.
Pour into a well buttered
9″ × 5″ × 3″ baking dish.
Cover top with foil, sealing
edges tightly. Place in large
baking pan. Pour boiling water
into baking pan to a depth of
2″. Bake in a 350° oven 1 hour.
Remove from oven and lift
off cover. Cool. Store covered
in refrigerator. Serve in ½″ slices.

Smörrebröd
H. C. Andersen

Hans Christian Andersen
sandwich

4 servings

    4 *slices rye or pumpernickel
        bread
        Margarine or butter*
    4 *slices liver paté page 15 or*
    8 *slices liverwurst*
    1 *tomato, sliced*
    8 *cooked bacon curls*
    4 *pickles, cut into fans
        Lettuce leaves*

Spread bread generously with
margarine; top with liver paté.
Garnish with tomato, bacon
curls and pickles. Serve on
lettuce leaves.

Smörrebröd Oliver Twist

Oliver Twist sandwich

6 servings

    6 *slices pumpernickel bread
        Margarine or butter*
    6 *slices cooked ham*
    1 *tablespoon horseradish*
    ½ *cup whipped cream or*
    ½ *cup sour cream*
    12 *cooked pitted prunes*
    6 *orange slices*

Spread bread with margarine.
Place folded slice of ham on
bread. Stir horseradish into
whipped cream. Heap spoonful
of cream in center of ham.
Place a prune on either side of
cream. Cut orange slices halfway
and twist; place in center of
cream. Serve immediately.

Sildcocktail

Herring cocktail

6 servings

- 6 *lettuce leaves*
- 3 *cooked, cold potatoes, peeled and sliced*
- 1 *(5½ ounce) can pickled matjes herring fillets*
- 4 *tablespoons mayonnaise*
- 2 *tablespoons chopped dill or chives*

Place lettuce leaves in small bowls or sherbet cups. Arrange sliced potatoes on lettuce leaf. Slice herring fillets; arrange over potatoes. Garnish each cocktail with mayonnaise. Sprinkle chopped dill or chives over mayonnaise. Serve cold.

Sherrysill

Herring in sherry pickle

4 servings

- 2 *salted schmalz herring, filleted and skinned*
- ⅓ *cup sherry wine*
- ¼ *cup water*
- 3 *tablespoons vinegar*
- ½ *cup sugar*
- ¼ *teaspoon ground allspice or*
- 3 *allspice berries, crushed*
- 2 *onions, thinly sliced Chopped fresh dill*

Cover herring with cold water; soak 24 hours. Drain and rinse. Place in a non-metallic bowl. Combine sherry, water, vinegar, sugar and allspice; pour over herring. Refrigerate about 24 hours. Serve garnished with sliced onions and dill.

Inlagd sild

Danish pickled salted herring

4 servings

- 2 *salted schmalz herring, filleted and skinned*
- 2 *medium onions, sliced*
- ½ *cup vinegar*
- ⅔ *cup water*
- 1 *cup sugar*
- 10 *allspice berries, crushed*

Cover fillets with cold water; soak 24 hours. Drain and rinse; cut into ½" pieces. Place in non-metallic bowl or glass jar. Combine remaining ingredients and bring to a boil; cool; pour over herring. Refrigerate several hours or overnight before serving.

Etikkasilliä

Finnish pickled herring

4 servings

- 4 *salted herring, filleted and skinned*
- 2 *cups vinegar*
- 1 *cup water*
- ½ *cup sugar*
- 3 *bay leaves*
- 1 *2" piece ginger root, sliced thinly*
- 2 *teaspoons mustard seed*
- 1 *tablespoon prepared horseradish*
- 4 *small red onions, thinly sliced*
- 1 *carrot, thinly sliced*

Soak herring in cold water at least 24 hours in a cool place. Drain; cut into ½" strips. Combine vinegar, water and sugar; bring to a boil over moderate heat. Simmer about 5 minutes until syrupy. In a non-metallic bowl, make alternate layers of herring, bay leaves, ginger root, mustard seed, horseradish, sliced onions and carrots. Pour vinegar syrup over fish; cover; refrigerate for 3 days.

Clams with olives

Mussels in spicy sauce

When the heat of the day has passed and the long awaited coolness of the evening at last arrives in Spain, it is the hour for sherry. Terraces overflow with people, wine cellars and cafes are crowded, and golden sherry is served everywhere. But no one ever drinks sherry by itself; an accompanying small white dish contains a delectable snack. This can be a few olives, a sliced hard-boiled egg with anchovies, a slice of sausage, pieces of cheese, nuts, a few shrimp, or even small fried squid. And a different hors d'oeuvre is eaten with each glass of sherry.

These snacks are called 'tapas', a Spanish word meaning 'small lid'. Originally a small dish was placed on top of the glass of sherry like a lid. According to one story, 'tapas' originated in the bull-fighters' cafes of Seville, where small gypsy boys would always come to hear the tales of what took place in the arena. Out of friendliness to their small admirers, the great matadors would offer them tasty snacks to eat. It is a charming story, but the tradition of the 'tapas' is probably quite ancient and may even have been brought to Spain by the Arabs.

Almejas con aceitunas

Clams with olives

   1 (7 ounce) can clams
   2 teaspoons wine vinegar
   1 small onion, finely chopped
   3 drops Tabasco
 10 black olives, pitted

Drain the clams and reserve the juices from the can. Combine vinegar, onion, Tabasco and can juices. Pour the mixture over the clams and garnish with black olives.

Mejillones con salsa picante

Mussels in spicy sauce

   1 cup canned mussels, drained
   2 tablespoons mayonnaise
   2 teaspoons mustard
   1 teaspoon sherry
 ½ teaspoon lemon juice
   1 (2½ ounce) jar chopped pimiento, cut into strips

Place the mussels in a glass dish. Combine the mayonnaise with the mustard, sherry and lemon juice. Stir in the pimiento. Spoon the sauce over the mussels.

Green pea soup

Watercress soup

4 servings

- *1 bunch watercress*
- *2 tablespoons butter*
- *1 onion, finely chopped*
- *1 stalk celery, chopped*
- *2 medium sized potatoes, cubed*
- *3 cups chicken broth, simmering*
- *1 tablespoon lemon juice*
- *½ teaspoon salt*
  Freshly ground black pepper
- *½ cup heavy cream*

Wash watercress. Reserve ½ cup of the leaves. Chop remaining leaves and stems into small pieces. Melt the butter in a saucepan and sauté onion and celery for 3 minutes. Add the watercress, potatoes, broth, lemon juice, salt and pepper. Cover and simmer for 30 minutes. Purée the soup in a blender. Strain blended soup and return to a clean saucepan. Add cream and heat to simmering point. Add reserved watercress leaves and serve hot or cold.

Cullen skink

Haddock and potato soup

6 servings

- *1 pound smoked haddock or other smoked salt water fish*
- *2½ cups cold water*
- *½ teaspoon salt*
- *3 medium sized potatoes, cut into quarters*
- *1 onion, chopped*
- *4 cups milk, simmering*
- *⅛ teaspoon nutmeg*
  Freshly ground black pepper
- *2 tablespoons finely chopped parsley*
- *6 slices freshly made toast*

Place the fish in a saucepan and add the cold water. Bring to simmering point and add salt, potatoes and onion. Cover and simmer for 25 minutes. Drain fish and potatoes and place in a blender. Add 1 cup of milk and turn on the motor. Blend until smooth. Add soup to the remaining simmering milk. Season with nutmeg and pepper. Stir over low heat for 5 minutes. Garnish with parsley. Serve hot with freshly made toast.

Lentil soup

6 servings

- *1¼ cups lentils*
- *4 strips bacon*
- *2 onions, finely chopped*
- *2 carrots, chopped*
- *2 stalks celery, chopped*
- *5 cups water*
- *1 bay leaf*
- *3 sprigs parsley*
- *½ teaspoon thyme*
- *1 teaspoon salt*
  Freshly ground black pepper
- *1 teaspoon tomato paste*
- *½ cup boiled ham, diced*

Wash lentils several times in cold water, then soak in cold water 2 hours. Drain the lentils. Fry the bacon until crisp. Drain on paper towels and discard all but 2 tablespoons of bacon fat. Fry onions, carrots and celery in bacon fat for 5 minutes. Transfer to a saucepan and add drained lentils, 5 cups water, bacon, bay leaf, parsley, thyme, salt pepper and tomato paste. Cover and simmer over low heat for 1½ hours. Purée the soup in a blender. Strain the soup and return to a clean saucepan. (Add ½ cup additional water or chicken broth if the soup is too thick. This depends on the type of lentils used.) Return soup to simmering point and garnish with diced ham. Serve hot.

Green pea soup

6 servings

- *½ pound dried split peas*
- *5 cups chicken broth*
- *2 tablespoons butter*
- *2 onions, finely chopped*
- *1 carrot, chopped*
- *2 stalks celery, chopped*
- *1 teaspoon sugar*
- *1 teaspoon dried mint*
- *½ teaspoon salt*
  Freshly ground black pepper
- *½ cup heavy cream*
- *3 slices bread, cut into croutons*
- *3 tablespoons butter or oil*

Wash the peas. Place in a bowl, cover with cold water and soak for 8 hours. Drain and rinse the peas. Place the peas in a saucepan. Add chicken broth. Bring to simmering point over low heat. Cover and cook for 1 hour until peas are tender. Heat the butter and sauté onions, carrot and celery for 5 minutes. Add to saucepan with peas. Add sugar, mint, salt and pepper and continue cooking for 20 minutes. Pureé the soup in a blender. Strain into a clean saucepan. Add the cream and heat 2 minutes until cream is hot. Fry croutons in hot butter or oil. Drain on paper towels. Garnish pea soup with croutons.

Hotch potch

Lamb and vegetable soup

8 servings

1½ *pounds stewing lamb with bones*
½ *cup flour seasoned with ¾ teaspoon salt*
Freshly ground black pepper
2 *tablespoons oil*
8 *cups cold water*
2 *onions, finely chopped*
2 *carrots, finely chopped*
1 *small turnip, diced*
½ *small cauliflower, separated into flowerets*
½ *cup lima beans, fresh or frozen*
½ *cups peas, fresh or frozen*
1 *cup lettuce leaves, shredded*
2 *tablespoons, finely chopped parsley*

Roll pieces of lamb in flour seasoned with salt and pepper. Sauté the meat in the oil until lightly browned. Place the lamb in a large saucepan and cover with cold water. Cover saucepan and simmer for 1½ hours. Add all the vegetables except the lettuce and peas. Simmer vegetables for 25 minutes. Add lettuce and peas and simmer another 10 minutes. Remove lamb. Discard the bones and shred meat into small pieces. Return meat to the saucepan and simmer 5 minutes. Add parsley and serve hot.
This is a summer soup, which makes use of tender, young vegetables. It should be very thick.

Scotch broth

6 servings

2 *pounds stewing lamb, with bones*
6 *cups cold water*
3 *tablespoons barley, washed*
2 *onions, finely chopped*
2 *carrots, diced*
2 *stalks celery, diced*
1 *bay leaf*
½ *teaspoon thyme*
3 *tablespoons finely chopped parsley*
½ *teaspoon salt*
Freshly ground black pepper

Place the lamb in a large casserole. Cover with cold water. Cover casserole and simmer for 1 hour. Add remaining ingedients and simmer for 1 more hour. Discard bay leaf. Remove lamb. Separate meat from the bones. Discard the bones and shred meat into small pieces. Return meat to the saucepan. Simmer for 5 more minutes.

Oxtail soup

6 servings

1 *(3½ pound) oxtail, cut into 2 inch joints*
½ *cup flour*
2 *tablespoons vegetable oil*
2 *onions, finely chopped*
2 *carrots, sliced*
2 *stalks celery, sliced*
6 *cups beef broth*
1 *bay leaf*
¼ *teaspoon thyme*
½ *teaspoon salt*
½ *teaspoon peppercorns*
1 *tablespoon finely chopped parsley*
3 *cloves*
⅛ *teaspoon nutmeg*

Garnish:
1 *carrot, diced*
1 *small onion, cut into slices and separated into rings*
1 *teaspoon lemon juice*
1 *tablespoon Worcestershire sauce*

Place oxtail joints in a large saucepan. Cover with cold water. Bring water to a boil and simmer for 10 minutes. Drain oxtail and dry the joints on paper towels. Roll joints in flour. Brown oxtail in hot oil. Add onions, carrots and celery and continue cooking for 5 minutes. Add broth, bay leaf, thyme, salt, peppercorns, parsley, cloves and nutmeg. Cover and simmer over low heat for 3 hours until meat is tender. Remove joints and strip off all the meat. Strain the broth and chill for 4 hours. Remove fat from the broth. Cook diced carrot and onion in simmering broth for 15 minutes. Add meat from oxtails. Add lemon juice and Worcestershire sauce. Simmer 5 minutes and serve hot.

Houbova polevka

Mushroom soup

6 servings

- *1 small onion, finely chopped*
- *1 carrot, peeled and finely chopped*
- *6 cups veal broth*
- *2½ tablespoons butter*
- *½ pound fresh mushrooms, coarsely chopped*
- *1 tablespoon finely chopped parsley*
- *1 tablespoon flour*
- *½ teaspoon salt*
  Freshly ground black pepper

Place the onion, carrot and broth in a saucepan and simmer 1 hour. Heat the butter in a large saucepan and sauté the mushrooms over low heat 6 minutes. Add the parsley, cover and cook 5 minutes. Sprinkle on the flour and cook, stirring, 2 minutes. Add the broth gradually, stirring constantly. Season with salt and pepper and simmer 10 minutes more.

Kminova polevka

Caraway seed soup

6 servings

- *2 tablespoons butter*
- *1½ tablespoons flour*
- *1 tablespoon caraway seeds, lightly crushed*
- *6 cups boiling water or chicken broth*
- *1 teaspoon salt*
  Freshly ground black pepper
- *½ pound macaroni, cooked al dente*

Heat the butter in a large pan, add the flour and stir until lightly browned. Add the caraway seeds. Add the water gradually, stirring constantly. Reduce the heat and simmer for 40 minutes. Strain the soup and season with salt and pepper. Add the macaroni, heat and serve.

Paradiessuppe

Paradise soup

4 servings

- *2 pounds tomatoes, cut into wedges*
- *4 cups beef broth*
- *6 tablespoons butter*
- *1 onion, chopped*
- *2 tablespoons flour*
- *2 carrots, sliced*
- *¼ cup chopped celery*
- *2 cloves*
- *1 bay leaf*
  Juice and rind of ½ lemon
- *1 tablespoon sugar*
- *1½ teaspoons salt*
- *¾ cup cooked rice*

Simmer the tomatoes in the beef broth for 15 minutes. Strain the broth. Heat the butter in a saucepan, add the onion and fry until lightly browned. Stir in the flour gradually and add the carrots and chopped celery. Stir in the tomato broth, cloves, bay leaf, lemon juice and rind, sugar and salt. Simmer for 30 minutes. Strain. Add the cooked rice, heat thoroughly and serve.

Gurkensuppe

Cucumber soup

4 servings

- *2 tablespoons butter*
- *1 onion, finely chopped*
- *½ tablespoon finely chopped parsley*
- *1 cucumber, peeled, seeded and chopped*
- *2 tablespoons flour*
- *¾ cup heavy cream*
- *5 cups chicken broth*
- *½ teaspoon salt*
  Freshly ground black pepper

Heat the butter in a large saucepan and sauté the onion, parsley and cucumber over low heat until the onion is soft. Add the flour and cook, stirring, 1 minute. Add the cream and broth gradually, stirring constantly. Bring to a simmer and add salt and pepper. Serve immediately.

Peking hot sour soup

4 to 6 American servings
4 to 6 Chinese servings

  4 *dried Chinese mushrooms*
  ½ *cup lean pork*
  ⅓ *cup canned bamboo shoots*
  2 *bean curd cakes*
  1 *egg*
  1 *tablespoon cornstarch*
  4 *tablespoons water*
  4 *cups chicken broth*
  2 *tablespoons white vinegar*
  1 *tablespoon soy sauce*
  ¼ *teaspoon salt*
  ¼ *teaspoon freshly ground*
     pepper
  ½ *teaspoon sesame oil*
  1 *scallion, minced*

Soak dried mushrooms in hot water for 20 minutes. Squeeze dry and remove stems. Cut mushroom caps into thin strips. Cut pork across the grain in ¼ inch thick slices and then in ⅛ inch wide strips. Cut bean curd and bamboo shoots into similar sized strips. Break egg in a bowl and beat lightly. Mix cornstarch and water until well blended. Bring the broth to the boil and add pork and mushrooms. Bring to the boil again, reduce heat and simmer for about 8 to 10 minutes. Add the bamboo shoots and bean curd and simmer another 4 to 5 minutes. Mix vinegar, soy sauce, salt and pepper and stir into soup. Stir in cornstarch mixture and cook stirring constantly until thickened. Stir in the beaten egg and remove from heat when egg threads are almost firm. Add sesame oil and scallion and serve immediately.

Watercress soup

4 American servings
4 Chinese servings

  ½ *bunch watercress*
  3 *cups chicken broth*

  ½ *teaspoon minced fresh*
     ginger root
  ½ *teaspoon soy sauce*
  ½ *teaspoon sherry*
  ¼ *cup slivered lean pork*
  1 *scallion, shredded*
  ¼ *teaspoon salt*

Wash watercress, discard tough stems and cut in 1½ inch lengths. In a saucepan, combine broth, ginger root, soy sauce and sherry and bring to a boil. Add pork, reduce heat and simmer for 10 minutes. Add watercress, scallion and salt and simmer for another 2 to 3 minutes. Serve immediately.

Pork and abalone soup

4 American servings
4 Chinese servings

  1 *(4 ounce) can abalone*
  ¾ *cup (4 ounces) lean pork*
  4 *cups chicken broth*
  2 *tablespoons sherry*
  ¼ *cup bamboo shoots*
  2 *tablespoons oil*
  ½ *teaspoon salt*
  2 *thin slices fresh ginger root*
  ⅛ *teaspoon freshly ground*
     black pepper
  4 *sprigs parsley*

Drain abalone and reserve the liquid. Cut the abalone and the pork into 1½ inch squares, ⅛ inch thick. Combine abalone liquid, chicken broth and sherry. Cut bamboo shoots into ⅛ inch thick slices and cut slices into match stick size strips 1½ inches long. Heat chicken broth mixture to boiling point. Heat the oil in a wok or skillet. Add salt. Add ginger root and stir fry for 2 minutes until lightly browned. Discard ginger root. Add the pork and stir fry for 2 minutes or until meat turns white and loses all its pink color. Do not let the pork brown. Transfer the pork to the saucepan containing boiling chicken broth. Add abalone and bamboo to the broth. Season with pepper. Cook only to heat through or abalone will toughen. Serve in individual bowls. Float a parsley sprig in each bowl.

Crab asparagus soup

6 American servings
6 Chinese servings

  8 *ounces fresh crabmeat*
  1 *pound fresh, thin stemmed*
     asparagus
  1 *tablespoon sherry*
  ½ *tablespoon soy sauce*
  6 *cups chicken broth*
  1 *tablespoon oil*
  1 *scallion, minced*
  1 *tablespoon cornstarch*
  3 *tablespoons water*
1½ *teaspoons chili sauce or*
  ½ *teaspoon Chinese chili paste*
  1 *tablespoon finely chopped*
     chives

Flake the crabmeat and remove hard membranes. Cut the top third of asparagus flowers and stems into pieces 1½ inches long. Parboil asparagus in boiling salted water for 3 minutes. Bring sherry, soy sauce and chicken broth to boiling point. Drain and rinse asparagus under cold running water. Heat the oil in a wok or skillet. Add scallion and stir fry for 30 seconds. Add crabmeat and asparagus and stir fry for 30 seconds. Add crabmeat and asparagus to chicken broth. Add chilli sauce. Stir in cornstarch dissolved in cold water. Stir 1 minute to thicken broth slightly. Ladle into bowls and garnish with chives.

Wonton soup

4 American servings
4 Chinese servings

For the wontons:
　8　wonton wrappers

　1　dried Chinese mushroom
　⅓　cup lean minced pork or beef
　¼　cup minced shrimp
　1　water chestnut, minced
　1　whole scallion, minced
　½　teaspoon soy sauce
　1　teaspoon sherry
　　Pinch of sugar
　¼　teaspoon salt
　1　egg, lightly beaten

For the soup:
　3　cups chicken broth

　*1　scallion, white part only,
　　thinly sliced*
　2　tablespoons egg garnish

Soak dried mushroom in warm
water 20 minutes. Squeeze dry.
Remove the stalk and mince the
cap. Combine mushroom, pork,
shrimp, water chestnut, scallion,
soy sauce, sherry, sugar and salt.
Let stand 30 minutes. Place
½ teaspoon of the filling barely
off center of each wrapper. Fold
wrapper in half and press the
edges together to seal them.
Again, fold the wrapper in half.
Pull the corners down into a
crescent shape, overlapping the
corners. Seal the overlap with a
little of the beaten egg. Bring
plenty of salted water to a
boil. Drop in the wontons one
by one and simmer 7 minutes.
(Make sure they do not stick to
the bottom of the pan.) Drain
the wontons. Bring the chicken

broth to a boil. Add wontons
and scallion. Top each serving
with a little of the egg garnish.

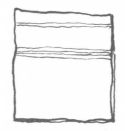

Egg drop soup

4 American servings
4 Chinese servings

　1　egg
　½　teaspoon water
　3　cups chicken or meat broth

　⅛　teaspoon sugar
　¼　teaspoon salt
　⅛　teaspoon sesame oil
　1　small scallion, minced
　*2　teaspoons finely chopped
　　chives*

In a small bowl, beat the egg
with the water. Bring the broth
to a simmer and stir in the sugar,
salt and sesame oil. Continue to
stir and slip the egg into the
simmering broth. As you stir,
the egg will coagulate and form
thin threads. Stir in the scallion
and remove from the heat. Pour
soup into individual bowls.
Garnish with chives and serve.

Sweet corn and chicken soup

4 American servings
4 Chinese servings

　1　(4 ounce) can creamed corn
　3　cups chicken broth
　¼　teaspoon salt
　*1　teaspoon cornstarch
　　dissolved in*
　1　tablespoon water
　½　recipe chicken velvet

　1　tablespoon ham garnish

Place corn in a blender and
blend until smooth. Bring the
broth to the simmering point.
Add the corn and salt and
simmer 3 minutes. Stir in
cornstarch mixture to thicken
slightly. Add chicken velvet and
simmer 1 minute, stirring
constantly. Pour into individual
soup bowls, top with ham
garnish and serve.

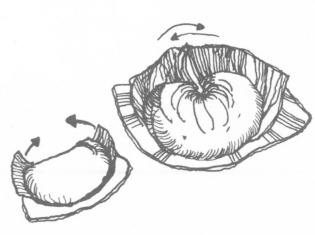

Soupe Meusienne

Soup from the Meuse

4 to 6 servings

- 3 tablespoons butter
- 1 head Boston lettuce, shredded
- 4 scallions, sliced
- 1 stalk celery, chopped
- 6 cups water
- ½ pound fresh green peas
- ½ pound cooked ham, in 1 piece
- 1 teaspoon thyme
- 1 bay leaf
- ¼–½ teaspoon salt (depending on saltiness of ham)
  Freshly ground black pepper
- ½ cup cream or milk
- 2 tablespoons finely chopped chervil or parsley

Heat the butter in a large saucepan and sauté the lettuce, scallions and celery slowly for 10 minutes. Add water, peas, ham, thyme, bay leaf, salt and pepper. Bring to a boil, lower the heat and simmer slowly for 1 hour. Remove the ham and cut into small pieces. Strain the broth and purée the vegetables in the blender. Return the ham and puréed vegetables to the broth. Add the cream and heat the soup thoroughly but do not boil. Serve in individual bowls and garnish each serving with a little chervil or parsley.

Humpkessoep

Vegetable soup

6 to 8 servings

- 8 cups water
- 1 pound green beans, cut into 1 inch pieces
- 1 pound smoked sausage or frankfurters
- 4 medium sized onions, chopped
- 4 medium sized potatoes, peeled and diced
- 1 cup mixed soup vegetables (celery tops, leeks, carrots, etc.)
- 1 teaspoon salt
  Freshly ground black pepper
- 2 tomatoes, peeled and cut into wedges
- 4 tablespoons finely chopped parsley

Bring the water to a boil in a large saucepan. Add the green beans, lower the heat and simmer 10 minutes. Add all the remaining ingredients except the tomatoes and parsley and simmer 30 minutes. Just before serving, stir in the tomatoes and parsley and simmer 2 minutes.

Soupe au lard

Bacon soup

6 servings

- ½ pound bacon, in 1 piece
- 6 cups cold water
- 12 peppercorns, crushed
- 2 bay leaves
- 1 teaspoon thyme
- 3 large carrots, peeled and sliced
- 2 small leeks, sliced
- 3 stalks celery, sliced
- 3 turnips, cubed
- ¼ small cabbage, shredded
  Salt, if necessary

Soak the bacon in cold water for 3 hours, changing the water frequently. (This will reduce the saltiness of the bacon.) Place the 6 cups cold water in a heavy pan and add the bacon, peppercorns, bay leaves and thyme. Bring to a boil, skim and lower the heat. Cover the pan and cook over the lowest possible heat for 30 minutes. Add the vegetables. Taste the broth and add salt, if necessary. This will depend on the saltiness of your bacon. Continue to simmer the soup, covered, for 1 hour. Remove the bacon from the pan. Discard the fat, cut the meat into small pieces and return to the soup. Refrigerate the soup and lift off the fat when it has risen to the top. When ready to serve, reheat the soup briefly.

Niersoep

Kidney soup

4 servings

- 1 veal kidney (about ½ pound)
- 4 cups beef broth
- ½ teaspoon salt
  Freshly ground black pepper
- 3 tablespoons butter
- 1 tablespoon finely chopped onion
- 4 tablespoons flour
- 1 cup cream
- 1 cup thinly sliced mushrooms
- 2 tablespoons Madeira or dry sherry

Soak kidney in cold water 2 hours, changing the water twice. Drain and slice kidney thinly. Add the slices to the beef broth and season with salt and pepper. Bring to a boil, lower the heat and simmer 30 minutes. Strain the broth. Heat the butter in a skillet and sauté the onion until golden. Add the flour and cook, stirring for 1 to 2 minutes. Add the cream and broth slowly, stirring with a wire whisk to form a smooth soup. Return the kidneys to the soup, add the mushrooms and cook 10 minutes more. Stir in the Madeira or sherry just before serving.

Mushroom soup

Chervil is the best loved soup in Belgium. You can buy bunches of fresh chervil all year round at any market and at any grocer's. The

pleasant odor of chervil soup is familiar to anyone who has stayed in a Belgian boarding house.

Champignonsoep

Mushroom soup

6 servings

- 4 tablespoons butter
- 1 pound fresh mushrooms, thinly sliced
- 2 tablespoons flour
- 6 cups beef broth, simmering
- ½ teaspoon salt
  Freshly ground black pepper
- 1 egg yolk combined with 2 tablespoons cream
  Juice of ½ lemon
- 2 slices white bread, diced and toasted in the oven until brown

Heat the butter in a large saucepan and sauté the mushrooms over medium heat for 3 to 4 minutes. Stir in the flour and cook 2 minutes. Add the hot broth gradually, stirring constantly. Season with salt and pepper and simmer slowly 10 minutes. Just before serving, stir in the egg yolk mixed with cream and the lemon juice. Heat the soup, but do not allow it to boil. Top each serving with toasted croutons.

Kervelsoep

Chervil soup

4 to 6 servings

- 3 tablespoons butter
- 2 tablespoons flour
- 6 cups beef broth
- ½ teaspoon salt
  Freshly ground black pepper
- 1 egg yolk
- ¼ cup cream
- 2 tablespoons finely chopped fresh chervil or parsley

In a saucepan, heat the butter, add flour and stir into a smooth paste. Add beef broth gradually, stirring constantly. Cook for 3 minutes. Season with salt and pepper. Combine egg yolk, cream and fresh chervil in a soup tureen and, stirring constantly, very carefully pour the hot soup over the mixture. Ladle the soup into individual bowls and serve at once.

Vegetable summer soup

Kippesoep met balletjes

Chicken soup with meat balls

4 servings

  2 *pounds stewing chicken*
3½ *cups water*
2½ *teaspoons salt*
   Freshly ground black pepper
 ¼ *teaspoon basil*
 1 *bay leaf*
 ¼ *teaspoon mace*
 1 *small clove garlic,*
   crushed
 ½ *pound small white onions*
 5 *small carrots, sliced*
 1 *tablespoon finely chopped*
   combined parsley and
   celery leaves

Place the chicken in the water
in a large saucepan. Add the
salt, pepper, basil, bay leaf,
mace and garlic. Bring to a boil,
lower the heat and simmer
slowly for 1½ hours or until the
chicken is just tender. Remove
chicken from the pan. Strain the
broth and carefully skim the fat
from the surface of the soup.
Bring the soup to a boil and add
the onions, carrots, parsley and
celery and simmer gently for
10 minutes.

For the meat balls:
 1 *cup finely minced pork*
 1 *egg*
 1 *slice crumbled white bread,*
   crusts removed
2½ *tablespoons flour*
 ½ *teaspoon salt*
   Freshly ground black pepper

Mix pork with egg, bread, flour,
salt and pepper. Form into
small meat balls, about ¾ inch
in diameter. Add the meat balls

to the soup and simmer for a
further 35 minutes. Meanwhile,
skin and bone the chicken. Cut
the meat into small pieces and
measure ½ cup. Garnish the
soup with the chicken and
serve. Save the remaining
chicken for use in salads or
sandwiches.

Zomer groentesoep

Vegetable summer soup

6 servings

- 3 *tablespoons butter*
- 6 *small carrots, peeled and sliced*
- 6 *cauliflower flowerets*
- 1 *leek, chopped*
- ½ *cup young green peas*
- 6 *cups beef broth, simmering*
- 3 *tablespoons uncooked rice*
- ½ *teaspoon salt*
  Freshly ground black pepper
- 1 *tablespoon finely chopped mixed garden herbs (chervil, chives, parsley, celery tops)*
- 1½ *tablespoons cornstarch dissolved in 3 tablespoons water*

For the meatballs:
- ½ *cup ground veal*
- ¼ *teaspoon salt*
  Freshly ground black pepper
  Dash of nutmeg
  Flour

Heat the butter in a large saucepan. Add the carrots, cauliflower, leek and peas and cook slowly for 10 minutes. Add the broth, rice, salt and pepper and bring to a boil. Reduce the heat and simmer slowly 15 minutes. Meanwhile, combine the veal, salt, pepper and nutmeg and form into balls ½ inch in diameter. Roll the meatballs in flour. Add the meatballs to the soup and simmer 15 minutes more. Stir in the garden herbs and cornstarch mixture and simmer a few minutes until the soup has thickened slightly. Serve immediately.

Preisoep

Belgian leek soup

4 to 6 servings

- 3 *tablespoons butter*
- ½ *pound leeks, sliced or*
- 4 *yellow onions, sliced*
- 1 *pound potatoes, peeled and cubed*
- 6 *cups beef broth*
- 1 *teaspoon salt*
- ½ *cup cream or milk*
- 4–6 *slices toasted French bread*

Heat the butter in a large saucepan. Add the leeks and sauté 3 minutes. Then add the cubed potatoes, beef broth and salt. Bring to a boil and cook for 40 minutes, stirring occasionally. Before serving, stir in cream or milk. Place a slice of toasted bread in each soup bowl and pour the hot soup over the bread.

Bruine bonensoep

Brown bean soup

6 servings (main course)

- 1½ *cups dried kidney beans*
- 3 *quarts water*
- 1 *bay leaf*
- 2 *cloves*
- 3 *medium sized potatoes, peeled and cubed*
- 3 *tablespoons butter*
- 1 *onion, chopped*
- ½ *tablespoon curry powder*
- 1 *teaspoon salt*
  Freshly ground black pepper
  Dash of Worcestershire sauce

Soak the beans in the water overnight. Bring to a boil, add the bay leaf and cloves and cook for 2 hours. Add potatoes and cook for another 30 minutes. In the meantime, heat the butter in a frying pan and sauté the chopped onion and curry powder until light brown. Remove bay leaf and cloves from the soup. Strain the broth and purée beans and potatoes in the blender. Add the purée to the broth. Add sautéed onion and cook for another 20 minutes, stirring occasionally. Season with salt, pepper and Worcestershire sauce. Serve the soup with toasted white bread.

Potage aux carottes

Carrot soup

6 to 8 servings

¼ *pound lean bacon, cut in small pieces*
1 *medium sized onion, finely chopped*
6 *cups water*
1 *stalk celery, chopped*
½ *pound carrots, peeled and sliced*
½ *pound potatoes, peeled and cubed*
½ *teaspoon salt*
 Freshly ground black pepper
1 *teaspoon sugar*
¼ *teaspoon mace*
¼ *teaspoon thyme*
1 *bay leaf*
½ *cup cream or milk*
1 *tablespoon finely chopped chervil or parsley*
2 *slices white bread, crusts removed*
2 *tablespoons butter*

Fry the bacon until the fat is rendered. Remove the bacon and discard all but 1 tablespoon bacon fat. Add the onion and sauté 5 minutes. In a saucepan, bring the water to a boil. Add the bacon, onion, celery, carrots, potatoes, salt, pepper, sugar, mace, thyme and bay leaf. Simmer, covered, for 1 hour. Purée the soup in a blender and pour it through a sieve back into the saucepan. Add the cream and chervil and heat the soup but do not boil. Cut the slices of bread in quarters diagonally and sauté in the butter until golden brown on both sides. Float the bread triangles on individual servings of soup.

Ossestaartsoep

Oxtail soup

4 to 6 servings

1 *small piece salt pork or bacon*
1 *oxtail, cut into pieces at the joints*
½ *teaspoon salt*
 Freshly ground black pepper
½ *teaspoon thyme*
1 *bay leaf*
1 *sprig parsley*
8 *cups water*
4 *tablespoons barley or rice*
1 *medium sized carrot, sliced*
1 *leek, thinly sliced*
1 *onion, coarsely chopped*
1 *stalk celery, sliced*
1 *medium sized potato, peeled and cubed*
¼ *pound lean bacon, finely chopped*
1 *tablespoon Madeira or sherry*
2 *tablespoons finely chopped parsley*

Rub a large heavy pan with the salt pork. Place it in the pan with the oxtail, salt, pepper, thyme, bay leaf, parsley and water and bring to a boil. Lower the heat, partially cover and simmer slowly 4 hours. Strain the broth and remove the meat from the oxtail joints. Return the meat to the strained broth and add the barley or rice. Cover and cook over low heat 30 minutes. Add the carrot, leek, onion, celery, potato and bacon and simmer, covered, 30 minutes more. Taste for seasoning and add Madeira. Garnish each serving with parsley.

Soupa lakhana

Cabbage soup

8 servings

- 2 pounds white cabbage
- 2 small onions, chopped
- 1½ tablespoons olive oil
- 4 medium sized ripe tomatoes, peeled, seeded and chopped
- ½ teaspoon salt
  Freshly ground black pepper
- 10 cups beef broth
- 1 cup croutons

Shred the cabbage finely, wash and drain. Fry the onions in the oil until golden brown and transfer to a large sauce pan. Add the cabbage, tomatoes, salt and pepper and cook for 1 minute. Add the beef broth and bring to a boil. Reduce the heat, partially cover and simmer for 30 minutes or until the cabbage is tender. Serve in individual bowls and garnish with croutons just before serving

Fasolada

Bean soup

8 servings

- 1 pound dried white beans
- 10 cups water
- 3 medium sized onions, chopped
- 1 carrot, finely chopped
- 1½ tablespoons chopped parsley
- 2 tablespoons chopped celery leaves
- 2 tablespoons tomato purée
- 1½ tablespoons olive oil
- ½ teaspoon salt
  Freshly ground black pepper

Soak the beans overnight. Wash, drain and place them in a large saucepan. Add the water and boil for 2 minutes. Pour off all the water and add the same quantity of fresh water. Bring to a boil, add the onions, carrot, 1 tablespoon parsley, celery leaves, tomato purée, oil, salt and pepper. Simmer for about 1 hour or until the beans are soft and tender. Season to taste, sprinkle on the remaining parsley and serve hot.

Makhluta

Lentil soup with chick peas

8 servings

- 1 cup chick peas
- ½ cup black beans
- 1 cup lentils
- 8 cups water
- 1 cup rice
- 2 tablespoons olive oil
- ½ cup chopped onion
- 1½ teaspoons salt
- ½ teaspoon crushed caraway seeds

Soak the chick peas and black beans together overnight in water to cover. Drain and place in a large, heavy pan with the lentils and water. Bring to a boil, lower the heat and simmer 1½ hours or until beans and peas are tender. Add the rice and simmer 20 minutes more. Meanwhile heat the olive oil in a small skillet and sauté the onions until golden brown. Drain off all the oil and add the onion to the bean soup. Stir in the salt and caraway seeds and simmer 5 minutes.

Fakki

Lentil soup

8 to 10 servings

- 1 pound yellow or brown lentils
- 10 cups water
- 2 onions, chopped
- 1 carrot, grated
- 2 cloves garlic, crushed
- 1 stalk celery, chopped
- 1 tablespoon olive oil
- 2 bay leaves
- 2½ teaspoons salt
  Freshly ground black pepper
- 2 tablespoons vinegar

Wash and drain the lentils. Place the lentils and water in a large saucepan. Add the onions, carrot, garlic, celery, oil, bay leaves, salt and pepper. Bring to a boil and simmer for 45 to 50 minutes until the lentils are tender. Remove the bay leaves. Purée the soup in the blender or force it through a strainer. Stir in the vinegar, reheat and serve.

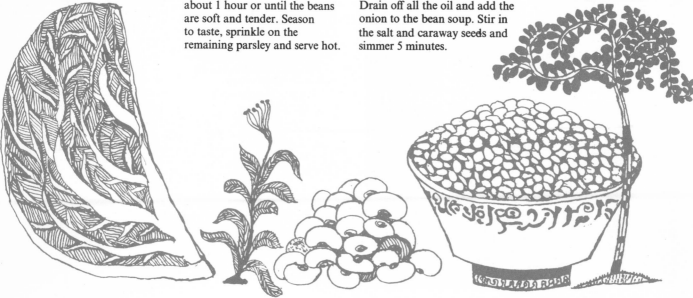

Weddings are still the occasion for festive and abundant eating. The many dishes set on the table are a traditional assurance that the marriage will prove fertile.

Dügün tshorbası

Wedding soup

6 servings

- 6 cups chicken broth
- 3 tablespoons butter
- 1 pound lean lamb, coarsley ground
- 2 tablespoons flour
- 1 onion, halved
- 1 teaspoon salt
   Freshly ground black pepper
- 2 teaspoons paprika
- 4 egg yolks, lightly beaten
   Juice of 1 lemon
- ¼ teaspoon cinnamon

Heat the chicken broth to boiling point. Melt the butter in a large skillet. Add the lamb and fry, stirring constantly until well browned. Stir in the flour and cook for 2 minutes. Add lamb, onion, salt, pepper and paprika to the hot broth. Bring to boiling point, reduce the heat and simmer for 1½ hours. Remove the onion. Beat the egg yolks and lemon juice together in a small bowl. Add egg yolk mixture to the soup, stirring constantly. Stir until hot but do not allow the soup to boil. Sprinkle with cinnamon and serve immediately.

Tchorba Toptsita

Traditional meatball soup

6 servings

- 2 pounds soup bones
- 6 cups water
- ½ cup ground beef
- ½ teaspoon salt
   Freshly ground black pepper
- 3 tablespoons finely chopped parsley
- 2 tablespoons olive oil
- 1 teaspoon paprika
- ½ cup rice
- 2 cloves garlic, crushed
- ¼ cup vinegar

Place the bones in a large saucepan. Add the water, cover and simmer for 3 hours. Skim off the foam which rises to the surface. Strain the broth and discard the bones. Add more water if necessary to make up the 6 cup quantity. Return the broth to a clean saucepan and bring to simmering point. Combine the beef with salt, pepper and 2 tablespoons chopped parsley. Form into small balls 1 inch in diameter. Add meat balls to broth and simmer for 15 minutes. Heat the oil in a small saucepan and stir in paprika. Cook the paprika in oil for 2 minutes and add to the soup. Add the rice. Cover the saucepan and simmer for 20 minutes. Stir in the remaining 1 tablespoon of parsley, the garlic and vinegar. Serve immediately.

Kakavia

Balık tshorbası

In Genesis the symbolic story is told of how Esau came home one day tired and hungry from hunting, and smelled what was probably lentil soup which his brother Jacob had cooked. Esau was so hungry he sold his birthright for some of the soup. Lentil soup is still a part of the daily diet throughout the Middle East, and it is probably the oldest dish in the world. Usually the soup is made with mutton or chicken, and the lentils are the small orange-red variety that can be bought at any Eastern market. With these lentils the soup becomes a beautiful vermilion-red color, much more attractive than the dull brown of the soup we know.

Certainly the most classic Greek soup is 'avgolemono', made from chicken broth, very slightly soured by lemon and thickened with a lightly beaten egg. It is a very fine gold-yellow soup, tasty and light and a necessary part of the Easter dinner.

And throughout the East when the summer comes, yoghurt soup is a refreshing dish. Yoghurt is one of the most ancient ingredients in the cooking of the entire Middle East. The soup is thinned with water or chicken broth.

Greek bouillabaisse

8 servings

2½ to 3 pounds assorted fish
    fillets
  1 teaspoon salt
    Juice of 1 lemon
    Heads, tails and bones of
    filleted fish
10 to 12 cups water
  4 tablespoons olive oil
  2 onions, thinly sliced
  1 potato, peeled and thinly
    sliced
  6 to 8 medium sized tomatoes,
    peeled, seeded and chopped
  2 tablespoons finely chopped
    celery leaves
  2 cloves garlic, crushed
 ¼ cup dry white wine
  1 bay leaf
    Freshly ground black pepper
  2 tablespoons finely chopped
    parsley

Wash the fish fillets, dry them and cut into small serving pieces. Sprinkle the fish with the salt and juice of ½ a lemon and set aside. Place the fish trimmings and the water in a large pan and bring to a boil. Lower the heat and simmer 20 minutes. (If fish trimmings are not available, use half clam juice and half water.) Strain and reserve the broth. Heat the olive oil in a large heavy pan. Add the onions, potato, tomatoes, celery leaves and garlic and sauté slowly 5 minutes. Add the reserved broth, wine and bay leaf and bring to a boil. Lower the heat, cover and simmer 40 minutes. Strain the broth, pressing down on the vegetables to extract all the

juices. Return the broth to the pan. There should be at least 10 cups. If not, add water to measure 10 cups. Bring the broth to a rolling boil and add the pepper, parsley and the firmest of the fish fillets. Cook 5 minutes and add the more delicate fish. Cook over moderate heat 10 minutes more. Just before serving, add the remaining juice of ½ a lemon and taste for seasoning.

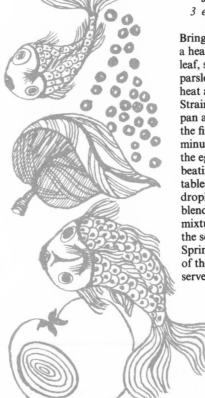

Fish soup

6 servings

  6 cups fish broth or half clam
    juice and half water
  1 bay leaf
 ¼ teaspoon salt
    Freshly ground black pepper
  3 tablespoons finely chopped
    parsley
    Pinch of saffron
  1 pound haddock fillets or
    fillets of other firm fleshed
    fish
    Juice of 1 lemon
  3 egg yolks, lightly beaten

Bring the fish broth to a boil in a heavy pan and add the bay leaf, salt, pepper, 2 tablespoons parsley and saffron. Reduce the heat and simmer 25 minutes. Strain the broth, return to the pan and bring to a simmer. Add the fish fillets and poach 15 minutes. Add the lemon juice to the egg yolks by droplets, beating constantly. Then add 4 tablespoons of the fish broth by droplets and beat until well blended. Stir the egg yolk mixture into the soup and ladle the soup into individual bowls. Sprinkle each serving with some of the remaining parsley and serve.

Psarosoupa

Fish soup

6 servings

- 6 cups fish broth or half clam juice and half water
- 4 medium sized tomatoes, peeled, seeded and chopped
- ½ teaspoon sugar
- ¼ teaspoon salt
  Freshly ground black pepper
- 1½ tablespoons olive oil
- ½ cup rice
- 1 tablespoon lemon juice
- 2 tablespoons finely chopped parsley

Place the fish broth, tomatoes, sugar, salt, pepper and olive oil in a heavy saucepan. Bring to a boil and cook 5 minutes over high heat. Reduce the heat and simmer 30 minutes. Bring to a boil, add the rice and cook over high heat 15 minutes. Stir in the lemon juice and parsley and serve immediately.

Sayadieh

Rice in fish broth

6 servings

- 2 pounds haddock, sea bass or cod fillets
- 1¼ teaspoons salt
- 4 tablespoons olive oil
- 2 small onions, chopped
  Head bones and other trimmings from filleted fish
- 4 cups water
  Freshly ground black pepper
- 1½ cups rice
- ½ cup combined almonds and pine nuts
- 1 tablespoon lemon juice

Sprinkle the fish fillets on both sides with 1 teaspoon salt and refrigerate for 2½ hours. Meanwhile, heat 1 tablespoon olive oil in a saucepan and sauté the onions until golden brown. Add the fish trimmings, water and pepper and bring to a boil. Reduce the heat and simmer 30 minutes. (If fish trimmings are not available, use half clam juice and half water.) Strain and reserve the broth. Soak the rice in water to cover for 30 minutes and drain. Bring 3 cups of the reserved fish broth to a boil, add the rice and stir once with a fork. Lower the heat, cover the pan and simmer until the rice has absorbed all the liquid (about 25 minutes). While the rice is cooking, heat the remaining olive oil in a skillet and sauté the fish fillets about 4 minutes on each side or until the flesh flakes easily with a fork. Remove from the pan and keep warm. Oil a shallow pan or ring mold and arrange the almonds and pine nuts on the bottom in a decorative pattern. Carefully place the cooked rice on the nuts and press down firmly with a wooden spoon or spatula. Unmold the rice on a serving dish and surround with the fish fillets. Bring the remaining fish broth to a boil and stir in the lemon juice and remaining salt. Pour into a sauce dish and serve with the fish and rice.

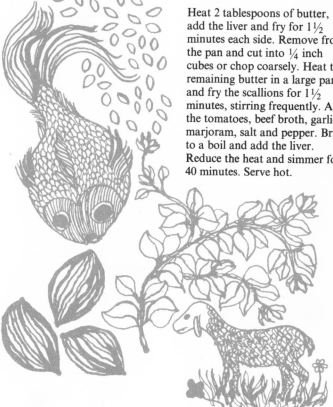

Kuzu ciger tshorbası

Liver soup

6 servings

- 4 tablespoons butter
- ½ pound lamb's liver
- 16 scallions, coarsely chopped
- 4 large ripe tomatoes, peeled, seeded and coarsely chopped
- 6 cups beef broth
- 2 cloves garlic, crushed
- ¼ teaspoon dried marjoram, crumbled
- 1 teaspoon salt
  Freshly ground black pepper

Heat 2 tablespoons of butter, add the liver and fry for 1½ minutes each side. Remove from the pan and cut into ¼ inch cubes or chop coarsely. Heat the remaining butter in a large pan and fry the scallions for 1½ minutes, stirring frequently. Add the tomatoes, beef broth, garlic, marjoram, salt and pepper. Bring to a boil and add the liver. Reduce the heat and simmer for 40 minutes. Serve hot.

Traditionally, this soup is made using 'offal meat' or the heart, liver, intestine, tripe and feet of a lamb.

Patsas

Lamb soup

6 servings

- 6 to 8 cups water
- 2 to 3 pounds lamb shanks
- 2 small onions, peeled
- 1 teaspoon salt
  Freshly ground black pepper
  Few springs parsley
- 3 eggs
  Juice of 2 lemons

Bring the water to a boil and add the lamb shanks. Bring to a boil again and skim the broth. Reduce the heat, add the onions, salt and pepper and simmer 1½ hours. Remove the lamb shanks, strip the meat from the bones and return the meat to the broth. Simmer ½ hour more. Remove and discard the onions. Prepare the egg and lemon juice mixture as described in the recipe for Avgolemono soup on page 25 and add it to the soup. Serve immediately.

Shorabat Kharoof

Lamb's soup with zucchini

6 servings

- 1 pound lamb with marrow bone
- 6 cups water
- 1 teaspoon salt
  Freshly ground black pepper
- 6 tablespoons raw rice
- ½ pound zucchini, peeled and chopped
- ¼ teaspoon cinnamon

Place the lamb in a medium-sized saucepan. Add the water, salt and pepper. Cover and simmer for 1½ hours. Discard the bone and cut the lamb into 1 inch cubes. Return the lamb to the saucepan with the cooking liquid. Add the rice and zucchini. Cover and simmer 20 minutes. Sprinkle with cinnamon just before serving.

Mayeritsa

Greek Easter soup

6 servings

- 3 tablespoons butter
- 1 pound lean lamb, cut into ¼ inch cubes
- 10 scallions, finely chopped
- 1 bunch fresh dill, finely chopped or
  1 tablespoon dried dill weed
- 2 tablespoons finely chopped parsley
- 1 tablespoon finely chopped fresh mint or
  1 teaspoon dried mint
- 6 cups water
- ½ teaspoon salt
  Freshly ground black pepper
- 6 tablespoons rice
- 3 eggs
  Juice of 2 lemons

Heat the butter in a large saucepan. Add the lamb, scallions, dill, parsley and mint and sauté 3 minutes. Add the water, salt and pepper and bring to a boil. Lower the heat, cover the pan and simmer 1 hour. Add rice and simmer 15 minutes more. Beat the eggs and add the lemon juice slowly, beating constantly. Stir a few tablespoons of the soup into the egg mixture and return to the soup. Do not allow it to boil or the eggs will curdle. Remove from the heat and serve immediately.

Koyun et suyu

Lamb's broth

8 servings

- 3 tablespoons butter
- 2 pounds boneless neck or shoulder of lamb, cubed
- 8 cups water
- 2 large onions, coarsley chopped
- 3 carrots, coarsley chopped
- 1 leek, coarsley chopped
- 2 tablespoons chopped celery leaves
- 4 scallions, coarsley chopped
- 1 bay leaf
- 1 teaspoon salt
  Freshly ground black pepper
- ¼ cup yogurt
- 1 teaspoon finely chopped parsley

Heat the butter in a large saucepan and sauté the lamb until lightly browned. Add the water, bring to a boil and skim the broth. Add all the remaining ingredients except the yogurt and parsley. Bring to a boil again, reduce the heat and simmer 1½ hours. Combine the yogurt with 2 tablespoons broth. Stir the yogurt mixture into the soup, sprinkle with parsley and serve.

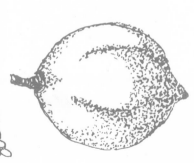

Onion soup is, among its other virtues, considered, a delicious remedy for a hangover after an evening of drinking. In Paris' better days the small bistros near the 'Halles', the splendid open-air market of the capital, had an early-morning clientele of partygoers in evening dress who mixed gaily with butchers and porters to share the benefits of onion soup. In those days the market was still held in the middle of the street and at night fresh fish, meat and vegetables arrived from the provinces. The bistros stayed open all night to serve wine and soup

Soupe à l'oignon

Onion soup

4 servings

  3 *tablespoons butter*
  3 *large onions, thinly sliced*
  1 *tablespoon flour*
½ *teaspoon salt*
     Freshly ground black pepper
  5 *cups beef broth*
  4 *thick slices French or*
     Italian bread
  4 *tablespoons grated*
     Parmesan cheese
  4 *tablespoons grated Swiss*
     or Gruyère cheese

In a heavy pan, melt the butter, add the sliced onions and cook slowly stirring occasionally, until golden. Sprinkle on the flour and stir for a few minutes to cook the flour. Season with salt and pepper. Add the broth, stirring constantly. Bring to a boil, lower the heat and let the soup simmer, partially covered, for 30 minutes. Toast the slices of bread in the oven until brown. Place them in a large ovenproof soup tureen or individual bowls. Preheat the broiler. Sprinkle the bread with Parmesan cheese. Pour the soup over the bread and top with the Swiss or Gruyère cheese. Brown the cheese under the broiler and serve immediately.

Potage Saint Germain

Fresh pea soup

4 servings

  1 *Boston lettuce*
  ¼ *pound butter*
  2 *pounds unshelled peas or*
     1 package frozen peas
  ½ *teaspoon salt*
  1 *teaspoon sugar*
  4 *cups water*
     Freshly ground black pepper

Wash lettuce and shred leaves into strips. Melt the butter in a saucepan. Add lettuce, shelled peas, salt and sugar. Cover and simmer over low heat for 10 minutes. Add water and simmer another 10 minutes until the peas are tender. Purée the soup in a blender. Return to a clean saucepan. Add pepper. Bring soup to simmering point. Serve hot.

Elzekaria

Soup from Alsace

6 servings

  ⅓ *cup lard or rendered*
     bacon fat
  1 *large onion, finely chopped*
  1 *medium white cabbage*
  2 *cloves garlic, crushed*
  1½ *teaspoons salt*
     Freshly ground black pepper
  ½ *pound kidney beans,*
     soaked overnight and
     drained
  1 *tablespoon cider vinegar*

Heat the lard in a heavy pan and cook the onions until brown. Wash the cabbage and chop into large pieces. When the onions are golden, add the cabbage and garlic and cook slowly for a few minutes. Sprinkle with the salt and pepper, add the beans and cover with water. Bring to a boil, lower the heat, cover and simmer for 3 hours. Just before serving add the vinegar and serve hot.

Potage de tomates

Fresh tomato soup

6 servings

  2 *tablespoons butter*
  1 *yellow onion, finely chopped*
  1 *clove garlic, crushed*
  5 *red ripe tomatoes*
  1 *tablespoon tomato paste*
  4 *cups chicken broth*
  1 *bay leaf*
  1 *teaspoon basil*
     Juice ½ lemon
  ½ *teaspoon salt*
     Freshly ground black pepper
  2 *tablespoons parsley, finely*
     chopped, for garnish

Sauté onion and garlic in hot butter for three minutes until softened. Add quartered tomatoes, tomato paste, chicken broth, bay leaf and basil. Cover and simmer for twenty minutes. Purée the soup in a blender and strain into a clean saucepan. Add lemon juice, salt and pepper. Return soup to simmering point and garnish with chopped parsley.

Garbure

Country style vegetable soup

8 servings

*4½ pounds vegetables in season
  such as: zucchini, cabbage,
  carrots, string beans, bell
  peppers, leeks, turnips,
  broccoli
1 piece cooked ham (about
  ½ pound)
1 piece lean bacon (about
  ½ pound)
½ teaspoon salt
  Freshly ground black pepper
1 bay leaf
½ teaspoon thyme
1 tablespoon chopped parsley
½ teaspoon dried marjoram
3 cloves garlic, crushed
2 ounces prosciutto or
  country ham, cut into small
  pieces
  Slices of rye bread*

Clean the vegetables and cut
into rough pieces. Place the
ham and bacon, fat side up,
in a large heavy pan. Add all
the vegetables (except cabbage,
if used), salt, pepper, bay leaf,
thyme, parsley, marjoram and
garlic; almost cover with
water and bring to a boil.
Lower the heat, cover the pan
and simmer 2 hours. Add the
proscuitto and cabbage, if used.
Cover and simmer another
hour. Strain the broth into a
warm soup tureen. Cut the
bacon and ham into pieces and
place the meats and vegetables
in a warm dish. In individual
soup bowls, place a slice of
rye bread, top with some of
the meat and vegetables and
pour over the hot broth.

Potage crécy

Carrot soup

4 servings

*3 tablespoons butter
1 pound carrots, peeled and
  diced
1 small onion, chopped
1 medium sized potato,
  peeled and diced
½ teaspoon salt
  Freshly ground black pepper
½ teaspoon sugar
3 cups beef broth
1 tablespoon chopped parsley
1 teaspoon chopped chervil
  or marjoram*

Melt the butter in a heavy
saucepan, add the carrots,
onion, and potato. Season with
the salt, pepper and sugar.
Cover and cook over low heat
for 15 minutes. Add the
broth and bring to a boil.
Lower the heat, cover and
simmer for another 15 minutes.
Purée the soup in a blender or
force it through a sieve. Serve
the soup hot, garnishing each
serving with some of the
chopped herbs.

Soupe au potiron

Pumpkin soup

6 servings

*3 tablespoons butter
1 medium onion, finely
  chopped
5 cups chicken broth
1 teaspoon salt
  Freshly ground black pepper
1 (1 pound) can pumpkin
½ cup heavy cream.*

Melt the butter in a heavy
saucepan and cook the onion
over moderate heat until soft.
Add the broth, salt and
pepper and bring to a boil.
Add the pumpkin, combine it
thoroughly, lower the heat
and simmer, covered for 45
minutes. Add the cream and
heat through. Serve hot.

Potage Parmentier

Potato soup

6 servings

*4 cups chicken broth
½ teaspoon salt
4 medium sized all purpose
  potatoes
3 yellow onions, chopped
3 fresh leeks, chopped or
  1 additional onion
½ teaspoon chervil or
  marjoram
2 tablespoons parsley,
  finely chopped
½ cup heavy cream
1 tablespoon butter*

Bring chicken broth to
simmering point and add salt.
Peel potatoes and cut into
eights. Add potatoes, onions
and leeks to broth. Cover and
simmer for 20 minutes. Mash
potatoes into the broth using
a potato masher to form
small pieces of potato. Add
chervil or marjoram, parsley
and cream. Add butter and
serve hot.
Note: To make vichyssoise,
purée the soup in a blender
adding one additional teaspoon
of salt. Chill the soup for at
least 4 hours. Add ½ cup
more chicken broth if soup
appears too thick.

Velouté laitue

Potage paysanne

Velouté laitue

Cream of lettuce soup

6 servings

    3 heads Boston lettuce
    2 tablespoons butter
 1½ teaspoons salt
       Freshly ground black pepper
    4 cups water
 ½ cup heavy cream
       Juice of ½ lemon
    6 thick slices French or
       Italian bread, toasted

Wash the lettuce, remove the
cores and quarter the heads.
Cook in boiling, lightly salted
water for 10 minutes. Drain
and chop the lettuce roughly.
Melt the butter in a saucepan,
add the lettuce, cover with a
circle of wax paper and cook
slowly for 5 minutes. Remove
the paper and sprinkle lettuce
with the salt and pepper; add
the water and bring to a boil.
Lower the heat and simmer,
partially covered, for 1 hour.
Purée the soup in a blender
or force through a sieve.
Return it to the pan, add the
cream and lemon juice, and
heat thoroughly before
serving. Float a round of
toasted bread in each bowl.
You may also chill the soup
for several hours and serve
it cold.

Potage paysanne

Vegetable soup

6 servings

 ½ pound lean bacon, cubed
    6 small breakfast sausage
       links
    1 onion, finely chopped
    3 medium onions, halved
    2 pounds potatoes, cubed
 ½ pound carrots, cubed
    1 teaspoon salt
       Freshly ground black pepper
 5½ cups beef broth
 ½ pound fresh or frozen
       green peas
 ½ pound fresh or frozen
       green beans

In a large heavy pot, cook the
bacon until crisp and the
sausage links until brown.
Remove the sausage links and
drain on paper towels. Strain
off all the fat from the pan,
add the onions, potatoes,
carrots, salt and pepper to the
bacon and combine thoroughly.
Lower the heat, cover and
simmer for 20 minutes. Pour
in the broth; add the peas,
beans and drained sausage
links, bring to a boil, cover and
simmer 20 minutes more.
Skim the fat from the soup or
refrigerate overnight and
lift off the congealed fat. Serve
the soup hot, placing a sausage
link and an onion half in each
bowl. This soup is really a
meal in itself.

Westerländer Fischsuppe

Westerländer Fischsuppe

Fish soup

6–8 servings

¼ cup margarine or butter
4 medium onions, chopped
2 (1 lb.) packages frozen fish
  fillets, cut into bite size
  pieces
2 medium potatoes, cubed
4 cups water
2 (8 oz.) bottles clam juice
4 tomatoes, peeled and
  quartered
1 cup broad noodles
¼ cup cooked diced bacon,
  drained
¼ pound shrimp, shelled and
  cleaned
1 small cucumber, peeled and
  chopped
1 teaspoon parsley flakes
1 pound mussels or clams,
  in shells

Melt margarine in large heavy
saucepan. Sauté onions until
transparent. Add fish, potatoes
and water. Bring to a boil;
reduce heat; simmer 15 minutes.
Add clam juice, tomatoes and
noodles; simmer 8–10 minutes.
Stir in bacon, shrimp, cucumber
and parsley. Add mussels.
Cook just until mussel shells
open.

Buttermilchsuppe

Buttermilk soup

4–6 servings

3 tablespoons cornstarch
4 cups buttermilk
1 tablespoon chives
1 teaspoon salt
1 egg yolk
1 hard cooked egg, chopped

Stir cornstarch into buttermilk
until smooth. Cook over
medium heat, stirring constantly,
until thick. Stir in salt and
chives. Beat a small amount of
hot mixture into egg; return
to buttermilk mixture; stir
well. Serve hot. Garnish with
chopped egg.

Ostpreußische Brotsuppe

East Prussian bread soup

4 servings

8 slices white bread, crusts
  removed and cubed
4 cups water
4 cloves
1 stick cinnamon
1 tablespoon sugar
½ teaspoon salt
½ cup sour cream
1 tablespoon lemon juice

Combine bread, water, cloves,
cinnamon, sugar and salt in
saucepan. Bring to a boil;
reduce heat; simmer 15 minutes.
Strain. Heat; stir in sour cream
and lemon juice.

Badische Lauchsuppe

Baden leek soup

6–8 servings

  4 *leeks*
½ *cup margarine or butter*
  2 *large onions, chopped*
  6 *cups water*
  6 *chicken bouillon cubes*
½ *teaspoon salt*
  1 *cup milk*
  1 *cup finely chopped ham,*
     optional

Slice leeks lengthwise; wash thoroughly under running water; cut into 1″ pieces. Melt margarine in heavy saucepan; sauté leeks and onions until leeks are soft. Add water, bouillon cubes, and salt. Bring to a boil; reduce heat; simmer 8–10 minutes, stirring occasionally. Add milk; heat. Ladle soup into serving dishes; sprinkle with chopped ham.

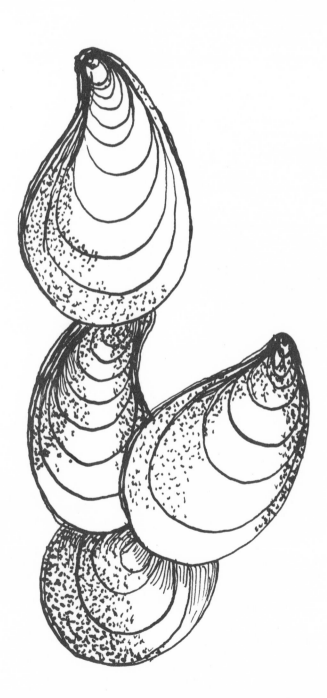

Muschelsuppe

Mussel chowder

4 servings

  2 *pounds mussels or clams*
     in shell
¼ *cup water*
  3 *slices bacon, diced*
  2 *medium onions, chopped*
  1 *stalk celery, chopped*
  3 *medium potatoes, peeled*
     and cubed
  1 *teaspoon salt*
⅛ *teaspoon black pepper*
  2 *cups milk*
     Margarine or butter

Wash and scrub mussels. Place mussels in large saucepot with the water. Cook just until shells open. Strain; reserve liquid. Remove mussels from shells and chop coarsely. In heavy saucepot fry out bacon. Sauté onions and celery until onions are transparent. Add potatoes, salt, pepper and 1 cup mussel broth. Cook until potatoes are tender about 15–20 minutes. Stir in milk and mussels; heat. Top each serving of chowder with a generous pat of margarine.

Pfälzer Rotweinsuppe

Pfälzer Rotweinsuppe

Red wine soup

4 servings

 2 *cups dry red wine*
 2 *cups water*
 4 *tablespoons minute tapioca*
 2 *tablespoons sugar*
½ *stick cinnamon*
 1 *piece lemon peel, ½″ thick*
 2 *egg whites*
 1 *tablespoon sugar*
  Ladyfingers or sweet wafers

Combine wine, water, tapioca, sugar, cinnamon and lemon peel in saucepan. Bring to a boil; reduce heat; simmer 8–10 minutes, stirring frequently. Beat egg whites until soft peaks form. Gradually beat in sugar; beating until stiff. Strain soup. Top each serving of soup with "icebergs" of egg white. Serve hot.

Stracciatella

Brodo con tortellini alla bolognese

Bouillon with tortellini Bolognese style

8–10 servings

- 4 cups sifted flour
- 6 eggs, slightly beaten
- 1 tablespoon salad oil
- 1 teaspoon salt
- 3/4 pound ground pork
- 1/4 pound ground beef
- 1/4 pound ground ham
- 1 egg yolk
- 1/4 cup grated Parmesan cheese
- 1/4 teaspoon nutmeg
- 12 cups beef bouillon
- 1 tablespoon tomato paste

Place flour in large bowl; add eggs, oil, and salt. Mix until dough can be gathered into a ball. Place dough on lightly floured board; knead until firm but elastic and smooth. Place dough in slightly dampened cloth; let stand 1/2 hour. Brown meat in large skillet; stir in ham. Remove from heat; blend in egg yolk, cheese and nutmeg. Form into 1″ balls. Roll out on lightly floured board, to 1/8″ thickness. Cut into 2″ circles; place one meatball in center of each circle. Fold dough over; forming a crescent. Moisten edges; seal with fork. Cover. Let stand 24 hours in a cool place. Just before serving bring bouillon to a boil; stir in tomato paste. Drop tortellini into bouillon; cook 15 minutes or until done. Serve with additional Parmesan cheese.

Zuppa pavese

Pavia soup

4 servings

- 2 (10 1/2 ounce) cans chicken consommé
- 1 soup can water
- 1/4 cup margarine or butter
- 1/4 cup grated Parmesan cheese
- 4 slices toast, crusts removed
- 4 poached eggs

Combine consommé and water; bring just to a boil. Reduce heat; simmer. Mix together margarine and cheese; blend well. Spread cheese mixture on toast. Place 1 slice toast in each soup bowl; top with egg. Ladle hot consommé into bowls. Serve immediately

Zuppa di lenticchie

Lentil soup

6 servings

- 1 pound lentils
- 2 quarts water
- 1/4 pound bacon, finely diced
- 1 medium onion, finely chopped
- 1 clove garlic, minced
- 1 1/2 teaspoons salt
- 1/2 teaspoon dried oregano

Rinse lentils. Combine lentils and water in large saucepot. Bring to a boil; simmer about 1 1/2 hours or until lentils are soft. Cook bacon until crisp in skillet. Remove bacon; pour off drippings, returning 3 tablespoons to skillet. Add remaining ingredients and bacon. Cook over medium heat, stirring constantly until onion is transparent. Press lentils through a fine sieve or blend smooth in blender. Add bacon mixture; stir well.

Stracciatella

Stracciatella

4 servings

- 4 cups chicken bouillon
- 2 eggs, slightly beaten
- 2 tablespoons flour
- 1/4 cup grated Swiss cheese
- 2 tablespoons grated Parmesan cheese
- 1/4 teaspoon salt
- Dash nutmeg
- 4 slices bread, toasted
- Chopped parsley

Bring 3 cups bouillon to a boil; reduce heat; simmer. Combine eggs and flour; stir in cheeses, mutmeg, and salt. Gradually stir in remaining bouillon. Stir a small amount of hot mixture into egg mixture. Slowly stir into hot bouillon. Reduce heat. Continue to cook, stirring constantly, until mixture thickens, about 3–4 minutes. Remove crusts from toast; cut into quarters; float on soup. Garnish with chopped parsley.

Minestra con broccoli

Broccoli soup

6 servings

>   3 tablespoons margarine or
>   butter
>   1 clove garlic, cut in half
>   2 (10 ounce) packages frozen
>   chopped broccoli
>   6 cups hot water
>   4 chicken bouillon cubes
>   1 tablespoon tomato paste
> $^1/_2$ teaspoon salt
>   Dash black pepper
>   Croutons

Melt margarine in large
saucepan over medium heat.
Brown garlic in margarine;
remove. Add broccoli; cook just
until heated. Add water,
bouillon cubes, tomato paste,
salt and pepper. Cook 5–10
minutes. Force through fine
sieve or blend smooth in
blender. Cook over medium
heat, stirring occasionally until
heated, about 10–15 minutes.
Serve with croutons.

Minestrone freddo

Cold minestrone

8-servings

>   2 tablespoons olive oil
>   1 medium onion, chopped
>   3 stalks celery, chopped
> $^1/_2$ teaspoon dried basil
>   3 potatoes, cubed
>   4 cups hot water
>   4 beef bouillon cubes
>   1 medium zucchini, chopped
>   2 (10 ounce) packages
>   frozen mixed vegetables

Heat oil in large saucepot. Sauté
onions, celery and basil until
onion is transparent. Add
potatoes, water, and bouillon
cubes. Simmer, covered, 30
minutes. Add zucchini and
mixed vegetables. Cook until
heated throughout, about 15–20
minutes. Chill. Serve chilled
with hot garlic bread.

Minestra di pasta e ceci

Chick pea soup

6 servings

>   2 tablespoons margarine or
>   butter
>   2 scallions, chopped
>   1 tablespoon parsley flakes
> $^1/_2$ teaspoon oregano
>   1 (1 pound) can tomatoes
>   1 (16 ounce) can chick peas
>   2 cups water
>   1 beef bouillon cube

Melt margarine in large
saucepan. Sauté scallions,
parsley and oregano in
margarine over medium heat,
2–3 minutes. Add remaining
ingredients. Cook over medium
heat, 5–10 minutes, or until
heated throughout.

Minestra d'orzo

Barley soup

6 servings

> $^1/_4$ pound bacon, diced
>   1 small leek, chopped
>   2 stalks celery, chopped
>   2 carrots, sliced
>   3 medium potatoes, cubed
> $^1/_2$ cup barley
>   1 tablespoon chopped parsley
> $^1/_2$ teaspoon salt
>   Dash black pepper
>   2 quarts beef bouillon

Cook bacon until crisp in large
heavy saucepot. Remove bacon;
pour off drippings, returning 3
tablespoons to pot. Add
vegetables; cook just until celery
softens slightly. Add remaining
ingredients and bacon. Cook
over medium heat, stirring
occasionally, until barley is
tender, about 1 hour.

This very characteristic soup comes from Genoa. It is prepared with another Genoese speciality, 'pesto' (which literally means pounded or crushed), a mixture of aromatic ingredients, green in color, because of the spinach and basil used in its preparation.

Minestrone alla genovese

Genoese minestrone

8 servings

$^1/_4$ *cup olive oil*
1 *clove garlic, minced*
1 *onion, finely chopped*
1 *leek, washed and diced*
1 *tablespoon parsley*
$^1/_2$ *teaspoon dried thyme*
1 *tablespoon tomato paste*
3 *medium tomatoes, peeled, seeded, and chopped*
2 *stalks celery, chopped*
2 *carrots, diced*
2 *potatoes, diced*
1 *(10 ounce) package frozen string beans*
6 *cups water*
6 *beef bouillon cubes*
1 *cup elbow macaroni or ditali*
$1^1/_2$ *cups drained, cooked, kidney beans*
Pesto, optional
Grated Parmesan cheese

Heat olive oil in large saucepot. Add garlic, onion, leek, parsley and thyme; cook until onion is transparent. Add tomato paste, tomatoes, celery, carrots, potatoes, string beans, water and bouillon cubes. Simmer covered, about 1 hour. Bring to a boil; add macaroni; cook until tender, about 8–10 minutes. Add beans; heat. Serve with pesto and Parmesan cheese.

For the pesto:

1 *(10 ounce) package frozen chopped spinach well drained*
1 *teaspoon dried basil*
3 *cloves garlic, minced*
1 *tablespoon parsley flakes*
4 *tablespoons salad oil*
2 *tablespoons margarine or butter*
$^1/_4$ *cup grated Parmesan cheese*

Combine all ingredients in top of blender; blend smooth. Or combine all ingredients in sauce pan; bring to a boil; press through fine sieve. Stir 1 or 2 tablespoons pesto into each bowl of minestrone.

Minestra alla romana

Roman soup

6 servings

1 *tablespoon margarine or butter*
1 *medium onion, chopped*
1 *clove garlic, minced*
2 *quarts beef bouillon*
1 *tablespoon tomato paste*
$^1/_2$ *teaspoon salt*
Dash black pepper
$^1/_4$ *teaspoon dried basil*
$^1/_4$ *pound fine noodles, broken into 2" pieces*

Melt margarine in large heavy saucepot; sauté onion and garlic in melted margarine until onion is transparent. Add bouillon, tomato paste, salt, pepper and basil; stir well. Bring to a boil; then simmer 10 minutes. Add noodles. Continue to cook, over medium heat, until noodles are done, about 5–6 minutes.

Minestrone all'italiana

Minestrone

12 servings

6 *slices bacon, finely diced*
1 *large onion, chopped*
2 *carrots, diced*
$^1/_2$ *pound ($1^1/_2$ cups) string beans, cut up*
1 *small head cauliflower, separated*
$^1/_4$ *pound ham, cut into strips*
1 *(10 ounce) package frozen lima beans*
2 *quarts beef bouillon*
2 *medium zucchini, chopped*
1 *pound spinach, finely chopped*
$^1/_4$ *pound spaghetti, broken into 2" pieces*
2 *tablespoons chopped parsley*
1 *teaspoon salt*
Dash black pepper
Grated Parmesan cheese

Cook bacon until crisp in large heavy saucepot. Remove bacon; pour off drippings, returning 3 tablespoons to saucepot. Sauté onion until slightly transparent. Add carrots, string beans, cauliflower, ham, lima beans and bouillon. Cook over medium heat until vegetables are tender, about 30 minutes. Add remaining ingredients and cook until spaghetti is done, about 8–10 minutes. Serve with grated Parmesan cheese.

Minestrone

In Italy, the noon-time meal begins with antipasto, but the evening meal begins with soup. The soup is made of a full-bodied chicken or meat broth, carefully skimmed of the fat; a handful of fresh vegetables adds flavor and texture. A generous amount of grated Parmesan cheese is sprinkled on at the table and sometimes, as in the 'zuppa pavese', a poached egg floats on top. A favorite soup is the 'pasta in brodo'. This is made by cooking any of the many thin spaghetti or noodle pastas in clear broth. Thick soups such as minestrone contain not only cooked pasta but also a variety of vegetables and meats. The typical taste of the Italian minestrone is obtained by first frying the vegetables in bacon fat and then cooking them in broth. Grated cheese is sprinkled on generously, and it isn't too much to say that a good minestrone is a meal in itself. In Tuscany a few drops light-green olive oil from the Tuscan hillside round out the flavor. In Genoa no soup is complete without basil and garlic. In Rome, Pecorino cheese is used to sprinkle over the soup, rather than Parmesan. Pecorino is a sharp sheep's cheese from the Albanese hills. Mint is often used as a garnish. Oregano is a favorite herb in Naples.

Minestra d'asparagi

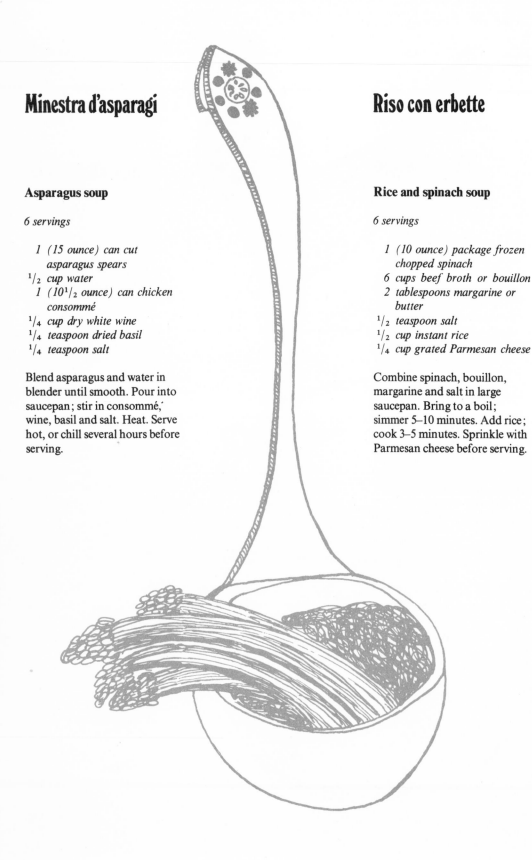

Asparagus soup

6 servings

*1 (15 ounce) can cut
   asparagus spears*
¹/₂ cup water
*1 (10¹/₂ ounce) can chicken
   consommé*
¹/₄ cup dry white wine
¹/₄ teaspoon dried basil
¹/₄ teaspoon salt

Blend asparagus and water in
blender until smooth. Pour into
saucepan; stir in consommé,
wine, basil and salt. Heat. Serve
hot, or chill several hours before
serving.

Riso con erbette

Rice and spinach soup

6 servings

*1 (10 ounce) package frozen
   chopped spinach*
6 cups beef broth or bouillon
*2 tablespoons margarine or
   butter*
¹/₂ teaspoon salt
¹/₂ cup instant rice
¹/₄ cup grated Parmesan cheese

Combine spinach, bouillon,
margarine and salt in large
saucepan. Bring to a boil;
simmer 5–10 minutes. Add rice;
cook 3–5 minutes. Sprinkle with
Parmesan cheese before serving.

Minestra di carciofi

Artichoke soup

6 servings

*3 tablespoons margarine or
   butter*
1 small onion, chopped
*1 (10 ounce) package frozen
   artichoke hearts*
4 cups water
1 thin strip lemon peel
4 chicken bouillon cubes
¹/₂ cup instant rice
1 egg, slightly beaten
¹/₄ cup grated Parmesan cheese

Melt margarine in large
saucepan. Sauté onion and
artichoke in margarine until
onion is transparent. Stir in
water, lemon peel and bouillon
cubes. Cook over medium heat,
stirring occasionally, about
10–15 minutes. Remove lemon
peel. Add rice; cook 3–5
minutes. Slowly stir a small
amount of hot mixture into
beaten egg; return to hot
mixture; blend well. Sprinkle
with Parmesan cheese before
serving.

Norrländsk laxsoppa

Norrlandsk salmon soup

4 servings

    5 cups liquid (drain liquid
       from salmon; add water
       to make 5 cups)
    3 tablespoons barley
    2 medium carrots, diced
    1 medium turnip, diced
    1 medium onion, chopped
    1 (16-ounce) can pink salmon
    1 teaspoon salt
       Dash black pepper
    2 tablespoons chopped parsley

Bring salmon liquid and water
to a boil. Add barley, boil 30
minutes. Add vegetables and
cook for 10–15 minutes, or until
tender. Add salmon pieces and
salt and pepper. Heat
thoroughly. Top with chopped
parsley. Serve hot.

Kalakeitto

Finnish fish soup

4 servings

    2 medium potatoes, peeled
       and cubed
    2 cups water
    1 teaspoon salt
    1 pound frozen haddock fillets,
       cut into bite size pieces
    3 tablespoons margarine or
       butter
    2 tablespoons flour
    2 cups milk
       Dash white pepper
    2 tablespoons chopped fresh
       dill or parsley

Cook potatoes in salted water
about 10 minutes; add fish;
simmer 15 minutes. In the
meantime, melt margarine in
saucepan. Stir in flour; add milk
gradually, stirring constantly.
Add to soup and cook, stirring
constantly, for another 3
minutes. Top with chopped dill
or parsley.

Köttsoppa

Swedish meat soup

6 servings

- 2 *pounds soup meat*
- 3 *quarts water*
- 2 *medium carrots, coarsely diced*
- 1 *turnip, cut into ½″ cubes*
- 1 *stalk celery, diced*
- 1 *medium onion, spiked with 2 cloves*
- 2 *scallions or leeks, sliced*
- 2 *teaspoons salt*
- 1 *teaspoon white pepper*

Place meat in large saucepan; add water. Bring to a boil; skim. Add salt; reduce heat and simmer about 2 hours. Add carrot, turnip, celery, onion and scallions; sprinkle with salt and pepper. Bring to a boil again; reduce heat and simmer 1 hour. Remove meat, cut into pieces, return to soup and heat thoroughly.

Spenatsoppa

Swedish spinach soup

4 servings

- 1 *(10½ ounce) can cream of chicken soup*
- 1 *cup milk*
- 2 *cups boiling water*
- 2 *chicken bouillon cubes*
- 1 *(10 ounce) package frozen chopped spinach, thawed*
- 1 *teaspoon salt*
- ¼ *teaspoon pepper*
- 2 *tablespoons chopped parsley*
- 2 *hard-cooked eggs*

In a large saucepan, combine soup, milk, and boiling water in which bouillon cubes have been dissolved. Add spinach. Place mixture in blender for a few seconds on medium speed just until spinach is very finely chopped; do not puree. Return to saucepan; simmer 10 minutes. Add salt and pepper. Garnish with chopped parsley and quarters of hard-cooked eggs.

Gule aerter

Danish pea soup

6 to 8 servings

- ¾ *pound dried yellow peas*
- 8 *cups water*
- 1 *(¾ to 1 pound) smoked pork shoulder, cut into small pieces*
- 1 *carrot, diced*
- 1 *medium onion, chopped*
- ¼ *teaspoon dried marjoram*
- 1 *teaspoon ginger*
- 1½ *teaspoons salt*

Soak peas in water about 12 hours, unless peas are quick-cooking variety. In a large saucepan, bring peas to a boil in the same water; skim. Add meat, carrot, onion and seasonings. Cover and simmer slowly about 1½ hours or until peas are tender. Season to taste.

Fiskesuppe

Norwegian fish soup

4 servings

- 2 *tablespoons margarine or butter*
- 2 *leeks or scallions, sliced*
- 4 *medium potatoes, diced*
- 1 *stalk celery, diced*
- 2 *teaspoons salt*
- 1 *teaspoon black pepper*
- 5 *cups water*
- 1 *pound fresh or frozen fish fillets*
- 1 *tablespoon chopped fresh dill or*
- 1 *teaspoon dried dill*

In a large, heavy skillet melt margarine; saute leeks, potatoes and celery about 5 minutes over low heat. Add salt, pepper, and water; bring to a boil and cook about 10 to 15 minutes or until vegetables are tender. Cut fish fillets into 1-inch pieces; add to soup about 10 minutes before vegetables are tender. Correct seasoning and sprinkle with dill. Serve immediately.

Danish pea soup *Swedish spinach soup*

Swedish meat soup

The name of this dish means 'fruits from the kettle'. It is a favorite supper of the fishermen who prepare their evening meal at sea by scooping up a few handfuls of the fish from their brimming nets. If your supermarket does not have mussels, use whatever fish is available and it will make a splendid dinner.

Sopa e caldeirada de enguias à pescadora

Although all good restaurants in Spain and Portugal serve thin, clear broth (in fact, the special soup of Madrid consists of broth with tomato puree), most of the soups in these two countries are hearty and most nourishing, meals in themselves. Both Spanish and Portuguese soups are prepared with inexhaustible imagination and variety. There are endless combinations of meat and fowl, or meat and fish, or meat and shellfish. The national soup of Portugal is 'caldeirada a fregateira.' The name literally means 'frigate cooking,' for the frigate in Portugal is a fishing boat. 'Caldeirada,' the soup that fisherman cook on board, is made of all the different kinds of fish that they have at that moment. Potatoes, olive oil, and garden herbs are then added to the pot. A good 'caldeirada' prepared with exquisite fish is a delightful meal, especially if accompanied by the light, softly sparkling white wine from northern Portugal, 'vinho verde.' In Andalusia, where the temperature seems almost to reach the boiling point in summer, and where the thermometer can still read 95° at the end of September, ice-cold 'gazpacho' is popular. With its raw pimentos, tomatoes and cucumbers, it is almost as much a salad as a soup. In the vineyards, when the grapes ripen and gypsies come from far and wide for the harvest, the famous 'ajo caliente' is readied. This is a hot garlic soup prepared for the grape-pickers, because Spaniards believe that garlic provides stamina and energy,

Fish soup mariners' style

6 servings

- 3 pounds mixed salt water fish (haddock, flounder, mullet, cod or other fish)
- 6 cups water
- ¾ cup dry white wine
- ½ teaspoon salt
- ½ teaspoon peppercorns
- ½ lemon, sliced
- 1 onion, chopped
- 1 leek, sliced, or 1 additional onion
- 1 carrot, sliced
- 2 bay leaves
- 3 sprigs parsley
- 2 large onions, thinly sliced
- 2 cloves garlic, finely chopped
- 1 (6 ounce) can tomato purée
- 1 teaspoon coriander seeds, crushed
- 6 medium-sized potatoes, peeled and sliced
- 1 pound mussels in their shells, scrubbed
- 1 cup shrimp, peeled and deveined

Have the fish cleaned and boned, but keep the heads and trimmings. Place the heads and trimmings in a large saucepan and add the water, wine, salt, peppercorns, lemon slices, onion, leek, carrot, bay leaves and parsley. Cover and simmer over low heat for 20 minutes. Do not allow the liquid to boil. Strain the broth. (If the fish trimmings are not available, substitute 2 cups clam broth, and 3 cups of water. Simmer the remaining ingredients in this liquid.) Cover the bottom of a casserole with onion slices, garlic, tomato purée, coriander seeds and potato slices. Add the fish broth and bring to a boil. Cover and cook for 15 minutes until the potatoes are almost done. Add the fish fillets. Cover and cook for 10 minutes. Add the mussels and shrimp. Cover and continue cooking 7 minutes until the mussel shells have opened. Serve with bread squares which have been rubbed with garlic and fried until crisp and golden in hot olive oil.

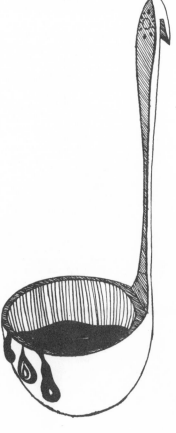

Ajo con uvas

Garlic soup with grapes

4 to 6 servings

2 cloves garlic, peeled
4 slices white bread, crusts removed
1 cup blanched almonds
1 tablespoon vinegar
2 tablespoons olive oil
1 teaspoon salt
¼ teaspoon white pepper
4 cups ice water
24 peeled white grapes

Place all the ingredients except the grapes in the jar of an electric blender and blend until smooth. Pour into individual soup bowls and top with grapes.

Ajo caliente

Hot garlic soup

4 servings

4 tablespoons olive oil
4 whole cloves garlic
4 thin slices firm textured bread, crusts removed
4 cups beef broth
¼ teaspoon hot red chili pepper
¼ teaspoon salt

Heat the oil in a suacepan. Add the cloves of garlic and cook until garlic is lightly browned. Discard the garlic. Fry the bread in the same oil until lightly browned. In the meantime heat the broth to boiling point. Season with hot pepper and salt. Add the broth to the bread and oil. Simmer for 20 minutes.

Gazpacho madrileño

Cold vegetable soup from Madrid

6 servings

2 green peppers, seeded and cubed
3 tomatoes, cut into wedges
1 clove garlic, peeled
4 tablespoons olive oil
4 cups ice water
2 tablespoons red wine vinegar
½ teaspoon salt
Freshly ground black pepper

For the garnish:
1 green pepper, seeded and finely chopped
2 tomatoes, peeled, seeded and chopped
1 small cucumber, finely chopped
2 slices bread, crusts removed and diced

Place the green peppers, tomatoes, garlic, olive oil and 1 cup of water in a blender and blend at high speed for 1 minute. Force the broth through a sieve and add the remaining water, vinegar, salt and pepper. Place the garnish ingredients in individual serving dishes. Serve the soup ice cold and pass the garnishes separately.

Gazpacho Alentejano

Cold vegetable soup Alentejo style

4 to 6 servings

1 clove garlic, crushed
½ teaspoon salt
3 tablespoons olive oil
½ teaspoon oregano
1 small red or green bell pepper, finely chopped
½ cucumber, peeled and cut into small cubes
2 tomatoes, peeled, seeded and chopped
4 cups chicken broth or cold water
8 thick slices brown bread, crusts removed and cut into strips
½ teaspoon salt
Freshly ground black pepper
2 tablespoons vinegar

Crush the garlic and add the salt. Mince the crushed garlic finely and place in a bowl. Add the olive oil, oregano, pepper, cucumber and tomatoes. Combine all these ingredients and add the chicken broth or water. Place the strips of bread in individual soup bowls and ladle the soup over the bread. When the bread has absorbed the liquid, season with salt and pepper. Sprinkle with vinegar just before serving. Sometimes sliced Spanish sausage is served with the soup and a few ice cubes are added just before serving.

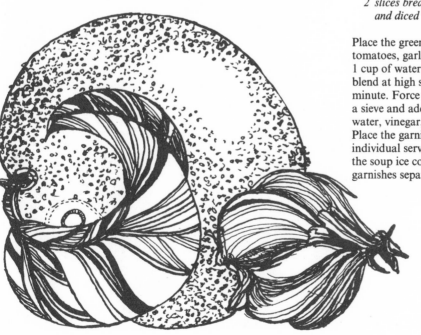

Sopa de lagosta à moda de Peniche

Lobster soup from Peniche

8 to 10 servings

  5 *cups water*
  1 *cup dry white wine*
  2 *large onions, finely chopped*
  2 *large carrots, peeled and*
     finely chopped
  3 *medium sized potatoes,*
     peeled and cubed
  1 *teaspoon salt*
12 *peppercorns*
  1 *(2 pound) lobster*
  2 *tablespoons olive oil*
  1 *cup tomato purée*
 ¾ *cup rice*
  1 *tablespoon finely chopped*
     parsley
 ½ *teaspoon ground coriander*
     Freshly ground black pepper
  3 *cloves garlic, crushed*
  2 *tablespoons brandy*

Place the water, wine, 1 onion, 1 carrot, potatoes, salt and peppercorns in a large saucepan and bring to a boil. Simmer 30 minutes. Add the lobster, cover the pan and simmer 20 to 30 minutes more or until the lobster is done. Heat the oil in another saucepan. Add the remaining onion and carrot and sauté until lightly browned. Stir in the tomato purée and set the mixture aside. Strain and reserve the lobster cooking liquid. Remove the meat from the lobster and cut into ½ inch pieces. Break the lobster shell into pieces, return it to the strained broth and simmer 15 minutes. Strain the broth again and add it to the tomato mixture. Stir in the rice, parsley, coriander, pepper, garlic and brandy and simmer 25 minutes. Add the lobster meat and simmer 5 minutes more. Taste for seasoning and serve immediately.

Sopa gaditana

Fish soup from Cadiz

6 servings

  2 *tablespoons olive oil*
  2 *cloves garlic, peeled*
  1 *onion, finely chopped*
  8 *cups boiling water*
  3 *pounds firm fleshed fish*
     fillets (haddock, cod,
     halibut, etc.)
  1 *teaspoon salt*
     Freshly ground black pepper
 ¼ *cup orange juice*
 ¼ *cup lemon juice*

Heat the oil in a large heavy pan and sauté the garlic cloves until brown. Discard the garlic. Add the onion and sauté until lightly browned. Add the water, fish, salt and pepper and simmer, covered, for 15 to 20 minutes. Strain the broth and return it to the pan. Skin and bone the fish, cut it into small pieces and return it to the broth. Add the orange and lemon juices and heat through. Serve immediately.

Sopa de amêijoas

Dried cod soup

4 servings

  1 *pound salt codfish*
  4 *cups water*
 ⅓ *cup oil*
  2 *cloves garlic, peeled*
  1 *pound leeks or*
     3 medium sized onions, sliced
  3 *medium sized potatoes,*
     peeled and sliced
  1 *bay leaf*
     Freshly ground black pepper
     Dash cayenne pepper

Soak the codfish overnight in cold water to remove excess salt. Drain cod and place in a saucepan. Add water, cover and simmer for 7 minutes. Drain cod and reserve the cooking water. Flake the cod into small pieces and discard the bones. Heat the oil and fry the garlic 3 minutes until lightly browned. Remove and reserve garlic cloves. Add the leeks or onions and potatoes. Fry for 3 minutes until softened but not browned. Add the flaked cod, bay leaf and black pepper. Add the reserved liquid. Cover and simmer for 20 minutes until potatoes are tender. Add a dash of cayenne pepper to the garlic and chop very finely. Add garlic and cayenne to the hot soup. Taste the soup and add salt if necessary. Discard the bay leaf before serving.

PASTA & RICE DISHES

Ziti alla carbonara

Sformato di tortelli

Polenta

Polenta

8 servings

1¹/₂ cups cornmeal
3 cups water
1 teaspoon salt

Combine cornmeal and 2 cups water in heavy saucepan; mix well. Stir in remaining water and salt. Bring to a boil, stirring constantly. Be sure cornmeal does not lump. Continue to cook, stirring constantly, until mixture is so thick, spoon will stand up, unsupported, in the middle of the pan. Pour into a buttered 1¹/₂ quart bowl or mold. Cool. Once cooled, polenta can be sliced and fried, baked or served with sauce.

Polenta lombarda

Lombardian polenta

6 servings

1 (10 ounce) package corn bread mix or
1 recipe Polenta, fried
4 tablespoons margarine or butter
2 (2–2¹/₂ pound) chickens, cut into 8 pieces
1 medium onion, chopped
1 (4 ounce) can sliced mushrooms
¹/₄ teaspoon dried sage
1 tablespoon flour
¹/₄ pound ham, diced
¹/₂ cup dry white wine

Prepare corn bread according to package directions or polenta according to recipe. Melt margarine in large skillet over medium heat. Brown chicken in margarine; remove. Add onion, mushrooms and sage to margarine; cook until onion is transparent. Add flour; stir until well blended. Add ham and chicken. Pour in wine. Cook over medium heat, stirring occasionally, about 25–30 minutes or until chicken is cooked. Serve over squares of corn bread or fried polenta.

Ziti alla carbonara

Anolini

Tortelli di ricotta

Sformato di maruzzelle

Ziti alla carbonara

4 servings

$^1/_2$ *pound bacon, diced*
  1 onion, chopped
$^1/_2$ *cup dry white wine*
  1 pound ziti
  3 eggs, slightly beaten
$^1/_4$ *cup grated Parmesan cheese*
$^1/_2$ *teaspoon salt*
    Dash black pepper

Cook bacon until crisp in heavy saucepot. Remove bacon; drain off drippings, returning 2 tablespoons to pot. Sauté onion in drippings until just transparent; add wine; cook until wine is reduced by half. Cook ziti according to package directions; drain well; return to pot. Add bacon, onion mixture, eggs, Parmesan cheese, salt and pepper. Toss lightly, until ziti is well coated. Serve immediately.

Anolini

6 servings

  1 recipe Pasta all'uova

$^1/_2$ *pound Italian sweet sausage*
  1 pound ground beef
  1 medium onion, chopped
  2 carrots, grated
  1 stalk celery, finely chopped
  1 cup bread crumbs
  3 eggs, slightly beaten
  1 teaspoon salt
$^1/_4$ *teaspoon nutmeg*
$^1/_4$ *teaspoon black pepper*
  8 cups beef bouillon or water
    Grated Parmesan cheese

Roll dough out into 2 sheets $^1/_8''$ thick. Break up sausage. Brown sausage and meat in large skillet. Add onion, carrot and celery; cook until onion is transparent. Drain off excess fat. Remove from heat; stir in bread crumbs, eggs, salt, nutmeg and pepper; mix well. Place a teaspoonful of filling at $1^1/_2''$ interval on one sheet of dough. Cover with second sheet. Cut out squares or circles with a knife or cookie cutter. Moisten edges; seal with fork. Cover; let stand 1 hour. Bring bouillon to a boil; add anolini; cook about 10 minutes or until tender. Serve in small amount of bouillon, topped with grated cheese.

Tortelli with Ricotta filling

4 servings

  1 recipe pasta all'uova

  1 (10 ounce) package frozen chopped spinach
$1^1/_2$ *cups Ricotta cheese*
  3 eggs
  3 tablespoons grated Parmesan cheese
$^1/_2$ *teaspoon salt*
$^1/_4$ *teaspoon nutmeg*
$^1/_8$ *teaspoon black pepper*
$^1/_2$ *cup margarine or butter*
$^1/_4$ *cup grated Parmesan cheese*
$^1/_4$ *teaspoon dried sage*

Roll dough out into 2 sheets $^1/_8''$ thick. Cover. Cook spinach; drain well. Combine spinach, Ricotta cheese, eggs, Parmesan cheese, salt, pepper and nutmeg; mix well. Place a teaspoonful of filling at $1^1/_2''$ intervals on one sheet of dough. Cover with second sheet. Cut out squares or circles with a knife or cookie cutter. Moisten edges; seal with fork. Cover; let stand 20 minutes. Cook in rapidly boiling salted water for 10 minutes or until tender. Drain well. Melt margarine; stir in remaining Parmesan cheese and sage. Pour margarine mixture over tortelli before serving.

Maruzelle mold

4 servings

$^1/_2$ *pound maruzzelle (shell) macaroni*
  4 tablespoons margarine or butter
  4 tablespoons grated Parmesan cheese
  2 eggs, slightly beaten
$^1/_2$ *pound ground beef*
  1 (4 ounce) can sliced mushrooms
  4 chicken livers
  2 tablespoons flour
$^1/_2$ *cup dry red wine or bouillon*
  1 (8 ounce) can tomato sauce
$^1/_2$ *teaspoon salt*
    Dash black pepper
  1 (10 ounce) package frozen peas, cooked

Cook macaroni according to package directions; drain. Add margarine, cheese, and eggs; toss lightly to blend. Spoon mixture into well buttered $1^1/_2$ quart ring mold. Set mold in pan of hot water. Bake in a moderate oven (375°) 20 minutes. Brown meat in large skillet; add mushrooms; cook 2–3 minutes. Cut chicken livers in half; dredge with flour. Add chicken livers to skillet; cook until browned. Add wine; cook until mixture begins to thicken. Stir in tomato sauce, salt and pepper. Simmer 15–20 minutes. Unmold macaroni mold; fill center with meat mixture. Place peas around bottom of mold.

Pasta all'uovo

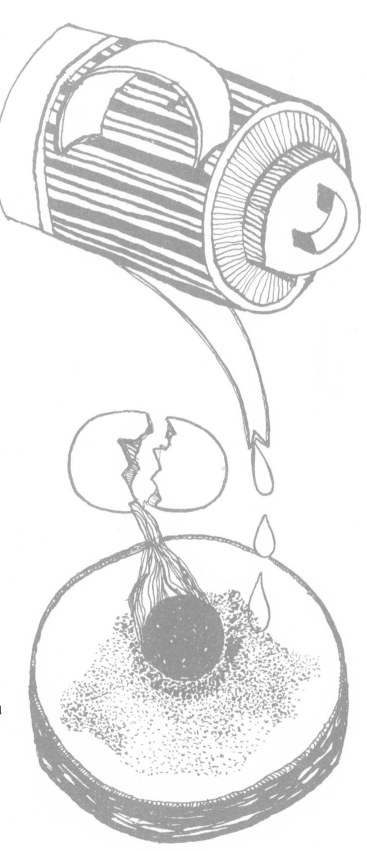

Cappelletti

Pasta dough made with eggs

2 pounds pasta

> *4 cups sifted flour*
> *6 eggs*
> *5 teaspoons salad oil*
> *1¹/₂ teaspoons salt*

Place flour in large bowl; add eggs, oil, and salt. Mix until dough can be gathered into a ball. Place dough on lightly floured board; knead until firm but elastic and smooth. Place dough in slightly dampened cloth; let stand ¹/₂ hour. Divide dough into quarters; roll out dough on lightly floured board to ¹/₈″ thickness. Fold dough over into a long roll; cut dough into desired size.

Fettucini: cut rolled dough into
          ¹/₄″ strips

Tagliatelle: cut rolled dough
          into ³/₈″ strips

Tagliarini: cut rolled dough
          into ¹/₈″ strips

Lasagne: cut dough into strips
          2″ wide and 8″ long

Manicotti: cut dough into
          4 × 4¹/₂″ squares

Cover cut dough; let dry 1 hour before cooking. To cook pasta bring 6–8 quarts water to a rapid boil. Add 2 tablespoons salt and 1 teaspoon salad oil Add pasta a few pieces at a time. As soon as pasta rises to the surface test for doneness. Pasta should still be firm ('al dente' or some resistance to the bite). Drain.

Little hats in tomato sauce

6 servings

> *1 recipe pasta all'uova*
>
> *1¹/₂ cups ground cooked*
>   *chicken*
> *1 cup Ricotta cheese*
> *2 eggs*
> *¹/₄ cup bread crumbs*
> *1 tablespoon chopped chives*
> *1 teaspoon salt*
> *¹/₂ teaspoon dried basil*
> *2 cups tomato sauce*
>
> *1 (16 ounce) jar spaghetti*
>   *sauce with mushrooms*

Roll dough out into 2 sheets ¹/₈″ thick. Cover. Combine chicken, cheese, eggs, bread crumbs, chives, salt and basil; mix well. Place a teaspoonful of filling at 1¹/₂″ intervals on one sheet of dough. Cover with second sheet. Cut out squares or circles with knife or cookie cutter. Moisten edges; seal with fork. Shape so that dough resembles a hat. Cook in rapidly boiling salted water, about 10 minutes or until tender. Drain well. Serve with hot sauce.

Different types of pasta

Fettucine con salsa di prezzemolo

Fettucini with parsley sauce

4 servings

- 1 *pound fettucini or thin noodles*
- $^1/_2$ *pound unsalted margarine or butter*
- $^1/_2$ *cup heavy cream*
- $^1/_2$ *cup chopped parsley*
- 1 *teaspoon dried basil*
- $^1/_2$ *teaspoon salt*
  Dash black pepper
- 2 *cups grated Parmesan cheese*

Cook noodles according to package directions. Slice half the margarine into warm bowl or chafing dish; add cream, parsley, basil, salt and pepper. Drain noodles quickly; pour into bowl. Slice in remaining margarine. Toss gently, turning noodles, over and over, until noodles are well coated. Add cheese; toss lightly until cheese coats noodles. Serve immediately.

Fusilli con fegatini

Fusilli with chicken livers

4 servings

- 4 *tablespoons margarine or butter*
- 1 *medium onion, chopped*
- $^1/_4$ *pound mushrooms, sliced*
- 1 *pound chicken livers*
- 2 *tablespoons flour*
- $^1/_2$ *cup dry red wine*
- 2 *cups Bolognese sauce*
- 2 *(8 ounce) cans beef gravy or Bolognese sauce*
- $^1/_2$ *teaspoon salt*
- $^1/_4$ *teaspoon black pepper*
- 1 *pound fusilli or spaghetti*

Melt margarine in heavy saucepot; sauté onion and mushrooms until onion is transparent. Cut chicken livers in half; dredge with flour. Add chicken livers and all the flour to saucepot; cook until chicken livers are lightly browned. Stir in red wine; cook, stirring constantly, until wine is reduced by half. Stir in Bolognese sauce, salt and pepper. Simmer 15–20 minutes. Cook fusilli according to package directions; drain well. Serve chicken livers over hot fusilli.

Farfalle al tonno

Farfalle and tunafish

6 servings

- 2 *($10^1/_2$ ounce) cans mushroom soup*
- 1 *soup can milk*
- 1 *(4 ounce) can sliced mushrooms*
- 1 *tablespoon chopped chives*
- 2 *teaspoons onion flakes*
- $^1/_2$ *cup sliced green olives*
- 8 *ounces American cheese, shredded*
- 2 *(7 ounce) cans tunafish, drained*
- 1 *large tomato, sliced*
- 12 *ounces farfalle (or bows) cooked and drained*

Combine soup, milk, mushrooms, onion flakes, and chives; mix well. Stir in olives, cheese and tunafish. Layer half the farfalle in buttered $2^1/_2$ quart casserole; then a layer of half the tuna mixture. Repeat. Arrange sliced tomatoes on top. Bake in a moderate oven (350°) about 25–30 minutes.

Mostaccioli con carciofi

Mostaccioli with artichoke hearts and Ricotta cheese

6 servings

- 1 *pound mostaccioli or elbow macaroni*
- 3 *tablespoons margarine or butter*
- 3 *tablespoons salad oil*
- 1 *small onion, sliced*
- 3 *frozen or canned artichoke hearts*
- 1 *cup dry white wine*
- $^1/_4$ *teaspoon black pepper*
- 1 *cup Ricotta or cottage cheese*
- $^1/_2$ *cup milk*
- 2 *egg yolks*
- $^1/_4$ *cup grated Parmesan cheese*
- 1 *teaspoon salt*
- $^1/_4$ *cup finely chopped parsley*

Cook macaroni according to package directions. Melt margarine in large skillet over medium heat; add oil. Sauté onion until transparent. Quarter artichoke hearts; add to saucepan. Stir in wine and pepper. Cook over medium heat until wine is reduced by half. Meanwhile, combine Ricotta cheese, milk, egg yolks, Parmesan cheese and salt; beat until well blended. Drain macaroni well; place in warmed serving dish. Add cheese mixture and artichoke mixture, toss lightly until well mixed. Garnish with finely chopped parsley.

Spaghetti con salsa di pollo

Spaghetti with chicken sauce

4 servings

- 6 *tablespoons margarine or butter*
- 1 *medium onion, chopped*
- 1 *small green pepper, chopped*
- $^1/_4$ *pound mushrooms, sliced*
- 2 *pimontos, diced*
- 1 *($10^1/_2$ ounce) can cream of chicken soup*
- 1 *cup milk*
- 2 *tablespoons sherry wine, optional*
- $^1/_2$ *teaspoon salt*
- *Dash nutmeg*
- 2 *cups cooked chicken, cubed*
- $^1/_4$ *cup bread crumbs*
- 1 *pound spaghetti*

Melt 4 tablespoons margarine in heavy saucepot. Sauté onion, pepper and mushrooms in margarine until onion is transparent. Stir in pimento, soup, milk, sherry, salt and nutmeg; blend well. Add chicken; simmer 5–10 minutes. Melt remaining margarine in small skillet; add bread crumbs; stir gently. Cook spaghetti according to package directions; drain well. Pour sauce over spaghetti; top with bread crumbs.

Spaghetti all'aglio

Spaghetti with garlic sauce

4 servings

- 1 *pound spaghetti*
- $^1/_2$ *cup margarine or butter*
- $^1/_2$ *cup olive oil*
- 4 *cloves garlic, minced*
- $^1/_4$ *cup finely chopped parsley*
- $^1/_2$ *teaspoon dried basil*
- $^1/_2$ *teaspoon dried oregano*
- $^1/_2$ *teaspoon salt*
- *Dash black pepper*
- *Grated Parmesan cheese*

Cook spaghetti according to package directions. Melt margarine in heavy saucepot; add oil; heat. Sauté garlic until lightly browned. Stir in parsley, basil, oregano, salt and pepper. Drain spaghetti well; return to pot. Add sauce; toss lightly. Serve with grated Parmesan cheese.

Spaghetti alla napoletana

Spaghetti Neapolitan style

4 servings

- 6 *slices bacon, diced*
- 1 *medium onion, chopped*
- 1 *pound ground beef*
- 1 *(1 pound) can tomatoes*
- 1 *(8 ounce) can tomato sauce*
- 1 *tablespoon tomato paste*
- 1 *teaspoon sugar*
- $^1/_2$ *teaspoon dried basil*
- $^1/_2$ *teaspoon dried oregano*
- 1 *pound spaghetti*

Fry out bacon in heavy saucepot. Sauté onion in bacon fat until transparent. Drain off excess fat. Brown meat. Add tomatoes, tomato sauce, tomato paste, sugar, basil and oregano; stir well. Simmer 15–20 minutes. Cook spaghetti according to package directions; drain well. Serve sauce over spaghetti.

Spaghetti marinara

Spaghetti with marinara sauce

4 servings

- 4 *tablespoons olive oil*
- 2 *onions, chopped*
- 2 *cloves garlic, minced*
- 2 *anchovy fillets*
- 1 *(29 ounce) can tomatoes*
- $^1/_2$ *cup dry white wine*
- $^1/_2$ *teaspoon salt*
- $^1/_4$ *teaspoon dried oregano*
- $^1/_4$ *teaspoon sugar*
- 1 *pound spaghetti*
- *Grated Parmesan cheese*

Heat oil in heavy saucepot; sauté onions and garlic in oil until onions are transparent. Add anchovies; stir to break up anchovies. Add tomatoes, wine, salt, oregano and sugar. Simmer 25–30 minutes. Meanwhile, cook spaghetti according to package directions; drain well. Pour sauce over spaghetti; sprinkle with grated Parmesan cheese.

Lasagne al forno

Baked lasagne

8–10 servings

> 3 tablespoons margarine or
> butter
> 2 (4 ounce) cans sliced
> mushrooms
> 1/4 pound ham, cut in strips
> 1 tablespoon parsley flakes
> 3 cups Bolognese sauce
> or
> 3 (8 ounce) cans beef gravy
>
> 1/2 cup heavy cream or
> evaporated milk
> 10 ounces lasagne noodles
> 1 1/2 cups grated Parmesan
> cheese

Melt margarine in large skillet;
sauté mushrooms, ham and
parsley flakes. Add Bolognese
sauce. Simmer uncovered, 15–20
minutes. Cook lasagne
according to package directions;
drain. Layer half the lasagne
noodles in a buttered
13 1/2″ × 8 3/4″ × 2″ baking dish.
Stir cream into sauce; spread
half the sauce over the noodles;
sprinkle with half the grated
cheese. Repeat. Bake in a
moderate oven (375°) about 30
minutes or until bubbly.

Lasagne con le vongole rosse

Lasagne with red clam sauce

8–10 servings

> 1/4 cup margarine or
> butter
> 2 cloves garlic, minced
> 3 (8 ounce) cans minced
> clams, drained
> 1 (29 ounce) can tomatoes,
> drained
> 2 eggs, slightly beaten
> 2 cups Ricotta cheese
> 1/2 cup grated Parmesan
> cheese
> 2 tablespoons parsley flakes
> 1 teaspoon salt
> 1/2 teaspoon black pepper
> 1 pound mozzarella
> cheese, sliced
> 10 ounces lasagne noodles

Melt margarine in skillet; sauté
garlic and clams until garlic is
lightly browned. Stir in
tomatoes. Cook over medium
heat, stirring occasionally,
about 15–20 minutes. Combine
eggs, Ricotta, Parmesan cheese,
parsley, salt and pepper; blend
well. Layer half the lasagne
noodles in a buttered
13 1/2″ × 8 3/4″ × 2″ baking dish;
spread with half the clam
mixture; top with half the
mozzarella cheese. Repeat. Bake
in a hot oven (375°) about 30
minutes or until hot and bubbly.

Spaghetti con prosciutto e uova

Spaghetti with ham and eggs

4 servings

> 1 pound spaghetti
> 4 tablespoons margarine or
> butter
> 1/2 pound ham, diced
> 2 eggs, slightly beaten
> 2 tablespoons cream,
> optional
> 2 tablespoons chopped
> chives
> 1/2 teaspoon salt
> 1/8 teaspoon black pepper
> 1/2 cup grated Parmesan
> cheese

Cook spaghetti according to
package directions. Melt
margarine in skillet; sauté ham
until lightly browned. Drain
spaghetti well; return to pot.
Immediately add ham, eggs,
cream, chives, salt and pepper;
toss lightly. (Heat from the
spaghetti cooks eggs). Add
Parmesan cheese; toss lightly.

Spaghetti con acciughe

Spaghetti with anchovies

4 servings

> 1 pound spaghetti
> 1/2 cup margarine or
> butter
> 1/4 cup olive oil
> 2 cloves garlic, minced
> 2 (1 3/4 ounce) cans
> anchovies with oil
> 1/2 cup chopped black olives
> 1 teaspoon capers
> 1/4 teaspoon dried oregano
> 1/4 teaspoon dried mint
> Grated Parmesan cheese

Cook spaghetti according to
package directions. Melt
margarine in saucepan; add oil;
heat. Add garlic, anchovies,
olives, capers, oregano and
mint. Cook 2–3 minutes, stirring
frequently, to break up
anchovies. Drain spaghetti.
Pour sauce over spaghetti; toss
lightly. Serve immediately with
grated Parmesan cheese.

Lasagne alla cacciatora

Lasagne hunters' style

8–10 servings

    4 tablespoons margarine or
       butter
    4 tablespoons olive oil
    1 large onion, chopped
    2 cloves garlic, minced
 $^1/_4$ pound mushrooms, chopped
    1 ($2^1/_2$–3 pound) chicken,
       cooked, boned and cubed
 $^1/_4$ pound chicken livers,
       chopped
 $^1/_4$ pound ham, diced
    1 teaspoon salt
 $^1/_4$ teaspoon black pepper
 $^1/_2$ cup red wine
    3 cups tomato puree
    1 teaspoon dried basil
 $^1/_2$ teaspoon dried rosemary
    1 teaspoon parsley flakes
   10 ounces lasagne noodles
 $^1/_2$ cup grated Parmesan
       cheese

Melt margarine in large skillet
over medium heat; add oil.
Sauté onion, garlic and
mushrooms in hot oil mixture
until onion is transparent. Add
chicken, chicken livers and ham.
Cook about 2–3 minutes.
Sprinkle with salt and pepper;
add wine. Continue to cook
until wine is reduced by half.
Skim off excess fat. Add tomato
puree and herbs; cook 25–30
minutes. Cook lasagne
according to recipe or package
directions; drain well. Butter a
$13^1/_2'' \times 8^3/_4'' \times 2''$ baking dish.
Arrange alternate layers of
noodles and meat mixture,
ending with meat mixture.
Sprinkle with Parmesan cheese.
Bake in a moderate oven (350°)
about 25–30 minutes or until
heated throughout.

Lasagne alla Paola

Lasagne Paula's style

8–10 servings

    1 pound sweet Italian sausage
    1 pound ground beef
    1 clove garlic, minced
    1 tablespoon dried basil
    1 teaspoon salt
    1 (1 pound) can tomatoes
    2 (6 ounce) cans tomato
       paste
 $^1/_2$ cup dry red wine
   10 ounces lasagne noodles
    2 eggs
    3 cups Ricotta or cottage
       cheese
 $^1/_2$ cup grated Parmesan
       cheese
    2 tablespoons parsley flakes
    1 teaspoon salt
 $^1/_8$ teaspoon black pepper
    1 pound mozzarella cheese,
       thinly sliced

Brown meat in heavy skillet;
spoon of excess fat. Add garlic,
basil, 1 teaspoon salt, tomatoes,
tomato paste and wine. Simmer,
uncovered, about 30 minutes,
stirring frequently. Cook
lasagne according to package
directions; drain. Beat eggs; add
Ricotta, Parmesan cheese,
parsley, salt and pepper. Blend
well. Layer half the lasagne in
a buttered $13^1/_2'' \times 8^3/_4'' \times 2''$
baking dish; spread with half
the Ricotta mixture. Add half
the mozzarella cheese; then half
the meat sauce. Repeat. Bake in
a moderate oven (375°) 30
minutes or until bubbly.

Ravioli

Ravioli

6 servings

3¹/₂ *cups sifted flour*
  ¹/₄ *teaspoon salt*
   3 *eggs, slightly beaten*
   2 *tablespoons soft margarine
      or butter*
  ¹/₂ *cup lukewarm water*
   1 *cup cooked ground
      chicken*
   1 *cup well drained
      spinach*
   2 *eggs, slightly beaten*
  ¹/₂ *cup bread crumbs*
  ¹/₄ *cup grated Parmesan
      cheese*
   2 *teaspoons parsley flakes*
   1 *clove garlic, minced*
  ¹/₂ *teaspoon salt*
  ¹/₄ *teaspoon black pepper*
   2 *cups tomato sauce*
         or
   1 *(16 ounce) jar meatless
      spaghetti sauce*

Place flour and salt in large
bowl; add 3 eggs, margarine and
water. Mix until dough can be
gathered into a ball. Place
dough on lightly floured board;
knead until firm but still smooth
and elastic. Cover; let stand 15
minutes. Meanwhile, combine
chicken, spinach, 2 eggs, bread
crumbs, cheese, parsley, garlic,
salt and pepper; mix well.
Divide dough in half; roll each
half out to ¹/₈″ thickness. Place
a teaspoonful of filling at 1¹/₂″
intervals on one sheet of dough.
Cover with second sheet. Cut
apart into squares or rounds

with a knife or cookie cutter.
Moisten edges; seal edges with
a fork. Allow to dry 1 hour.
Cook in batches in 6 quarts
boiling salted water, about 5–10
minutes or until done; drain.
Serve with hot sauce.

Manicotti

Macaroni muffs

4 servings

   1 *pound manicotti tubes or*
  22 *(4″) squares home-made
      pasta all'uova*
   2 *cups Ricotta cheese*
   2 *eggs, slightly beaten*
  ¹/₄ *pound ham, ground*
  ¹/₂ *cup grated Parmesan
      cheese*
   1 *tablespoon chopped chives*
   2 *teaspoons parsley flakes*
   1 *teaspoon salt*
  ¹/₄ *teaspoon black pepper*
   2 *cups tomato sauce
         or*
   1 *(16 ounce) jar marinara
      sauce*

Cook manicotti tubes according
to package directions, or cook
squares of home-made pasta in
6 quarts boiling salted water,
about 4 minutes. Remove with
slotted spoon; drain well on
cheesecloth. Combine Ricotta
cheese, eggs, ham, Parmesan
cheese, chives, parsley, salt and
pepper. Mix well. Fill manicotti
tubes with filling, or spread
filling on cooked dry pasta
squares; roll up tightly. Moisten
edges and seal tightly. Spoon
small amount of sauce on
bottom of buttered
13¹/₂″ × 8³/₄″ × 2″ baking pan.
Place manicotti in baking pan.
Pour remaining sauce over
manicotti. Bake in a moderate
oven (375°) about 20–25 minutes
or until hot and bubbly.

'Pasta' identifies the multitude of products made from semolina or flour and water and then dried in various shapes and forms, each one of which has its own, mostly very descriptive name. Each region of Italy has its special shape, the variations limited only by the imagination. Italian grocery stores carry all types of dried pasta, the pasta secca. It's a tempting adventure to make your own pasta fresca, the fresh or homemade pasta. However, if you prefer, ready-made pasta (available at all supermarkets) may be substituted. Pasta is a regular part of the Italian menu. It is usually served as a first course. At lucheon a modest dish of pasta serves as the main course.

acimi di pepe: 'peppercorns' tiny pieces of round or square pasta; used in soups.

agnolotti: round *ravioli*, filled with meat.

anelli and **anellini:** 'rings' and 'little rings' (for soups).
cannelloni: flat squares of pasta rolled around a stuffing.
cappelletti: 'little hats', flat or round squares with filling.

cavatelli: a short curled noodle, formed like a shell.
conchiglie: shaped like sea shells. Sometimes called *maruzze, maruzelle* or *conchigliette.*

ditali: 'thimbles'; macaroni cut in short lengths, about $1/4$ inch in diameter and $1/2$ inch long.
ditalini: same shape as ditali but cut in $1/4$ inch lengths. Used in soups.
farfalle, farfallette or **farfalloni:** 'butterflies'. Small and large ribbon bows.

fettuccine, fettuccelle: 'ribbons'. About $1/4$ inch wide. Easy to make as a fresh pasta.

fusilli: a spiral, curly spaghetti, twisted like a corkscrew.

lasagne: a very wide flat pasta used most often in baked dishes. Also sold with one or two sides rippled.

maccheroni (or macaroni): hollow or pierced pasta products. There are more than 20 sizes of hollow pastas. Most often used is *mezzani*, a smooth, curved tubular pasta about 1 inch long and $1/4$ inch in diameter. Other sizes are *bucatini, mezzanelli, ziti, zetoni, cannelle,* and *tufoli.*

mafalde: long twisted ribbon noodles.
ravioli: pasta squares, stuffed with eggs, vegetables or cheese. Other sizes are called *anolini, anolotti or raviolini* (small ravioli).

rigatoni: large, ribbed, tubular pasta cut into 3 inch lengths.

spaghetti: pasta dried in long, thin, round strands, as distinguished from the *macaronis* (round but hollow) and noodles like *lasange* (flat). Listed as *spaghetti's* are *capellini, fedelini, vermicelli, spaghettini,* and *spaghettoni.*

tagliatelle: narrow egg noodles, not different from the fettucine. The tagliatelle is $3/4$ inch wide in the home-made version. The 4 names in this family ranging from $3/4$ inch to $1/8$ inch are *tagliatelle, tagliolette, tagliolini* and *tagliarini.*

tortellini: 'small twists', to be stuffed.

vermicelli: Very thin *spaghetti.* Vermicelli is sold not only in straight rods, but also sometimes 15 or 20 strands are twisted to form a bow knot.

Spaghetti con le vongole

Spaghetti with white clam sauce

4 servings

$^1/_2$ *cup margarine or*
  butter
$^1/_4$ *cup salad oil*
  3 cloves garlic, minced
  2 (8 ounce) cans minced
  clams, drained
$^1/_4$ *cup finely chopped parsley*
$^1/_4$ *teaspoon dried basil*
$^1/_4$ *teaspoon dried oregano*
$^1/_4$ *teaspoon salt*
  Dash black pepper
  1 pound spaghetti
  Grated Parmesan cheese

Melt margarine in saucepot;
add oil; heat. Sauté garlic and
clams in hot oil mixture over
medium heat, 2–3 minutes. Stir
in parsley, basil, oregano, salt
and pepper. Simmer 5–10
minutes. Cook spaghetti
according to package directions;
drain well. Return to pot; add
sauce; toss lightly. Serve with
grated Parmesan cheese.

Spaghetti al tonno

Spaghetti with tuna sauce

4 servings

  3 tablespoons margarine or
  butter
  1 medium onion, chopped
  1 clove garlic, minced
$^1/_4$ *pound mushrooms*
  sliced
  2 anchovy fillets, optional
  2 (7 ounce) cans tunafish
  2 (8 ounce) cans tomato
  sauce
$^1/_4$ *cup sliced green*
  olives
  1 pound spaghetti

Melt margarine in heavy
saucepot. Sauté onion, garlic
and mushrooms until onion is
transparent. Add anchovies and
tunafish; stir in tomato sauce.
Simmer 15–20 minutes. Cook
spaghetti according to package
directions; drain well. Pour
sauce over spaghetti. Garnish
with olive slices.

Tagliarini con fegatini

Noodles and chicken livers

4 servings

$^1/_2$ *cup margarine or*
  butter
  1 medium onion, chopped
$^1/_2$ *pound mushrooms,*
  sliced
$^1/_4$ *cup flour*
$^1/_2$ *teaspoon salt*
$^1/_8$ *teaspoon black pepper*
  1 pound chicken livers
$^1/_2$ *cup Marsala wine*
$^1/_4$ *cup water*
  1 pound tagliarini or
  medium noodles

Melt margarine in large skillet;
sauté onion and mushrooms in
margarine until onion is
transparent. Combine flour, salt
and pepper. Cut chicken livers
in half; dredge with flour. Add
chicken livers and all the flour
mixture to skillet. Cook until
chicken livers are lightly
browned. Stir in wine and water.
Cook over low heat, stirring
occasionally, until chicken livers
are cooked, 5–10 minutes. Cook
noodles according to package
directions; drain well. Serve
chicken livers over noodles.

Tagliatelle ai funghi

Tagliatelle and mushrooms

4 servings

  1 pound tagliatelli or
  fettucini noodles
$^1/_2$ *cup margarine or*
  butter
$^1/_4$ *cup salad oil*
  1 pound mushrooms, sliced
  2 teaspoons parsley flakes
  1 teaspoon salt
$^1/_4$ *teaspoon black pepper*
  Grated Parmesan cheese

Cook noodles according to
package directions. Melt
margarine in heavy saucepot;
add oil; heat. Sauté mushrooms
in hot oil mixture; stir in
parsley, salt and pepper. Drain
noodles well; return to pot. Add
mushroom sauce; toss lightly.
Serve with grated Parmesan
cheese.

Frankfurter Nudelpfanne

Frankfurter Nudelpfanne

Frankfurt noodle casserole

6 servings

   1 *(8 oz.) package noodles,*
      cooked and drained
   1 *(10 oz.) package frozen*
      peas, thawed
   4 *tablespoons margarine or*
      butter
   1 *(10 oz.) package frozen*
      spinach, cooked and drained
   1 *pound frankfurters, sliced*
   1 *(10½ oz.) can cream of*
      mushroom soup
  ½ *cup sour cream*
  ½ *cup milk*
   4 *slices bacon, cooked and*
      crumbled

Combine noodles, 1½ cups peas,
and margarine; mix lightly.
Place spinach in bottom of
buttered 2½ qt. casserole.
Spread noodle mixture over
spinach. Combine frankfurters,
soup, sour cream, and milk;
mix well; pour over noodles.
Bake in a hot oven (400°) about
25 minutes. Sprinkle bacon and
peas over top; bake 5 minutes
more.

Eight jewel fried rice

6 American servings
6 Chinese servings

  4 cups cold cooked rice
  4 eggs
½ teaspoon salt
  1 tablespoon water
3½ tablespoons oil
  2 scallions
  4 large shrimp
½ cup diced lean pork
½ cup diced cooked boiled ham
    or uncooked smoked ham
½ cup diced chicken breast
  4 fresh mushrooms, finely
    chopped
  3 water chestnuts, sliced
    thinly
½ cup cooked peas
¼ teaspoon salt
  1 tablespoon soy sauce
  2 to 3 tablespoons chicken
    broth

Loosen the cold rice with chopsticks or your fingers to separate it into individual grains. Combine the eggs, salt and water in a small bowl and beat lightly. Scramble the eggs in 1 tablespoon oil until just set. Remove the eggs from the pan. Cut the scallions into pieces ½ inch long. Shell, devein and chop the shrimp into small pieces. Heat the remaining oil in a wok or a skillet. Add scallions and stir fry for 30 seconds. Add pork and stir fry for about 2 minutes or until it has lost any trace of pink. Add ham, chicken breast and mushrooms and stir fry for 1 minute. Add shrimp and water chestnuts and stir fry for another 1 minute. Add rice and stir fry for 1 minute.

Add peas, salt, soy sauce and chicken broth. Add scrambled eggs to pan. Stir fry gently to allow rice to heat through. Serve hot.

Sizzling rice

4 American servings
4 Chinese servings

This dish, sometimes called singing rice or crackling rice, is made with the crusts of rice which remain sticking to the pan when cooking rice. As this is normally only 1 or 2 tablespoons, you have to "collect" these crusts from several batches of cooked rice until you have the cup and a half you need for this recipe. Rice crusts may be reserved in any airtight capped container in the refrigerator for several weeks.

1½ cups rice crusts
  1 pound shrimp
1½ tablespoons sherry
  ¼ teaspoon salt
  1 tablespoon cornstarch
  2 tablespoons oil or lard
  ¾ cup chicken broth
  ¼ teaspoon salt
  1 tablespoon sugar
  4 tablespoons tomato purée
    or catsup
½ tablespoon sherry
  1 tablespoon cornstarch
  2 tablespoons water
    Oil for deep frying

Break the rice crusts into bite size pieces and dry on a baking sheet in a 300 degree oven for 10 minutes or until completely dry. Shell the shrimp and take out the black vein. Combine sherry, salt and cornstarch and mix with the shrimp. Leave for 20 minutes. Heat the oil or lard in a wok or other pan. Add the shrimp and stir fry for about 1 minute or until pink but not completely done. Remove shrimp from pan and keep warm. Combine chicken broth, salt, sugar, tomato purée or catsup and sherry in a saucepan and bring to a boil. Mix cornstarch and water and stir into the sauce to thicken. Add shrimp, reduce heat a little and simmer for 2 minutes or until heated through. Heat the oil for deep frying, when oil is quite hot, add rice crusts and deep fry for about 1 minute or until floating and golden brown. Remove rice from pan with a skimmer, drain quickly and place on a hot serving dish. Bring rice and shrimp sauce to the table. Pour the sauce over the hot rice and you will hear the rice sizzle and sing with happiness.

Basic preparations

Rice cooking I

4 American servings
4 Chinese servings

1 cup raw long grain white rice
1½ to 1¾ cups water

Put the rice in a large saucepan. Add enough cold water to cover the rice by 2 inches. Wash the rice by rubbing it gently between your fingers. Drain and cover rice with fresh water. Continue washing the rice until the water is clear. This washing process removes dust and excess starch from the rice. Put the rice into a large saucepan. Add the water and bring to boiling point over moderately high heat. Stir rice occasionally until most of the water has been absorbed and the rice is visible, bubbling and foaming. Cover the pan and reduce heat to simmering point. Continue cooking for 20 minutes until the rice is dry and fluffy.

Note: You may need to adjust the quantity of water and the length of the cooking time depending on the type of rice which you are using. Unfortunately, exact timing can only be judged after a few experiments.

Rice cooking II

4 American servings
4 Chinese servings

1 cup raw long grain white rice
Water

Wash the rice as directed in the previous recipe. Place the rice in a large saucepan in an even layer. Add enough cold water to cover the rice by 1 inch. Bring to a boil over high heat. Stir once. Cover and simmer over low heat for 25 minutes until all the water has been absorbed. Do not raise the lid while the rice is simmering. Stir cooked rice gently to separate and fluff the grains. If the rice is not used immediately, leave it covered over the lowest possible heat. Do not turn off the heat and then turn it on again or the rice will become soft and pasty.

Rice steaming

4 American servings
4 Chinese servings

1 cup raw long grain white rice
Water

Wash the rice as described in recipe for rice cooking I. Place in a pan with plenty of water. Bring to a boil over high heat and boil for 5 to 7 minutes, stirring occasionally. Drain in a sieve. Transfer rice to a steamer lined with a piece of cloth. Cover with the lid and steam for about 20 minutes. Little holes can be made in the rice with a chopstick to ensure better steaming.

Fried rice I

Fried rice II

Rice and noodles are the staple food of the Chinese people. Rice is grown and eaten primarily in the Southern part of China where it is important not only for its taste but because it is often the only barrier against starvation. But even apart from the basic necessity of eating rice, to the Chinese, the pure white grains and bland taste seem to be the perfect accompaniment to all other foods. When sampling all the myriad taste elements of a Chinese meal, a spoonful of rice taken with the other food as well as in between, brings a neutral element into play so that every new morsel can unfold all its full flavor and character.

Long grain rice is suitable for most dishes. When properly cooked, it absorbs a great deal of water and will be dry and fluffy. Short grain rice, because it does not absorb as much water as the long grain variety, will generally be softer and more moist and the grains will tend to stick to one another. The so called instant rice is not suitable for Chinese cooking; it has less taste and is less nutritious. Rice is either boiled or steamed, though even in boiling there is actually a steaming process going on in the pan for most of the time. It is very important to wash the rice well to get ride of the excess starch which otherwise would make the rice too sticky. After it has been boiled or steamed, left over rice can be fried. It should be completely cooled before it is fried. Sometimes rice is not cooked alone, but may be topped with other foods, the flavors of

which are allowed to permeate the rice.

4 American servings
4 Chinese servings

3 cups cold cooked rice
3 eggs
¼ teaspoon salt
½ tablespoon water
2 tablespoons oil
2 scallions, cut into ½ inch pieces
2 tablespoons soy sauce

Separate the grains of rice with chopsticks or a fork. Lightly beat the eggs, salt and water. Heat the oil in a wok. Add the scallions and stir fry ½ minute. Add the rice and stir fry until heated through and each grain is coated with oil. Pour in the egg mixture and continue stirring until the egg is nearly set. Add soy sauce and stir until well combined. Serve. immediately.

4 American servings
4 Chinese servings

3 cups cold cooked rice
2 eggs
¼ teaspoon salt
½ tablespoon sherry
2 tablespoons oil
4 scallions, cut into ½ inch pieces
½ cup diced roast pork

½ cup diced cooked smoked ham
½ cup cooked peas
2 tablespoons chicken broth
1 tablespoon soy sauce

Separate the grains of rice with chopsticks or a fork. Lightly beat the eggs, salt and sherry. Heat the oil in a wok. Add the scallions, roast pork and ham and stir fry ½ minute. Add the rice and stir fry until heated through and each grain is coated with oil. Add the peas and pour in the egg mixture. Continue stirring until the egg is nearly set. Add chicken broth and soy sauce and stir until well combined. Serve immediately.

Soft fried noodles, pork and shrimp

4 American servings
8 Chinese servings

1 recipe soft fried noodles

½ pound lean pork
½ pound shrimp
1 stalk celery, cut diagonally in ¾ inch pieces
3 tablespoons oil
¼ teaspoon salt
1 tablespoon soy sauce
1 tablespoon sherry
1 clove garlic, crushed
1 slice fresh ginger root, minced
½ red pepper, seeded and cut into ½ inch long pieces
1½ tablespoons chicken broth or water
1 recipe egg-garnish

6 onion brushes

Cut pork in strips 1½ inches long, ½ inch wide and ⅛ inch thick. Shell shrimp and take out the black vein. Blanch the celery in boiling water for 3 minutes. Rinse under cold running water and drain. Heat 2 tablespoons oil in a wok or other pan. Add salt and stir fry for about 30 seconds. Add pork and stir fry for about 2 minutes or until it has lost any trace of pink. Add shrimp and stir fry for about 1 minute. Add soy sauce and sherry and stir fry for another 30 seconds. Remove pork and shrimp mixture from pan. Add remaining oil and heat. Add garlic and ginger root and stir

fry for 30 seconds. Discard garlic, add celery and red pepper and stir fry for about 1½ minutes. Add broth and stir fry for another minute. Return pork and shrimp to the pan and heat through briefly. Add soft fried noodles and toss to mix. Transfer to a serving dish, garnish with egg-garnish and onion brushes and serve.

Mixed tossed noodles

4 American servings
6 Chinese servings

1 pound egg noodles
1 tablespoon oil
4 scallions
2 dried Chinese mushrooms
½ cup cooked chicken
½ cup roast pork
3 tablespoons oil
1 clove garlic, crushed
1 thin slice fresh ginger root, minced
½ cup bamboo shoots, shredded
½ cup bean sprouts
½ cup chicken broth
3 tablespoons soy sauce
1 tablespoon sherry
½ teaspoon sugar
1 tablespoon cornstarch
2 tablespoons water
2 tablespoons ham garnish

Cook the noodles.
Drain noodles and rinse under cold running water. Toss with 1 tablespoon oil. Cut scallions into pieces ½ inch long. Soak dried mushrooms in hot water for 20 minutes. Squeeze mushrooms dry. Discard stems and cut caps into strips 1 inch long and ¼ inch wide. Cut chicken into slices ¼ inch thick. Cook pork. Cut pork into ¼ inch thick slices. Heat the oil in a wok or large skillet. Add garlic and ginger and stir fry for 30 seconds. Add scallions and stir fry for 30 seconds. Add bamboo shoots and mushrooms and stir fry for 1½ minutes. Add chicken and pork and stir fry for 1 minute. Add bean

sprouts and stir fry for 20 seconds. Add chicken broth, soy sauce, sherry and sugar. Bring to a boil over high heat. Combine cornstarch and water and add to thicken sauce. Immerse noodles in boiling water for 2 minutes until very hot. Drain noodles and place in a serving dish. Add stir fried mixture and toss gently. Serve immediately.

Noodles in soup, served in a Nga Po casserole dish and soft fried rice noodles which has tea melon as one of its interesting ingredients.

Noodles in soup

4 American servings
4 Chinese servings

　¼　pound egg noodles
　1　dried Chinese mushroom
　2　ounces lean pork (butt or
　　　shoulder)
　½　tablespoon sherry
　¼　teaspoon salt
　1　teaspoon cornstarch
1½　tablespoons oil
　1　thin slice fresh ginger root,
　　　minced
　2　fresh mushrooms, thinly
　　　sliced
　1　tablespoon soy sauce
　3　cups boiling chicken broth
　4　onion brushes

Parboil noodles as directed in recipe on page 19 and keep warm. Soak dried mushroom in warm water for about 20 minutes. Squeeze dry, remove stem and shred cap. Cut pork into ⅛ to ¼ inch thick slices across the grain. Mix sherry, salt and cornstarch. Add pork and toss to coat. Heat the oil in a wok or frying pan. Add the ginger root and stir fry for 30 seconds. Add the pork and stir fry for about 1½ minutes. Add fresh and dried mushrooms and stir fry for another half minute. Add soy sauce to the boiling broth. Place the noodles in individual bowls and pour over the broth. Top with stir fried pork and mushrooms, garnish each serving with an onion brush and serve.

Plain soft fried noodles

Soft fried rice noodles

Noodles in soup

6 American servings
6 Chinese servings

1 pound egg noodles
1 tablespoon oil
2 scallions
3 tablespoons oil
½ teaspoon salt
1 teaspoon soy sauce

Drain, rinse
under cold running water and
mix with 1 tablespoon oil.
Cut scallions in ½ inch long
pieces. Heat the oil in a wok
or other pan until quite hot.
Add scallions and stir fry for
30 seconds. Add noodles and
stir fry for 2 minutes, separating
the noodles with chopsticks.
Add salt and soy sauce and stir
fry for another ½ to 1 minute
or until completely heated
through and lightly browned.
Serve plain or combine with a
stir fried mixture as indicated
in other recipes.

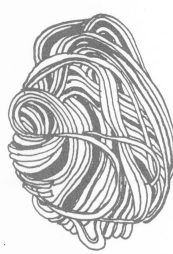

4 American servings
8 Chinese servings

1 pound rice noodles
1 tablespoon oil
¼ cup dried shrimp (optional)
2 to 3 dried Chinese mushrooms
½ pound lean pork
*¼ cup preserved tea melon or
   preserved sweet cucumber*
4 tablespoons oil
*3 scallions, cut into ½ inch
   pieces*
1 tablespoon soy sauce
*¼ cup shredded bamboo
   shoots*
*4 fresh mushrooms, thinly
   sliced*
¼ cup sliced water chestnuts
*1 tablespoon chicken broth
   or water*

Parboil rice noodles for 7 to
8 minutes. Drain, rinse under
cold running water and mix
with 1 tablespoon oil.
Meanwhile, soak dried shrimp
and dried mushrooms separately
in warm water for about 30
minutes. Drain shrimp and
squeeze mushrooms dry.
Remove mushroom stems and
shred caps. Cut the pork into
pieces 1 inch long, ¾ inch wide
and ½ inch thick. Drain tea
melon and cut into ½ to ¾
inch long pieces. Heat 2
tablespoons oil in a wok or
other pan. Add scallions and
stir fry for about 30 seconds.
Add pork and stir fry for
about 2 minutes or until it has
lost any trace of pink. Add
dried shrimp and stir fry for
another 30 seconds. Add soy
sauce, bamboo shoots,
mushrooms, dried mushrooms

and water chestnuts and stir
fry for 1½ minutes. Add broth
and tea melon and stir fry
for another ½ minute. Remove
from pan and keep warm.
Add remaining oil to the pan
and heat until very hot. Add
noodles and stir fry for 1 to
1½ minutes or until heated
through and very lightly
browned. Return meats and
vegetables to the wok and toss
to mix. Serve immediately.

4 American servings
4 Chinese servings

3 cups chicken broth
*¼ cup shredded Chinese
   cabbage or spinach*
½ cup shredded roast pork

*1 scallion, cut in 1 inch
   pieces*
1 teaspoon soy sauce
¼ pound egg noodles, cooked

4 sprigs fresh parsley

Bring broth to the simmer.
Add cabbage and simmer 3
minutes. Add pork and scallion
and simmer 1 minute. Stir in
soy sauce. Place noodles in
individual soup bowls. With a
slotted spoon, place some of the
pork and vegetables in each
bowl. Pour the broth into the
bowls, garnish with parsley
and serve.

Arroz con costrada de huevos estilo Alicante

Crusted rice with eggs

6 to 8 servings

  1 *(2 to 3 pound) chicken, cut into 8 pieces*
  ½ *pound boneless ham*
  2 *small chorizos or substitute pepperoni*
  1 *cup dried chick peas, soaked overnight*
  8 *cups water*
  ½ *teaspoon salt*
     Freshly ground black pepper
  2 *tablespoons olive oil*
  ½ *onion, finely chopped*
  1 *sweet sausage*
  2 *cups converted rice*
  4 *eggs*

Place the chicken, ham, chorizos, chick peas, water, salt and pepper in a heavy pan. Bring to a boil, reduce the heat and simmer, uncovered, for about 2½ hours or until the chick peas are tender. Drain and reserve the cooking liquid. Heat the olive oil in a paella pan or other large, shallow pan. Sauté the onion and sausage for about 8 minutes. Remove the sausage and slice into bite sized pieces. Slice the chicken, ham and chorizos. Add the rice to the paella pan and stir for 3 minutes. Reheat the reserved cooking liquid. Add the sliced meats, chick peas and 4 cups of the cooking liquid. Stir once and boil 3 minutes over high heat. Reduce the heat and simmer uncovered 15 to 20 minutes more or until the rice has absorbed all the liquid and is tender. Beat the eggs until foamy and pour them over the rice. Bake in a preheated 400° oven for 3 to 5 minutes or until the eggs begin to brown. Serve from the pan.

Arroz com tomate à Portuguesa

Rice with tomatoes Portuguese style

6 servings

  3 *tablespoons butter*
  1 *onion, finely chopped*
  1 *cup raw rice*
  2 *cups beef broth*
  1 *(8 ounce) can tomato sauce*
  ½ *teaspoon salt*
     Freshly ground black pepper

Heat the butter in a saucepan. Add the onion and fry over moderately high heat for 3 minutes. Add the rice and stir until it begins to brown. Add beef broth, tomato sauce, salt and pepper. Simmer uncovered over low heat for 20 minutes without stirring until the rice is tender and all the liquid has been absorbed.

Arroz de salmão à Lisboeta

Rice with salmon Lisbon style

4 servings

  2 *cups water*
  ½ *teaspoon salt*
  1 *cup raw rice*
  1 *pound fresh salmon, cut into 4 slices*
  2 *tablespoons melted butter*
  3 *tablespoons butter*
  3 *tablespoons flour*
1½ *cups milk*
  3 *egg yolks*
  1 *teaspoon curry powder*
  ½ *teaspoon salt*
     Freshly ground black pepper

Bring the water to a boil and add the salt and rice. Stir once with a fork, cover and cook over low heat about 25 minutes or until all the liquid is absorbed. Brush the slices of salmon with 2 tablespoons melted butter and broil 6 to 10 minutes. The fish is done when it flakes easily with a fork. Melt the remaining butter in a saucepan and stir in the flour. Cook over low heat for 1 minute. Add the milk gradually, stirring constantly. Beat the egg yolks and add 1 tablespoon of the hot sauce. Stir the egg yolks and curry powder into the sauce. Season with salt and pepper. Cut the salmon into small pieces. Arrange the rice on a platter, place the pieces of salmon on top and pour the sauce over the fish.

Arroz con pescado a la catalana

Rice with fish Catalan style

4 servings

    24 steamer (soft shell) clams
  1½ cups cold water
    ½ pound squid (optional)
    ½ pound firm fleshed fish fillets,
        such as cod, halibut or
        haddock
    ½ pound large shrimp
    1 green pepper, peeled, seeded
        and chopped
    3 tablespoons oil
    1 onion, finely chopped
    1 clove garlic, crushed
    2 ripe tomatoes, peeled,
        seeded and chopped
  1½ cups converted rice
    ¼ teaspoon saffron powder or
        ½ teaspoon saffron threads
    ¼ teaspoon salt
    1 cup green peas
    2 tablespoons finely chopped
        parsley

Scrub the clams and soak them in 3 changes of cold water for 1 hour to remove the sand completely. Steam the clams over 1½ cups water for 10 minutes until they have opened. Discard the empty shell from each clam. Strain the broth. Cut the squid into 1 inch rings. Discard the head, ink sacs and cartilage from the squid. Cut the fish fillets into 8 pieces. Remove the shells and veins from the shrimp. Parboil the green pepper in 3 cups water for 5 minutes. Drain and rinse the green pepper under cold water. Heat 2 tablespoons of oil and fry the squid, fish fillets and shrimp for 5 minutes until the fish is lightly browned and the

shrimp is pink. Remove all the fish. Add the remaining 1 tablespoon oil to the skillet and fry the onion and garlic for 3 minutes until softened. Add the tomatoes and immediately remove from the heat. Add the fish to the skillet. When you are ready to serve the dish, reheat all these ingredients until they are hot. Transfer them to a paella pan or a large casserole. Add the rice and strained clam broth adding enough water or white wine to make up 3 cups liquid. Add saffron and salt. Stir once and cook on top of the range uncovered for 10 minutes. Do not stir again or the rice will become gummy. Add green pepper, peas and clams. Do not stir but continue cooking uncovered for 5 minutes. Sprinkle with parsley. The fish will be completely cooked and the rice will have absorbed all the liquid. Allow the dish to stand for 5 minutes and serve with a tossed salad.

Arroz de manteiga

Rice cooked in bouillon

4 servings

    6 tablespoons butter
    1 onion, finely chopped
    1 cup raw rice
    2 cups beef broth

Heat 4 tablespoons of the butter in a saucepan. Fry the onion in the butter for 3 minutes, but do not let the onion brown. Add the rice and stir for 3 minutes until the grains of rice are lightly browned, Add the beef broth and the remaining butter. Simmer, uncovered, over low heat for 20 minutes until the rice is tender. Do not stir the rice while it is simmering.

Arroz de caril de camarão

Rice with shrimp

6 to 8 servings

   10 peppercorns, crushed
    1 clove garlic, crushed
    1 teaspoon powdered ginger
    ½ teaspoon ground anise
    1 teaspoon ground coriander
    1 teaspoon ground cumin
    2 cups grated coconut
    3 tablespoons butter
    2 medium-sized onions, finely
        chopped
    2 pounds shrimp, shelled and
        deveined
  1½ cups dry white wine
    ½ cup water
    1 teaspoon salt
    ¼ cup tomato purée

In a bowl, combine the peppercorns, garlic, ginger, anise, coriander, cumin and coconut. Heat the butter in a large skillet and sauté the onions until softened. Add the shrimp and cook, stirring, 4 minutes or until they turn pink. Add the coconut mixture, wine, water and salt and bring to a simmer. Stir in the tomato purée and cook 1 to 2 minutes to blend the flavors. Serve on a bed of rice.

EGG & CHEESE DISHES

According to tradition, cheese fondue was created by a Swiss winegrower's wife during the vintage. As she was very busy picking grapes, she had no time to prepare the normal type of meal.

Fondue

Käse Beignet

Gâteau au fromage Fribourgeoise

Cheese fondue is now probably as popular abroad as it is in Switzerland itself. But its origins are uniquely Swiss. Fondue was most likely invented by a wine grower's wife somewhere near Neuchâtel during the weeks of the grape harvest. This has always been a very busy time for the whole family, and the work is hard. There is no time to prepare a full meal, but everyone must still eat heartily to cope with the grape picking. The famer's wife hit upon the idea of melting cheese in wine in a large pan and setting it in the middle of the table. Everyone would sit around the pan, dipping pieces of bread stuck onto a fork into the soft, hot cheese mixture and enjoying a substantial meal prepared quickly. Because cheese fondue is so easy to make, and with no dishes to wash afterwards, it has naturally become popular around the world in recent years. But it needs a healthy stomach to digest this heavy mixture. Therefore, it's important to remember to add Kirsch (cherry liqueur) to make the fondue easier to digest. And it's also a good idea to drink hot tea with the fondue; this helps it go down more easily.

Cheese fondue

6 servings

- 1 clove garlic, cut in half
- 2 cups dry white wine
- 1 pound Gruyère cheese, grated
- 1 pound Emmenthal (Swiss) cheese, grated
  Freshly ground black pepper
- 3 tablespoons cornstarch dissolved in
  3 tablespoons kirsch
- 1 loaf French bread, cut into cubes

Rub garlic all over the inside of an earthenware fondue pot. Pour in the wine and place over moderate heat until the wine begins to bubble. Add the cheese a little at a time, stirring constantly as if making a figure 8. When the cheese has melted, sprinkle with pepper and stir in the dissolved cornstarch. Place the fondue pot over a portable burner at the table. Provide each guest with a long fork. (A bread cube is speared on the fork and dipped into the melted cheese.) Serve a dry white wine with the fondue.

Cheese steak

8 servings

- 1¾ cups flour
- 1 cup beer
- ⅔ cup water
- 2 egg whites
- 8 ½ inch thick slices Gruyère cheese, each weighing about 2 ounces
- ½ cup flour for dredging
  Oil for deep frying

Sift the flour into a bowl. Add the beer and water and beat until smooth. Cover and let the batter stand 1 hour. Beat the egg whites until soft peaks form and fold into the batter. Dredge each cheese slice in flour and dip into the batter. Fry the cheese in hot (375°) oil until golden brown. Drain on paper towels and serve immediately.

Cheese pie from Fribourg

4 to 6 servings

- 1½ cups flour
- ½ teaspoon salt
- 6 tablespoons butter
- 4 tablespoons water
- 2 tablespoons butter
- 1 onion, chopped
- 2 cups grated Gruyère cheese
- 4 eggs, beaten
- ½ teaspoon salt
  Freshly ground black pepper
- ⅛ teaspoon nutmeg
- 1 cup light cream

Place the flour and salt in a bowl. Blend in the butter with a pastry blender until it resembles fine breadcrumbs. Add the water and stir with a fork to form a smooth dough. Roll out the pastry ⅛ inch thick and line a 9 inch pie pan. Heat 2 tablespoons butter in a skillet and fry the onion until softened. Remove from the heat and add the grated cheese. Spread the mixture over the pastry shell. Mix the beaten eggs with the salt, pepper, nutmeg and cream. Pour over the onion and grated cheese and bake in a preheated 350° oven for 30 minutes. Serve hot.

Scrambled eggs with pork, onion and chives

3 American servings
6 Chinese servings

  5 *eggs*
  1 *teaspoon water*
  ½ *teaspoon salt*
  ⅛ *teaspoon white pepper*
  2 *tablespoons finely chopped chives*
1½ *tablespoons oil*
  2 *slices fresh ginger root*
  1 *scallion, minced*
  1 *medium onion, shredded lengthwise*
  ½ *cup shredded lean pork*
  1 *tablespoon ham garnish*

Combine eggs, water, salt, pepper and chives in a bowl and beat until well blended. Heat oil in a frying pan until very hot. Add ginger root and stir fry 1 minute. Remove ginger root from the pan and add scallion and onion. Stir fry ½ minute. Add pork and stir fry 2 minutes. Reduce the heat and add the eggs. Stir as for scrambled eggs until soft curds form. Serve immediately topped with ham garnish.

Soy colored eggs

4 American servings
4 Chinese servings

  4 *eggs*
  ½ *cup soy sauce*
  ½ *cup chicken broth or water*
  6 *tablespoons sugar*
  ¼ *teaspoon sesame oil*
  1 *tablespoon minced onion*
16 *to 20 radishes*

Place the eggs in a saucepan. Cover with cold water and boil gently for 5 minutes. Remove from the heat and put under cold running water for 5 minutes. Remove the shells carefully. Place the soy sauce, chicken broth, sugar, sesame oil and onion in a small saucepan. Bring the mixture to boiling point. Add the eggs, cover the pan and simmer for 10 minutes. Remove from the heat and allow the eggs to cool in the sauce for 30 minutes. Turn the eggs during the cooking and cooling to ensure that they are colored evenly. Drain the eggs and cut into quarters lengthwise. Serve with radishes and plum sauce. These eggs may be served either as a hot accompaniment to a meal or cold as an appetizer.

Tea eggs

4 American servings
4 Chinese servings

4 *eggs*
3 *cups boiling water*
2 *tablespoons black tea*
1 *teaspoon salt*
2 *cloves star anise*

Place the eggs in a pan and cover with cold water. Bring to a boil over high heat. Reduce heat and simmer 5 minutes. Remove from the heat, drain the eggs and run cold water over them for several minutes. Dry the eggs and tap the shells gently on all sides to crack them evenly. Place the 3 cups boiling water in a saucepan with the tea, salt and star anise. Add the eggs, cover and simmer gently for 1½ hours. Let the eggs cool in the flavored water ½ hour. The eggs may be made in advance but do not shell them until ready to serve. Serve halved or quartered as an appetizer or as a garnish for a luncheon salad.

Steamed eggs

4 American servings
4 Chinese servings

1 *cup chicken broth*
½ *cup minced lean pork or beef*
2 *scallions, minced*
2 *teaspoons sherry*
¼ *teaspoon salt*
¼ *teaspoon sugar*
1 *teaspoon oil*
4 *eggs*
1 *teaspoon oil*

Heat the broth until hot but not boiling. Combine pork or beef, scallions, sherry, salt, sugar and oil in a bowl and mix until well blended. In another bowl stir the eggs just long enough to blend the yolks and whites. Add the sherry mixture and then the broth gradually, stirring gently all the time. Oil a shallow heatproof dish with the remaining oil and pour in the mixture. Steam over water that is just kept at boiling point for about 15 to 20 minutes or until of a custard-like consistency. Start testing for doneness with a toothpick after 10 minutes. When it comes out clean, the eggs are done. A little soy sauce may be sprinkled onto the eggs before serving to enhance the flavor.
Note: Minced chicken, shrimp or flaked crabmeat can be substituted for pork or beef.

Shiny brown soy eggs and marbled tea eggs show the fascinating ways the Chinese have with eggs.

It is not difficult to see why Crab Foo Young is a very popular dish in China and abroad once you have made it yourself.

Crab foo young

Plain boiled or fried eggs, are seldom eaten in China. Usually they are seasoned one way or another when boiled, and are combined with numerous other ingredients when steamed, scrambled or fried. Lard is sometimes used as a cooking agent in the preparation of eggs. Eggs are frequently served as a garnish in soups or with other dishes. They play an important role in fried rice dishes and are used in batters for deep fried foods.

3 American servings
6 Chinese servings

4 eggs
½ teaspoon salt
⅛ teaspoon freshly ground pepper
2 teaspoons sherry
1 cup fresh or canned crabmeat
3 to 3½ tablespoons oil
2 scallions, minced
6 medium sized mushrooms, sliced
1 tablespoon finely chopped chives
1 recipe Foo Young sauce

Beat the eggs lightly in a bowl. Stir in salt, pepper and sherry. Shred the crabmeat and remove any hard pieces. Heat 1½ tablespoons oil in a wok or frying pan. Stir fry scallions, mushrooms and chives for 2 minutes over moderate heat. Add crabmeat and stir fry for 1 more minute over high heat. Remove the pan from the heat and allow the mixture to cool for a few minutes. Add the egg mixture. Heat 2 tablespoons of oil in a wok or frying pan with sloping sides. Add the crab and egg mixture and cook the omelette until

just set and lightly browned on the underside. Fold the omelette and continue cooking for 1 minute. Place omelette on a serving plate. Serve immediately with Foo Young sauce.
Note: A few choice pieces of crabmeat may be reserved to decorate the omelette.

Chicken omelet

3 American servings
6 Chinese servings

  1 dried Chinese mushroom
  Breast of ½ a small
  chicken, skinned, boned
  and shredded
¼ teaspoon salt
1½ teaspoons cornstarch
  3 tablespoons oil
  1 scallion, minced
  5 thin slices bamboo
  shoot, shredded
  1 tablespoon ham garnish

  2 tablespoons chicken broth
  5 eggs
½ teaspoon salt
  Freshly ground black pepper
  1 tablespoon finely chopped
  chives

Soak the mushroom in warm water for 20 minutes. Remove and discard the stem and shred the cap. Mix the chicken with the salt and cornstarch. Heat 1 tablespoon oil in a wok or frying pan with sloping sides. Add chicken and stir fry for 1 or 2 minutes or until all traces of pink disappear. Remove chicken from the pan. Add 1 more tablespoon oil and stir fry scallion, bamboo shoot, ham and mushroom 2 minutes. Return chicken to to the pan and add broth, scraping up the browned bits clinging to the pan. Remove mixture from the pan and wipe the pan out with paper towels. Beat the eggs with the salt, pepper and chives. Add the chicken mixture and stir to combine. Heat the remaining 1 tablespoon oil in the pan

until very hot. Pour in the omelette mixture and stir with a fork until the eggs begin to set. Lift the edge of the omelette so that the uncooked egg will run under the cooked part. With the aid of a large spatula, fold the omelette in half. Serve immediately.

Shrimp foo young

3 American servings
6 Chinese servings

  4 eggs
½ teaspoon salt
⅛ teaspoon freshly ground
  pepper
  2 teaspoons sherry
  3 to 3½ tablespoons oil
  2 scallions, shredded
  1 tablespoon finely shredded
  bamboo shoots
  1 cup peeled small shrimp
  1 cup bean sprouts, loosely
  packed
½ tablespoon soy sauce
  1 recipe Foo Young sauce

Beat eggs lightly in a bowl and stir in salt, pepper and sherry. Heat 1 to 1½ tablespoons oil in a wok or large frying pan and stir fry scallions and bamboo shoots for 1½ minutes. Add shrimp, bean sprouts and soy sauce and stir fry for another 1 minute. Remove from heat, let cool for a few minutes, then stir into egg mixture. Heat 2 tablespoons oil in a frying pan, with sloping sides. Add the egg mixture and cook the omelette until set and lightly browned on the underside. Fold the omelette and continue cooking for a few seconds. Invert the omelette onto a serving dish.

Uova fiorentina

Eggs Florentine

6 servings

$^1/_4$ *cup margarine or butter*
$^1/_4$ *cup flour*
1 *teaspoon salt*
2 *cups milk*
2 *(10 ounce) packages frozen
   chopped spinach*
$^1/_4$ *teaspoon nutmeg*
12 *poached eggs*
$^1/_4$ *cup grated Parmesan
   cheese*

Melt margarine in saucepan;
blend in flour and salt.
Gradually add milk, stirring
constantly until well blended.
Cook over medium heat, stirring
constantly until thickened.
Cook spinach; drain well.
Combine $^1/_2$ cup white sauce
and spinach; stir in nutmeg.
Pour mixture into 6 ramikins or
heat proof baking dishes.
Arrange 2 eggs on top of each.
Spoon remaining sauce over
eggs. Sprinkle top with cheese.
Bake in a hot oven (400°) until
browned, about 10 minutes.

Uova affogate alla casalinga

Poached eggs on toast

4 servings

1 *(8 ounce) can tomato sauce*
4 *eggs*
2 *tablespoons margarine or
   butter*
1 *teaspoon anchovy paste*
4 *slices toast*
   Grated Parmesan cheese

Heat tomato sauce in skillet.
Break eggs carefully into sauce;
cover; poach over low heat
about 5 minutes. Combine
margarine and anchovy paste;
blend well; spread on toast. Put
one egg and some of the sauce
over each slice of toast. Sprinkle
with Parmesan cheese.

Uova e peperoni con salsicce

Eggs and pepper with sausages

4 servings

2 *tablespoons margarine or
   butter*
2 *tablespoons chopped onion*
4 *tablespoons chopped green
   pepper*
2 *tablespoons chopped
   pimento*
$^1/_4$ *teaspoon oregano*
6 *eggs*
6 *tablespoons water*
6 *sweet Italian sausages,
   cooked*
$^1/_2$ *cup tomato sauce, heated*

Melt margarine in large skillet
over medium heat. Sauté onion,
pepper, pimento and oregano
until onion is transparent.
Combine eggs and water; beat
with a fork until light and
foamy. Pour eggs into skillet.
Cook slowly, gently lifting from
bottom and sides with spoon as
mixture sets, so liquid can flow
to bottom. Do not stir. Cook
until set but still moist. Arrange
on serving platter with cooked
sausages; spoon hot tomato
sauce over eggs.

Frittata alla savoiarda

Savoy omelette

4 servings

4 *tablespoons margarine or
   butter*
$^1/_2$ *cup diced ham*
1 *scallion, finely chopped*
1 *(4 ounce) can chopped
   mushrooms*
8 *eggs*
2 *tablespoons cold water*
$^1/_2$ *teaspoon salt*
$^1/_4$ *teaspoon dried basil*
2 *teaspoon parsley flakes*
2 *tablespoons grated
   Parmesan cheese*
4 *ounces mozzarella cheese,
   cubed*

Melt 2 tablespoons margarine in
skillet; sauté ham, scallions and
mushrooms. Melt remaining
margarine in 10″ skillet or
omelet pan. Tilt skillet back and
forth to grease well. Combine
eggs, water, salt, basil, parsley
and 1 tablespoon Parmesan
cheese; beat thoroughly with a
fork until light and foamy. Pour
egg mixture into skillet. As
mixture sets at edge, with fork
draw this portion toward center
so uncooked portions flow to
bottom. Shake skillet to keep
omelet sliding free. Cook until
eggs are still soft on top.
Remove from heat. Spoon ham
mixture over eggs; top with
mozzarella cheese. Sprinkle with
Parmesan cheese. Bake in a very
hot oven (450°) just until cheese
melts.

Uova alla cacciatora

Eggs hunters' style

4 servings

- 4 tablespoons margarine or butter
- 2 tomatoes, thickly sliced
- 1 tablespoon chopped onion
- 4 chicken livers, cut into 4 pieces
- $1/4$ teaspoon salt
- $1/8$ teaspoon oregano
- 4 eggs
- 4 slices hot toast

Melt 2 tablespoons margarine in skillet; sauté tomatoes, turning once, until golden brown. Remove; keep warm. Cook onion and chicken livers in margarine until chicken livers are cooked; stir in salt, and oregano. In a separate skillet, melt remaining margarine. Break eggs gently into skillet. Gently cook eggs over low heat, spooning margarine over them 3–4 minutes or until of desired firmness. To serve, top each slice of toast with chicken livers, then with tomato slices and then egg.

The 'uova alla paesana', or fried eggs country style, are a delicious variation on bacon and eggs as we know it. They are a familiar farmer's breakfast from the Po valley in the North of Italy. Place a thick, tasty, golden-yellow slice of crispy bacon on the polenta, and crown with eggs fried sunny-side up, garnish with fried tomatoes, or serve with tomato sauce.

The Spanish omelette, the 'tortilla', could be called the national dish of Spain. There are as many versions as there are cooks and housewives. It is the simplest and probably the most *common dish throughout Spain, solid, filling and capable of endless variations.*

Egg dish a la Flamenca

Tortilla a la española

Spanish omelette

4 servings

  4 small potatoes
  ½ cup oil
  ½ teaspoon salt
  8 eggs

Peel the potatoes and cut into very thin slices. Dry the slices on paper towels. Fry in hot oil until tender and lightly browned. Drain off the excess oil and season the potatoes with ¼ teaspoon salt. Beat the eggs in a bowl, add remaining salt and pour over the potatoes to form a round flat omelette. Brown the omelette on both sides. Serve with a tossed salad or endive salad, or with a salad made with lettuce, tomato, onion, olives and tuna fish.

Greixera de macarrones

Eggs and macaroni

4 servings

- ¾ *pound macaroni*
- *1 cup milk*
- *1 cup grated sharp cheddar cheese*
- ⅛ *teaspoon cinnamon*
- ½ *teaspoon salt*
  Freshly ground black pepper
- *4 hard boiled eggs, halved*
- *3 tablespoons butter*

Cook the macaroni in plenty of boiling salted water for 5 to 7 minutes or until almost tender. Drain. Bring the milk to a simmer and add the macaroni, ¾ cup cheese, cinnamon, salt and pepper. Transfer to a buttered casserole and arrange the eggs on top. Sprinkle with the remaining cheese and dot with butter. Place in a 400° oven for 5 to 10 minutes or until lightly browned.

Huevos al plato a la flamenca

Egg dish à la Flamenca

4 servings

- *3 tablespoons olive oil*
- *1 medium sized onion, finely chopped*
- ½ *cup cubed Serrano ham*
- *1 large potato, peeled and cubed*
- *1 large tomato, peeled, seeded and chopped*
- *2 tablespoons cooked peas*
- *2 tablespoons chopped cooked green beans*
- ¼ *cup cooked asparagus tips*
- *1 sweet pepper, cubed*
- *8 thin slices chorizo sausage or substitute pepperoni*
- ¼ *cup sherry*
- *1 tablespoon tomato sauce*
- ½ *teaspoon salt*
  Freshly ground black pepper
- *8 eggs*
- ¼ *teaspoon salt*
  Freshly ground black pepper
- *2 tablespoons finely chopped parsley*
- *2 tablespoons melted butter*

For the garnish:
- *8 thin slices Serrano ham*
- *8 thick slices chorizo sausage*
- *2 sweet peppers, cut into 8 triangles*

Heat the oil in a heavy saucepan. Add the onion, ham and potato and sauté until the potatoes are almost tender. Add the tomato and cook, stirring, 2 minutes. Add the peas, beans, asparagus tips, sweet pepper, chorizo, sherry, tomato sauce, salt and pepper. Bring to a simmer and cook 6 minutes. Divide the mixture between 4 shallow ovenproof dishes. Break 2 eggs into each dish. Sprinkle with salt, pepper and parsley and baste with butter. Bake in a preheated 375° oven for 8 minutes or until the whites are set. Garnish each dish with ham, chorizo and sweet pepper and serve.

Huevos al nido

Eggs in their nest

4 servings

- *4 small rolls*
- *4 tablespoons milk*
- *4 teaspoons butter*
- *4 eggs, separated*
- ½ *teaspoon salt*
- *1 tablespoon slivered almonds*
- ½ *cup oil*

Cut the tops off the rolls. Scoop out most of the soft bread, to form a nest. Into each roll add 1 tablespoon of milk, then a teaspoon of butter and then an egg yolk. Sprinkle yolk with salt. Beat the egg whites until stiff. Pile egg whites on top of the yolks and sprinkle with almonds. Fry the rolls in hot oil. Spoon the hot oil over the whites until they puff even higher. Serve immediately as the whites fall quickly.

Tortilla murciana

Omelette Murcian style

4 servings

½ *small eggplant*
2 *teaspoons salt*
4 *tablespoons oil*
1 *small onion, finely chopped*
1 *green pepper, finely chopped*
1 *zucchini, diced*
2 *small tomatoes, peeled, seeded and chopped*
¼ *pound boiled ham, diced*
8 *eggs*
½ *teaspoon salt*
Freshly ground black pepper

Cut the eggplant into slices 1 inch thick. Score the flesh with a sharp knife, sprinkle with salt and allow it to stand for 10 minutes to drain off the bitter juices. Rinse the slices, pat dry on paper towels and cut into 1 inch square pieces. Heat the oil in a large skillet. Fry the onion and green pepper for 3 minutes. Add the eggplant and zucchini and cook for 5 minutes. Stir the vegetables occasionally and add a little more oil if necessary. Add the tomatoes and ham and continue cooking until all the vegetables are tender and the tomato juices have boiled down. Beat the eggs lightly. Add salt and pepper. Pour the eggs over the vegetables to form a flat, round omelette. Brown the omelette on both sides. This dish is usually served with a tossed green salad.

Omeleta de atum com cogumelos

Omelette with tuna and mushrooms

4 servings

5 *tablespoons butter*
¼ *pound fresh mushrooms, thinly sliced*
1 *(7 ounce) can tuna fish, drained and flaked*
6 *eggs*
½ *teaspoon salt*
Freshly ground black pepper

Melt 2 tablespoons butter in a skillet and sauté the mushrooms over high heat for 3 to 4 minutes. Add the tuna and combine thoroughly. Beat the eggs with the salt and pepper and add the mushroom-tuna mixture. Heat the remaining butter in a large skillet until very hot. Pour in the egg mixture and stir with the flat of a fork until the eggs begin to set. Run the omelette under the broiler for a few seconds to cook the top of the omelette. Serve straight from the pan and pass a bowl of rice separately.

Ovos estrelados com queijo da Serra da Estrela

Fried eggs with cheese

1 serving

1 *tablespoon butter*
2 *slices goat cheese, ⅛ to ¼ inch thick*
2 *eggs*
⅛ *teaspoon salt*
Freshly ground black pepper

In an individual ramekin, melt ½ tablespoon of butter and add the slices of cheese. Heat slowly and, when the cheese begins to melt, break the eggs over the cheese. Sprinkle with salt and pepper and cook just until the whites begin to set around the edges. Melt the remaining butter and baste the eggs with it. Place under a preheated broiler for 1 to 2 minutes or until the whites are completely set. Serve immediately.

Ovos mexidos com tomate

Scrambled eggs with tomatoes

6 servings

¼ *pound lean salt ham (country ham)*
4 *tablespoons butter*
2 *large onions, sliced*
3 *medium sized tomatoes, peeled, seeded and chopped*
Freshly ground black pepper
6 *sprigs parsley*
12 *eggs, lightly beaten*
½ *teaspoon salt*

Soak the ham in cold water for at least 1 hour to remove excess salt. Drain. Heat the butter and add the ham and onions. Fry over low heat for 7 minutes. Add the tomatoes. Season with pepper and add parsley sprigs. Simmer for 5 minutes. Pour the eggs over the tomatoes and scramble the eggs. Discard the ham and parsley sprigs. Season with salt and pepper and serve immediately.
Note: The ham and parsley are added to give flavor to the dish.

Eggs à la Soller

Eggs and macaroni

Huevos al modo de Sóller

Eggs à la Soller

4 servings

   3 *tablespoons butter*
   1 *medium sized leek, thinly*
      sliced
   1 *medium sized carrot, thinly*
      sliced
   1 *medium leek, thinly sliced*
   1 *medium carrot, thinly sliced*
  ⅓ *cup peas*
  ½ *teaspoon salt*
      Freshly ground black pepper
  ½ *teaspoon sugar*
   1 *cup milk*
   1 *tablespoon dry white wine*
   4 *small ham steaks, ¼ inch*
      thick
   2 *tablespoons oil*
   8 *eggs*

Melt the butter in a saucepan, add the leek, carrot and peas and sauté until golden brown. Add the salt, pepper, sugar, milk and wine and simmer gently 15 to 20 minutes or until the vegetables are tender. Purée the mixture in a blender until smooth. Keep warm. Sauté the ham steaks in the oil and place on a serving dish. Fry the eggs and place on the ham. Pour the sauce over the eggs and serve hot.

FISH & SEAFOOD DISHES

Mussels or clams in broth

4 servings

  2 *quarts fresh mussels or*
    clams or 2 (1 pound) cans
    mussels or clams
  1 *cup dry white wine*
  1 *cup water*
½ *teaspoon salt*
  4 *scallions, finely chopped*
½ *teaspoon dried thyme*
  2 *bay leaves*
  4 *tablespoons finely chopped*
    parsley
  1 *stalk celery, very finely*
    chopped
  1 *tablespoon butter, softened*
  1 *tablespoon flour*

Scrub the mussels with a stiff brush and clean well. Remove beards. Place mussels in a large bowl and cover with cold water. Discard any open mussels. Soak mussels 15 minutes to allow sand to soak out. Rinse mussels and place in a saucepan. Add wine and water. Add salt, scallions, thyme, bay leaves, parsley and celery. Cover and simmer 5 minutes. Strain liquid from the pan into a small saucepan and return to simmer. Combine butter and flour into a paste. Stir paste into simmering broth. Remove top shells from each mussel. Place in individual soup bowls and cover with the sauce.

Oysters

4 servings

24 *fresh oysters*
  1 *lemon, cut into wedges*
    Tabasco sauce or cayenne
    pepper
  4 *slices brown bread*
    Butter

Insert the oyster knife close to the hinge in the shell. Twist the knife upwards across the hinge to open the oyster. Slip the knife under the oyster to release it from the shell. (This will also kill the oyster). Place the shells on serving plates filled with crushed ice. Garnish the plates with lemon wedges. Serve tabasco sauce or cayenne pepper separately. Serve the oysters immediately accompanied with buttered brown bread.

Baked trout and bacon

2 servings

  2 *(¾ pound) trout, filleted*
  8 *slices bacon*
  2 *tablespoons butter*
  2 *tablespoons chopped parsley*
½ *teaspoon salt*
    Freshly ground black pepper

Dry trout thoroughly on paper towels. Line a baking dish with half of the bacon. Place half of the butter and parsley in each trout cavity and season with salt and pepper. Lay trout on the bacon and cover with remaining bacon. Bake in 350° oven for 15 minutes. Discard bacon and serve trout with boiled potatoes.

Finnan haddie is a traditional dish originating on the east coast of Scotland in Kincardineshire. For generations the Scots smoked the haddock over seaweed, though now pine and oak chips are more commonly used. Finnan haddie is frequently served topped with either a pat of butter or a poached egg. It is always accompanied by large quantities of brown bread and butter.

Old English baked cod

4 servings

    4 (6 ounce) cod-fish steaks
    2 tablespoons butter
    1 onion, finely chopped
    4 mushrooms, finely chopped
    3 tablespoons finely chopped
      parsley
    ¼ teaspoon thyme
    1 bay leaf
    ½ teaspoon salt
      Freshly ground black pepper
    2 cups milk
    1½ tablespoons cornstarch
      dissolved in 2 tablespoons
      cold water
    ½ cup breadcrumbs
    4 strips bacon, fried until crisp
    4 lemon wedges
      Watercress or parsley for
      garnish

Heat the butter in a skillet. Sauté onions and mushrooms 5 minutes. Transfer to a baking dish. Arrange cod over the mixture and add parsley, thyme, bay leaf, salt, pepper and milk. Cover dish with foil and bake in a 350° oven for 20 minutes. Remove the fish and keep it warm. Strain milk into a saucepan. Bring milk to simmering point and stir in cornstarch paste. Cook 2 minutes to thicken into a sauce. Arrange cod on a clean baking dish. Cover with sauce. Top with breadcrumbs and crumbled bacon. Place under the broiler for 3 minutes until crumbs are lightly browned. Garnish dish with lemon wedges and watercress or parsley.

Flounder poached in cider

6 servings

    2 pounds flounder, filleted
    1 teaspoon butter
    4 scallions, finely chopped
    ½ teaspoon salt
      Freshly ground black pepper
    1 cup cider
    2 tablespoons apple brandy
    1 tablespoon lemon juice
    2 tablespoons butter
    2 tablespoons flour
    ⅓ cup heavy cream
    4 tablespoons Parmesan
      cheese, freshly grated

Butter a baking dish and sprinkle dish with scallions. Arrange flounder fillets in a single layer in the dish. Season fish with salt and pepper. Add cider, apple brandy and lemon juice. Cover dish with aluminum foil. Place dish in a 350° oven and poach fish for 12 minutes. Strain off the liquid carefully. Keep the fish warm. Melt the butter. Stir in the flour and cook for 1 minute. Add strained liquid and cream. Pour sauce back over the fish. Sprinkle with cheese and brown under the broiler for 3 minutes.

Finnan haddie

Poached smoked haddock

4 servings

    1 small onion, sliced thinly
    1½ pounds smoked haddock
    2 cups milk
    1 bay leaf

Sauce:
    2 tablespoons butter
    2 tablespoons flour
    1 teaspoon prepared (Dijon
      type) mustard
    2 tablespoons finely chopped
      parsley

Place onion slices in a shallow buttered baking dish. Lay fish on the onion and add milk and bay leaf. Cover dish with aluminum foil and poach the fish in a 350° oven for 15 minutes. Remove fish and keep it warm. Strain and reserve poaching liquid. To prepare the sauce, heat the butter in a small saucepan. Stir in the flour and cook for 1 minute. Add reserved poaching liquid. Stir constantly until a medium thick sauce is formed. Stir in mustard and parsley. Serve the sauce separately.

Lobster salad

4 servings

    3 (1½ pound) lobsters
    1 Boston lettuce
    2 medium sized ripe tomatoes,
      sliced
    1 small cucumber, sliced
    2 hard boiled eggs, sliced
    12 black olives, pitted
    1 cup mayonnaise
    ½ teaspoon finely chopped
      parsley
    ¼ teaspoon tarragon
    1 teaspoon chives

Boil the lobsters for 18 minutes. Remove the lobster meat. Cut the meat into small pieces and reserve the coral (if you have selected lady lobsters). Wash the lettuce and arrange the leaves on a large platter. Arrange alternating slices of tomato, cucumber and egg around the edge of the platter. Decorate the platter with black olives. Arrange the lobster in the center of the platter. Combine the mayonnaise with the herbs. Mash the reserved coral and add it to the mayonnaise. Serve the mayonnaise separately.

Fish cakes

4 servings

- *1 pound cod*
- *1 tablespoon butter*
- *½ teaspoon salt*
- *Freshly ground black pepper*
- *1 teaspoon lemon juice*
- *4 medium sized potatoes, boiled and peeled*
- *¼ cup milk*
- *½ cup all purpose flour*
- *2 eggs, lightly beaten*
- *½ cup breadcrumbs*
- *Oil for deep frying*

Place the fish in a buttered baking dish. Dot with remaining butter. Season with salt, pepper and lemon juice. Cover dish with a piece of aluminum foil. Bake 20 minutes in a 350° oven. Remove skin and bones from the fish and flake into small pieces. Force potatoes through a strainer or potato ricer. Add potatoes to fish. Add enough milk to allow mixture to hold together. Form mixture into 8 flat patties. Dredge patties with flour, dip quickly into egg and finally into breadcrumbs. Fry fish cakes for 4 to 5 minutes in deep hot fat until golden brown on both sides.

Potted shrimp

4 servings

- *½ cup butter*
- *¾ pound very small shrimp, peeled*
- *¼ teaspoon salt*
- *Dash cayenne pepper*
- *¼ teaspoon ground mace*
- *¼ teaspoon nutmeg*
- *¼ teaspoon allspice*

Heat the butter in a small saucepan. When butter is hot and foaming, remove from the heat and strain through a double thickness of cheesecloth to remove deposits. Reserve 2 tablespoons clarified butter. Heat remaining butter in a small skillet. Add shrimp seasonings and spices. Cook over high heat for 5 minutes, taking care to prevent the butter from burning. Place in a small pot and chill in the refrigerator. Pour on reserved clarified butter to seal the pot. Serve as a cocktail spread on freshly made toast or crackers.

Shrimp with mustard and eggs

6 servings

- *2 pounds small shrimp, peeled and deveined*
- *4 scallions, finely chopped*
- *3 tablespoons butter*
- *2 tablespoons finely chopped parsley*
- *½ teaspoon tarragon*
- *1 tablespoon mild (Dijon type) mustard*
- *6 hard boiled eggs, finely chopped*
- *¼ cup heavy cream*
- *3 tablespoons grated Parmesan cheese*
- *1 additional teaspoon butter*

Melt the butter and sauté the shrimp and scallions over high heat for 3 minutes until shrimp are pink and almost tender. Reserve 6 partially cooked shrimp. Add the parsley, tarragon, mustard, eggs and cream. Continue cooking for 2 minutes until the eggs are hot. Transfer all the ingredients to a buttered baking dish. Sprinkle with cheese, dot with remaining butter and add reserved shrimp. Place under the broiler for 3 minutes until lightly browned.

Crab salad

4 servings

- *1¼ pounds fresh backfin crabmeat*
- *1 tablespoon lemon juice*
- *1 cup mayonnaise*
- *½ cup sour cream*
- *1 teaspoon Worcestershire sauce*
- *3 tablespoons prepared shrimp cocktail sauce*
- *2 ripe tomatoes, sliced*
- *1 small cucumber, sliced*
- *3 hard boiled eggs, sliced*
- *⅓ cup English walnuts, chopped*
- *1 avocado, sliced*

Clean the crab carefully to remove hard membranes. Sprinkle crabmeat with lemon juice. Combine mayonnaise, sour cream, Worcestershire sauce and shrimp cocktail sauce. Allow the sauce to stand for 1 hour if possible. Arrange the tomato, cucumber and egg slices around the edges of 4 plates. Place the crabmeat in the center of the circle. Top crab with walnuts. Arrange avocado around the crabmeat.

Kippers are generally served for breakfast accompanied with freshly made toast or brown bread and butter.

Baked salmon

12 servings

1 (6–7 pound) whole salmon
4 tablespoons butter, melted
1 teaspoon salt
   Freshly ground black pepper
2 tablespoons lemon juice
½ cup white wine
½ cup water

Cut a piece of aluminum foil large enough to envelop the salmon. Brush the foil generously with butter. Brush salmon on both sides with remaining butter. Sprinkle fish with salt, pepper and lemon juice. Wrap the salmon in foil and place in a roasting tin, or on a baking sheet. Bake in a 350° oven allowing 10 minutes per pound and 10 minutes extra. Pour combined wine and water over the fish after 20 minutes; this will prevent fish from drying out. Remove the fish from the oven. (The salmon will stay hot for several minutes if it remains wrapped in foil.) If it is served cold, keep the fish wrapped in foil to retain its shape.

Grilled kippers

4 servings

4 kippers
4 tablespoons butter
4 teaspoons lemon juice
   Fresh parsley for garnish

Remove kippers from packages and discard oil. Place kippers on a broiler rack lined with aluminum foil. Dot each fish with butter and sprinkle with lemon juice. Broil fish 5 minutes on each side until skin is crisp and golden brown. Serve garnished with sprigs of parsley.

Herrings fried in oatmeal

4 servings

4 fresh herrings, cleaned
   or 1½ pounds salt water fish
½ cup milk
8 tablespoons oatmeal
1 teaspoon salt
   Freshly ground black pepper
3 tablespoons butter or
   margarine

Mustard sauce:
2 tablespoons butter
2 tablespoons flour
1¼ cups milk
2 teaspoons prepared (Dijon type) mustard
1 teaspoon lemon juice

Dry the fish on paper towels. Dip fish first in milk and then in oatmeal. Season fish with salt and pepper. Heat the butter in a large skillet. Fry herrings 5 minutes on each side, adjusting the heat to prevent the butter from burning. Serve with mustard sauce prepared as follows: Heat 2 tablespoons butter in a small saucepan. Stir in the flour and cook 1 minute. Add milk gradually stirring constantly to form a smooth sauce. Add mustard and lemon juice. Season with salt and pepper. Serve sauce separately.

Carp is the great fish of the Donau, and carp prepared in a piquant paprika sauce is the crowning pride of any good Hungarian restaurant.

Paprika Karpfen

Paprika carp

4 servings

>   3 tablespoons butter
>   2 onions, finely chopped
>   1 clove garlic, crushed
>   2 teaspoons paprika
>   1 green pepper, seeded
>   and chopped
>   1 (2 to 3 pound) carp,
>   cleaned and cut into pieces
>   ½ teaspoon salt
>   Freshly ground black pepper
>   1 tablespoon chopped parsley
>   ¼ cup white wine
>   2 tablespoons tomato paste

Heat the butter in a casserole and fry the onions and garlic until soft and golden. Add the paprika and green pepper and fry for 5 minutes. Add the fish and season with salt, pepper and chopped parsley. Add the wine and stir in the tomato paste. Simmer gently for about 15 minutes until the fish is tender and flakes easily. Add a little water during cooking if necessary.

Heringe Böhmer Art

Herring fillets Bohemian style

4 servings

- 8 *salted herring*
- 1½ *cups water*
- ½ *cup wine vinegar*
- 2 *bay leaves*
- 6 *peppercorns, crushed*
- 2 *tablespoons chopped parsley*
- 1 *stalk celery, chopped*
- 2 *carrots, sliced*
- 2 *onions, cut into rings*
- 1 *cup milk or cream*
   Grated rind of 1 lemon
- 2 *teaspoons capers*

Soak the herring in water for 3 hours. Bring the water and vinegar to a boil. Add the bay leaves, peppercorns, parsley, celery and carrots. Simmer for 20 minutes. Drain the herring and arrange in a dish. Cover with onion rings. Add the milk or cream to the marinade and pour over the herrings. Finally add the lemon rind and capers. Cover and refrigerate for 6 days.

Hal keszthely

Pike or perch Keszthely

4 servings

- 4 *whole (¾ pound) pike or perch*
- 1 *teaspoon salt*
- 1 *tablespoon paprika*
- 4 *tablespoons butter*
- 4 *large cooked potatoes, sliced*
- 1 *cup whipping cream*
- 2 *tablespoons chopped parsley*

Make incisions in the skin of the fish and rub with salt and paprika. Place the fish in a buttered baking dish. Add the remaining butter. Bake in a preheated 375° oven for 8 minutes until half done. Arrange the sliced potatoes around the fish and bake for another 8 minutes or until the fish is tender. Pour the cream over the fish and heat the cream to the simmering point. Arrange the potatoes on a warm serving dish, place the fish on top of the potatoes and pour over the pan juices. Garnish with chopped parsley.

Hal gombaval

Fish and mushrooms

4 servings

- 4 *medium sized potatoes, peeled and cut in half*
- 1½ *pounds white fish fillets*
- ½ *teaspoon salt*
   Freshly ground black pepper
- ⅓ *cup flour*
- ¼ *pound mushrooms, finely chopped*
- 1 *tablespoon finely chopped parsley*
- 1 *tablespoon flour*
- ¼ *cup heavy cream*
- 1 *cup chicken broth*
   Juice of ½ lemon

Place the potatoes in a pan and add cold salted water to cover. Place the lid on the pan, bring to a boil and cook 12 to 15 minutes until the potatoes are almost tender. Drain and set aside. Sprinkle the fish fillets on both sides with salt and pepper and dredge in flour. Arrange in a buttered ovenproof casserole and surround with the potatoes. Sprinkle the mushrooms and parsley on top. In a bowl, combine the flour and cream until the mixture is smooth. Add the broth and lemon juice, beating constantly with a wire whisk. Pour into the casserole and bake in a 350° oven 8 minutes. Reduce the heat to 300° and bake 25 minutes more. Serve from the casserole.

Stir fried oysters

2 American servings
4 Chinese servings

   2 teaspoons soy sauce
   1 teaspoon cornstarch
  12 oysters, shucked
   1 cake bean curd
   1 clove garlic, crushed
   1 slice fresh ginger root,
     minced
  ¼ teaspoon salt
   2 tablespoons soy sauce
   2 tablespoons sherry
   4 tablespoons chicken broth
     or water
   1 teaspoon cornstarch
     Oil for deep frying
   2 tablespoons oil
   2 slices fresh ginger root,
     shredded
   4 whole scallions, cut into
     ½ inch strips
   2 tablespoons ham garnish

Combine 2 teaspoons soy sauce
and 1 teaspoon cornstarch in a
small bowl. Add the oysters
and coat them with the mixture.
Let stand 10 minutes. Cut the
bean curd into strips ½ to
¾ inch long. Combine garlic,
ginger root and salt. Gently
toss the bean curd in this
mixture and let stand 5 minutes.
In a small bowl, combine the
soy sauce, sherry, chicken broth
and 1 teaspoon cornstarch.
Heat oil for deep frying.
Carefully wipe off the garlic
and ginger clinging to the
bean curd. Fry the pieces of
bean curd until golden brown
and crisp on the outside but
tender inside. Drain on paper
towels. Heat 2 tablespoons
oil in a wok. Add shredded
ginger root and scallions and
stir fry 1 to 1½ minutes. Add
oysters with their liquid and
stir fry 1½ to 2 minutes.
Remove oysters from the wok.
Add soy sauce mixture and
bring to a boil. Add bean
curd and heat 1 minute.
Return oysters to the wok and
heat briefly. Transfer to a
serving dish and sprinkle with
ham garnish.

Stir fried scallops and bamboo

4 American servings
8 Chinese servings

   1 pound scallops
  ¾ cup bamboo shoots
   2 cakes bean curd
   2 tomatoes
   1 scallion
   1 clove garlic
   3 tablespoons oil
  ½ teaspoon salt
   1 tablespoon soy sauce
  ½ tablespoon sherry
  ½ teaspoon sugar
  ¼ cup chicken broth
  ⅛ teaspoon sesame oil
   2 teaspoons cornstarch
   1 tablespoon water

Cut scallops in ¼ inch thick
slices. Cut bamboo shoots into
slices 1 inch long, ½ inch wide
and ⅛ to ¼ inch thick. Cut
bean curd cakes in half and
then crosswise into ¼ to ½ inch
thick slices. Peel, seed and
drain tomatoes. Mince scallion
and garlic. Heat 2 tablespoons
oil in a wok or other pan,
add scallops and stir fry for
about 1 to 1½ minutes. Remove
from pan and keep warm.
Add 1 tablespoon oil, heat and
add salt and garlic. Stir fry
for 30 seconds. Add bean curd
and stir fry gently for about
2 minutes or until lightly
browned. Add bamboo and stir
fry for another ½ minute.
Add soy sauce, sherry, sugar
and tomatoes and stir fry for
30 seconds. Return scallops to
the pan and stir fry to heat
through. Add broth and bring
quickly to a boil. Mix sesame
oil, cornstarch and water and stir
in to thicken. Serve immediately.

Stir fried scallops and chicken livers

2 American servings
4 Chinese servings

  ½ pound chicken livers, cleaned
  ½ cup chicken broth
   2 tablespoons soy sauce
   1 tablespoon sherry
  ¼ teaspoon sugar
   2 tablespoons oil
  ¾ pound scallops, sliced ¼
     inch thick
   1 thin slice fresh ginger root,
     minced
   2 whole scallions, minced
  ½ tablespoon cornstarch
     dissolved in
  1½ tablespoons water

Place chicken livers in a bowl.
Cover with boiling water and
let stand 3 to 4 minutes.
Drain, dry carefully on paper
towels and set aside. Combine
the chicken broth, soy sauce,
sherry and sugar in a small
bowl. Heat the oil in a wok.
Add scallops and stir fry 2
minutes. Remove from the pan.
Add ginger and scallions and
stir fry ½ minute. Add livers
and stir fry 2 minutes. Add
chicken broth mixture and bring
to a boil. Stir in the cornstarch
mixture to thicken. Return
scallops to the wok and heat
through. Serve immediately.

The Steamed sea bass recipe is originaly prepared with carp. Fragrant steamed carp is surrounded by refreshing onion brushes.

Steamed sea bass

6 American servings
10 Chinese servings

  1 (3 pound) sea bass or other firm fish
  1 teaspoon salt
1½ to 2 tablespoons fermented black beans
  1 clove garlic, crushed
  2 thin slices ginger root, shredded
  2 scallions, minced
  3 tablespoons soy sauce
  1 tablespoon sherry
  ½ teaspoon sugar
  1 tablespoon oil
  6 onion brushes

Have the fish cleaned and scaled but left whole with head and tail on. Score crosswise on both sides and sprinkle with salt. Soak the fermented black beans in water for about 20 minutes. Drain and mash together with the garlic. Place fish in a shallow heatproof dish. Mix all ingredients except onion brushes until blended and spread over fish. Place in a steamer and steam for 30 to 35 minutes or until done. Remove from steamer. Decorate with onion brushes and serve.

Simmered mullet

4 American servings
6 Chinese servings

  2 small (¾ to 1 pound)
    mullets
  2 teaspoons salt
  6 cups water
  2 scallions, minced
  2 thin slices fresh ginger
    root, minced
  2 tablespoons sherry
  1 teaspoon salt
  2 tablespoons oil

Have the fish cleaned and
scaled but leave head and tail
on. Score, sprinkle with the
salt on both sides and leave for
20 minutes. Rinse under cold
running water and drain.
Bring the water to a boil.
Add scallions, ginger root,
sherry, salt and oil to the water
and return to a rolling boil.
Place fish on a skimmer and
lower into the boiling liquid.
Reduce heat, cover and simmer
for 5 minutes. Turn off heat
completely and leave, covered,
for 20 to 25 minutes. Remove
the fish carefully and serve hot.

Steamed cod steak

4 American servings
8 Chinese servings

  6 dried Chinese mushrooms
  2 pounds cod steaks, 1½ to 2
    inches thick (or other firm
    white fish)
  ½ teaspoon salt
  2 slices fresh ginger root,
    minced
  2 tablespoons soy sauce
  1 tablespoon oil

Soak the mushrooms in warm
water for 20 minutes. Squeeze
dry, remove stalks and leave
caps whole. Place fish and
mushroom caps in a shallow
heatproof dish and sprinkle
with salt. Combine ginger root
with soy sauce and oil. Sprinkle
over fish. Place fish in a
steamer and steam for about
15 minutes. Remove from
steamer and serve immediately.

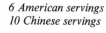

Fish balls

6 American servings
10 Chinese servings

  2 pounds raw fish fillets, such
    as flounder, cod or haddock
  2 thin slices fresh ginger root
  6 to 8 tablespoons water
  1 tablespoon sherry
  2 tablespoons minced onion
    or scallion
  ½ teaspoon salt
  2 egg whites ·
  1 teaspoon cornstarch

Mince or grind the fish and
place in a bowl. Chop the ginger
root and, using a garlic press,
squeeze the juice over the fish.
Beat the fish until smooth,
adding half of the water
gradually. Add sherry, onion
and salt. Beat until well blended.
Add the egg whites and the
cornstarch and beat vigorously
for 1 minute. Continue beating
for another few minutes,
adding more water gradually if
the mixture seems very stiff.
Divide the mixture into 4
equal parts and form each part
into 5 small balls. Bring 1½ to 2
quarts of water to a boil.
Reduce heat a little, drop in
the fish balls and poach them
for about 6 minutes. Remove
them with a skimmer and use as
directed in recipes. If they are
not to be used immediately,
drop them into cold water and
refrigerate until used.

Fish balls in bouillon

6 American servings
10 Chinese servings

  1 recipe fish balls (see
    previous recipe)
  2 cups chicken broth
  1 tablespoon sherry
  ½ teaspoon salt
  2 egg yolks
  1 scallion, minced or 2
    tablespoons chopped chives

Prepare fish balls as described
in previous recipe and reserve
the egg yolks used in this
preparation. Poach the fish
balls and drain. Bring chicken
broth to a boil. Add sherry
and salt. Reduce the heat a
little, add the fish balls and heat
through. Remove from the heat,
stir in egg yolks and sprinkle
on the scallion or chives.
Serve immediately.

For this recipe carp can be substituted by equal quantity sea bass, perch, trout or salmon.

Fried sole and peppers

3 American servings
6 Chinese servings

  1 pound flounder fillets
    (or substitute haddock or
    other firm, white fish)
  2 thin slices fresh ginger
    root, minced
  ½ teaspoon salt
  ¼ teaspoon sugar
  ½ teaspoon sesame oil
  1 tablespoon sherry
  1 small red pepper
  1 small green pepper
  1 medium onion
  1 egg, lightly beaten
  1 tablespoon cornstarch
  5 tablespoons oil
  1 slice fresh ginger root
  1 clove garlic
  1 teaspoon sherry
  1 teaspoon soy sauce

Cut sole fillets across the grain into 1½ inch long pieces. Mix minced ginger, salt, sugar, sesame oil and sherry in a bowl. Add the fish and marinate for 2 hours. Cut peppers in half lengthwise, remove membranes and seeds and cut into 1½ inch long diamond shapes, 1 inch wide. Peel and cut the onion in half lengthwise. Cut each half into 1 inch wide sections. Separate onion sections into strips. Drain fish and wipe dry with paper towels. Dip the fish into egg to coat. Sprinkle evenly with cornstarch. Heat 1 tablespoon of oil in a skillet or large frying pan until quite hot. Add ginger root and garlic and let brown slightly. Remove ginger and garlic, add pepper and onion and stir fry for about 1½ to 2 minutes over medium heat. Add sherry and soy sauce, stir and remove all the ingredients from pan and keep hot. Add remaining oil and increase the heat. Add the fish and fry until crisp and golden on both sides. Remove from pan and drain on paper towels. Transfer to a serving plate, add pepper and onion mixture and serve immediately.

Deep fried sweet and sour fish

4 American servings
8 Chinese servings

  1 recipe sweet sour sauce

  2 pounds fish fillets of any
    firm, white fish
  1 egg
  1 egg white
  2 to 2½ tablespoons cornstarch
  1 teaspoon salt
  1 teaspoon sherry
    Flour
    Oil for deep frying

Prepare sweet sour sauce as directed and keep warm. Cut fish fillets in ¾ to 1 inch cubes. Mix egg, egg white, cornstarch, salt and sherry into a smooth batter. Dredge fish very lightly in flour and lightly coat with the batter. Heat the oil for deep frying. Add fish cubes, one at a time in several batches. Deep fry until golden brown. Remove from the pan with a skimmer and drain on paper towels. Transfer to a serving dish. Pour sweet sour sauce over and serve.

Braised carp and bean curd

4 American servings
8 Chinese servings

  1 (2 to 3 pound) carp or
  1 teaspoon salt
  1 tablespoon flour
  3 tablespoons oil
  2 thin slices fresh ginger root
  2 scallions, minced
  3 tablespoons soy sauce
  1 tablespoon sherry
  ⅛ teaspoon white pepper
  ½ to ¾ cup chicken broth
  1 teaspoon sugar
  ¼ teaspoon sesame oil or ½
    tablespoon oyster sauce
  1½ to 2 cakes bean curd, cut
    into 1 inch cubes

Have the fish man clean and scale the fish. Remove head, fins and tail, if desired. Wash fish under cold running water, drain and wipe dry with paper towels. Make a few incisions or scores on both sides. Sprinkle with salt and set aside for 15 minutes. Sprinkle the fish evenly with flour. Heat the oil in a heavy pan just large enough to hold the fish. Add the ginger root and stir fry for 30 seconds. Add the scallions and stir fry for about 45 seconds. Add the fish and fry over high heat until brown on both sides. Sprinkle with soy sauce, sherry and pepper. Reduce the heat to medium and cook for about 1½ minutes. Add chicken broth, sugar and sesame oil or oyster sauce and bring to a boil quickly. Reduce heat, cover and simmer for 8 to 10 minutes. Add bean curd to the sauce and simmer for another 7 minutes. Serve immediately.

Brusselse karper

Carp Brussels style

4 servings

1 (2 pound) carp
6 tablespoons vinegar
1 small slice pork rind
2 carrots, sliced
1 leek or 1 medium sized
  onion, sliced
1 stalk celery, sliced
¼ teaspoon thyme
1 bay leaf
1 sprig parsley
1 cup beer
½ teaspoon salt
  Freshly ground black pepper
2 teaspoons sugar
  Dash of nutmeg
1 thick slice pound cake
2 teaspoons honey
¼ teaspoon powdered ginger
1 tablespoon cornstarch
  dissolved in
  2 tablespoons cooking liquid
3 tablespoons butter

Place the fish in just enough
water to cover. Add vinegar and
let stand for 1 hour. Drain the
carp. Place pork rind, carrots,
leek, celery, thyme, bay leaf and
parsley in a pan. Place carp on
top. Pour in the beer and
enough water to just cover the
fish. Sprinkle with salt, pepper,
sugar and nutmeg. Bring to a
boil and immediately lower the
heat. Poach at a slow simmer for
30 minutes. Carefully remove
fish and place on a warm dish.
Remove pork rind, parsley and
bay leaf. Add the pound cake,
honey and ginger and let the
pound cake soak until saturated.
Strain and rub the solids through
a sieve. Return the purée to

the sauce. Thicken the sauce with
the cornstarch mixture. Swirl
in the butter. Pour the sauce over
the fish and serve.

Truite à l'Ardennaise

Trout Ardenne style

4 servings

4 whole trout (each about
  ¾ pound)
1 cup white wine
1 cup water
2 carrots, peeled and sliced
1 leek, sliced
1 sprig parsley
¼ teaspoon thyme
1 bay leaf
1 clove
½ teaspoon salt
6 peppercorns, crushed
2 teaspoons cornstarch
3 tablespoons butter, softened
1 tablespoon finely chopped
  parsley

Pour the wine into a pan and
add the water, carrots, leek,
parsley, thyme, bay leaf, clove,
salt and peppercorns. Bring
to a boil, lower the heat and
simmer for 30 minutes. Poach
the trout in this court bouillon
for 6 to 10 minutes. Carefully
remove the trout from the broth
and place on a warm serving
dish. Strain the broth, place
over high heat and reduce to
1 cup. Thicken the liquid with
the cornstarch dissolved in
2 tablespoons of cold water.
Add the butter and beat it in
with a wire whisk until the
butter is dissolved. Pour the
sauce over the trout and sprinkle
with parsley.

Moules à la Bruxelloise

Mussels Brussels style

4 servings

10 pounds mussels, cleaned and
  brushed
3 tablespoons butter
  Celery leaves from 1 bunch
  celery, chopped
10 sprigs parsley
1 onion, chopped
1 cup white wine
  Freshly ground black pepper

Heat the butter in a large pan
over low heat and add celery
leaves, parsley, onion, wine and
pepper. Add the mussels and
cover the pan. Simmer until the
shells open, 7 to 10 minutes.
Strain the broth. Transfer the
mussels and the broth to a
warm serving dish and serve
immediately.

Waterzooi van vis

Waterzooi of fish

6 servings

- 3 *pounds fresh fish, filleted (pike, carp or bass)*
  Leafy tops from 1 bunch celery
- 2 *tablespoons butter*
- 1 *teaspoon salt*
  Freshly ground black pepper
- 3 *egg yolks*
- 3 *tablespoons cream*
- 12 *slices rye bread*
  Butter

Cut the fish into 2 inch pieces. Place in a pan and just cover with water. Add celery leaves, butter, salt and pepper and cook over moderate heat about 8 to 10 minutes or until fish flakes easily. Do not overcook. Remove the fish and keep warm. Strain the broth, discard celery leaves and reduce fish broth to 2 cups. Beat the egg yolks with the cream. Stir 1 tablespoon of the broth into the egg yolks, then add this mixture to the hot broth, stirring constantly. Continue cooking until broth has thickened slightly but do not allow it to boil or the egg yolks will curdle. Pour the sauce over the fish and serve with buttered rye bread.

Gestoofde kabeljauwstaart

Stewed cod

4 servings

- 4 *cod steaks*
- 1 *teaspoon salt*
- ½ *cup water or fish broth*
  Juice of ½ lemon
- 2 *tablespoons butter*
- 3 *tablespoons fine dry bread crumbs*
- ½ *lemon, sliced*
  Parsley sprigs

Rub the cod with salt and let stand for 30 minutes. Place in an ovenproof dish with the water or fish broth. Sprinkle with lemon juice, dot with butter and sprinkle with bread crumbs. Cover with aluminum foil and bake in a preheated 300° oven for about 30 minutes. Garnish with lemon slices and parsley. Serve with small new potatoes or mashed potatoes and a salad.

Marine stokvis

Dried cod navy style

4 servings

- 1 *pound salt cod*
- 4 *cups water*
- ½ *teaspoon salt*
- 1 *cup rice*
- 6 *tablespoons butter*
- 3 *tablespoons flour*
- 2 *tablespoons prepared mustard*
- 2 *onions, cut into rings*
- 4 *eggs*
- 4 *potatoes, cooked*
- 2 *gherkins, chopped*

Soak the fish in water for 4 hours. Remove the bones, if any, and cut the meat into strips. Roll up and tie the strips. Bring the water to a boil, add the salt and cod and lower the heat. Simmer slowly for 1 hour. Keep the cod warm and reserve the cooking liquid. Cook the rice, following the directions on the package. Heat 3 tablespoons butter in a saucepan, stir in the flour and add 2 cups of the cooking liquid, stirring constantly until a smooth sauce is formed. Stir in mustard. In a frying pan heat the remaining 3 tablespoons butter and sauté the onion rings until golden brown. Serve cod, raw eggs, potatoes, rice, onion rings, gherkins and mustard sauce separately. In the Dutch navy, this dish is eaten as follows: In a deep plate combine raw egg with a potato. Mash well. Then mix the potato with the cod and rice. Spoon over the fried onion rings, gherkins and mustard sauce.

Vlaamse kabeljauw

Flemish cod

4 servings

- 4 *cod fillets, ½ pound each*
- ¼ *cup butter*
- 1 *onion, thinly sliced*
- ½ *cup warm water*
- 1 *tablespoon lemon juice*
- 1 *tablespoon freshly chopped parsley*

Butter an ovenproof dish with 2 tablespoons butter and place the cod fillets in the dish. Heat the remaining butter in a saucepan and sauté the onion over low heat until golden. Add the warm water and simmer 10 minutes. Spoon onions and liquid over the fish fillets. Cover the dish with aluminum foil and place in a preheated 300° oven for about 30 minutes. Uncover and sprinkle on the lemon juice and chopped parsley.

The best way to prepare really fresh fish is to roast it over a glowing-hot charcoal fire that has been sprinkled with fine dried herbs from the hills. Grilled mullet.

Grilled fish with oregano

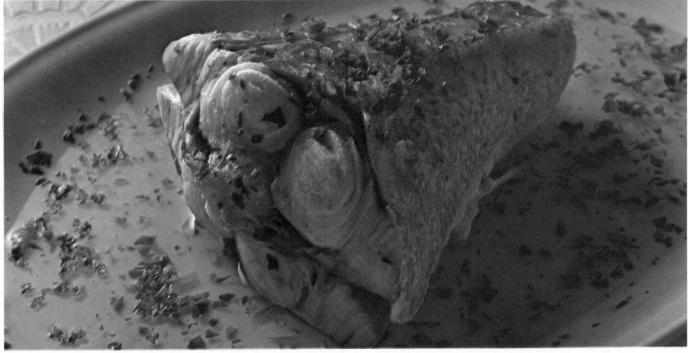

Balık köftesi

Fish balls

4 to 6 servings

1½ pounds haddock or cod fillets
2 slices stale bread, crusts removed
1 onion, finely chopped
1 egg, beaten
2 tablespoons finely chopped parsley
½ teaspoon salt
   Freshly ground black pepper
½ teaspoon cumin
   Pinch of saffron soaked in 1 teaspoon water
   Cornstarch
   Oil for deep frying

Remove skin and bones from the fish and blend to a paste in an electric blender. You will have to do this in 2 or 3 batches. Place the fish in a mixing bowl and add all the remaining ingredients except the cornstarch and oil. Mix until thoroughly combined. Shape into small balls and roll in cornstarch. Heat the oil for deep frying and fry the balls for 4 to 5 minutes until golden brown. Drain on paper towels and serve immediately.

Psari me kolokitia

Fish with zucchini

6 servings

1 (3 to 4 pound) whole striped bass
1 teaspoon salt
   Freshly ground black pepper
2 tablespoons olive oil
2 onions, sliced
2 cloves garlic, minced
2 tablespoons chopped parsley
1 tablespoon chopped fresh mint or
   ½ teaspoon dried mint
3 medium sized tomatoes, peeled, seeded and chopped
½ teaspoon sugar
⅛ teaspoon cinnamon
¾ cup water
6 small zucchini, cut into 1 inch pieces
   Juice of ½ lemon

Wash and dry the fish and sprinkle inside and out with ½ teaspoon salt and pepper. Heat the oil in a large skillet and fry the onions until light golden and soft. Add the garlic, parsley, mint, tomatoes, remaining salt and pepper, sugar and cinnamon. Fry for 1 minute. Add water, cover and simmer for 30 minutes. Add the zucchini and the whole fish. Cover and cook in a preheated 350° oven for 20 to 25 minutes until the fish is tender. Sprinkle with lemon juice and serve hot.

Barbounia sti-skara

Grilled mullet

4 servings

4 small red mullet
½ teaspoon salt
   Freshly ground black pepper
4 tablespoons olive oil
1 tablespoon lemon juice
1 tablespoon finely chopped parsley

Have the mullet cleaned but leave them whole. Sprinkle on both sides with salt and pepper and set aside 10 minutes. Combine the olive oil and lemon juice. Preheat the broiler and oil the broiler rack. Place the mullet on the rack, brush with the oil mixture and broil about 5 minutes on each side or until nicely browned. Brush frequently with the oil mixture. Place the fish on a serving plate, sprinkle with parsley and serve with a tomato sauce.

Psari me rigani

Grilled fish with oregano

4 servings

1 (2 pound) striped bass or other salt water fish
1 teaspoon salt
   Freshly ground black pepper
½ teaspoon oregano
4 teaspoons lemon juice
3½ tablespoons olive oil
1 small onion, sliced into thin rings
2 teaspoons chopped parsley

Wash and dry the fish. Combine the salt, pepper and oregano and rub the fish with this mixture inside and out. Mix 2 teaspoons lemon juice with 3 tablespoons olive oil and brush over the fish. Place on an oiled rack and broil for 15 minutes, turning once during the cooking. Baste with the lemon-oil mixture several times. Sprinkle the onion rings with the remaining 2 teaspoons lemon juice and ½ tablespoon of oil. Remove the fish and place on a heated serving dish. Garnish with the marinated onion rings and chopped parsley and serve.

Mahi Polou

Fish with rice

4 servings

  3 *tablespoons butter*
  1 *tablespoon cumin seeds*
     Pinch of saffron
½ *cup raisins, soaked in hot*
     water and drained
  2 *cups cooked rice*
¾ *pound cooked firm white*
     fish, flaked
  1 *tablespoon finely chopped*
     parsley
½ *teaspoon salt*
     Freshly ground black pepper
  2 *tablespoons water*

Heat the butter, add the cumin seeds, saffron and raisins and fry gently for 3 minutes. Add the rice and stir until each grain is shiny with butter. Mix in the fish, parsley, salt, pepper and 2 tablespoons water. Cover and bake in a preheated 300° oven for 1 hour.

Kibbet Samak

Mashed fish

8 servings

  1 *pound bass, filleted*
1½ *cups bulgar or cracked wheat*
  3 *cups hot water*
  2 *teaspoons salt*
  2 *small onions, finely chopped*
     Freshly ground black pepper
     Thin peel of ½ an orange,
     finely chopped
  1 *teaspoon ground coriander*
  4 *tablespoons olive oil*
  3 *small onions, sliced*
     Few threads saffron

Chop the fish into small pieces. Soak the bulgar in the hot water with 1 teaspoon salt for ½ hour. Drain. Place onions, pepper, orange peel and coriander in a bowl. Add fish and bulgar and mix thoroughly. Heat 2½ tablespoons oil in a heatproof casserole. Add the sliced onions, remaining salt, pepper and saffron. Cook for 5 to 10 minutes until the onion is soft. Spread the fish mixture over the onions. Brush with the remaining oil and bake in a preheated 400° oven for 30 minutes. Let cool. Cut into serving pieces and serve with Yakni Samak. (Recipe page 47.)

Kababe Mahi

Stuffed baked fish

4 to 6 servings

  1 *(4 pound) striped bass or*
     other firm fleshed white fish
  4 *tablespoons butter, melted*
¼ *cup dried apricots, soaked,*
     drained and chopped
¼ *cup raisins, soaked and*
     drained
  3 *tablespoons chopped walnuts*
  2 *tablespoons chopped*
     pistachios
¼ *teaspoon salt*
     Freshly ground black pepper
½ *teaspoon ground cloves*
     Pinch of saffron
¼ *teaspoon ground cardamom*
     Pinch of cinnamon
     Grated peel of 1 orange
  1 *tablespoon lemon juice*
  1 *tablespoon finely chopped*
     parsley

Clean the fish, leaving head and tail intact. Heat 2 tablespoons butter in a skillet, add all the remaining ingredients except the lemon juice and parsley and sauté over low heat 4 minutes. Stuff the fish with this mixture and secure the opening with skewers. Place the fish in a buttered baking pan and brush with the remaining butter and lemon juice. Cover the pan with aluminum foil and bake in a 375° oven for 25 minutes. Uncover and bake 10 minutes more. Carefully transfer to a serving platter, sprinkle with parsley and serve.

There is an old French saying that fish without wine is poison, and another that says 'Fish must swim three times, once in water, then in butter, and finally in wine'. All of which confirms the classical gastronomic rule that fish and wine are inseparable. A corollary of the same rule is that fish is normally accompanied by a dry white wine. The only exception to the rule is fish prepared in a very rich sauce, with which a demi-sec white wine is drunk. A refinement of the rule is that the more delicate the fish the better the wine has to be. A fine white wine is always drunk cool – but never chilled. In fact, anything ice cold that passes over the tongue deadens the taste buds to the subtleties of the meal. A good white wine should therefore never be cooler than cellar

Moules marinière

Mussels mariners' style

6–8 servings

6–8 dozen mussels, fresh or
    canned with shells, if
    available
2 tablespoons butter
1 stalk celery, chopped
1 medium leek or three
    scallions, sliced thinly
1 carrot, chopped
¼ cup chopped parsley
1 bay leaf
    Coarsley ground black
    pepper
1½ cups dry white wine

If using fresh mussels, scrub the shells with a stiff brush, cleaning them well. Remove the beards with a sharp knife, rinse under cold running water, and soak in cold water for 10 to 15 minutes to remove excess sand. Discard any mussels that are open. In a large pot, melt the butter and cook the celery, leek or scallion and carrot until soft. Add the remaining ingredients and bring to a simmer. Rinse the mussels and add to the pot. Cover and steam the mussels, shaking the pan occasionally, until the shells open—about 5 to 10 minutes. Cook for 5 minutes if using canned mussels. Remove the mussels to a large warm bowl. Continue simmering the liquid for three minutes more and strain into the bowl over the mussels. Serve hot with French bread.

Crevettes à l'estragon

Shrimp with tarragon

4 servings

2 tablespoons butter
4 scallions, finely chopped
2 cloves garlic, crushed
2 green peppers, finely
    chopped
1½ pounds shrimp, shelled
    and deveined
2 medium sized tomatoes,
    peeled, seeded and chopped
½ teaspoon tarragon
2 tablespoons lemon juice
¼ teaspoon salt
    Freshly ground black pepper
⅓ cup white vermouth
½ cup white wine
1 tablespoon cornstarch,
    dissolved in 2 tablespoons
    cold water
2 tablespoons parsley,
    finely chopped

Cut the shrimp through the back but keep the tail attached. Heat the butter in a skillet. Sauté scallions, garlic and green pepper 3 minutes until softened. Add shrimp and cook over high heat for 3 minutes. Add tomatoes, tarragon, lemon juice, salt and pepper, vermouth and wine. Simmer 5 minutes. Stir in cornstarch dissolved in cold water. Garnish with parsley and serve hot on a bed of rice.

Maquereaux au fenouil

Mackerel with fennel

6 servings

3 (1½ pound) mackerel
¾ cup butter, softened
6 scallions, finely chopped
2 tablespoons lemon juice
2 tablespoons fresh fennel,
    or dill weed or
1 teaspoon fennel seeds
    or dill seeds
1½ tablespoons olive oil or
    vegetable oil
1 teaspoon salt
    Freshly ground black pepper
6 cherry tomatoes

Sauce:
¼ cup dry white wine
4 scallions, finely chopped
2 egg yolks
½ cup hot butter
    Fennel, dill or parsley
    for garnish

Dry fish inside and out with paper towels. Combine butter, scallions, lemon juice and fennel. Stuff the fish with this mixture. Sew or skewer the edges together. Brush the fish with oil and sprinkle with salt and pepper. Place under the broiler for ten minutes on each side. Continue cooking for ten minutes in a 400° oven. During the last five minutes add the whole tomatoes. In the meantime, prepare the sauce. Pour the wine into a small saucepan. Add the scallions and simmer over low heat for three minutes until scallions are softened and almost all the wine has boiled away. Remove the pan from the heat. Beat the egg yolks into the wine. Place the pan over very low heat. Beat in the hot butter stirring constantly. Remove the pan from the heat as soon as the sauce is thickened. Season the sauce with salt and pepper. Remove skewers from the fish and place on a hot platter. Garnish platter with tomatoes, fresh fennel, dill or parsley. Serve hot. Serve the sauce separately.

Poissons aux câpres

Rougets farcis aux échalotes

Maquereaux au fenouil

Buissons d'éperlans

Sole Bercy

Fillet of sole Bercy

4 servings

1¾ pounds sole or flounder
    fillets with skin removed
- ½ *teaspoon salt*
    Freshly ground black pepper
3 *scallions, finely chopped*
2 *tablespoons parsley,*
    finely chopped
½ *cup white wine*
2 *tablespoons butter*

Season fish with salt and
pepper. Butter a large oval
baking dish. Add the scallions
and parsley. Add wine and
place the dish in a 350° oven
for 5 minutes. Take the dish
out of the oven. Arrange
fillets in a single layer in the
dish, top with pats of butter.
Cover the fish with aluminum
foil. Place in the oven for 15
minutes. Remove paper.
Drain off the poaching liquid.
Place under the broiler for
2 minutes. Serve hot.

Sole Deauvilloise

Fillet of sole au gratin in cider sauce

4 servings

¼ *cup butter*
½ *pound onions, chopped*
½ *cup heavy cream*
1½–2 *pounds fillets of sole or*
    one large flounder, head
    and tail intact
1¼ *cups fish broth or 1*
    chicken bouillon cube
    dissolved in 1¼ cups water
¾ *cup apple cider or juice*
½ *teaspoon salt*
    Freshly ground black pepper
    Peel of one lemon
1½ *tablespoons butter*
2 *tablespoons flour*
    Dash of nutmeg
1 *teaspoon dry mustard*
    Drops of lemon juice
3–4 *tablespoons fine dry*
    breadcrumbs

In a small saucepan, heat the
butter, add the onions and
cook until soft. Purée the
mixture in the blender with
2 tablespoons of cream or
force through a sieve. Place
the fillets, folded in half, or the
whole fish in a shallow, lightly
buttered flame proof serving
dish. Combine the broth,
cider, salt, pepper and lemon
peel and bring to a simmer.
Simmer 10 minutes and strain
onto the fish. Cover the fish
with a buttered piece of wax
paper cut to fit the pan.
Bring the liquid to a simmer on
top of the stove, place in a
400° oven and poach for 5 to
10 minutes. The whole fish
will require the longer time.

Strain off the poaching liquid
and reserve. Melt 1 tablespoon
butter, add the flour and cook
for a few minutes over medium
heat. Add 1¼ cups of the
poaching liquid, stirring
constantly until smooth. Add
the puréed onions, remaining
cream, nutmeg, mustard and
a few drops of lemon juice.
Bring to a boil, stirring,
and simmer a few minutes.
Pour the sauce over the fish,
sprinkle with breadcrumbs,
dot with butter and place
under the broiler for about
2 minutes or until golden.
Garnish with parsley and
serve hot.

Poissons aux câpres

Fish fillets with capers

4 servings

2 *pounds salt water fish*
    fillets: e.g. haddock,
    cod, etc.
2 *cups fish broth or 2 chicken*
    bouillon cubes dissolved
    in 2 cups water
½ *cup butter*
    Juice of 1 lemon
½ *cup capers*
2 *teaspoons red wine vinegar*
1 *tablespoon chopped parsley*

Place the fillets in a lightly
buttered flameproof dish, pour
on the broth and cover with
buttered wax paper, cut to
fit the pan. Bring to a simmer
on top of the stove. Place in
a 375° oven and poach for
10–12 minutes or until the fish
flakes easily. While the fish
cooks, melt the butter in a
small pan, stir in the lemon
juice, capers, and vinegar and
heat until bubbling. When the
fish is done, drain it and
place on a warmed serving
dish. Pour the butter over and
garnish with chopped parsley.

Cotriade

Fish soup

6 servings

*3 pounds fish: such as a
combination of sea bass,
mullet, haddock, mackerel,
devil fish, whiting, sardine*
2 tablespoons olive oil
2 large onions, chopped
*6 cups fish broth
or 3 chicken bouillon
cubes dissolved in 6 cups
water*
*2 teaspoons salt
Freshly ground black pepper*
*1 tablespoon parsley, finely
chopped*
¼ teaspoon dried sage
¼ teaspoon marjoram
¼ teaspoon dried thyme
1 bay leaf
*1 pound potatoes cut into
large cubes
French or Italian bread*

Clean the fish and cut into
thick slices. In a large pan,
heat the oil, add the onions
and sauté over medium heat
until brown. Add the broth
and bring to a boil over high
heat. Add the salt, pepper,
parsley, sage, marjoram,
thyme and bay leaf and simmer
3 minutes. Add the potatoes,
cover and cook over medium
heat 5 to 7 minutes. Add the
fish slices, lower the heat and
cook, covered, for 7 to 10
minutes or until the fish
flakes easily. Place fish on a
warm platter and surround
with the potatoes. Place thick
slices of bread in individual
soup bowls and pour over
the bouillon.

Saumon diable

Deviled salmon

4 servings

1½ pounds salmon steaks
½ cup butter, softened
*1 tablespoon mild (Dijon)
mustard*
*1 tablespoon lemon juice
Dash cayenne pepper*
*2 tablespoons parsley, finely
chopped*
1½ tablespoons vegetable oil
*¼ teaspoon salt
Freshly ground black pepper*

Beat butter with mustard,
lemon juice, cayenne pepper
and parsley. Place in the
refrigerator to harden. Brush
salmon with oil and season
with salt and pepper. Broil 4
minutes on each side. Top hot
salmon with a pat of cold
flavored butter. Serve hot.

Bouillabaisse

Fish soup from Marseilles

6 servings

*3 pounds assorted salt
water fish (cod, haddock,
red snapper, sea bass, etc.)*
2 cups bottled clam broth
2 cups water
1 onion, chopped
2 carrots, chopped
2 stalks celery, chopped
2 stalks parsley
*3 tablespoons olive oil or
vegetable oil*
1 onion, finely chopped
2 cloves garlic, crushed
*3 medium sized tomatoes,
peeled, seeded and chopped
or 1 (1 pound) can
tomatoes, drained and
chopped*
1 bay leaf
*1 teaspoon fennel seeds,
crushed*
*⅛ teaspoon saffron, soaked
in 1 tablespoon hot water
for 5 minutes
Peel from ½ orange,
finely chopped*
*½ teaspoon salt
Freshly ground black pepper*

Remove skin and bones from
the fish. Cut fish into 2 inch
slices and lay to one side.
Put clam broth, water,
1 onion, carrots, celery and
parsley in a large saucepan.
Cover and simmer for 30
minutes. Strain the broth and
discard the vegetables. Fry fish
in hot oil, three minutes on
each side, until lightly browned.
Transfer fish to the broth.
In the same skillet sauté
onion and garlic for two
minutes until softened. Add
tomatoes, bay leaf, fennel,
saffron with its soaking water,
and orange peel. Season with
salt and pepper. Simmer
these ingredients uncovered for
5 minutes. Transfer to the
broth with the fish. Bring
broth to simmering point.
Ladle into soup bowls and
serve with French bread.

Saumon poché

Poached salmon

4 servings

  1 *cup dry white wine*
  2 *cups water*
  1 *medium onion, sliced*
  2 *carrots, sliced*
 ¾ *teaspoon salt*
  1 *bay leaf*
  4 *salmon steaks*
    Watercress
    Hollandaise sauce

Place the wine, water, onion,
carrots, salt and bay leaf in a
heavy saucepan. Bring to a
boil, lower the heat and simmer
45 minutes. Place the salmon
in a lightly buttered shallow
pan, strain on the liquid and
cover with buttered wax
paper cut to fit the pan.
Bring the liquid to a simmer on
top of the stove, place in a
375° oven and poach for
10–15 minutes depending on
the thickness of the steaks.
Drain the fish and place on a
serving platter. Garnish with
watercress and serve warm
with Hollandaise sauce.

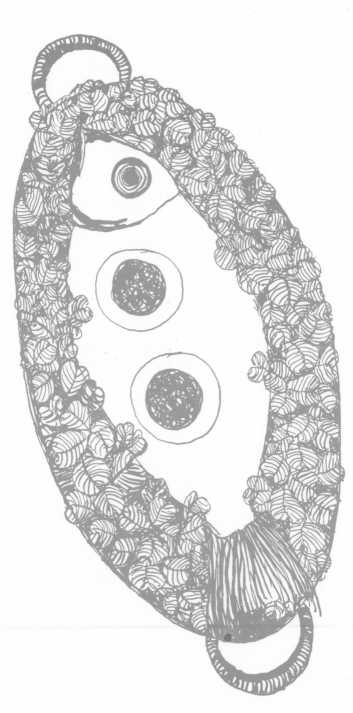

Salade de tourteau

Crab salad

6 servings

  2 *pounds crabmeat, cleaned*
  6 *mushrooms, sliced*
  2 *tablespoons lemon juice*
  6 *tablespoons olive oil or*
    vegetable oil
 ¼ *teaspoon salt*
    Freshly ground black pepper
  4 *hard boiled eggs*
  2 *tomatoes, cut into wedges*
  2 *green peppers, cut into*
    strips
 12 *black olives, pitted*
 ¼ *cup English walnuts,*
    chopped
  2 *tablespoons parsley,*
    finely chopped

Combine crabmeat and
mushrooms in a bowl. Stir
together the lemon juice, oil,
salt and pepper. Moisten
crabmeat and mushrooms
with 2 tablespoons lemon juice
and oil. Place crabmeat in the
center of a serving dish.
Cut eggs into wedges and
arrange around the crabmeat.
Place tomatoes in a bowl.
Simmer green pepper strips for
four minutes in boiling water.
Drain and rinse in cold water.
Add green pepper and olives
to tomatoes. Toss with
remaining lemon juice and oil.
Drain and arrange around
crabmeat. Sprinkle crabmeat
with walnuts and parsley.

Merlan au vin rouge

Whiting in wine sauce

4 servings

> 2 tablespoons olive oil
> 1 medium onion, finely
>   chopped
> 1 tablespoon flour
> 1 cup dry red wine
> 1 cup water
> ¾ teaspoon salt
>   Freshly ground black pepper
> 2 cloves garlic, crushed
> ¼ teaspoon thyme
> 1 bay leaf
> 1 tablespoon chopped parsley
> 2 teaspoons tomato paste
> 2 large whiting, cut into 1"
>   thick slices
> 1 cup flour seasoned with
>   ½ teaspoon salt
>   Freshly ground black pepper
> 3 tablespoons olive oil
> 1 tablespoon capers

Heat the olive oil in a heavy saucepan and sauté the onion until golden. Add the flour, stir and cook for 1 minute. Pour on the wine and water, stirring vigorously. Bring to a boil and add salt, pepper, garlic, thyme, bay leaf, parsley and tomato paste. Lower the heat and simmer until the sauce is reduced to about 1¼ cups. While the sauce is reducing, dredge the fish slices in seasoned flour. Heat the olive oil until it sizzles and sauté the fish on both sides until done and golden. Drain on paper towels and place on a warmed serving platter. When the sauce is ready, remove the bay leaf, stir in the capers and pour over the fish.

Grenouilles

Frog legs

4 servings

> 24 frog legs
> ½ cup milk
> ½ cup flour, seasoned with
>   ½ teaspoon salt
>   Freshly ground black pepper
> 3 tablespoons butter
> 3 cloves garlic, crushed
> 2 tablespoons white vermouth
> 2 hard boiled eggs, chopped
> 2 tablespoons parsley, finely
>   chopped
> 1 teaspoon capers (optional)
> 2 tablespoons lemon juice

Dip frog legs in milk and then in seasoned flour. Shake off excess flour. Sauté frog legs and garlic in butter for ten minutes until lightly browned. Transfer frog legs to a hot serving dish. Add vermouth to the skillet and stir in eggs, parsley, capers and lemon juice. Pour all these hot ingredients over the frog legs. Serve hot.

Buissons d'éperlans

Fried smelts

4 servings

> 1½ pounds smelts or fresh
>   sardines
> 1 cup milk
> 1 cup flour
>   Oil for deep frying
>   Salt
>   Sprigs of parsley
> 2 lemons, thinly sliced

Clean the smelts and dry thoroughly on paper towels. Heat the oil to 375° or until almost smoking. Dip the smelts into the milk, then the flour and fry a few at a time, until golden brown. As they are done, remove and drain on paper towels. Sprinkle with salt and keep warm. When all are done, transfer to a heated bowl, mounding them slightly. Fry sprigs of parsley, drain and garnish the smelts with the parsley and lemon slices.

Barbue Mornay

Halibut with Mornay sauce

6 servings

> 3 pounds halibut steaks
> 2 cups water
> ½ teaspoon salt
> 2 tablespoons lemon juice
> 2 tablespoons butter
> 2 tablespoons flour
> 2 cups milk
> ¼ cup Swiss cheese, grated
> ¼ cup Parmesan cheese,
>   grated
> ¼ teaspoon salt
>   Freshly ground black pepper
> 1 teaspoon mild (Dijon)
>   mustard
> ½ cup breadcrumbs

Place fish in a large skillet and cover with water. Add salt and lemon juice. Simmer uncovered for 15 minutes until fish is white and flakes easily. Drain fish and keep it warm. Melt the butter in a saucepan. Stir in the flour and add the milk gradually. Add cheeses and season the sauce with salt, pepper and mustard. Place fish in a baking dish. Cover with sauce and top with breadcrumbs. Bake 5 minutes in a 400° oven until sauce is lightly browned and bubbling.

Rougets farcis aux échalotes

Stuffed striped mullet

3 servings

  3 *(one pound) striped
      mullets or other small salt
      water fish, cleaned*
 ¼ *pound bacon, fried until
      crisp, and drained*
  6 *scallions, finely chopped*
  3 *teaspoons butter, melted*
 ¼ *teaspoon salt
      Freshly ground black pepper*

Sauce:
  2 *tablespoons butter*
  2 *tablespoons flour*
  2 *cups milk*
  1 *tablespoon tomato paste*
 ¼ *cup heavy cream*
  1 *bunch parsley, finely
      chopped*
  9 *boiled small potatoes*

Crumble the bacon, combine with the scallions and stuff the mullets. Butter three pieces of aluminum foil and place mullets on the foil. Sprinkle with salt and pepper and fold foil into little packets. Bake in a 350° oven for 20 minutes. In the meantime, heat 2 tablespoons butter in a small saucepan. Stir in the flour and add the milk gradually. Stir in the tomato paste and cream. Season with salt and pepper. Simmer sauce, uncovered over low heat for ten minutes and then keep it warm. Take fish out of the packets and broil for 3 minutes on each side. Sprinkle parsley over a platter. Place mullets on top of the parsley and arrange the hot boiled potatoes on the platter. Serve the sauce separately.

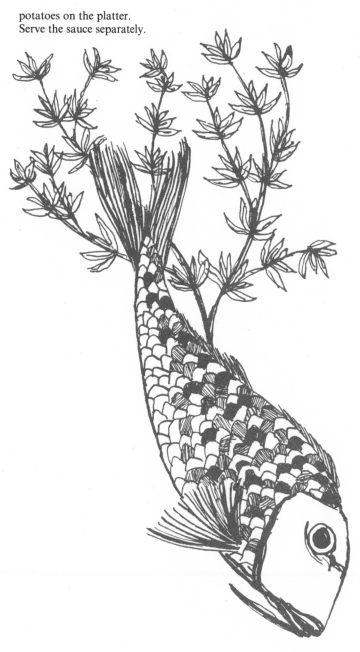

Rougets aux fines herbes

Riviera mullet

4 servings

  2 *pounds mullet*
 ¼ *cup butter
      Sprigs of parsley*
  3 *shallots or scallions,
      finely chopped*
 ¼ *teaspoon dried thyme*
  1 *bay leaf*
 ¼ *teaspoon fennel seed*
  1 *carrot, grated*
  1 *lemon, thinly sliced*
  8 *black olives, chopped*
 ¼ *teaspoon salt
      Freshly ground black pepper*
  2 *teaspoons lemon juice*
 ½ *cup dry sherry*
  2 *tablespoons fine dry
      bread crumbs*
  1 *tablespoon butter*
  2 *tablespoons finely chopped
      parsley*

Clean the fish and dry thoroughly with paper towels. Melt the butter in an ovenproof dish large enough to hold the fish and add the parsley, shallots, thyme, bay leaf, fennel, carrot, lemon slices and olives. Season the fish inside and out with salt and pepper. Place in the dish, sprinkle with lemon juice and pour the sherry over all. Cover tightly with aluminum foil and bake in a 375° oven for 25 minutes or until done. Sprinkle the fish with bread crumbs, dot with butter and place under the broiler until the bread crumbs are golden. Sprinkle with parsley and serve hot.

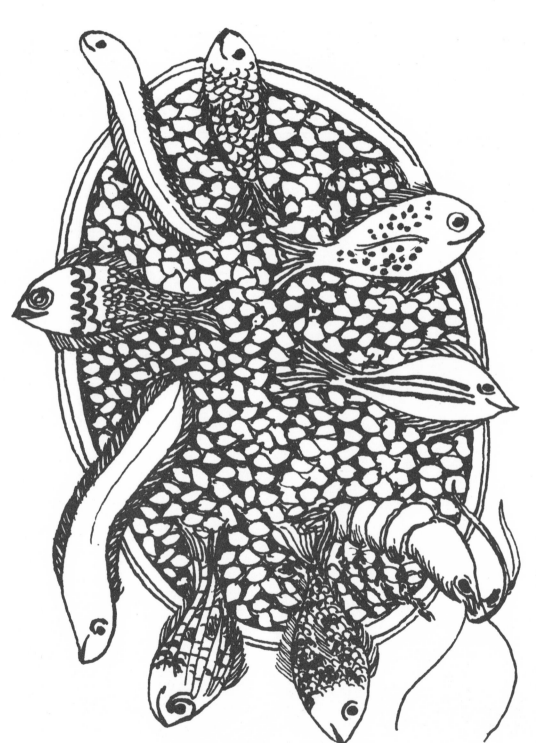

Hamburger Kasserolle

Fish casserole

6 servings

  *2 tablespoons margarine or
    butter*
  1 medium onion, chopped
  *1 (16 oz.) package frozen
    fish fillets, cut into
    bite-size pieces*
  ½ pound scallops
  *½ pound shrimp, shelled and
    cleaned*
  *1 (10 oz.) package frozen
    artichoke hearts, thawed*
  *1 (3 oz.) can sliced
    mushrooms, drained*
  *1 (10½ oz.) can mushroom
    soup*
  1 cup dry white wine
  ½ teaspoon salt
  2 cups cooked rice
  2 teaspoons parsley flakes
  *2 tablespoons grated Parmesan
    cheese*

Melt margarine in large skillet;
sauté onion in margarine until
transparent. Add fish,
scallops, shrimp, artichoke
hearts, mushrooms, soup,
wine and salt; mix well.
Combine rice and parsley in
greased 2½ qt. casserole.
Pour fish mixture over rice.
Bake in a moderate oven (350°)
20 minutes. Sprinkle cheese
over top; bake 10 minutes
longer.

Büsumer Fischsuppe

Hamburger Kasserolle

Büsumer Fischsuppe

Fish stew Büsum style

6–8 servings

- 4 *medium onions, sliced*
- 1 *stalk celery, chopped*
- 2 *(1 lb,) packages frozen perch fillets, cut into serving size pieces*
- 1 *tablespoon salt*
- 2 *tablespoons margarine or butter*
- 5 *cups milk*
- ½ *cup sour cream*
- 2 *tablespoons chopped dill pickle*
- 4 *teaspoons horseradish*
- 1 *teaspoon parsley flakes Fresh chopped dill*

Place onions, celery, fish, salt and margarine in large heavy saucepan; add milk. Bring to a boil; reduce heat; simmer 15–20 minutes. Add sour cream, pickle, horseradish and parsley; stir to blend; heat. Garnish with dill.

Fischklopse in Specksauce

Fish patties with sweet-sour sauce

6 servings

- 1 *cup croutons*
- ¼ *cup milk*
- 1 *pound cooked fish, ground*
- 1 *egg*
- 1 *tablespoon grated onion*
- ½ *teaspoon salt*
- 1 *cup fine bread crumbs*
- 2 *tablespoons margarine or butter*
- 1 *(10½ oz.) can cream of shrimp soup*
- ½ *cup milk*
- 2 *teaspoons vinegar*

Soak croutons in milk until soft; drain well. Combine croutons, fish, egg, onion and salt; mix well. Add ¼–½ cup bread crumbs as needed to make a firm mixture. Shape into 2″ × 1″ patties. Roll in remaining bread crumbs. Melt margarine in large skillet, brown patties in margarine. Combine soup, milk and vinegar in saucepan; blend well. Heat. Serve sauce over patties.

Flunder, Hamburger Art

Whole flounder, Hamburg style

4 servings

- ½ *pound bacon, diced*
- 4 *flounder (about 12 oz. each) cleaned, pan-ready*
- 2 *teaspoons lemon juice*
- 1 *teaspoon salt*
- ¼ *cup flour*
- ¼ *cup margarine or butter Parsley sprigs Lemon wedges*

Fry diced bacon until crisp; drain on paper towels. Sprinkle each flounder with lemon juice and salt; coat with flour, shaking off excess. Melt margarine in large frying pan over moderately high heat. Fry fish slowly, about 5 minutes on each side, until golden brown. Arrange fish on platter, garnished with bacon pieces, parsley sprigs and lemon slices. Serve with potato sald.

Bremer Aalfrikassee

Eel fricassee

6 servings

- 1 *tablespoon beef extract*
- 3 *(1-pt.) bottles clam broth*
- 2 *pounds fresh eel, cleaned, skinned and cut into 1½" pieces, or*
- 1½ *pounds red snapper or haddock fillet, cut into 1½" × 1" pieces*

Fish balls:

- 2 *onions, peeled and cut into 6 wedges each*
- ½ *pound haddock fillet*
- 2 *egg whites*
- ½ *cup half-and-half*
- ½ *teaspoon salt*
- ⅛ *teaspoon pepper*

Sauce:

- 2 *tablespoons margarine or butter*
- 4 *tablespoons flour*
- 2 *cups poaching liquid*
- 2 *egg yolks*
- ½ *cup half-and-half*
- ½ *cup dry white wine*
- 1 *(8 oz.) can sliced mushrooms, drained*
- ½ *pound frozen cooked, cleaned shrimp*
- 1 *(8 oz.) can cut asparagus pieces, drained*

Combine beef extract and clam broth in large, wide skillet or saucepan. Add eel or other fish pieces. Poach for 15 minutes or until fish flakes easily when tested with fork. Carefully remove fish. Keep warm. Reserve 2 cups liquid. Put onions and haddock fillet through finest blade of food

grinder. Beat in egg whites, half-and-half and salt and pepper. Form into 1" balls. Poach fish balls in hot, but not boiling water for about 10 minutes. Drain. Melt margarine in saucepan, stir in flour and reserved 2 cups broth; cook over medium heat, stirring constantly, until mixture thickens. Combine egg yolks with half-and-half; add small amount of the hot mixture, stirring well. Return to saucepan, stirring briskly. Stir in wine, mushrooms, shrimp and asparagus. Add reserved poached fish and fish balls. Blend carefully. Serve hot with rice and cucumber salad.

Gedünste Fisch-Filets in Dillsauce

Poached fish fillets in dill sauce

4 servings

- 1½ *cups water*
- 1 *teaspoon salt*
- 1 *medium onion, sliced*
- 1 *bay leaf*
- 1 *(16 oz.) package frozen fish fillets, thawed*
- 2 *tablespoons margarine or butter*
- 2 *tablespoons flour*
- ½ *cup sour cream*
- 2 *tablespoons fresh dill, chopped*

In a large skillet, combine water, salt, onion, and bay leaf; bring to a boil. Turn down heat so that water is simmering. Carefully add fish fillets. Poach for 8–10 minutes or until fillets flake when tested with a fork. Gently remove fillets from pan; keep warm on serving platter. Strain fish broth and reserve 1 cup. In a small saucepan, melt margarine. Stir in flour; gradually add fish broth, stirring constantly. Cook until thickened. Remove from heat and stir in sour cream and dill. Serve sauce over fillets.

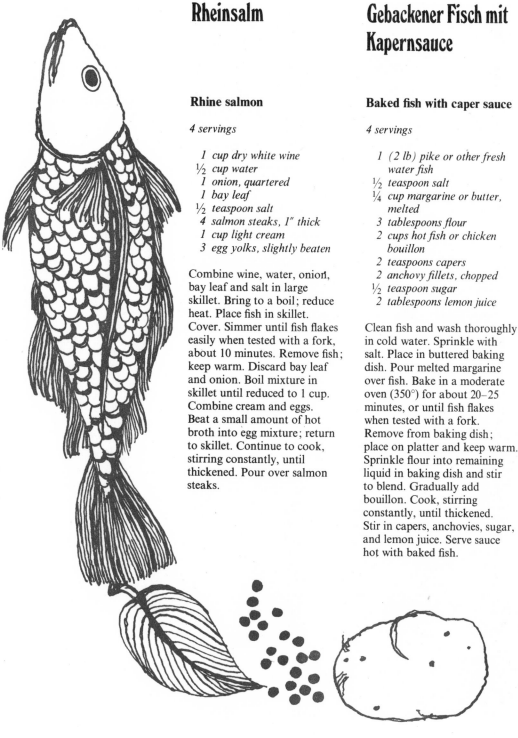

Rheinsalm

Rhine salmon

4 servings

  1 cup dry white wine
½ cup water
  1 onion, quartered
  1 bay leaf
½ teaspoon salt
  4 salmon steaks, 1″ thick
  1 cup light cream
  3 egg yolks, slightly beaten

Combine wine, water, onion, bay leaf and salt in large skillet. Bring to a boil; reduce heat. Place fish in skillet. Cover. Simmer until fish flakes easily when tested with a fork, about 10 minutes. Remove fish; keep warm. Discard bay leaf and onion. Boil mixture in skillet until reduced to 1 cup. Combine cream and eggs. Beat a small amount of hot broth into egg mixture; return to skillet. Continue to cook, stirring constantly, until thickened. Pour over salmon steaks.

Gebackener Fisch mit Kapernsauce

Baked fish with caper sauce

4 servings

  1 (2 lb) pike or other fresh water fish
½ teaspoon salt
¼ cup margarine or butter, melted
  3 tablespoons flour
  2 cups hot fish or chicken bouillon
  2 teaspoons capers
  2 anchovy fillets, chopped
½ teaspoon sugar
  2 tablespoons lemon juice

Clean fish and wash thoroughly in cold water. Sprinkle with salt. Place in buttered baking dish. Pour melted margarine over fish. Bake in a moderate oven (350°) for about 20–25 minutes, or until fish flakes when tested with a fork. Remove from baking dish; place on platter and keep warm. Sprinkle flour into remaining liquid in baking dish and stir to blend. Gradually add bouillon. Cook, stirring constantly, until thickened. Stir in capers, anchovies, sugar, and lemon juice. Serve sauce hot with baked fish.

Friesischer Pfannfisch

Poached codfish

4–6 servings

  2 pounds fresh codfish fillet or steak
10 peppercorns, crushed
  1 bay leaf
  1 tablespoon chopped parsley
  2 cups water
  2 tablespoons margarine or butter
  2 tablespoons cornstarch
1½ tablespoons lemon juice
    Salt and pepper
1½ pounds hot, cooked potatoes, cut into 1″ cubes
    Chopped parsley

Place fish, peppercorns, bay leaf, parsley and water into a wide skillet or saucepan. Bring to the boiling point. (Do NOT allow to boil.) Poach until fish is tender, about 5–10 minutes. Carefully remove the fish to warm platter. Strain liquid, reserving 2 cups. Melt margarine in saucepan; blend in cornstarch. Gradually add the reserved fish stock. Cook over medium heat, stirring constantly, until thickened, about 3–5 minutes. Stir in lemon juice. Season to taste with salt and pepper. Stir in potato cubes. Serve the sauce with the fish, or break the fish into approximately 1″ cubes and stir very gently into the sauce. Serve garnished with additional chopped parsley.

Gedünste Forelle

Gedünste Forelle

Poached trout

4 servings

> 2 cups water
> 1 tablespoon parsley flakes
> 1 onion, quartered
> 2 bay leaves
> 3 cloves
> 1 teaspoon salt
> 4 trout, cleaned and pan-ready
> ½ cup melted margarine or
>   butter
>   Parsley sprigs
>   Lemon wedge

Combine water, parsley, onion, bay leaves, cloves and salt in large skillet. Bring to a boil; add fish. Reduce heat; cover; simmer 12–15 minutes or until fish flakes easily when tested with a fork. Carefully remove fish to serving dish; pour over melted margarine. Garnish with parsley sprigs and lemon wedges.

Gebackene Forelle
Starnberger Art

Gebackene Forelle Starnberger Art

Pan-fried trout Starnberg style

4 servings

  4 *trout, cleaned and pan-ready*
  2 *teaspoons Worcestershire*
    sauce
  2 *teaspoons salt*
  4 *tablespoons flour*
  4 *tablespoons salad oil*
  4 *tablespoons margarine or*
    butter
  3 *shallots, finely minced or*
    1 small onion, finely chopped
  2 *tablespoons lemon juice*
  1 *teaspoon parsley flakes*
½ *teaspoon dried tarragon*

Rub insides of fish with
Worcestershire sauce, then with
salt. Dredge fish with flour.
Heat oil in large skillet. Fry fish
in hot oil 3 minutes on each
side. Remove fish; keep warm.
Pour off oil. Melt margarine
in skillet; stir in shallots, lemon
juice, parsley, and tarragon;
heat. Pour over fish.

Ostpreußische Bierfische

**Fish in beer,
East Prussian style**

6 servings

2 cups water
1 (12 oz.) bottle dark beer
1 tablespoon finely chopped
  parsley
½ cup celery, chopped
1 medium onion, chopped
2 teaspoons salt
1 teaspoon pickling spice
1 teaspoon margarine or
  butter
3 pounds flounder fillet,
  carp or pike, cut into
  serving pieces
3 tablespoons cornstarch
¼ cup water
1 teaspoon lemon juice
  Sugar
  Parsley sprigs

Combine water, beer, parsley, celery, onion, salt, pickling spice, and margarine in large skillet or wide saucepan. Bring to boiling point; do not allow to boil. Add fish pieces. Poach until fish flakes easily when tested with fork, about 3–5 minutes, depending on thickness of pieces. Carefully remove fish to heated platter with slotted spoon. Strain broth. Combine cornstarch and water. Add to broth. Bring to a boil and cook until thickened, stirring constantly. Add lemon juice. Season to taste with a little sugar. Serve fish and sauce separately with boiled potatoes. Garnish with parsley sprigs.

Ratsherren-Fisch

"Councellors" fish

4 servings

1½ pounds frozen fish fillets,
  thawed
½ teaspoon salt
¼ teaspoon black pepper
¼ cup margarine or butter,
  melted
¼ cup milk
1 tablespoon flour
⅔ cup grated cheddar cheese
1 tablespoon snipped parsley

Place fish fillets in buttered shallow casserole (7″ × 10″). Sprinkle with salt and pepper. Pour melted margarine over fillets. Bake in a hot oven (400°) for 15–20 minutes or until fish flakes when tested with fork. Mix milk, flour, and cheese together. Pour over fillets and return them to oven until top is browned, about 10–12 minutes. Sprinkle with parsley.

Wriezener Makrelen

Poached mackerel with herbs

4 servings

4 whole mackerel, cleaned
1 tablespoon vinegar
1 teaspoon salt
¼ teaspoon black pepper
1 onion, quartered
½ cup water
1 cup white wine
3 peppercorns, crushed
½ bay leaf
1 whole clove
½ teaspoon thyme
2 tablespoons cornstarch
¼ cup water
½ cup cream
2 tablespoons margarine or
  butter
1½ tablespoons chopped chives
1½ tablespoons chopped parsley

Sprinkle fish with vinegar, salt, and pepper. In large skillet mix onion, water, wine, peppercorns, bay leaf, clove, and thyme; bring to a boil Carefully add fish; reduce heat and cover. Poach for 15–20 minutes or until fish flakes when tested with fork. Remove fish and keep warm. Strain fish broth; measure 1 cup. Return to skillet. Blend cornstarch into cold water; add fish broth. Cook until thickened and clear. Stir in cream, margarine, chives and parsley. Serve hot over fish.

For the 'zuppa di pesce'-recipe use as many different kinds of fish as possible

Zuppa di pesce

Fish soup

4 servings

1 pound fish fillets
2 cups water
2 tablespoons margarine or
    butter
1 small onion, chopped
1 clove garlic, minced
2 tablespoons chopped green
    pepper
1 stalk celery, chopped
2 medium potatoes, diced
1 (1 pound) can tomatoes
1 bay leaf
1 teaspoon salt
$^1/_8$ teaspoon black pepper
$^1/_4$ teaspoon dried oregano

Cut fish into serving pieces; place in saucepan. Add water. Cook over medium heat about 10 minutes or until fish flakes easily with a fork. Drain, reserving broth. Melt margarine in saucepot over medium heat. Sauté onion, garlic, pepper, and celery until onion is transparent. Stir in remaining ingredients and fish broth. Cook until potatoes are tender. Add fish; cook until heated throughout.

Zuppa di pesce alla genovese

Genoese fish soup

6 servings

1 pound fish fillets
4 cups water
2 tablespoons margarine or
    butter
1 medium onion, chopped
1 clove garlic, minced
1 (1 pound) can tomatoes
1 teaspoon dried sage
$^1/_2$ teaspoon salt
    Dash black pepper
$^1/_2$ pound shrimp, shelled and
    cleaned
2 tablespoons chopped parsley

Cut fish into bite-size pieces; place in saucepan. Add water. Cook over medium heat about 10 minutes or until fish flakes easily with a fork. Drain, reserving broth. Melt margarine in saucepot over medium heat. Sauté onion and garlic in margarine until onion is transparent. Stir in tomatoes, broth, sage, salt and pepper. Cook 3–5 minutes. Add shrimp and fish; cook just until shrimp turn pink. Garnish with parsley.

A visitor to an Italian fish market can see a harvest of sea food far richer than one could imagine. Fish from all over the Mediterranean lie on the stone slabs, their scales glittering in the bright sunshine, among them strange creatures that one would never have imagined could have come from the depths of such a beautiful, sparkling sea. Here are flashing blue and silver mackerel, elegantly flat sole, deep red mullet; there are monster-headed black rays, hideous John Dory's and squid with long purple fangs. Dark gray crabs crawl about in large boxes and lobsters, their claws bound, turn their untrusting beady eyes on passing shoppers. Mussels and other shellfish are piled in mounds. Adding to the color, the Italian merchants have decorated their counters with seaweed and bright yellow lemons.

Perhaps the most beautiful fishmarket in all Italy is the one in Venice. Imagine it early in the morning: there is a salty tang in the air as the fishing boats come through the mist, returning from their night on the Adriatic Sea to make their way up the Grand Canal to the market quay. The boats gently jostle against each other as they unload and the mist slowly rises revealing the ancient city.

Soon the market is full of housewives going from counter to counter inspecting the catch and selecting their purchases. Italian women are very choosy when it comes to buying; the poorer they are the more particular they are about what they buy. They carefully count each precious lira that they must spend. Right in the middle of the housewives are the cooks from the small trattorias and from the big restaurants. In Venice, even the chefs from the famous restaurants, such as the Gritti Palace, do their own shopping at the market. Choosing the ingredients is too important an affair to let someone else do the buying and they are determined that they will find the finest of the bright pink scampi and small rock lobsters which are among the most delicious in the world. You can eat these tasty shrimps in small or luxury restaurants in Venice and be sure of getting a delicacy. Scampi are the pride of Venice and from them each cook can prepare a meal fit for a king.

Anguille

Herbed eels

6 servings

2 pounds large eels
1 cup flour
1 tablespoon parsley flakes
$^1/_2$ teaspoon salt
   Dash black pepper
4 tablespoons margarine or
   butter
$^1/_2$ cup dry white wine
$^1/_2$ cup water
1 teaspoon lemon juice
2 tablespoons parsley flakes
1 tablespoon chopped chives
$^1/_4$ teaspoon salt
$^1/_4$ teaspoon dried mint

Clean, skin and cut eels into
$2^1/_2''$ pieces. Combine flour, 1
tablespoon parsley, $^1/_2$ teaspoon
salt and pepper in large clean
brown paper bag. Drop eels in
bag, 2 or 3 pieces at a time;
shake until coated. (If there is
time let dry on rack 15–20
minutes). Melt margarine in
large skillet. Sauté eels in
margarine until lightly browned.
Add wine, water, lemon juice,
parsley, chives, salt and mint.
Cook over medium heat, about
10–15 minutes, basting eels
frequently.

Carpio arrosto

Baked carp

4 servings

$^1/_4$ cup salad oil
$^1/_4$ cup dry white wine or
   vinegar
2 tablespoons lemon juice
1 tablespoon chopped parsley
$^1/_4$ teaspoon salt
4 (1 pound) carp or perch
   fillets
1 lemon, thinly sliced

Combine oil, wine, lemon juice,
parsley and salt; pour over fish.
Cover; refrigerate 1 hour.
Remove fish from marinade;
place in $11^3/_4'' \times 7^1/_2'' \times 1^3/_4''$
baking dish. Bake in a moderate
oven (350°), basting frequently
with marinade, until fish are
done about 15–20 minutes.
Garnish with lemon slices.

Pesce alla paesana

Fish peasant style

4 servings

2 pounds fish fillets
$^1/_4$ teaspoon paprika
2 tablespoons melted
   margarine or butter
1 teaspoon fennel seed,
   crushed
1 teaspoon parsley flakes
$^1/_4$ teaspoon dried thyme
1 tablespoon lemon juice
$^1/_2$ cup dry white wine or
$^1/_4$ cup water

Cut fish into serving pieces;
arrange in $11^3/_4'' \times 7^1/_2'' \times 1^3/_4''$
baking pan. Sprinkle fish with
paprika. Combine remaining
ingredients, pour over fish. Bake
in a moderate oven (375°) about
15–20 minutes or until fish
flakes easily with fork. Baste
frequently

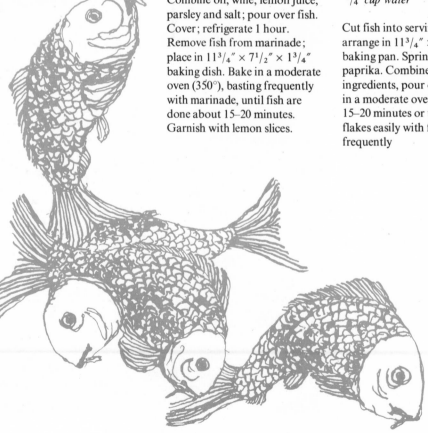

Fritto misto

Aragosta
Italians enjoy steamed or boiled
lobsters served with mayonnaise
or lemon butter

Fritto misto di pesce

Mixed fish-fry

6 servings

   1 *cup flour*
$^1/_4$ *teaspoon salt*
   3 *tablespoons salad oil*
$^3/_4$ *cup warm water*
   1 *egg white*
   1 *pound fish fillets*
 12 *shrimp, shelled and cleaned*
 12 *shucked clams*
      Oil or shortening for deep
      fat frying
      Lemon wedges

Combine flour and salt; stir in oil; mix well. Add water; blend well. If possible, let batter rest 2 hours, although it may be used at once. Beat egg white until stiff, but not dry; fold into batter. Cut fish fillets into bite-size pieces. Heat oil to 375°. Dip fish into batter; drop into fat. Deep-fry turning once, about 5–6 minutes or until golden brown. Remove from fat with tongs. Drain on absorbent paper; keep warm while remaining fish is fried. Garnish with lemon wedges.

Filetti di pesce all'anice

Broiled fish fillets with anise

4 servings

$^1/_4$ *cup margarine or butter*
$^1/_4$ *teaspoon anise seed, crushed*
$^1/_2$ *cup dry white wine*
$^1/_8$ *teaspoon salt*
2 *pounds fish fillets*
1 *tablespoon chopped parsley*

Melt margarine in small skillet over medium heat, add anise seed; heat 1–2 minutes, stirring constantly. Add wine and salt; simmer 5–10 minutes. Cover broiler pan with aluminium foil; rub foil lightly with oil. Place fillets on foil; brush with margarine mixture. Broil 2″ from heat about 6–10 minutes. Do not turn. Place fish on serving platter; pour remaining sauce over fish. Garnish with chopped parsley.

Triglie alla livornese

Livornese Mullet

4 servings

4 *(8 ounces each) mullets*
2 *tablespoons margarine or butter*
1 *(1 pound) can tomatoes*
2 *strips lemon peel,* $^1/_4$″ *wide*
1 *bay leaf*

Clean and dry fish. Melt margarine in large skillet over medium heat. Sauté mullets in margarine, turning once, until lightly browned. Add remaining ingredients; cook over low heat, basting fish frequently, about 8–10 minutes or until fish flakes easily with a fork. Remove peel and bay leaf before serving.

Triglie alla graticola con finocchio

Mullet with fennel 'en papillote'

4 servings

$^3/_4$ *cup salad oil*
3 *tablespoons lemon juice*
4 *(8 ounces each) mullets, cleaned*
1 *large fennel bulb, thinly sliced or*
4 *stalks celery, thinly sliced*
1 *(6 ounce) package ham slices, cut in strips*
1 *teaspoon parsley flakes*
1 *lemon, thinly slices*

Combine oil and lemon juice; pour over fish. Cover; refrigerate 1 hour. Blanch fennel strips in boiling water about 1 minute; drain. Remove fish from marinade. Place 1 fish on large piece of foil; arrange fennel and ham strips on fish; sprinkle with parsley; top with 2 lemon slices. Close foil securely, using a drugstore wrap. Repeat with remaining ingredients. Bake in a moderate oven (350°) about 20–25 minutes.

Granchi

Crabmeat

2 servings

1 *(7 ounce) can crabmeat*
2 *tablespoons margarine or butter*
1 *lemon*
$^1/_8$ *teaspoon salt*
  Dash black pepper
  Hot cooked brown rice
1 *tablespoon chopped parsley*

Place crabmeat in 2 small ramikins or flame proof baking dishes. Dot with pats of margarine. Squeeze juice of half a lemon over each. Sprinkle with salt and pepper. Broil, 3″ from heat, until lightly browned and bubbly, about 4 minutes. Serve over hot rice. Garnish with chopped parsley.

Gamberi con riso

Shrimp and rice

4 servings

> 4 tablespoons margarine
>   or butter
> 1 medium onion, chopped
> $^1/_4$ cup finely chopped celery
> 1 (1 pound) can tomatoes
> $^1/_2$ teaspoon dried basil
> $^1/_2$ teaspoon salt
>   Dash black pepper
> 20 large shrimp, shelled
>   and cleaned
> 1 (10 ounce) package
>   frozen peas
>   Hot cooked rice

Melt margarine in skillet; sauté
onion and celery in margarine
until onion is transparent. Stir
in tomatoes, basil, salt and
pepper; bring to a boil. Reduce
heat; add shrimp and peas.
Cook over low heat until shrimp
are pink and tender, about 8–10
minutes. Serve over hot rice.

Gamberi alla mario

Shrimp Mario

4 servings

> 4 tablespoons margarine
>   or butter
> 1 medium onion, sliced
> 1 green pepper, chopped
> 1 medium tomato, quartered
> $^3/_4$ cup dry white wine
> 20 large shrimp, shelled
>   and cleaned
> $^1/_4$ teaspoon salt
>   Dash black pepper
>   Hot cooked rice

Melt margarine in large skillet;
sauté onion and green pepper
until onion is transparent. Add
tomato and wine; cook 3–5
minutes. Add shrimp, salt and
pepper. Cook over medium
heat, stirring constantly, until
shrimp are pink and tender,
about 8–10 minutes. Serve over
hot rice.

Vongole alla siciliana

Steamed clams Siciliana

4 servings

> 24 hard shell clams
> 2 tablespoons salad oil
> 2 cloves garlic, minced
> $^1/_4$ cup dry white wine
> $^1/_4$ cup water
> 1 tablespoon parsley
>   flakes
> $^1/_4$ teaspoon salt
>   Dash black pepper
>   Lemon wedges

Scrub clams under running
water until free of sand. Heat oil
in large saucepot; sauté garlic in
hot oil. Stir in remaining
ingredients. Place clams in
saucepot. Cover; steam until
shells just open. Heap clams in
soup dish. Spoon sauce over
clams, Garnish with lemon
wedges.

Aragosta oreganata

Lobster oregano

2 servings

2 (1¹/₂–2 pounds) lobsters
¹/₂ cup melted margarine
   or butter
¹/₂ cup seasoned bread
   crumbs
2 tablespoons grated
   Parmesan cheese
1 teaspoon grated onion

Split and clean lobster; crack claws. Place lobster, meat side up on broiler rack, 4″ from heat. Brush well with margarine. Broil 10–12 minutes, brushing with margarine now and then. Combine bread crumbs, cheese and onion. Sprinkle lobster with crumb mixture. Pour remaining margarine over crumbs; broil 5 minutes longer. Garnish with lemon wedges and parsley, if desired.

Aragosta alla marsala

Lobster in wine

2 servings

2 (1¹/₂–2 pound) lobsters
3 tablespoons oil or
   margarine
1 small onion, finely
   chopped
1 small clove garlic,
   cut in half
1 cup dry white wine
2 tomatoes, quartered
   and seeded
1 tablespoon parsley
   flakes
¹/₂ teaspoon dried oregano
¹/₂ teaspoon salt
   Dash cayenne pepper

Split lobster in half lengthwise; remove stomach sacks and intestinal tubes. Remove and crack claws and joints. Separate tails from chests. Heat oil or margarine in large skillet. Add lobster pieces, meat-side down; sauté for several minutes, turning with tongs, until shells are bright red. Remove lobster and keep warm. Sauté onion and garlic in skillet. Add remaining ingredients. Bring mixture to a boil; cook until liquid is reduced by half. Add lobster; simmer 8–10 minutes, basting every few minutes. Arrange lobster pieces on a warm platter and spoon sauce over them. Garnish with watercress and lemon wedges, if desired.

Passera con peperoni

Flounder with peppers

6 servings

4 tablespoons margarine
   or butter
2 medium onions, sliced
1 green pepper, cut
   into rings
1 red pepper, cut into
   rings
1 cup dry white wine
³/₄ teaspoon chervil
¹/₄ teaspoon salt
   Dash black pepper
2 pounds flounder
   fillets

Melt margarine in large skillet. Sauté onions and peppers just until onions are transparent. Stir in wine, chervil, salt and pepper. Simmer 5 minutes. Place fish fillets in buttered 11³/₄″ × 7¹/₂″ × 1³/₄″ baking dish; pour onion mixture over fish. Bake, basting frequently, in a moderate oven (350°) about 25–30 minutes or until fish flakes easily when tested with a fork.

Merluzzo con erbe

Haddock with herbs

6 servings

2 pounds haddock fillets
1 (1 pound) can tomatoes
1 clove garlic, minced
1 tablespoon salad oil
1 teaspoon parsley flakes
¹/₄ teaspoon dried oregano
¹/₄ teaspoon dried thyme

Place fish in buttered 11³/₄″ × 7¹/₂″ × 1³/₄″ baking dish. Combine remaining ingredients; pour over fish. Bake, basting frequently, in a moderate oven (350°) about 25–30 minutes or until fish flakes easily when tested with a fork.

1) Whole squid.
2) Separate the head from the tail.
3) Remove the ink sac and cut off the tentacles.
4) Discard intestines, cartilage and head.

5) Cut off fins. Rinse fins, tail and tentacles under cold running water to remove red, lacelike membrane.
6) Turn tail inside out and wash carefully.

Although lobster is the pride and glory of the coasts of Spain and Portugal, it is very expensive.

Chipirones

Langosta del pobre

Squid

Poor man's lobster

4 servings

2 pounds squid
½ teaspoon salt
½ cup flour
1 cup oil
2 onions, finely chopped
2 cloves garlic, finely chopped
2 tomatoes, peeled, seeded and chopped
1 bay leaf
½ cup dry white wine
½ cup water
2 tablespoons finely chopped parsley

Clean the squid and reserve the ink sacs. Stuff the tentacles into the body cavities and close with toothpicks. Sprinkle with salt and dredge in flour. Fry in hot oil for 4 minutes until lightly browned. Drain the squid and transfer to a casserole. Pour 3 tablespoons of the cooking oil into a skillet. Add the onions and garlic and fry for 3 minutes. Add the tomatoes, bay leaf, white wine and ¼ cup water. Simmer for 10 minutes. Stir the ink from the reserved sacs into remaining ¼ cup water. Add to the tomato mixture. Pour this mixture over the squid in the casserole. Cover the casserole and cook in a preheated 350° oven for 10 minutes until the squid is tender. Remove the squid, discard the toothpicks and strain the sauce. The sauce will be thick. Spoon the sauce over the squid, sprinkle with parsley and serve hot with fried rice.

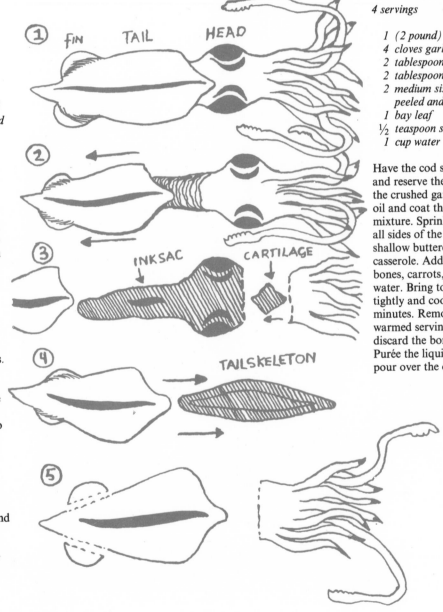

4 servings

1 (2 pound) piece cod
4 cloves garlic, crushed
2 tablespoons olive oil
2 tablespoons paprika
2 medium sized carrots, peeled and sliced
1 bay leaf
½ teaspoon salt
1 cup water

Have the cod skinned and boned and reserve the bones. Combine the crushed garlic with the olive oil and coat the fish with the mixture. Sprinkle the paprika on all sides of the fish and place in a shallow buttered heatproof casserole. Add the reserved fish bones, carrots, bay leaf, salt and water. Bring to a simmer, cover tightly and cook slowly 20 minutes. Remove the cod to a warmed serving plate and discard the bones and bay leaf. Purée the liquid in a blender and pour over the cod.

Bacalao a la manchega

Salt codfish à la Mancha

4 to 6 servings

    1 pound boneless salt cod
    ⅓ cup flour
    ½ cup olive oil
    2 medium sized onions, chopped
    1 bay leaf
    1 large clove garlic, chopped
    2 tablespoons chopped parsley
       Few threads saffron
    4 medium-sized tomatoes,
       peeled, seeded and chopped
    ½ teaspoon salt
       Freshly ground black pepper
    3 medium-sized green peppers
    8 eggs
       Paprika

Soak the codfish overnight, changing the water 2 or 3 times. Cut into ½ inch slices. Dry the fish and dredge in flour. Sauté in the oil until golden brown and tender. Cool and flake the fish. Sauté the onions with the bay leaf in the oil in which the fish was fried. When brown, add the garlic, parsley, saffron and tomatoes. Season with salt and pepper and simmer gently about 10 minutes or until the tomatoes are cooked. Remove the bay leaf. Broil the peppers, turning frequently, for 5 minutes or until brown. Wrap in a damp towel for 2 to 3 minutes, then slide off the skins. Remove the stems and seeds and cut peppers into thin strips. Cover the bottom of a fireproof casserole with ⅓ of the tomato mixture, add a layer of ½ of the flaked fish and ½ of the pepper strips. Repeat these layers, ending with the tomato mixture. Bake in a preheated 350° oven for 15 minutes. Remove from the oven, break the eggs over the top and return to the oven for 10 to 15 minutes or until the eggs are set. Sprinkle with paprika and serve hot.

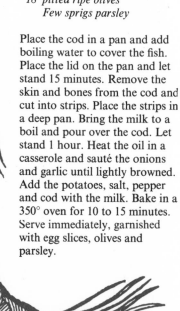

Bacalhau a Gomes de Sá

Cod Gomes de Sá

6 servings

    2 pounds cod
    1¾ cups milk
    3 tablespoons olive oil
    4 medium sized onions, thinly
       sliced
    2 cloves garlic, crushed
    2 pounds potatoes, peeled and
       boiled until tender
    ½ teaspoon salt
       Freshly ground black pepper
    4 hard boiled eggs, sliced
    18 pitted ripe olives
       Few sprigs parsley

Place the cod in a pan and add boiling water to cover the fish. Place the lid on the pan and let stand 15 minutes. Remove the skin and bones from the cod and cut into strips. Place the strips in a deep pan. Bring the milk to a boil and pour over the cod. Let stand 1 hour. Heat the oil in a casserole and sauté the onions and garlic until lightly browned. Add the potatoes, salt, pepper and cod with the milk. Bake in a 350° oven for 10 to 15 minutes. Serve immediately, garnished with egg slices, olives and parsley.

Bacalao a la vizcaína

Biscayan cod

4 servings

    2 pounds cod, cut into 4 slices
    2 cups water
    ½ teaspoon salt
    2 fresh chili peppers
    2 tablespoons cold water
    4 tablespoons olive oil
    1 onion, finely chopped
    3 cloves garlic, crushed
    1 raw potato, peeled and grated
    1 ripe tomato, peeled, seeded
       and chopped

Place the cod in a skillet. Add water and salt and simmer over low heat for 5 minutes. Drain the cod and reserve the cooking water. Pound the chili peppers to a paste with 2 tablespoons water. Heat the olive oil in a skillet. Add the onion and garlic and cook for 3 minutes until lightly browned. Stir in chili pepper paste and cook 2 minutes. Cover with a layer of grated potato and the tomato, forced through a strainer to form a pulp. Place the cod on top and add 1 cup of the reserved cooking water. Cover and simmer over low heat for 45 minutes. Add more water if necessary to form a sauce.

Tumbet de pescado

Fish tumbet

4 servings

   1 *medium sized eggplant*
   1 *tablespoon salt*
   8 *tablespoons olive oil*
   1 *medium sized onion, chopped*
   1 *clove garlic, crushed*
   1 *bay leaf*
   2 *large tomatoes, cut into
      wedges*
 1/8 *teaspoon cinnamon*
 1/2 *teaspoon sugar*
   1 *teaspoon salt*
     Freshly ground black pepper
   4 *potatoes, peeled and sliced*
   1 *pound haddock fillets*
 1/4 *cup flour seasoned with
      1/4 teaspoon salt
      Freshly ground black pepper*
   2 *medium sized green peppers
      Juice of 1/2 lemon*
   3 *tablespoons white wine*

Peel the eggplant and cut into
1/2 inch slices. Lightly score both
sides of the slices, sprinkle with
salt and place on a rack to let
the bitter juices drain from the
eggplant. Heat 1 tablespoon oil
in a saucepan and sauté the
onion, garlic and bay leaf until
the onion is golden. Add the
tomatoes, cinnamon, sugar,
1/2 teaspoon salt and pepper and
simmer gently for 20 minutes.
Meanwhile, heat 3 tablespoons
oil in a large skillet. Dry the
potato slices thoroughly, add to
the skillet and sprinkle with 1/2
teaspoon salt. Cover the skillet
and cook, stirring occasionally,
until the potatoes are brown and
tender. Transfer to a shallow
buttered ovenproof dish and
arrange the fish fillets on top of
the potatoes. Add 3 tablespoons
oil to the skillet. Rinse and dry
the eggplant slices thoroughly.
Dredge in the seasoned flour
and sauté over medium heat
until nicely browned. Arrange
the eggplant on top of the fish.
Add the remaining 1 tablespoon
oil to the skillet. Remove the
stem, seeds and membranes from
the peppers and cut into thin
strips. Sauté the strips, stirring
constantly, until softened. Place
the peppers on top of the
eggplant. Purée the tomato sauce
in the blender and force through
a sieve. Stir the lemon juice and
wine into the tomato sauce and
pour over the tumbet. Bake in a
preheated 350° oven for 25 to 30
minutes. Serve immediately.

Filetes de linguado com molho de ostras e camarões

**Fillet of sole with oyster/
shrimp sauce**

4 servings

 1 1/2 *pounds sole or flounder fillets*
 3/4 *cup dry white wine*
 1/2 *teaspoon salt
     Freshly ground black pepper*
   2 *carrots, chopped*
   1 *onion, chopped
     Sprig of parsley*
   1 *bay leaf*
 1/4 *teaspoon salt*
   1 *cup water*
  30 *oysters*
   2 *tablespoons butter*
   3 *tablespoons flour*
 1/2 *teaspoon lemon juice*

Marinate the fish in 6
tablespoons of the wine, 1/2
teaspoon salt and pepper for
30 minutes. Simmer the chopped
carrots, onion, parsley, bay leaf
and salt in 1 cup water and the
remaining wine for 30 minutes.
Strain and reserve the broth.
Add broth to the fish and
simmer gently for 15 minutes.
Transfer the fish to an ovenproof
serving dish, strain the broth and
keep warm. Simmer the oysters
in their own liquor for 5
minutes. Melt 2 tablespoons
butter in a pan, stir in 3
tablespoons flour and cook 2
minutes. Add 6 tablespoons of
the oyster juice, 3/4 cup of fish
liquid and 1/2 teaspoon lemon
juice and cook, stirring, until
smooth. Arrange the oysters on
top of the fish fillets and pour
on the sauce. Place in a 350°
oven for 5 to 10 minutes until
sauce is bubbling.

Lenguado con salsa de nueces

Sole in nut sauce

4 servings

 1/2 *cup almonds*
 1/2 *cup filberts*
   1 *slice toasted bread*
   1 *tablespoon finely chopped
      parsley*
   1 *clove garlic*
   2 *pounds sole or flounder
      fillets*
 1/4 *teaspoon salt
     Freshly ground black pepper*

Place the almonds, filberts,
bread, parsley and garlic in the
blender and blend until nuts are
finely chopped and breadcrumbs
are formed. Place the fish fillets
in a large skillet. Cover with cold
water and poach the fish,
uncovered, for 8 minutes or
until almost cooked. Drain the
fish and place in a baking dish.
Reserve the cooking water. Add
cooking water a tablespoon at a
time to the nut mixture. Add
enough liquid to form a light
sauce (roughly 1 cup water).
Season sauce with salt and
pepper. Pour the sauce over the
fish and heat in a preheated 350°
oven for 8 minutes until fish is
cooked and the sauce is
bubbling.

Merluza con ajo

Hake with garlic

4 servings

   2 *cups water*
 ¼ *teaspoon salt*
   4 *medium sized potatoes, peeled and thinly sliced*
   1 *medium sized onion, thinly sliced*
 1½ *to 2 pounds hake or cod fillets*
   4 *tablespoons olive oil*
   4 *cloves garlic, crushed Pinch of cayenne pepper*

Place the water and salt in a shallow casserole and bring to a boil. Add the potatoes and onion and simmer, covered, for 20 minutes or until the vegetables are tender. Add the fish fillets and more water if necessary to cover fish and vegetables. Cover and simmer slowly for 8 to 10 minutes or until fish is done. Do not over cook. Drain off all the liquid and keep the fish and vegetables hot. Heat the oil in a small skillet. Add the garlic and sauté until it begins to brown. Stir in the cayenne pepper and pour over the fish. Serve from the casserole.

Budín de merluza con mayonesa

Hake pudding with mayonnaise

6 servings

   2 *pounds hake, cod or other white fish, filleted*
   1 *onion, sliced*
   2 *sprigs parsley*
 ½ *teaspoon salt*
 ½ *teaspoon peppercorns*
   2 *tablespoons lemon juice*
   2 *cups water*
   6 *slices white bread, crusts removed*
 ½ *cup hot milk*
   3 *tablespoons oil*
   2 *onions, finely chopped*
   1 *clove garlic, finely chopped*
   2 *tomatoes, peeled, seeded and chopped*
   5 *eggs, separated*
 12 *boiled, unpeeled shrimp*
 1½ *cups mayonnaise*

Place the fish, onion, parsley, salt, peppercorns, lemon juice and water in a skillet. Simmer the fish for 20 minutes until white and tender. Remove the fish from the cooking liquid and flake it with a fork. Soak the bread in hot milk. Heat the oil in a saucepan and fry the onions and garlic for 3 minutes. Add the tomatoes and continue cooking for 10 minutes. Force the mixture through a strainer to form a purée. Add the flaked fish and bread. Stir in the egg yolks. Beat the egg whites until they stand in soft peaks. Fold egg whites into the fish mixture. Fill into a buttered baking dish. Bake in a preheated 375° oven for 20 minutes. Garnish with shrimp. Serve the pudding with warm mayonnaise.

MEAT DISHES

Roast beef

North country beef

North country beef

3 servings

- 1½ pounds flank steak
- 1 onion, finely chopped
- 1 tablespoon finely chopped parsley
- ½ cup red wine
- 1 tablespoon Worcestershire sauce
- ½ cup beef broth
- 1 tablespoon cornstarch dissolved in 2 tablespoons cold water

Draw criss cross lines across the steak with a sharp knife. Combine the onion and parsley and press the mixture into the scored beef. Place the beef in a shallow dish. Add the wine and Worcestershire sauce. Allow the beef to marinate in the wine for 1 hour, or longer if possible. Turn the beef once. Remove the beef from the marinade. Dry on paper towels. Broil the beef 4 minutes on each side. In the meantime, place the wine and Worcestershire sauce in a small saucepan. Add the beef broth and bring to boiling point. Stir in the cornstarch dissolved in cold water and allow the mixture to thicken into a sauce. Slice the beef thinly, holding the knife almost flat and parallel to the beef. Cut long thin slices of beef, cutting across the grain. Serve the sauce on the beef.

Roast beef

6 servings

- 6 pound standing rib roast

Sauce:
- 2 tablespoons fat from roast
- 3 scallions, finely chopped
- 2 tablespoons flour
- ½ cup beef broth
- ½ cup red wine
- ¼ teaspoon thyme
- ¼ teaspoon salt
  Freshly ground black pepper

Stand beef, fat side up, in a roasting pan. Insert a meat thermometer taking care that the thermometer does not touch the bone. Roast the beef uncovered in a 450° oven for 15 minutes. Lower the heat to 350°. Allow 18 minutes to the pound for rare beef (thermometer reading 130°); 25 minutes (150°) for medium rare beef and 30 minutes for well done beef (165° on the thermometer). Remove the beef from the oven and wrap in aluminum foil. Allow the beef to stand for 15 minutes before carving. While the beef is reeassembling all its juices, prepare the sauce. Place 2 tablespoons of fat from the roast in a small saucepan. Sauté scallions in the fat 3 minutes. Stir in the flour and allow the flour to brown in the fat for 1 minute. Add beef broth, wine and thyme. Season with salt and pepper. Simmer sauce uncovered for 10 minutes.

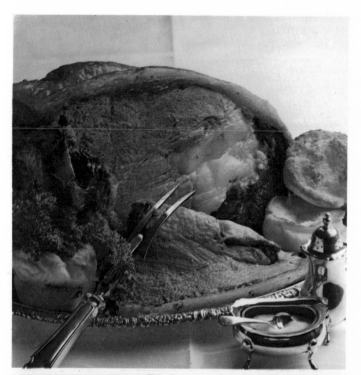

Boiled beef with horseradish

Shropshire herb roll

Scenes from the world-famous twelfth-century tapestry about the Battle of Hastings between William the Conqueror and the English, representing the slaughtering of the cattle, the roasting of the meat, the laying of the table and the enjoying of the meal.

8 servings

4 *pounds fresh or salt brisket
  or corned beef*
4 *onions, sliced*
4 *carrots, sliced*
3 *stalks celery, sliced*
2 *bay leaves*
3 *sprigs parsley*
1 *teaspoon thyme*
1 *teaspoon black peppercorns*
3 *cups water*

Sauce:
½ *cup heavy cream, whipped*
½ *cup sour cream*
4 *teaspoons prepared
  horseradish*
½ *teaspoon salt*

Place the beef in a heavy casserole. Add the remaining ingredients. Add enough water to cover the beef. This quantity will vary, depending on the size of the casserole. Add 1 teaspoon salt if fresh beef was used. Cover casserole and simmer for 3 hours until the meat is tender when pierced with a fork. Chill the meat in the strained broth overnight. Remove the fat which will have risen to the surface of the broth. Slice the beef thinly. Reheat the sliced beef in the broth until it is just hot. Do not over cook the beef. Combine the ingredients for the sauce. Arrange slices of meat on a serving plate. Serve a variety of boiled vegetables separately. Serve the sauce separately.

4 servings

Pastry:
2 *cups sifted all purpose flour*
1 *teaspoon salt*
½ *pound beef suet, chilled and
  chopped into small pieces*
1 *tablespoon lemon juice*
6 *tablespoons water*

Filling:
2 *tablespoons finely chopped
  parsley*
¼ *teaspoon thyme*
1 *tablespoon finely chopped
  chives*
½ *teaspoon marjoram*
½ *teaspoon chervil*
1 *onion, finely chopped*
1 *egg, lightly beaten*
½ *pound bacon, fried until
  crisp*
2 *cups leftover chicken, cut
  into small pieces*
2 *tablespoons milk*

Sauce:
1 *tablespoon butter*
1 *tablespoon flour*
½ *cup beef broth*
1 *tablespoon Madeira*

Baked ham

Stewed oxtail

Pot roast beef

Place the flour and salt in a bowl. Add the suet and blend the suet into the flour with a pastry blender or fingertips. Add the lemon juice. Stir the water into the flour with a fork, adding just enough water to form the pastry into a ball. Wrap the ball in waxed paper and chill it for 1 hour. Dust the pastry with flour and roll it into a rectangle about 12 inches by 8 inches in size. Combine the herbs, onion and egg and spread onto the pastry. Add crumbled bacon and chicken. Season with salt and pepper. To prepare the sauce, melt the butter and add the flour. Stir in the beef broth gradually to form a thick sauce. Add the Madeira. Pour sauce over the bacon and chicken and roll the pastry lengthwise as for a jelly roll. Pinch the ends together to contain the filling. Place the roll on a buttered and floured cookie sheet. Brush the roll with milk and bake in a 400° oven for 15 minutes. Reduce the heat to 350° and continue cooking for 30 minutes or until golden brown.

10 servings

5–6 pound smoked tenderized ham
2 cups orange juice
4 cloves
1 (2 pound) can apricots
½ cup apricot preserves
2 tablespoons sherry
2 tablespoons mild (Dijon type) mustard
1 cup brown sugar

Place the ham in a roasting pan, fat side up. Add orange juice and cloves. Add syrup from canned apricots. Roast uncovered in a 350° oven allowing 30 minutes to the pound. One hour before the estimated cooking time has elapsed, take the ham from the oven. Remove the rind and leave a layer of fat about ¼ inch thick. Draw criss cross lines in the fat. Heat and then strain the apricot preserves. Add sherry and mustard. Brush ham with mixture and then press sugar over the ham. Return the ham to the oven to complete the cooking. Serve the ham hot or cold with a garnish of apricot halves.

4 servings

1 (2½ pound) oxtail, cut into joints
½ cup flour seasoned with 1 teaspoon salt
Freshly ground black pepper
3 tablespoons vegetable oil
2 onions, finely chopped
2 carrots, sliced
1 small turnip, diced (optional)
2 stalks celery, chopped
2 cups beef broth
1 bay leaf
½ teaspoon thyme
1 tablespoon lemon juice
1 tablespoon tomato paste
2 tablespoons finely chopped parsley

Dredge the oxtail joints in seasoned flour and then brown the joints in hot oil. Transfer the joints to a casserole. Fry the onions, carrots, turnip and celery in the same oil. Stir in 1 tablespoon seasoned flour. Add the beef broth and all the remaining ingredients except the parsley. Cover and cook in a 300° oven for 3 hours until the meat is tender. Chill the stew overnight. Remove the fat which has risen to the surface. Reheat the casserole in a 350° oven for 20 minutes. Garnish with parsley and serve with boiled potatoes.

6 servings

3 pounds boneless chuck steak or bottom round, cut in 1 piece and tied
2 tablespoons oil
3 onions, chopped
3 carrots, chopped
1½ cups beef broth
1 tablespoon tomato paste
1 bay leaf
3 sprigs parsley
½ teaspoon thyme
Freshly ground black pepper
1 teaspoon salt
1½ tablespoons butter, softened
1½ tablespoons flour

Brown the beef on all sides in very hot oil. Remove the beef. Add onions and carrots to the same oil and cook for 5 minutes. Place beef and vegetables in a casserole. Add broth, tomato paste, bay leaf, parsley, thyme, pepper and salt. Cover and cook in a 350° oven for 2½ hours until beef is tender. Discard bay leaf and parsley. Combine butter and flour in a custard cup, blending until smooth. Stir into liquid in the casserole. Cook 4 minutes until liquid is thickened into a sauce. Slice the beef, spoon the sauce over the beef and serve with boiled potatoes and freshly cooked vegetables.

Oysters and lamb are a strange combination: but in Lancashire, they have both and so why not put them in the same pot? The result is suprisingly good.

Lancashire hot pot

6 servings

  2 *tablespoons butter*
  6 *baking potatoes, peeled and sliced ¼ inch thick*
  2 *pounds stewing lamb, cut into slices 1 inch thick*
  1 *teaspoon salt*
    Freshly ground black pepper
  2 *onions, sliced thinly*
  3 *lambs kidneys, cut into small pieces*
12 *oysters*
  1 *cup beef broth*
  2 *tablespoons finely chopped parsley*

Butter a 1½ quart casserole. Place a layer of ¾ of the potato slices in the dish and cover with the lamb. Season with salt and pepper. Cover with a layer of ½ of the onion slices. Add the kidneys, then a layer of remaining onions. Add the oysters and top with a layer of potatoes. Add the beef broth. Brush potatoes with melted butter. Cover and cook in a 350° oven for 2 hours. Remove the lid and return the dish to the oven for 30 minutes to allow the potatoes to become crisp and brown.

Goulash is Hungarian in origin, but all the countries surrounding Hungary, including Austria, have adopted this dish.

Znaimer Goulasch

Goulash with pickled cucumbers

6 servings

2½ to 3 pounds rump steak,
　 cut into 2 inch cubes
½ cup flour seasoned with
　 ½ teaspoon salt
　 Freshly ground black pepper
2 tablespoons butter
2 tablespoons oil
6 onions, coarsely chopped
1 tablespoon paprika
2 cups beef broth
3 tablespoons tomato purée
½ teaspoon marjoram
¼ teaspoon caraway seeds
1 clove garlic, crushed
　 Grated rind of 1 lemon
　 Pickled cucumbers
　 Boiled potatoes

Dredge the cubes of meat in seasoned flour and sauté over high heat in the hot combined butter and oil until nicely browned on all sides. Transfer to a casserole with a slotted spoon. Add the onions to the butter and oil and sauté over medium heat until golden brown. Add paprika, ½ cup broth, tomato purée, marjoram, caraway seeds, garlic and lemon rind and simmer 3 minutes. Add the remaining broth and pour over the meat in the casserole. Bring to a simmer, cover and cook slowly 1½ hours or until the meat is tender. Serve from the casserole and pass bowls of pickled cucumbers and boiled potatoes separately.

Gulyas

Goulash

6 servings

2 pounds sirloin steak, cut into
　 1 inch cubes
1 teaspoon salt
　 Freshly ground black pepper
3 tablespoons butter
4 onions, coarsely chopped
2 cups beef broth or water
4 medium sized potatoes,
　 peeled and cubed
1 clove garlic, crushed
1 teaspoon caraway seeds
1 tablespoon paprika
2 green peppers, seeded and cut
　 into rings
4 medium sized tomatoes,
　 peeled, seeded and sliced

Season the beef with salt and pepper. Heat the butter and fry the onions until soft and golden. Add the beef and fry over high heat for 5 minutes until browned on all sides. Add the beef broth, cover and simmer for 1¼ hours. Add the potatoes, garlic and caraway seeds and sprinkle with paprika. Arrange the peppers and tomatoes on top. Cover and continue cooking for 25 minutes until the vegetables are tender. In Hungary, goulash is served with "scipethe," flake-formed pasta, for which wide noodles can be substituted.

Reisfleisch

Székely gulyas

The Hungarian word 'gulyás' means cow herder, and goulash, the dish prepared with meat, onions and paprika that has become famous throughout the world, has been for centuries the traditional meal of the cattlemen on the wide Hungarian plains. When the sun goes down and the cattle have been watered, a fire is built beside the whitewashed cabin of the cattlemen. Over the flames stands a tripod holding a heavy iron pot in which the 'gulyás' is cooked. This classical 'gulyás' is called 'bográcsgulyás', kettle goulash, and in most restaurants it is served from an iron pot at the table. This traditional goulash is more a kind of soup than a stew, and it is much thinner than the goulash eaten in most restaurants outside Hungary. The so-called goulash as we know it, with its thick brown sauce, is called 'pörkölt' in Hungary. As is the case with so many traditional dishes, there are any number of varieties. The cattlemen naturally use beef, but mutton can also be used, or even pork. If it is prepared with pork and sauerkraut, it becomes the famous 'Székelygulyás.' The cook in one famous restaurant in Budapest also adds green beans, and during the grape harvest wine is sometimes added to the goulash served to grapepickers.

In the summer the visitor can go to small outdoor eating places called 'guláscarda', or goulash inns. Three different kinds of goulash are served, spooned piping hot out of pots and eaten with brown bread and caraway seeds.

Pork with rice

6 servings

>   3 tablespoons butter
>   1 onion, finely chopped
>   1 clove garlic, crushed
>   2 pounds pork shoulder, cut
>   into ½ inch cubes
>   1 tablespoon paprika
>   ½ teaspoon salt
>   Freshly ground black pepper
>   5 cups beef broth
>   1½ cups rice
>   4 tablespoons heavy cream
>   12 thin strips pimiento

Heat the butter in a casserole and sauté the onions and garlic until softened. Add the pork and sauté until brown. Pour off the accumulated fat and add the paprika, salt, pepper and 2 cups broth. Cover and simmer 1 hour. Meanwhile, cook the rice in the remaining broth until all the liquid has been absorbed. Strain the pork and onions and reserve the cooking liquid. Combine the rice with the strained pork and onions and mold firmly into individual serving dishes. Stir the cream into the reserved cooking liquid and bring to a simmer. Pour a little of the sauce over each serving. Garnish with 2 strips of pimiento and serve immediately.

Pork goulash

6 servings

>   3 tablespoons butter
>   4 onions, sliced
>   1 teaspoon caraway seeds
>   1 clove garlic, crushed
>   1 tablespoon chopped fresh
>   dill or
>   1 teaspoon dried dill weed
>   ½ teaspoon salt
>   Freshly ground black pepper
>   2½ pounds shoulder of pork,
>   cut into 1 inch cubes
>   ½ cup water
>   1 tablespoon paprika
>   2 pounds sauerkraut
>   ½ cup sour cream

Heat the butter in a casserole and sauté the onions until golden brown. Stir in the caraway seeds, garlic, dill, salt and pepper. Arrange the pork on top of the onion mixture and pour in the water. Cover and simmer gently 30 minutes. Check occasionally to see if the mixture is sticking to the pan and add water, 1 tablespoon at a time, if necessary. Add the paprika and sauerkraut and combine thoroughly. Cover and cook over very low heat 1 hour or until the pork is tender. Remove from the heat and stir in the sour cream. Serve from the casserole with boiled potatoes.

Kümmelfleisch

Caraway goulash

4 servings

- 2 *pounds lean beef, cut into*
  ¾ inch cubes
- 1 *onion, quartered*
- ½ *teaspoon salt*
  Freshly ground black pepper
- 1 *teaspoon crushed caraway*
  seeds
- ½ *teaspoon paprika*
  Pinch of ground cloves
- 2 *teaspoons vinegar*
  Beef broth or water

Place the beef, onion, salt, pepper, caraway seeds, paprika, cloves and vinegar in a heavy casserole. Add beef broth or water to just cover the ingredients, bring to a boil and skim the broth. Reduce the heat, cover and simmer 2 hours until beef is tender. Serve with boiled potatoes or buttered noodles.

Koloszvári gulyas

Goulash Klausenburg style

6 servings

- 2 *tablespoons butter*
- 2 *pounds beef chuck or round,*
  cut into ¾ inch cubes
- 2 *onions, coarsely chopped*
- 1 *clove garlic, crushed*
- 1 *tablespoon paprika*
- ½ *teaspoon caraway seeds*
- ¼ *teaspoon marjoram*
- 1 *teaspoon salt*
  Freshly ground black pepper
- 1½ *cups beef broth or water*
- 4 *medium sized potatoes,*
  peeled and cubed
- 2 *green peppers, seeded and*
  cut into strips
- 4 *tomatoes, peeled, seeded and*
  sliced
- 4 *cups shredded white cabbage*

Heat the butter in a casserole. Add the beef and cook for 5 minutes until brown. Add the onions, garlic, paprika, caraway seeds, marjoram, salt, pepper and beef broth. Bring to a boil, reduce the heat and simmer, covered, for 1½ hours. Add the potatoes, peppers, tomatoes and cabbage and more water or broth if necessary. Cover and simmer for 25 minutes until the vegetables are tender.

Majoran tokany

Meat stew with sour cream

6 servings

- 6 *tablespoons butter*
- 3 *onions, chopped*
- 2 *pounds rib steak or sirloin*
  steak, cut into strips
- 1 *teaspoon salt*
  Freshly ground black pepper
- ½ *teaspoon marjoram*
- ¾ *cup white wine*
- ¾ *cup water*
- ½ *pound boiled ham, cut into*
  strips
- 1 *cup sour cream*

Heat the butter in a large skillet. Add the onions and fry 4 to 5 minutes until golden. Add the beef and season with salt, pepper and marjoram. Sauté 3 to 4 minutes. Add the wine and water, bring to a boil and simmer, covered, for 1 hour. Add the ham and simmer for 30 minutes. Stir in the sour cream. Heat but do not boil. Serve with noodles.

Krautfleisch

Pork and cabbage stew

6 servings

- 2 *pounds pork shoulder, cut*
  into squares
- 1 *teaspoon salt*
  Freshly ground black pepper
- 6 *tablespoons butter*
- 2 *onions, chopped*
- 1 *clove garlic, crushed*
- 1 *tablespoon paprika*
- ½ *tablespoon wine vinegar*
- 1 *head white cabbage, shredded*
- 2 *cups chicken broth*
- 6 *tablespoons heavy cream,*
  lightly beaten
- 1 *tablespoon chopped chives*

Season the pork with salt and pepper. Heat 3 tablespoons of the butter in a skillet and brown the pork on all sides. Remove from the pan. Heat the remaining butter and fry the onions with the garlic until golden. Add the paprika and wine vinegar and simmer for 1 minute, stirring constantly. Place the pork, onion mixture and cabbage in a casserole. Add the chicken broth and simmer gently for 1 hour. Transfer to a heated serving dish. Spoon the cream into the center of the dish and garnish with chives. Serve with boiled potatoes.

Gespickte Kalbsvögerl

Tafelspitz

Larded veal birds

6 servings

- 2 pounds veal, cut from the leg
  into 6 equal sized portions
- 1 teaspoon salt
  Freshly ground black pepper
- 6 slices bacon
- 3 tablespoons butter
- 1 onion, finely chopped
- 1 tablespoon tomato paste
- 1 cup chicken broth or water
- 1 tablespoon cornstarch
- ½ cup dry white wine
- 1 teaspoon lemon juice

Season the veal with salt and
pepper. Pound each piece until
very thin and roll up tightly.
Wrap a strip of bacon around
each roll and secure with string.
Heat the butter in a frying pan,
add the onion and cook until
soft and golden. Add the veal
rolls and fry 5 to 10 minutes.
Reduce heat and stir in tomato
paste and chicken broth. Cover
and simmer gently for 1 hour.
Remove veal from pan, discard
strings and keep warm. Combine
cornstarch and wine and add to
pan juices. Continue cooking for
3 to 5 minutes until sauce has
thickened. Add lemon juice and
pour sauce over veal rolls. Serve
with rice and mushrooms.

Boiled beef

6 servings

- 6 cups water
- 2 teaspoons salt
- 2 onions
- 2 carrots
- 3 sprigs parsley
- 6 peppercorns, crushed
- 1 bay leaf
- 3 pounds top or bottom round
  of beef
- 3 tablespoons chopped chives
- 1½ cups mayonnaise

Place the water, salt, onions,
carrots, parsley, peppercorns
and bay leaf in a saucepan and
bring to a boil. Add the beef,
cover and simmer for 1½ to 2
hours. Remove the beef from
the saucepan and cut into slices
½ inch thick. Arrange the beef
on a heated serving dish and
pour over 1 cup of the beef broth.
Stir the chopped chives into the
mayonnaise and serve separately
as a sauce. Serve with boiled
potatoes and applesauce.

Pork is delicious with sauerkraut, but in early summer, when the tender garden beans are ready, no one in Austria hesitates to substitute them for the more traditional accompaniment.

Bosnian black pot

Schweinekotelett auf Sauerkraut

Pork chops with sauerkraut

4 servings

　4　tablespoons butter
　2　onions, chopped
1½　pounds sauerkraut
　½　cup beef broth
　½　cup red wine
　1　green pepper, seeded
　　　and chopped
　2　bay leaves
　2　teaspoons paprika
　⅛　teaspoon white pepper
　4　pork chops
　½　teaspoon salt
　　　Freshly ground black pepper

Heat 2 tablespoons butter in a casserole and sauté the onions until golden brown. Add the sauerkraut and broth and simmer 30 minutes. Add the wine, green pepper, bay leaves, paprika and white pepper and simmer 30 minutes more. Meanwhile, heat the remaining butter in a skillet. Sprinkle the pork chops with salt and pepper and sauté over medium heat about 15 minutes on each side until golden brown and done. Arrange the chops on top of the sauerkraut in the casserole. Serve with broiled tomatoes, and corn on the cob or boiled potatoes.

Gekochter Schweinschlegel

Boiled fresh ham

8 servings

    1 fresh ham
    2 onions, sliced
    2 carrots, sliced
    1 parsnip, cubed
    1 small turnip, cubed
    1 clove garlic, crushed
1½ teaspoons salt
    8 peppercorns, crushed
 ¼ teaspoon allspice
    6 tomatoes, peeled and
       quartered
 ½ teaspoon salt
1½ cups dry white wine

Place the ham in a pan. Add
boiling water to cover and let
stand for 3 minutes. Pour off the
water. Add more water to cover,
bring to a boil and skim off the
scum that rises to the surface.
Add the onions, carrots,
parsnip, turnip, garlic and
seasonings. Bring to a boil,
reduce the heat and simmer
gently for 3 to 3½ hours or until
the ham is tender (30 minutes to
the pound). Place the tomatoes
in a pan. Sprinkle with salt and
add the white wine. Bring to a
boil, reduce the heat and simmer,
stirring occasionally, until
reduced to a thick sauce. Force
through a strainer and keep
warm. Pour the liquid off the
ham when cooked and reserve
for use in soups. Transfer the
ham and vegetables to a
serving dish, pour over the
tomato sauce and serve.

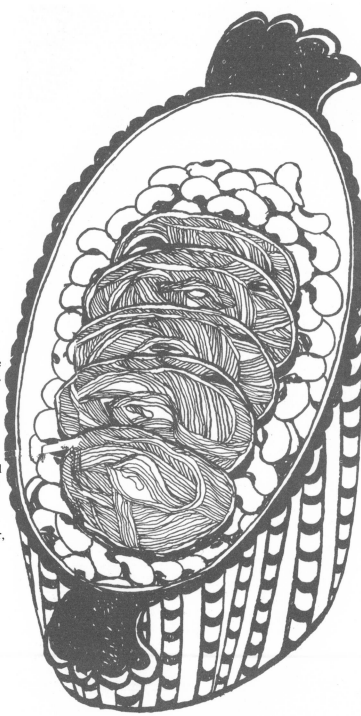

Bosnische schwarze Pfanne

Bosnian black pot

6 to 8 servings

    4 pounds pork belly (fresh
       bacon), with rind
    2 tablespoons coarse salt
    1 to 2 cups water
 ¼ pound bacon, diced
    1 onion, chopped
    1 cup beef broth
    2 green peppers, seeded and
       cut into strips
    2 (16 ounce) cans broad
       beans, drained
 ½ teaspoon salt
       Freshly ground black pepper
 ¼ teaspoon marjoram
    1 cup heavy cream
    2 tablespoons finely chopped
       parsley

Make diamond shaped incisions
in the pork rind and rub the
rind with coarse salt. Pour
water to a 1 inch depth into a
roasting pan and add the pork,
rind side down. Roast in a
325° oven 1 hour. Turn and
roast 1 hour more until the
rind is crisp and brown.
Meanwhile, fry the bacon until
the fat is rendered. Add the
onion and fry until the bacon
is crisp and the onion is golden
brown. Add broth and green
peppers and simmer 15 minutes.
Add the beans, salt, pepper
and marjoram and transfer
to a casserole. Stir in the cream
and parsley and simmer 10 to
15 minutes. Slice the meat and
arrange on top of the beans.

Eingemachtes Kalbsfleisch

Veal ragout

4 servings

1½ *pounds veal, cut into 1½ inch cubes*
1 *teaspoon salt*
  Freshly ground black pepper
3 *tablespoons butter*
1 *onion, chopped*
2 *tablespoons flour*
1½ *cups chicken broth or water*
1 *cup mushrooms, sliced*
4 *tablespoons green peas*
1 *tablespoon chopped parsley*
1 *egg yolk*
2 *tablespoons milk*
1 *teaspoon lemon juice*

Season the veal with salt and pepper. Heat the butter and brown the meat over high heat for 5 minutes. Remove the veal from the pan. Add the onion to the butter and fry until soft and golden. Stir in the flour and add the chicken broth gradually, stirring constantly until the sauce is thickened. Add the veal and mushrooms. Bring to a boil and simmer gently for 45 minutes. Add water if the sauce becomes too thick. Add the peas and parsley and cook for 10 minutes. Before serving, stir in the egg yolk combined with the milk and lemon juice. Heat thoroughly and serve.

Teleci gulas

Veal stew

4 servings

4 *tablespoons butter*
1¾ *pounds stewing veal, cubed*
1 *teaspoon salt*
  Freshly ground black pepper
2 *teaspoons caraway seeds, crushed*
½ *onion, chopped*
1 *carrot, diced*
2 *cups chicken broth*
2 *tablespoons flour*
1 *tablespoon chopped parsley*

Heat the butter in a saucepan. Add the veal and fry until lightly browned on all sides. Season with salt, pepper and caraway seeds. Reduce the heat, cover and continue cooking for 7 to 8 minutes. Add the diced vegetables and fry for another 2 minutes, stirring occasionally. Add ½ of the broth, bring to a boil. Reduce the heat, cover and simmer for 1 hour or until the meat is tender. Remove the lid, increase the heat and allow almost all the broth to evaporate. Stir in the flour and add the parsley and remaining broth. Bring to a boil and simmer for another 10 minutes.

Pieds de porc

Pork hocks Geneva style

4 to 6 servings

3 *tablespoons oil*
6 *fresh pork hocks*
½ *teaspoon salt*
  Freshly ground black pepper
2 *carrots, chopped*
2 *large onions, chopped*
2 *cloves garlic, crushed*
1 *cup white wine*
4 *tomatoes, peeled, seeded, drained and chopped*
  White part of 1 leek, chopped
1 *cup beef broth*
¼ *teaspoon dried rosemary*
¼ *teaspoon dried tarragon*
1½ *teaspoons mild (Dijon type) mustard*
2 *tablespoons fine dry breadcrumbs*
1 *tablespoon butter*
½ *pound mushrooms, chopped*
1½ *tablespoons cornstarch*
¼ *cup Madeira*

Heat the oil in a large pan and fry the pork hocks 10 to 15 minutes until lightly browned. Season with salt and pepper, remove from the pan and keep warm. In the remaining oil, fry the carrots, onions and garlic until soft. Add the wine, tomatoes, leek, beef broth, rosemary and tarragon. Return the pork to the pan, cover and simmer for 3 hours. Remove the pork, drain and cut the meat from the bones. Reserve the cooking liquid. Place the meat in a buttered casserole, spread with mustard and sprinkle with breadcrumbs. Add the drained vegetables and bake in a preheated 400° oven for 20 minutes. (It will not dry out.) Heat 1 tablespoon butter in a frying pan and fry the mushrooms until lightly browned. Add 2 cups of the reserved cooking liquid. Dissolve the cornstarch in the Madeira and stir into the sauce. Simmer 2 minutes until thickened. Serve the sauce separately.

Tender veal tongue is one of the pride and joys of Viennese cooking. Perhaps this has something to do with the white wine grown on the hills around Vienna that tastes so good with it.

Kalbszunge

Veal tongue

4 servings

1   (2 pound) veal tongue
1   teaspoon salt
1   carrot, sliced
1   onion, quartered
1   sprig parsley
1   bay leaf
1   clove
4   peppercorns, crushed
1   package frozen French cut green beans, cooked and chopped
1   package frozen asparagus tips, cooked
2   oranges, peeled and thinly sliced
6   tablespoons cranberry jelly

Soak the tongue in cold water 2 to 3 hours. Rinse thoroughly and sprinkle with salt. Place the tongue in a large casserole with the carrot, onion, parsley, bay leaf, clove and peppercorns and add water to cover. Bring to a boil, lower the heat and simmer, covered, 2½ hours until the tongue is tender. Drain the tongue, remove the skin and cut into ½ inch thick slices. Arrange the slices on a warm serving dish alternately with the green beans and asparagus tips. Surround with orange slices and top the orange slices with a spoonful of cranberry jelly. Serve with mashed potatoes.

Fermented black beans add an interesting flavor to beef.

Beef balls are first rolled in shiny white glutinous rice and then steamed to savory tenderness.

Stir fried beef in black bean sauce

4 American servings
6 Chinese servings

½ *pound flank steak, sirloin*
 steak or top round beef
 1 *tablespoon fermented black*
 beans
 2 *small red peppers*
 1 *small onion*
 3 *tablespoons oil*
 1 *clove garlic, crushed*
 2 *thin slices fresh ginger root*
 1 *tablespoon sherry*
 1 *tablespoon cornstarch*
½ *cup chicken broth*

Slice beef across the grain in
⅛ inch thick slices about 2
inches square. Soak fermented
black beans in water for about
10 minutes. Drain and mash with
the back of a spoon. Remove
membranes and seeds from
peppers and cut into 2 inch long
and ¼ inch wide strips. Cut the
strips into 1 inch diamonds.
Cut onion in the same way. Heat
2 tablespoons of oil in a wok
or large skillet and, when hot,
add garlic and ginger root.
Stir fry for 1 minute. Remove
garlic. Add beef slices and stir
fry for about 2 minutes. Remove
from pan and keep warm. Add
remaining oil and heat until hot.
Add pepper and stir fry for
about 2 minutes. Remove from
pan and add to the beef. Add
black beans to the pan and stir
for about ½ minute. Mix sherry
and cornstarch in a bowl until
well blended. Pour chicken broth
into the pan and heat quickly
until boiling. Return beef and
peppers and reheat. Stir in
cornstarch mixture until
thickened.

Steamed beef balls

4 American servings
6 Chinese servings

    1 cup uncooked long grain rice
    1 pound top round beef
    1 scallion, minced
    1 teaspoon finely minced fresh
       ginger root
    2 water chestnuts, minced
       (optional)
    1 egg, lightly beaten
    1 tablespoon soy sauce
    ½ tablespoon sherry
    ½ teaspoon salt
    ½ teaspoon sugar

Place the rice in a bowl, add
water to cover and soak for
about 1 to 1½ hours. Drain well
and spread out on a large plate
or rolling board. Remove all fat
and trimmings from beef and
mince the beef finely. Add
scallion, ginger root, water
chestnuts, egg, soy sauce, sherry,
salt and sugar and mix until
well blended. Form the mixture
into balls about 1½ inches in
diameter. Roll each ball in rice
until completely covered. Place
balls on a shallow, heatproof
dish, taking care that they are
½ inch or more apart from each
other. Place in a steamer and
steam for about ½ hour. Serve
immediately. They may be
dipped in soy sauce.

Stir fried beef and bean sprouts

4 American servings
8 Chinese servings

    ½ pound flank steak, sirloin
       steak or top rump of beef
    1 green pepper
    1 onion
    2 cups bean sprouts
    ½ tablespoon soy sauce
    1½ tablespoons sherry
    1 tablespoon cornstarch
    4 tablespoons oil
    1 clove garlic, crushed
    2 thin slices fresh ginger root,
       minced
    ¼ teaspoon salt
    3 to 4 tablespoons chicken
       broth

Slice the beef across the grain
into ⅛-inch thick slices and cut
these slices into 2 inch long and
1-inch wide strips. Remove
membrane and seeds from green
pepper and cut into strips,
2-inches long and ¼-inch wide.
Halve the onion lengthwise
and then cut into long, thin
strips. If fresh bean sprouts are
used, blanch them in boiling
water for 30 seconds. Rinse
under cold running water and
drain. If canned bean sprouts
are used, put them in ice water
for ½ hour to restore their
crispness and drain. In a bowl,
mix soy sauce, sherry and
cornstarch until well blended.
Add the beef, toss to coat and
leave for about 10 minutes.
Heat half of the oil in a wok or
large skillet and, when hot, add
the beef. Stir fry for about
2 minutes, then remove from pan
and keep warm. Add remaining
oil and heat. Put garlic, ginger
root and salt into the pan and

stir fry for about 1 minute.
Remove garlic. Add pepper and
onion and stir fry for about
1 minute. Add bean sprouts and
stir fry for 1 more minute.
Pour in the chicken broth and
heat until boiling. Return the
beef and stir fry for 30 seconds
to reheat. Serve immediately.

Braised pork

4 American servings
8 Chinese servings

  2 pounds boneless fat pork
    (fresh ham or shoulder),
    in 1 piece
  2 tablespoons oil
  2 slices fresh ginger root,
    minced
  1 clove garlic, crushed
  2 scallions, cut diagonally
    into 1 inch pieces
  6 tablespoons soy sauce
  3 tablespoons sherry
  3 cups boiling water
1½ tablespoons brown sugar

Heat oil in a heavy casserole. Brown pork on all sides. Add ginger root, garlic, and scallions and cook 1 minute. Add soy sauce, 2 tablespoons sherry and water and bring to a simmer. Reduce heat, cover the pan and simmer 45 minutes, turning the meat every 10 minutes. Add the remaining sherry and the brown sugar and cook 45 minutes to 1 hour, turning the meat every 20 minutes. Slice and serve moistened with a little of the cooking liquid.

Red simmered pork

6 American servings
10 Chinese servings

  ½ pound dried Chinese squid,
    cleaned (optional)
  ¼ cup Chinese lily buds
    (optional)
  3 pounds pork, preferably butt
2½ to 3 cups water
  1 clove garlic, minced
  3 slices fresh ginger root,
    minced
  6 tablespoons soy sauce
  1 tablespoon sherry
  1 teaspoon salt
  3 teaspoons brown sugar

If both squid and lily buds are available, they give this dish a very authentic character. On the other hand, the pork will taste excellent on its own. Soak squid in warm water. Cut the body in half lengthwise. Score the inside with a sharp knife in a small diamond pattern. Soak the lily buds in warm water for about 1 hour. Rinse under cold water and drain. Remove tough parts. Cut pork into 1 to 1½ inch cubes. Place in a heavy pan or casserole, add the water and bring to a boil over high heat. Add garlic, ginger root, soy sauce, sherry and salt. Bring to a boil again. Reduce the heat, cover and simmer for about ½ hour. Add the squid, cover and simmer 40 minutes more. Add lily buds and sugar. Cover and simmer for another 30 to 40 minutes.

Tung po pork

4 American servings
8 Chinese servings

  2 pounds pork loin with skin
  2 tablespoons salt
  4 cups water
  2 scallions, cut into 1 inch
    pieces
  4 tablespoons soy sauce
  2 tablespoons sherry
  1 thin slice fresh ginger root,
    minced
  1 tablespoon sugar
  1 cup shredded Chinese
    cabbage
  1 tablespoon cornstarch
    dissolved in
  3 tablespoons water

Cut pork in 3 inch squares and rub with salt. Let stand 1 hour. Rinse pork under cold running water, place in a heavy pan with the 4 cups water and bring to a boil. Remove the pork with a slotted spoon and rinse under cold running water. Skim the scum from the water and return the pork to the pan. Cover and simmer ½ hour. Add scallions, soy sauce, sherry and ginger root. Simmer, covered, 1½ hours. Remove the pork from the broth and place, skin side down, in a shallow heatproof dish. Sprinkle with sugar, place in a steamer and steam 45 minutes. Meanwhile add the cabbage to the broth and simmer 20 minutes. With a slotted spoon, transfer cabbage to a serving plate. Top with the pork, skin side up. Add the dissolved cornstarch to the simmering broth and stir until thickened slightly. Pour a few spoonfuls of the sauce over the pork and serve.

Deep fried pork balls

4 to 6 American servings
4 to 6 Chinese servings

1½ pounds pork (loin, butt or
    shoulder) with some fat,
    minced
  1 slice fresh ginger root,
    minced
  3 water chestnuts, minced
  ½ medium onion, minced
  1 teaspoon sugar
  1 tablespoon soy sauce
  2 teaspoons sherry
2½ tablespoons cornstarch
  1 egg
    Oil for deep frying
    Shredded lettuce

Combine the minced pork, ginger, water chestnuts and onion. Place these ingredients in a bowl and mix thoroughly with sugar, soy sauce, sherry, cornstarch and egg. Form the mixture into 10 to 15 balls and place balls on a plate. Chill the balls until ready to fry. Heat the oil for deep frying. Add a few balls at a time. Fry for about 3 minutes. Remove and drain on paper towels. Continue frying remaining pork balls a few at a time. Reheat the oil until it is very hot. Deep fry all the balls together a second time for about 2 minutes until lightly browned and crisp. Drain and serve on a bed of shredded lettuce. Serve plain or with a sweet sour sauce

Sweet sour pork

Sweet sour pork hardly needs any recommendation.

4 American servings
8 Chinese servings

1 recipe sweet sour sauce

1 pound lean pork
¼ teaspoon salt
¼ teaspoon sugar
1 tablespoon soy sauce
2 tablespoons sherry
⅛ teaspoon freshly ground
   black pepper
1 small onion
1 green pepper
2 slices canned pineapple
2 carrots, cut diagonally into
   1 inch pieces
1 egg
2 tablespoons flour

½ teaspoon salt
1 tablespoon water
2 tablespoons oil
2 thin slices fresh ginger root,
   minced
1 clove garlic, crushed
   Oil for deep frying

Combine ingredients for sweet sour sauce in an enamelled saucepan. Mix cornstarch and water for the sauce but do not add it yet. Cut the pork in pieces 1 to 1½ inches square and ¾ inch thick. Mix salt, sugar, soy sauce, sherry and pepper. Add pork, toss to coat and marinate for about 20 minutes, turning meat twice.

Cut the onion in half lengthwise and then cut into 1 to 1½ inch long and ¾ inch wide pieces. Remove membrane and seeds from pepper, cut in 1 inch wide strips and then in 1 to 1½ inch diamond shapes diagonally. Cut the pineapple rings into 1 inch pieces. Bring plenty of salted water to a boil, add the carrots and parboil for 3 to 4 minutes. Rinse under cold running water and drain. Combine egg, flour, salt and water to make a batter. Heat 2 tablespoons of oil in a wok or other pan. Add ginger and garlic and stir fry for 30 seconds. Discard garlic. Add vegetables and stir fry for about

2½ minutes. Meanwhile, heat the sweet sour sauce in a saucepan. Add sauce to the vegetables and stir in cornstarch mixture to thicken. Remove from heat and keep warm. Heat the oil for deep frying. Coat pork pieces lightly with the batter. Drop into the hot oil one by one and deep fry for about 3½ minutes or until golden brown. Drain, add to the sauce and stir to coat. Serve immediately.

Stir fried pork, nuts and vegetables

3 American servings
6 Chinese servings

  3 dried Chinese mushrooms
½ pound lean pork (tenderloin, butt or shoulder)
½ cup bamboo, sliced
  6 water chestnuts
  2 scallions
  4 fresh mushrooms
  4 tablespoons oil
½ teaspoon salt
  1 clove garlic, crushed
  2 thin slices fresh ginger root
½ cup bean sprouts
½ teaspoon salt
  1 tablespoon sherry
½ cup chicken or meat broth
  1 tablespoon soy sauce
  1 tablespoon cornstarch dissolved in
  3 tablespoons water

Soak the dried mushrooms in hot water for about 30 minutes. Squeeze dry, remove stalks and cut caps in ¼ to ½ inch wide strips. Cut the pork across the grain into ⅛ inch thick slices. Cut the bamboo in ⅛ to ¼ inch slices and the water chestnuts cut in ¼ inch thick slices. Cut the scallions in 1 inch long pieces diagonally. Cut mushrooms in ¼ inch thick slices. Heat 2 tablespoons oil in a wok or other pan. Add the salt and stir fry for 30 seconds. Add the garlic and ginger and stir fry for about 45 seconds or until lightly browned. Remove garlic from pan. Add bamboo, water chestnuts, mushrooms and Chinese mushrooms and stir fry for 1 minute. Add bean sprouts and stir for another 30 to 45 seconds. Remove from the pan.

Add remaining oil and heat. Add salt and scallions and stir fry for 30 seconds. Add the pork and stir fry for about 2½ minutes. Stir in sherry and stir fry to blend. Return vegetables to the pan, add broth and soy sauce and bring quickly to a boil. Reduce heat, cover and simmer for about 2 minutes or until tender. Stir in the cornstarch mixture to thicken and serve immediately.

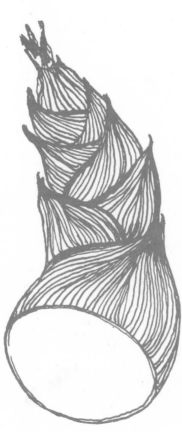

Stir fried pork and eggplant

4 American servings
8 Chinese servings

  1 large eggplant
  3 tablespoons salt
  1 tablespoon sherry
½ teaspoon salt
  2 teaspoons cornstarch
½ pound lean pork, cut diagonally across the grain into ⅛ inch slices
  3 tablespoons oil
¼ cup chicken broth
  2 tablespoons soy sauce
¼ teaspoon sugar
  2 cloves garlic, crushed
  1 thin slice fresh ginger root, minced
  4 scallions, cut diagonally into 1 inch pieces
  3 firm ripe tomatoes, peeled, seeded and cut into ½ inch slices

Remove the leaves from the eggplant and cut a ½ inch slice off both ends. Quarter the eggplant lengthwise, then cut into ½ inch slices. Sprinkle both sides of the pieces with salt and let stand 20 minutes to release the bitter juices. Rinse under cold running water and dry on paper towels. Combine the sherry, ½ teaspoon salt and cornstarch. Toss the pork strips in this mixture to coat them evenly. Heat half of the oil in a wok over high heat. Add the eggplant and stir fry 2 minutes. Add the broth, soy sauce and sugar. Reduce the heat a little, cover and cook 10 minutes. Remove eggplant and liquid from the pan. Wipe the wok dry with paper towels. Add remaining oil to the wok and

heat until very hot. Add garlic and ginger root and stir fry 1 minute. Discard garlic. Add pork and stir fry 1 minute. Add scallions and stir fry 2 minutes. Add tomatoes and stir fry ½ minute. Finally, return eggplant with its cooking liquid to the wok and stir about 1 minute. Transfer to a serving dish and serve immediately.

The meats used in Chinese cookery are pork, beef and lamb. Veal is almost never used, and lamb is rarely served except in the North. In the course of time the Chinese have developed numerous ways of preparing pork. It can be steamed, braised, red simmered, clear simmered stir fried, barbequed, roasted and deep fried, and it combines well with a vast number of other ingredients. Butt, shoulder and loin are good choices for almost any of these ways of preparing pork. Other parts of the pig including the feet, kidneys, pork belly, etc. are also used extensively in Chinese cooking. The color of the meat should be a bright pink.

Beef has historically always been scarce because cattle themselves are not raised extensively, and the small number of cattle that are found, are used to work on the fields. Beef is also prepared in many ways in Chinese cooking. Top round steak, flank steak, sirloin steak and tenderloin are the cuts most generally used. Flank steak is preferred because of its easily recognizable muscular structure. The color of the beef should be a beautiful red, and all the fat is trimmed away before it is cooked or served. Pork is done when all its pink color has gone and beef is done when there is no longer any trace of red and the meat is slightly browned. These color changes are important to watch for, especially in stir fried dishes.

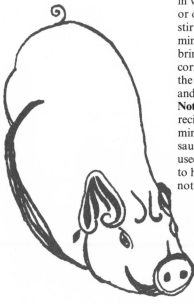

Crisp roast belly of pork and bean curd

6 American servings
10 Chinese servings

1 recipe roast belly of pork

2 cakes bean curd
2 to 3 tablespoons soy sauce
½ cup chicken broth
½ teaspoon salt
¼ teaspoon sugar
1 tablespoon cornstarch
2 tablespoons water
1½ tablespoons oil
Few sprigs parsley

Prepare roast belly of pork as directed in previous recipe. Cut the pork into 1 to 1½ inch cubes. Cut bean curd cakes in 1½ inch long and ½ inch thick slices. Combine soy sauce, broth, salt and sugar in a saucepan and heat until salt and sugar are dissolved. Dissolve cornstarch in water. Heat the oil in a wok or other pan, add bean curd and stir fry for about 1 to 1½ minutes. Add soy sauce mixture, bring to the boil and stir in cornstarch to thicken. Stir in the pork. Decorate with parsley and serve.

Note: The bean curd in this recipe may be deep fried for 1½ minutes and added with the soy sauce mixture. If this method is used, just allow the bean curd to heat through again but do not stir fry.

Crisp roast belly of pork

6 American servings
8 Chinese servings

2 pounds fresh belly of pork (fresh bacon)
1 teaspoon salt
1 tablespoon sugar or brown sugar
3 tablespoons soy sauce
1 tablespoon hoisin sauce
1 thin slice fresh ginger root, minced
1 small bunch watercress
6 to 8 onion brushes

Prick the skin side of the pork belly with the point of a sharp knife and rub salt into the skin. Mix sugar, soy sauce, hoisin sauce and ginger and rub into the meat side. Place the meat, skin side up, on a rack under a preheated broiler and broil for 15 to 20 minutes or until skin is crisp and brown. Fill a pan with boiling water and place on the bottom of the oven. Place the broiler pan in the middle of the oven and roast the pork in a medium hot oven (350 to 375°) for about 1 hour or until done. Let cool to room temperature. Cut the pork into 1 inch cubes in such a way that every piece of meat has a piece of the skin. Place on a serving dish, surround with watercress and onion brushes and serve.

Szechuan style twice cooked pork

4 American servings
8 Chinese servings

  *1 pound fresh belly of pork
     (fresh bacon)*
1½ quarts water
  2 tablespoons oil
  ¼ teaspoon salt
  1 clove garlic, crushed
  *2 thin slices fresh ginger root,
     minced*
  *1 green pepper, seeded and cut
     into thin strips*
  *2 scallions, cut into ½ inch
     pieces*
  *1 tablespoon Chinese canned
     brown bean sauce, mashed*
  ½ teaspoon sugar
  1 tablespoon sherry
  *1 teaspoon hoisin sauce
     combined with*
  1 teaspoon water
  *⅛ teaspoon cayenne pepper,
     combined with*
  1 teaspoon oil

Leave pork whole. Bring the
water to a boil and add pork.
Reduce heat, cover and simmer
for about 45 minutes to 1 hour.
Drain pork and cut into ¹⁄₁₆ to
⅛ inch thick slices.
Heat oil in wok or other pan.
Add salt, garlic and ginger root
and stir fry for 30 seconds. Add
pepper and scallions and stir fry
for 30 seconds. Add brown bean
sauce and stir fry for 1 more
minute. Add pork, sugar and
sherry and stir fry for 1½
minutes. Stir in hoisin sauce and
stir fry for another 1 to 1½
minutes. Stir in pepper-oil
mixture and serve.
Note: Originally, Szechuan
pepper oil was used and
sprinkled on just before serving.

Red pepper and oil are used as
substitutes here. Instead, a fresh
red chili-pepper, minced, can be
added with the green pepper.

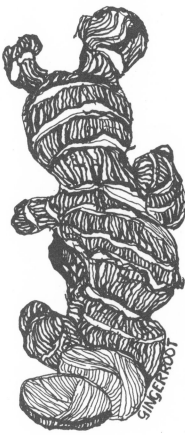

Pork balls and broccoli

2 American servings
4 Chinese servings

  *1 recipe for deep fried pork
     balls*
  1 pound fresh broccoli
  2 tablespoons oil
  ½ teaspoon salt
  1 clove garlic, peeled
  1 thin slice ginger root
  ½ cup chicken broth
  1 teaspoon soy sauce
  ½ teaspoon sugar
  2 teaspoons cornstarch
  1 tablespoon water

Prepare pork balls according to
the directions in the recipe, but
deep fry for only 1 minute for
the second frying. Cut flowerets
from the broccoli. Discard lower
half of tough stems. Cut wide
stems in half lengthwise and
then cut diagonally into 2 inch
pieces. Parboil broccoli flowers
and stems in plenty of boiling
salted water for 4 minutes.
Drain and rinse under cold
running water until completely
cooled. Heat the oil in a wok or
skillet. Add salt and stir for 30
seconds. Add peeled clove of
garlic and ginger root. Stir fry
for 1 minute. Discard garlic and
ginger root. Add broccoli and
stir fry for 1 minute. Add pork
balls and stir fry for 1 minute.
Add chicken broth, soy sauce
and sugar and cook to heat
through. Stir in cornstarch
dissolved in cold water. Serve
immediately.

Stir fried pork kidneys

4 American servings
6 Chinese servings

  2 pork or veal kidneys
  *1 cup fresh peas, shelled (or
     equal quantity canned peas)*
  2 tablespoons oil
  *4 thin slices fresh ginger root,
     shredded*
  *4 whole scallions, cut in 1 inch
     pieces*
  4 tablespoons soy sauce
  2 tablespoons sherry
  ½ teaspoon sugar
  *3 tablespoons chicken or meat
     broth*
  *2 teaspoons cornstarch
     dissolved in*
1½ tablespoons water

Cut the kidneys in half and
remove fat and veins. Bring
plenty of salted water to the boil.
Drop in the kidneys and parboil
for 7 to 8 minutes. Rinse under
cold running water and drain or
wipe dry on paper towels. Cut
into ¼ inch thick slices. Place
fresh peas in a bowl and pour
boiling water over them. Leave
for 5 minutes and drain. Heat
2 tablespoons of the oil in a wok
or other pan. Add ginger root
and stir fry for 30 seconds.
Add kidneys and scallions and
stir fry for 1 minute. Stir in soy
sauce, sherry and sugar and stir
fry until sugar is dissolved. Add
peas and broth and bring to a
boil. Reduce heat a little, cover
and cook for 4 to 5 minutes.
Stir in cornstarch mixture to
thicken and serve. If canned peas
are used, add them only at the
last minute and stir to heat
through.

Collared beef

Rollade

Collared beef

8 servings

2 pounds sirloin steak in
  1 piece
1 teaspoon salt
  Freshly ground black pepper
1 pound filet mignon steak in
  1 piece
4 tablespoons butter
½ teaspoon thyme
1 onion, finely chopped
1 bay leaf
1 cup milk

Have the sirloin steak flattened
to a thickness of ½ inch. Rub
the meat with salt and pepper.
Place the filet mignon steak over
the sirloin steak, roll up and tie
in several places. Heat the butter
in a heavy casserole until very
hot. Brown the meat quickly on
all sides over high heat. Lower
the heat and add thyme, onion
and bay leaf. Cover the pan
and simmer for 1½ hours,
turning occasionally. Add a bit
of butter now and then if the
meat tends to stick. Remove the
meat from the pan and cool
slightly before slicing. Remove
the bay leaf and add the milk,
stirring up the brown bits
clinging to the bottom of the
pan. Serve the sliced rollade on
a warm platter and pass the
sauce separately. Serve mashed
potatoes and fresh vegetables
with this dish.

Slavinken

Ground pork rolls

4 servings

2 slices day-old bread,
  crusts removed
¼ cup milk
1 pound ground pork or
  sausage meat
½ teaspoon salt
  Freshly ground black pepper
  Dash of nutmeg
½ onion, finely chopped
8 thin slices lean bacon
2 tablespoons butter
½ cup milk

Crumble the bread and soak
in ¼ cup milk. Squeeze bread
as dry as possible and combine
with ground pork or sausage
meat, salt, pepper, nutmeg and
onion. Knead mixture until
well blended. Form 4 cylinders,
3″ long and wrap 2 slices
bacon around each cylinder
cross-wise. Tie at intervals with
thread to secure the bacon.
Heat butter in a frying pan and
fry the cylinders over medium
heat 8 minutes. Turn and fry
another 8 minutes. Remove the
meat from the pan and keep
warm. Pour out the accumulated
fat. Add the milk to the pan
and cook over high heat
scraping up the brown bits
clinging to the bottom. Serve
the pork rolls with mashed
potatoes and a salad and pass
the milk gravy separately.

Pork chops with apricots

Ground pork rolls are called 'slavinken' in Dutch. The word literally means 'salad birds'

because the small rolls suggest the form of a small roasted bird and are eaten in the fall with a tender, fresh lettuce salad.

Varkenslapjes met abrikozen

Pork chops with apricots

4 servings

- 4 thick pork chops
- ¼ teaspoon powdered ginger
- 1 teaspoon salt
  Freshly ground black pepper
- 2 tablespoons butter
- 2 small onions, finely chopped
- 1 teaspoon tomato paste
- ½ cup red wine
- 8 canned apricot halves
- 3 tablespoons fine dry breadcrumbs
- 1 tablespoon butter

Season the chops with ginger, salt and pepper. Fry the chops in the butter over high heat until evenly browned. Place the chops in an ovenproof dish and surround with the chopped onions. Discard the fat from the frying pan and add the tomato paste and wine. Pour this mixture over the pork chops. Cover with apricot halves, sprinkle with breadcrumbs and dot with butter. Cook in a preheated 325° oven for 45 minutes. Serve with rice and green beans.

Kalfstong met zure saus

Veal tongue with sour sauce

6 servings

 1 veal tongue (about 3 pounds)
 1 teaspoon salt
 1 carrot, peeled and sliced
 1 onion, sliced
   Leafy tops from 1 bunch
   celery
 1 sprig parsley
 ¼ teaspoon mace
 4 peppercorns, crushed
 1 clove
 1 bay leaf

For the sauce:
 4 tablespoons butter
 4 tablespoons flour
 2 cups cooking liquid
 2 eggs
 3 tablespoons wine vinegar

Soak the tongue in cold water for several hours. Rinse the tongue under cold running water and rub lightly with salt. Place in a pan with water to cover and add the vegetables, herbs and spices. Bring to a boil and cook over low heat for about 3 hours or until tender. Remove the tongue from the pan and remove the skin. Strain the cooking liquid and reserve 2 cups for the sauce. Keep the tongue warm in the remaining cooking liquid. Melt half of the butter, stir in the flour, and add the cooking liquid, stirring constantly until a smooth sauce is formed. Combine the eggs with a little of the warm sauce and add this mixture to the sauce, stirring constantly. Then, over very low heat, add the remaining butter and vinegar stirring constantly. Do not allow the sauce to boil after the eggs are added. Slice the tongue, arrange on a warm dish and serve lima beans and the sauce separately.

Filet de porc à l'escavèche

Marinated fillet of pork

6 servings

For the marinade:
 ¾ cup white wine
 ¾ cup vinegar
 1 teaspoon thyme
 2 bay leaves
 1 clove garlic, crushed
 ½ teaspoon dried tarragon
 6 juniper berries, crushed

 2 pounds fillet of pork, 1 piece
 2 tablespoons oil
 2 medium sized carrots,
   peeled and sliced
 1 medium sized onion, sliced
 1 stalk celery, sliced
 1 sweet red or green pepper,
   seeded and cut into strips
 1 tablespoon chopped parsley
 1 pound tomatoes, peeled,
   seeded and sliced
 2 cloves garlic, crushed
 1 teaspoon salt
   Freshly ground black pepper
 2 tablespoons butter

Combine marinade ingredients. Add pork and marinate overnight. Heat oil in a skillet and sauté carrots, onion, celery, red pepper and parsley for 5 minutes. Add tomatoes, garlic, salt and pepper and cook 2 minutes. Strain and add marinade and simmer 20 minutes. Meanwhile heat butter in a heavy casserole. Dry pork well with paper towels and brown on all sides in hot butter. Add vegetable mixture and bring to a simmer. Cover and cook 45 minutes to 1 hour or until pork is tender. Slic pork and serve vegetables sep rately.

Côtelettes de porc à la Liègeoise

Pork chops from Liège

4 servings

 4 pork chops
 ½ teaspoon salt
 2 juniper berries, finely crushed
 ¼ cup flour
 1½ tablespoons butter
 1 tablespoon oil

Season the pork chops with the salt and juniper berries. Dredge the chops in the flour. Sauté in hot combined butter and oil until tender and golden brown on both sides.

Lever met spek en uien

Liver with bacon and onions

4 servings

- 8 *slices bacon*
- 1 *large onion, finely chopped*
- 4 *thin slices calves' liver*
- ½ *teaspoon salt*
  Freshly ground black pepper

Fry bacon until crisp. Drain on paper towels and keep warm. Sauté the onion in the rendered bacon fat until golden. Remove from the pan with a slotted spoon and keep warm. Sprinkle the liver with salt and pepper. In the same fat, brown the liver 3 to 4 minutes on each side. Transfer to a serving dish and cover with the bacon and onions. Serve with applesauce and mashed potatoes.

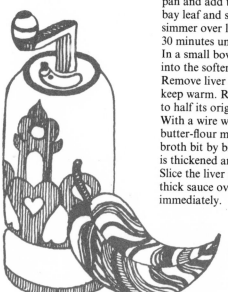

Foie de porc de Tournaisais

Pork liver Tournai style

6 servings

- 2 *pounds pork or beef liver*
- 1 *teaspoon salt*
  Freshly ground black pepper
- 3 *tablespoons bacon fat or oil*
- 1 *medium sized onion, thinly sliced*
- 3 *cups beef broth*
- 1 *teaspoon thyme*
- 1 *bay leaf*
- 1 *tablespoon sugar*
- 3 *tablespoons flour*
- 3 *tablespoons butter, softened*

Sprinkle the liver with salt and pepper. Heat the bacon fat until very hot and brown the liver quickly. Remove liver from the pan and sauté the onion in the same fat over medium heat. Return liver to the pan and add the broth, thyme, bay leaf and sugar. Cover and simmer over low heat 25 to 30 minutes until liver is tender. In a small bowl, blend the flour into the softened butter. Remove liver from the pan and keep warm. Reduce the broth to half its original quantity. With a wire whisk, beat the butter-flour mixture into the broth bit by bit until the sauce is thickened and smooth. Slice the liver and pour the thick sauce over. Serve immediately.

L'Atte

Atte (specialty of Ath)

6 servings

- 2 to 2½ *pounds boneless loin of pork**
- 2 *cloves garlic, cut into slivers*
- 4 *whole cloves*
  Coarse salt
- 2 *bay leaves, crushed*
- 1 *teaspoon thyme*
- 3 *cups beef broth*

Make deep incisions all over the pork and insert the garlic slivers and cloves in the incisions. Rub the salt, bay leaves and thyme all over the surface of the pork. Place the pork in a shallow dish, cover with aluminum foil or plastic wrap and refrigerate 4 days. Wipe as much salt as possible from the pork and place in an ovenproof casserole. Pour in the broth. Bake in a preheated 350° oven for 1½ to 2 hours or until the pork is done and tender. Serve cold, in thin slices.

*Traditionally, pork breast is used for this dish, but it is not usually available in America so we have substituted pork loin.

Lever met pruimen

Liver with prunes

4 servings

- ½ *pound dried pitted prunes*
- 1 *strip lemon rind*
- ¼ *cup sugar*
- 2 *tablespoons bacon fat or butter*
- 1 *large onion, thinly sliced*
- 1¼ *pounds calves' liver, diced*
- 1 *tablespoon flour*
- 1 *cup beef broth*
- 2 *tablespoons vinegar*
- ½ *teaspoon salt*
  Freshly ground black pepper
- ½ *teaspoon thyme*
- 1 *bay leaf*

Soak prunes overnight in cold water. Drain. Barely cover with water, add lemon rind and sugar and simmer 5 to 10 minutes. In a large skillet, heat the bacon fat and sauté the onion over medium heat until light brown. Add the liver and sauté 3 minutes. Sprinkle on the flour and cook 1 to 2 minutes. Add the broth, stirring to scrape up the brown bits clinging to the pan. Add the remaining ingredients and the prunes with their liquid. Simmer 15 minutes and serve.

Calves' liver with red wine

Pork fillets with cream sauce

Foie de veau au vin rouge

Calves' liver with red wine

4 servings

½ teaspoon salt
   Freshly ground black pepper
1 bay leaf, crumbled
1 teaspoon thyme
1 tablespoon flour
1¼ pounds calves' liver, in
   1 piece
2 tablespoons butter
1 onion, finely chopped
1½ cups dry red wine
2 tablespoons sugar

Combine the salt, pepper, bay leaf, thyme and flour and rub into the liver. Heat the butter and sauté the liver and onions over moderately high heat until liver is brown. Add the wine and sugar. Reduce heat, cover and simmer slowly for 1 hour. Slice the liver and arrange on a warm serving dish. Cook the liquid over high heat until reduced by half. Strain and pour over the sliced liver.

Varkenshaasje in roomsaus

Pork fillets with cream sauce

4 servings

1½ pounds pork fillets cut
   from the loin
1 teaspoon salt
   Freshly ground black pepper
3 tablespoons butter
1 small onion, finely chopped
½ cup sliced mushrooms
½ cup white wine
2 tablespoons flour
¾ cup cream, heated

Season the pork fillets with salt and pepper. Heat the butter and brown the meat 8 minutes on both sides. Remove the meat and keep warm. Sauté the onion and the mushrooms in the same butter for 2 minutes. Add wine and simmer, covered, for 10 minutes. Combine the flour with 4 tablespoons cream. Add the remaining cream to the pan. Add the flour mixture, stirring constantly, until the sauce is smooth. Cover the fillets with a little of the sauce and pass the rest separately.

'Moussaka', eggplant-and-meat pie, can be found anywhere the Turks have set foot, from Rumania and Greece to deep into Asia. It is a substantial dish for which a number of different recipes exist. Poor people prepare it with potatoes, those who have more money prepare it with meat.

Moussaka

Meat and eggplant pie

4 servings

      4 small eggplants
 1½ teaspoons salt
 1½ tablespoons oil
      3 tablespoons butter
 1½ pounds minced lamb or beef
      2 onions, chopped
          Freshly ground black pepper
      ¼ teaspoon cinnamon
      4 ripe tomatoes, peeled,
          seeded and chopped
      3 tablespoons chopped parsley
      2 to 3 tablespoons water
      6 tablespoons dry breadcrumbs
      6 tablespoons grated
          Parmesan cheese
      3 egg yolks
      2 cups Béchamel sauce

Peel eggplants and cut into thick slices. Sprinkle with 1 teaspoon salt and set aside for 15 minutes. Wash off excess salt and drain. Heat the oil in a skillet. Add the eggplant slices and fry until lightly browned on both sides. Remove and drain on paper towels. Heat the butter in a frying pan and brown the meat. Add the onions and fry until soft and golden. Season with remaining salt, pepper and cinnamon. Add tomatoes, parsley and water. Bring to a boil and simmer for 20 minutes. Sprinkle ½ the breadcrumbs into a buttered baking dish and cover with ½ the meat mixture. Add ½ the eggplant slices. Sprinkle with ⅓ of the grated cheese. Repeat with layers of remaining meat, eggplant and ½ the remaining cheese. Beat the egg yolks in a bowl. Beat in a few tablespoons of hot Béchamel sauce and add to remaining sauce. Pour sauce over the dish, sprinkle with remaining cheese and breadcrumbs and bake in a preheated 350° oven for 45 minutes or until crust is crisp and brown. Serve with yogurt and a salad.

Béchamel sauce

      2 tablespoons butter
      2 tablespoons flour
      2 cups milk
    ½ teaspoon salt
          Freshly ground black pepper

Melt the butter, stir in the flour and cook over low heat for 1 minute. Add the milk gradually, stirring with a wire whisk to form a smooth medium thick sauce. Season with salt and pepper.

Ossetong met rozijnesaus

Ox tongue with raisin sauce

8 servings

   1 beef tongue (4 pounds)
   1 teaspoon salt
   1 carrot, peeled and sliced
   1 onion, sliced
     Few celery tops
   1 sprig parsley
   6 peppercorns, crushed
   1 bay leaf
   1 clove

Soak the tongue for at least 3 hours in cold water. Rinse under cold running water. Combine the remaining ingredients in a large pot. Add the tongue and cover with water. Bring to a boil, cover and simmer gently for at least 3 hours or until meat is tender. Remove the skin from the tongue and cut the meat into slices ½ inch thick. Keep warm. Strain liquid and reserve 2½ cups for the sauce. Serve with rice, assorted vegetables and a raisin sauce.

For the sauce:
   ½ cup seedless raisins
   ½ cup red port wine
   3 tablespoons butter
   3 tablespoons flour
2½ cups cooking liquid
   1 tablespoon tomato purée
   ¼ teaspoon sugar
   ½ teaspoon vinegar
     Salt
     Freshly ground pepper

Soak the raisins in the port for at least 1 hour. Heat the butter and stir in flour. Gradually add the reserved cooking liquid, stirring constantly until a smooth sauce is formed. Strain raisins and add the port, tomato purée, sugar and vinegar to the sauce. Reduce sauce over medium heat to ⅔ its original quantity. Add raisins, season to taste with salt and pepper and simmer for a few minutes.

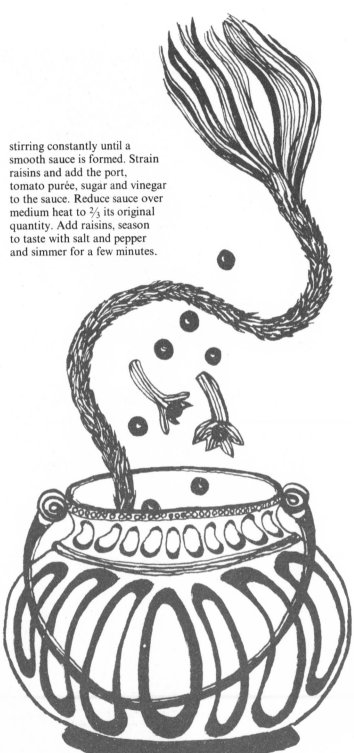

Vlaamse ossestaart

Flemish oxtail

4 servings

   *1 oxtail, cut into pieces at
     the joints*
   2 cloves
   4 juniper berries, crushed
   1 onion
   4 cups water
½ teaspoon salt
     Freshly ground black pepper
   *3 medium sized carrots,
     peeled and sliced*
   2 stalks celery, sliced
¼ small cabbage, shredded
½ pound lean bacon, in 1 piece
   *1 pound potatoes, peeled
     and cubed*
   1 garlic sausage

Soak the oxtail in boiling water for 5 minutes and rinse under cold, running water. Tie the cloves, juniper berries and onion in a cheesecloth bag. Place the water in a heavy pan, bring to a boil and add the oxtail, ingredients in the cheesecloth, salt and pepper. Cover and simmer 2 hours. Add carrots, celery, cabbage and bacon and simmer, covered, 1 hour. Add potatoes and cook, covered, 30 minutes more. Add the sausage during the last 10 minutes of cooking time. Discard cheesecloth bag. Remove the vegetables with a slotted spoon and place on a serving dish. Slice the bacon and sausage and arrange them and the oxtail on top of the vegetables. Serve immediately.

Qa'meh

Minced meat

4 servings

  6 tablespoons butter
  2 onions, chopped
  1 pound minced lamb
     Freshly ground black pepper
  ½ teaspoon turmeric
  5 small tomatoes, boiled,
     peeled and forced through
     a sieve
  ½ cup beef broth
  ½ cup yellow split peas
  3 tablespoons lime or lemon
     juice
  1 teaspoon salt
     Pinch of saffron
  ¼ cup dried apricots, minced

Heat 4 tablespoons butter in a
heavy pan. Add the onions and
fry until lightly browned.
Remove the onions. Add the
lamb to the same butter
and fry until lightly browned.
Sprinkle with pepper and
turmeric. Add the tomatoes
and beef broth. Bring to a boil
and simmer for 10 minutes.
Add the split peas, lime juice,
salt and saffron. Cover and
simmer 1 hour. Heat the
remaining butter in a pan, add
the apricots and stir over low
heat for 4 minutes. Add to
the meat and simmer 20 minutes.

Motanjen Khoreshe

Meatballs with fruits and nuts

4 servings

  1 pound ground lean lamb
  1 onion, finely chopped
  ¼ teaspoon salt
     Freshly ground black pepper
  4 tablespoons oil
  2 cups beef broth
  ¼ cup yellow split peas,
     soaked overnight and drained
  1 cup combined almonds and
     pistachios, chopped
  ½ pound combined dried
     apricots and prunes, chopped

In a bowl combine the lamb,
onion, salt and pepper. Form
small meatballs and sauté
in 2 tablespoons oil until nicely
browned on all sides. Add the
broth and split peas and bring
to a boil. Lower the heat,
cover and simmer 40 minutes.
Meanwhile, heat the remaining
oil in a skillet and sauté the
nuts and dried fruits until
lightly browned. Add these
ingredients to the meatballs
and simmer uncovered 40
minutes more. Transfer to a
serving dish and serve with rice.

Kababe barg

Leaf kebab

4 to 6 servings

  2 pounds top round of beef
  3 tablespoons onion juice
  3 tablespoons lemon juice
  ½ teaspoon salt
     Freshly ground black pepper

Cut the meat into long thin
slices and pound the slices
until they are even thinner.
Combine the remaining
ingredients in a shallow pan.
Add the meat and let it marinate
overnight in the refrigerator.
Thread the meat on skewers and
cook over a hot charcoal fire
or under the oven broiler for
10 minutes or until nicely
browned. Turn frequently so
that the meat browns evenly.

Tas kebab

Meat with pilaf

6 servings

  4 tablespoons butter
  2 onions, thinly sliced
  6 medium sized tomatoes,
     peeled, seeded and mashed
  2 cloves garlic, crushed
  1 teaspoon salt
     Freshly ground black pepper
  ¼ teaspoon cinnamon
  ¼ teaspoon sugar
  1 bay leaf
  2 pounds veal, cut in 1 inch
     cubes
  2½ cups beef broth

Heat the butter, add the onions
and fry until soft and golden.
Add the tomatoes, garlic, salt,
pepper, cinnamon, sugar and
bay leaf and fry for 3 minutes.
Add the veal and beef broth and
bring to a boil. Cover, reduce
the heat and simmer for
1 hour. Serve with pilaf rice.

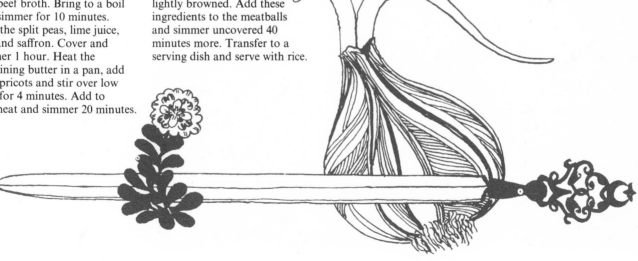

*Wholesome yogurt is served
everywhere from Greece to
regions much farther east. It is
also used to prepare fine, slightly
sour meat sauces.*

Meat with pilaf

Khoreshe mast

Meatballs with yogurt

4 servings

> 1 pound lamb, ground
> 1 teaspoon salt
>   Freshly ground black pepper
> 1 teaspoon turmeric
> 3 tablespoons oil
> 2 teaspoons ground cumin
> 1 teaspoon ground coriander
> ½ teaspoon ground cloves
> 1 teaspoon ground cardamom
> ½ teaspoon ground cinnamon
> 1 onion, finely chopped
> ¾ cup hot water
> 1½ cups yogurt

Combine the lamb with salt,
pepper and turmeric and form
into small balls. Heat the oil in a
heavy pan, add the spices and
onion and fry until the onion is
soft. Add the meatballs and fry
until browned. Add ¾ cup hot
water, bring to a boil and
simmer gently for about 40
minutes or until the water has
evaporated. Add the yogurt, stir
and heat without boiling for
5 minutes until heated through.
Serve hot.

'Kebab', meat on the spit, is the symbol of Turkish cooking.

Kufteh mo'alla

Big meatballs

4 servings

    1 pound ground lean lamb
    1 onion, finely chopped
    ½ cup yellow split peas, cooked
    1 cup rice, cooked
    4 scallions, sliced
    3 tablespoons finely chopped
       parsley
    ½ teaspoon salt
       Freshly ground black pepper
    2 tablespoons combined
       currants and raisins, soaked
    ½ cup pitted prunes, soaked
       and chopped
    3 hard boiled eggs, chopped
    ½ cup pistachio nuts
    3 tablespoons chopped walnuts
    1 onion, chopped and sautéed
    4 cups beef broth
    3 tablespoons rice, pounded
       between 2 sheets of waxed
       paper
    3 tablespoons lemon juice
       Pinch of saffron soaked in
    1 teaspoon water
       Pinch of sugar
    1 tablespoon oil
    1 tablespoon finely chopped
       fresh mint or
       1½ teaspoons dried mint
    1 tablespoon finely chopped
       fresh basil or
       1½ teaspoons dried basil

In a bowl, thoroughly combine
the lamb, onion, split peas, rice,
scallions, parsley, salt and
pepper. Divide the mixture in
half. Shape one of the halves
into a ball with a large hollow
in the center. Combine the
currants and raisins, prunes,
2 eggs, pistachio nuts, walnuts
and sautéed onion and fill the

hollow with the mixture. Form
the remaining meat into a ball
and form over the stuffing.
Carefully place the meatballs in
a casserole just large enough to
hold them. Pour in enough broth
to just cover the meatballs. Add
the rice and bring to a boil.
Lower the heat, cover and
simmer 1 hour. Add the lemon
juice, saffron and sugar and
simmer 10 minutes more. Heat
the oil in a small skillet and
sauté the mint and basil for 2
minutes. Carefully lift out the
meatballs and place on a
serving dish. Top with the fried
mint and basil and the remaining
hard boiled egg. Serve the broth
separately.

Kufteh Tabrizi

Stuffed meat Tabriz style

6 servings

    1 cup rice, cooked
    ½ cup yellow split peas, soaked
       and cooked
    1 pound ground lamb
    3 medium sized onions, finely
       chopped
    ½ teaspoon salt
       Freshly ground black pepper
    ½ teaspoon turmeric
    ¼ teaspoon cinnamon
    ¼ teaspoon ground cloves
    ½ cup dried pitted prunes,
       chopped
    ¼ cup chopped almonds
    1 tablespoon butter
    1 tablespoon chopped parsley
    1 teaspoon crushed dried mint
    ½ cup beef broth

Combine the rice, split peas,
lamb, 2 onions, salt, pepper,
turmeric, cinnamon and cloves
until well blended. Place ½ this
mixture in a buttered 9 inch
square baking dish. Fry the
prunes, almonds and remaining
onion in 1 tablespoon butter for
5 minutes. Add parsley and mint.
Spread this stuffing over the
rice mixture and cover with
remaining rice. Add the beef
broth and bake in a preheated
350° oven for 45 minutes.

Yogurtlu kebab

Meat with yogurt

4 servings

    1½ to 2 pounds boneless leg of
       lamb
    2 tablespoons olive oil
    1 small onion, grated
    ½ teaspoon salt
       Freshly ground black pepper
    6 tablespoons yogurt
    2 to 3 tablespoons butter
    2 medium sized tomatoes,
       peeled, seeded and mashed
    4 thin slices whole wheat or
       any brown bread, toasted
    1½ cups yogurt, heated
    1½ teaspoons paprika

Cut the lamb into ½ inch cubes.
In a bowl, combine the olive oil,
onion, salt, pepper and yogurt.
Add the lamb cubes and
marinate 12 hours. Drain the
lamb and dry it thoroughly.
Heat the butter in a skillet and
sauté the lamb over high heat
until well browned on all sides.
Remove with a slotted spoon
and keep warm. Spread the
tomatoes over the toasted bread,
top with the lamb and pour on
the heated yogurt. Reheat the
butter remaining in the skillet.
Add the paprika and cook,
stirring, 2 minutes. Pour the
mixture over the lamb and serve.

Fillet wusach Matsadah

Fried fillet of beef in puff pastry

6 servings

> 2 pounds fillet of beef, cut into
>   1 inch steaks
> 4 tablespoons butter
> 1¾ cups mushrooms
> ½ pound chicken livers
> 1 teaspoon salt
>   Freshly ground black pepper
> 1 package frozen individual
>   patty shells, thawed
> 1 egg, beaten

Sauté the beef for 2 minutes in hot butter. Remove from the pan. Wash the mushrooms and slice thinly. Cut the chicken livers into small pieces. Add salt and pepper and sauté mushrooms and livers in the same butter in which the meat was browned. Remove and cool. Roll each patty shell to a ⅓ inch thick round. Put each piece of meat in the middle of the pastry. Cover with the mixture of livers and mushrooms. Pinch the pastry closed around the fillet and brush with beaten egg. Bake in a preheated 400° oven for 20 to 25 minutes. Serve with baked tomatoes.

Patlıcan kebabı

Lamb with eggplants

4 servings

> 4 small eggplants, sliced
> 1 tablespoon salt
> 4 tablespoons butter
> 2 onions, thinly sliced
> 1½ pounds lean lamb, cut into
>   1 inch cubes
> 4 tomatoes, peeled, seeded and
>   chopped
> ½ teaspoon salt
>   Freshly ground black pepper
> 1 cup water
> 1 tablespoon finely chopped
>   parsley

Sprinkle the eggplant slices with salt and set aside on a rack for 15 minutes. (This will drain the bitter juices from the eggplants.) Heat ½ the butter in a casserole and sauté the onions until soft. Add the lamb and sauté until well browned on all sides. Add tomatoes, salt and pepper and simmer 15 minutes. Meanwhile, rinse the eggplant slices and pat dry with paper towels. Heat the remaining butter in a skillet and sauté the slices over low to medium heat about 2 minutes on each side. Place on top of the lamb and add water and parsley. Cover the pan and simmer 50 minutes. Serve from the casserole.

Arni me domates

Lamb and tomatoes

4 servings

> 1½ pounds lamb
> 1 teaspoon salt
>   Freshly ground black pepper
> 4 tablespoons butter
> 6 ripe tomatoes, peeled,
>   seeded and chopped
> ¼ teaspoon cinnamon
> ½ teaspoon sugar
> ¾ cup beef broth

Cut the lamb into 4 pieces, rub with salt and pepper and set aside for 20 minutes. Heat the butter in a pan, add the lamb and brown on all sides. Add the tomatoes, cinnamon and sugar and 2 tablespoons beef broth. Simmer for 10 minutes. Continue cooking for 1 hour or until the meat is tender. Add the beef broth as needed during the cooking period, keeping only a small quantity of liquid in the pan. Serve with noodles.

Pilav kuzulu

Lamb pilaf

4 servings

> 4 tablespoons butter
> 1 onion, finely chopped
> 1 pound lamb, cut in small
>   cubes
> 1 teaspoon salt
>   Freshly ground black pepper
> ¼ teaspoon cinnamon
> 3 ripe tomatoes, peeled, seeded
>   and chopped
> 2 tablespoons pine nuts
> 2 tablespoons raisins
> 1 green pepper, seeded and
>   sliced
> 1½ cups raw rice
> 2 tablespoons chopped parsley
>   Pinch of saffron soaked in
>   3 cups beef broth

Heat the butter, add the onion and fry until soft and golden. Add the lamb and brown it on all sides. Add salt, pepper and cinnamon. Add the tomatoes, pine nuts, raisins and green pepper, cover and simmer for 10 minutes. Add the rice and stir for 2 minutes. Add parsley, saffron and broth. Cook over moderate heat until all the liquid has been absorbed and small holes appear on the surface of the rice. Reduce the heat to low, cover, put an asbestos pad under the pan and cook for 20 to 30 minutes until the rice is tender.

Meat casserole (photo below)

There is very little liquid called for in this recipe, though some juices will be formed by the vegetables. This is intended to be an extremely thick stew.

Güvec

Qormeh sabzi

Meat casserole

6 servings

- 2 small eggplants, sliced
- 2 teaspoons salt
- 4 tablespoons butter
- 2 pounds lamb, cut in 1 inch cubes
- 2 onions, sliced
- ½ pound green beans, broken in half
- 3 small zucchini, cut in thick slices
- 4 medium sized tomatoes, peeled and quartered
  Freshly ground black pepper
- 1 teaspoon paprika
- 2 tablespoons chopped parsley

Sprinkle the eggplant slices with 1 teaspoon salt and set aside for 15 minutes. Rinse and drain. Heat the butter in a casserole and fry the lamb until browned. Add the onions and fry for another 2 minutes. Arrange all the vegetables on top and sprinkle with the remaining salt and pepper. Add water to almost cover the vegetables. Sprinkle with paprika and bring to a boil over moderate heat. Transfer to a preheated 350° oven and bake for 50 to 60 minutes. Sprinkle with parsley and serve.

Meat and vegetable stew

4 servings

- 5 tablespoons oil
- 1½ pounds shoulder of lamb, finely diced
- 1 onion, chopped
- ½ teaspoon salt
  Freshly ground black pepper
- ½ teaspoon turmeric
- ⅓ cup lemon juice
- ½ cup water
- 10 scallions, thinly sliced
- 3 tablespoons finely chopped celery leaves
- ½ pound spinach, chopped
- 3 tablespoons chopped parsley
- ⅔ cup canned chick peas (garbanzos), drained

Heat 2 tablespoons oil in a heavy casserole and sauté the lamb until well browned on all sides. Add the onion and sauté until soft. Add salt, pepper, turmeric, lemon juice and water and bring to a boil. Lower the heat, cover and simmer very slowly 15 minutes. Heat the remaining oil in a skillet and sauté the scallions, celery leaves, spinach and parsley for 2 minutes, stirring constantly. Add these vegetables and the chick peas to the meat and combine thoroughly. Bring to a boil and lower the heat. Cover and simmer very slowly another 20 minutes.

Estouffade de boeuf

Estouffade de boeuf

Beef casserole

8 servings

½ pound lean sliced bacon
3½ pounds bottom round of
    beef, cubed
½ cup all purpose flour
    seasoned with ¼ teaspoon
    salt
    Freshly ground pepper
2 shallots or green onions,
    sliced
2 medium sized onions,
    roughly cut
2 large carrots, thickly sliced
2 cups dry red wine
¼ cup brandy
2 cloves garlic, crushed
½ teaspoon thyme
1 bay leaf, crumbled
1 tablespoon finely chopped
    parsley
½ teaspoon salt
    Freshly ground pepper
1 tablespoon tomato paste
½–1 cup beef broth

Simmer the bacon in water
for 10 minutes to render the
fat. Drain, reserve 3 slices and
roughly chop the remainder.
In a heavy flameproof casserole
just large enough to hold the
ingredients, lay the 3 bacon
strips on the bottom. Roll the
beef cubes in seasoned flour
and place half of them close
together in a layer on top of
the bacon. Cover the beef
with half of the vegetables and
chopped bacon. Repeat the
layers with the remaining
beef, vegetables and bacon.
Warm the wine in a small pan.
Add the brandy, garlic, thyme,
bay leaf, parsley, salt, pepper
and tomato paste. Combine
thoroughly and pour into the
casserole. Use beef broth as
needed to almost cover the
contents of the pan. Bring to a
simmer on top of the stove.
Cover with aluminum foil and
then a lid and place in a 300°
oven for 3 hours. Skim off the
fat, taste for seasoning and
serve from the casserole.

Pot au feu

Beef stew

6–8 servings

3 pound piece of beef (sirloin, bottom round, rump, etc.)
2 marrow bones (optional)
1 teaspoon salt
10 peppercorns
½ teaspoon thyme
1 bay leaf
1 tablespoon chopped parsley
2 medium onions
4 cloves
2 stalks celery, sliced
½ pound carrots, sliced
½ pound turnips, cubed
2 leeks or 6 scallions, sliced
½ pound potatoes, cubed
1 small cabbage, roughly cut
½ cup red wine
Pickles
Mild (Dijon) mustard
Coarse sea salt

Place the beef, marrow bones, salt, peppercorns, thyme, bay leaf and parsley in a heavy pan. Almost cover with water, bring to a boil and skim. Reduce the heat, partially cover and simmer for 2 to 2½ hours, skimming occasionally. Spike one of the onions with the cloves and slice the other. Add these to the pot along with the celery, carrots, turnips, leeks and potatoes. Simmer, partially covered, another hour. Add the cabbage and continue simmering for ½ hour. Remove the meat and vegetables from the broth. Slice the meat and place on a platter with the vegetables. Spoon the optional marrow over slices of French bread and discard the bones. Skim any fat from the broth, add the wine and transfer to a warm bowl. Serve the meat and vegetables from the platter and pass the broth, French bread, pickles, mustard and sea salt separately.

Boeuf à la mode

Beef braised in wine

8 servings

8 carrots, sliced thinly
1 onion, chopped finely
1 bay leaf
½ teaspoon thyme
3 sprigs parsley
¼ teaspoon salt
  Freshly ground black pepper
3 pounds top sirloin or eye round roast
1½ cups red wine
2 tablespoons olive oil or vegetable oil
3 onions, finely chopped
4 cloves garlic
12 large mushrooms, finely chopped
1 teaspoon lemon juice
½ pound bacon
½ cup beef broth
3 tablespoons flour

Place carrots, onion, bay leaf, thyme and parsley, salt and pepper in a bowl. Add the beef and wine. Cover and marinate the beef in the refrigerator for 24 hours. Turn the beef every 8 hours. Remove the meat. Dry on paper towels. Strain and reserve the marinade. Heat the oil in a heavy casserole and brown the meat on all sides over high heat. Lower the heat and fry onions and garlic in the same oil for 3 minutes. Add mushrooms and lemon juice and continue cooking for 5 minutes. In the meantime, fry bacon until almost crisp. Drain and leave to one side. Heat reserved marinade with beef broth. Stir flour into onions and mushrooms. Add bacon. Replace beef in the casserole and stir in warm wine and broth. Cover and cook 2½ hours in a 350° oven.

Beckenoff

Pork and lamb baked with potatoes

6 servings

    2 tablespoons butter
    6 Idaho potatoes, peeled and
      sliced thinly
    2 large onions, sliced thinly
    1 teaspoon salt
      Freshly ground black pepper
1½ pounds pork tenderloin,
      trimmed and sliced thinly
1½ pounds lamb shoulder,
      trimmed and sliced thinly
    ½ teaspoon thyme
    1 bay leaf
    4 tablespoons finely chopped
      parsley
    ½ cup white wine
    ½ cup chicken broth
    1 tablespoon cornstarch
      dissolved in 2 tablespoons
      cold water
    1 tablespoon butter
    2 tablespoons finely chopped
      parsley

Butter a large baking dish with 1 tablespoon of butter. Cover with half of the potatoes, then arrange half of the onion rings on top of the potatoes. Season lightly with salt and pepper. Place half of both kinds of meat on top of the onions. Season with salt and pepper. Add thyme, bay leaf and half of the parsley. Add remaining meats and season again with salt and pepper. Add a layer of onion rings, a layer of potatoes and again season with salt and pepper. Pour in wine and chicken broth. Dot with remaining tablespoon of butter.

Cover tightly with aluminum foil. Bake in a 350° oven for 2 hours. Remove foil, stir in cornstarch paste and heat until sauce is thickened. Dot surface with butter. Brown potatoes under the broiler for 3 minutes. Garnish with finely chopped parsley and serve hot.

Côte de boeuf à la Bordelaise

Rib steak in Bordelaise sauce

6 servings

3½ pounds rib steak with the
      bone or 2½ pounds
      boneless sirloin steak cut
      1 inch thick
    2 tablespoons butter
    1 tablespoon olive oil or
      vegetable oil
    ½ teaspoon salt
      Freshly ground black pepper
    4 tablespoons finely chopped
      scallions
    1 clove garlic, crushed
    ½ cup red wine
    ¼ teaspoon thyme
    1 tablespoon lemon juice
    1 tablespoon brandy
    4 tablespoons butter, softened
    2 tablespoons finely chopped
      parsley
    2 tablespoons beef marrow,
      (diced and simmered in
      boiling water for 3 minutes),
      if available

Sauté steak in a heavy skillet in combined, hot butter and oil. Adjust the heat to prevent the butter from burning. Cook steaks 4 to 5 minutes on each side. Transfer to a hot plate. Season with salt and pepper and keep hot. Stir scallions and garlic into the same skillet. Sauté scallions for three minutes. Add wine, stirring in all the browned juices from the bottom of the pan. Add thyme, lemon juice and brandy. Boil over high heat until the wine is reduced to about 3 tablespoons. Remove skillet from the heat

and beat in the butter and finely chopped parsley. Add beef marrow if available. Serve sauce separately.

Gigot d'agneau à la Bretonne

Côte de boeuf à la Bordelaise

Veau à la Niçoise

Veal Riviera style

6 servings

2½ pounds boneless veal roast
 2 cloves garlic, quartered
 ½ teaspoon salt
     Freshly ground black pepper
 3 tablespoons olive oil or
     vegetable oil
 3 medium sized onions, sliced
 3 large ripe tomatoes, peeled,
     seeded and chopped
 1 tablespoon finely chopped
     parsley
 ½ teaspoon marjoram

Make deep slits in the veal and
insert garlic quarters. Brown
meat lightly in hot oil. Remove
meat from the pan. Add onions
and simmer over medium heat
for 3 minutes. Add tomatoes,
parsley and marjoram.
Season veal with salt and
pepper. Place veal on the bed
of vegetables. Roast in a 300°
oven for 1½ hours. Slice and
serve hot or cold.

Côte de veau Vallée d'Auge

Veal cutlets with mushrooms

4 servings

 4 veal cutlets, 4 ounces each,
     pounded thin
 2 tablespoons butter
 ¼ pound mushrooms, thinly
     sliced
 ¼ pound small white onions,
     blanched in boiling salted
     water for about 8 minutes
     or until tender
 ¾ cup heavy cream
 ½ teaspoon salt
     Freshly ground black pepper
 ¼ cup apple brandy
 1 teaspoon lemon juice
 1 tablespoon cornstarch
     dissolved in 2 tablespoons
     water

In a heavy skillet, heat the
butter until foaming and sauté
the cutlets for about 2 minutes
on each side. Transfer them
to a warm serving plate.
Add the mushrooms and onions
to the skillet and sauté 3
minutes until softened. Pour
on the cream. Season with salt
and pepper and simmer 3
minutes. Add the apple brandy
and simmer another 3 minutes.
Add lemon juice to taste and
thicken into a sauce with the
cornstarch mixture. Pour the
sauce over the veal and
serve hot.

Filet de boeuf en croûte

Selle d'agneau bouquetière

Rognons de veau aux tomates

Veal kidneys with tomatoes

4 servings

1½ pounds calves' or lamb
   kidneys
1 onion, finely chopped
2 tablespoons butter
8 button mushrooms
1 teaspoon paprika
1 tablespoon mild (Dijon)
   mustard
1½ tablespoons flour
1 cup beef broth
2 tomatoes, peeled, seeded
   and chopped
¼ cup heavy cream
¼ teaspoon salt
   Freshly ground black pepper
2 tablespoons parsley,
   finely chopped

Cut kidneys into small pieces, cutting around white inner core. Sauté onion in butter for 3 minutes until softened. Add and sauté kidneys and mushrooms for 3 minutes over high heat. Lower the heat and stir in paprika, mustard and flour. Add beef broth, tomatoes and cream. Season with salt and pepper. Simmer 5 minutes until kidneys are tender. Garnish with finely chopped parsley.

Boeuf à la Bourguignonne

Entrecôte marchand de vin

Steak au poivre

Beef Bourguignon

6 servings

    3 pounds lean boneless
       chuck, cubed
    1 large onion, thinly sliced
    ½ teaspoon thyme
    1 bay leaf
    1 tablespoon chopped parsley
    1 clove garlic, crushed
    ½ teaspoon salt
       Freshly ground black pepper
    1 cup dry red wine
    2 tablespoons olive oil
    ¼ pound lean salt pork
       or sliced bacon, cut into
       thin strips
   18 small white onions
    2 tablespoons flour
 1½ cups beef broth or bouillon
    ½ pound mushrooms
    2 tablespoons butter

Place the meat, onion, thyme,
bay leaf, parsley, garlic, salt
and pepper in a bowl. Combine
the wine and olive oil, pour
over the beef and marinate
for 4 or more hours, stirring
occasionally. Place the salt
pork or bacon strips in a
heavy casserole and sauté until
the fat is rendered. Add the
small white onions and sauté
until tender and browned and
the salt pork or bacon is crisp.
Remove from the pan. Dry the
cubes of beef well with paper
towels and reserve the
marinade. Sauté the beef in
the hot fat, browning well on
all sides. Sprinkle on the flour,
cook for a few minutes and
pour on the marinade and
beef bouillon. Bring to a
simmer, cover and cook for

2 hours or until beef is tender.
In the meantime, lightly sauté
the mushrooms in the butter.
When the beef is done, taste
for seasoning, add the salt
pork or bacon, onions and
mushrooms to the casserole
and simmer another 15 minutes
to blend the flavors. Serve
from the casserole. This dish
is best prepared one day before
it is to be served.

Steak in red wine

4 servings

    4 fillet mignon steaks
       (6–8 ounces each, cut
       1½ inches thick)
    1 tablespoon butter
    1 tablespoon vegetable oil
    ½ teaspoon salt
       Freshly ground black pepper
    ¾ cup red wine
    4 tablespoons scallions,
       chopped
    ½ teaspoon thyme
    1 bay leaf
    ¼ teaspoon Bovril
    3 tablespoons butter, softened

Sauté steaks in hot butter and
oil over high heat for 3 minutes
on each side. Place on a hot
serving dish. Season with salt
and pepper and keep warm.
In the meantime, prepare the
sauce: Pour the wine into a
small saucepan. Add scallions,
thyme and bay leaf. Boil over
high heat until reduced to ½
cup. Stir in Bovril (meat glaze)
and butter. Boil 2 more
minutes. Remove the bay leaf.
Pour sauce over steaks and
serve immediately.

Pepper steak

4 servings

    4 boneless tenderloin or
       sirloin steaks
    2 tablespoons oil
 1½ tablespoons peppercorns or
       1 tablespoon cracked pepper
    4 tablespoons butter
    2 shallots or scallions,
       finely chopped
    ⅓ cup dry white wine
    ¼ cup beef broth
    ⅓ cup brandy

Dry the steaks well with paper
towels. Rub them on both
sides with 1 tablespoon oil.
Crush the peppercorns and
press firmly into both sides
of the steaks. Let stand 1 to 2
hours. In a heavy pan, heat the
remaining oil and 2 tablespoons
of the butter until very hot.
Sauté the steaks over high heat
for about 3 minutes on each
side for rare meat. Transfer
them to a hot platter and
sprinkle with salt. Add the
shallots to the pan and sauté
for a few minutes. Pour in the
wine and broth and boil rapidly,
scraping up the meat juices
clinging to the pan. Warm the
brandy, ignite it and add to the
pan. When the flames have
died down, remove the pan
from the heat and beat in the
remaining butter. Pour the
sauce over the steaks and serve.

Foie de veau Véronique

Calves liver with grapes

6 servings

> 6 *slices calves' liver*
> ½ *cup flour seasoned with*
>   *½ teaspoon salt*
>   *Freshly ground black pepper*
> 1 *tablespoon oil*
> 2 *tablespoons butter*
> ¼ *cup sweet vermouth*
> 1 *cup beef broth*
> ¼ *teaspoon thyme*
> ½ *cup white seedless grapes*

Dredge the liver slices in the seasoned flour. Melt the butter and oil in a large skillet. When the butter is foaming, sauté the liver slices for 2 or 3 minutes on each side. Remove to a heated platter. Add the vermouth, broth and thyme to the skillet. Boil over high heat, scraping up the browned bits clinging to the bottom of the pan. When the sauce has reduced to about ¾ cup, add the grapes and heat through. Taste for seasoning. Pour the sauce over the liver and serve hot.

Boeuf aux champignons

Beef with mushrooms

4 servings

> 2 *pounds fillet of beef*
> 1 *tablespoon butter*
> 1 *tablespoon olive oil or*
>   *vegetable oil*
> 1 *onion, finely chopped*
> 1 *clove garlic, crushed*
> 4 *mushrooms, thinly sliced*
> 2 *tablespoons flour*
> 1 *teaspoon tomato paste*
> ½ *cup red wine*
> ¾ *cup beef broth*
> ½ *teaspoon salt*
>   *Freshly ground black pepper*
> ½ *teaspoon thyme*
> 2 *tablespoons parsley,*
>   *finely chopped*

Cut beef into thin slices and then into strips. Sauté beef strips in a skillet in combined butter and oil over high heat for 5 minutes. Stir beef to prevent it from sticking. Stir in onion and garlic. Cook 3 minutes. Add mushrooms and cook 2 minutes. Fold in flour and tomato paste. Stir in wine and beef broth. Season with salt and pepper. Add thyme and simmer 3 more minutes. Garnish with parsley. Serve hot.

Selle d'agneau bouquetière

Roast lamb with garden vegetables

8 servings

> 6 *pound leg or shoulder*
>   *of lamb*
> 2 *cloves garlic, slivered*
> 1 *teaspoon thyme*
> 1 *teaspoon salt*
>   *Freshly ground black pepper*
>   *Juice of 1 lemon*
> 2 *tablespoons olive oil*
> 1 *cauliflower*
> 2 *pounds green beans*
> 1 *pound asparagus*
> 1 *pound new potatoes*
> ¼ *cup butter*
> 8 *small tomatoes*
> 8 *medium sized mushroom*
>   *caps*
> 2 *tablespoons butter*
> ¼ *teaspoon salt*
>   *Freshly ground black pepper*
> 1 *bunch watercress, washed*
>   *and thoroughly dried*

Make slits in the roast and insert garlic slivers. Sprinkle with thyme, salt and pepper and rub with lemon juice and olive oil. Place the meat in a roasting pan and cook uncovered in a 450° oven for 15 to 20 minutes or until nicely browned. Reduce the heat to 350°, insert a meat thermometer and roast, basting occasionally with the pan drippings, until the meat reaches the desired degree of doneness. The total time will be 10 to 12 minutes per pound for medium rare, which is the preference in France, or 13 to 15 minutes per pound for well done. In the meantime, prepare the vegetables, dividing the cauliflower into sections. Cook the cauliflower, green beans, and asparagus separately in boiling salted water until tender but still firm. If frozen vegetables are used, follow the package directions. Canned vegetables should simply be heated through. Boil the potatoes, covered, until not quite done, then sauté in the butter until golden. Blanch the whole tomatoes in boiling water for 2 to 3 minutes, making sure they remain firm. Remove the cores and slip off the skins. Sauté the mushroom caps in 2 tablespoons butter for 3 to 5 minutes and season with salt and pepper. When the roast is done, place on a warmed platter and surround with the vegetables. Garnish with watercress and serve.

Gigot d'agneau à la Bretonne

Leg of Lamb Brittany style

6 to 8 servings

> 6 *pound leg of lamb, boned and tied*
> 2 *cloves garlic, slivered*
> 4 *tablespoons olive oil*
> 1 *teaspoon salt*
> *Freshly ground black pepper*
> 1 *teaspoon rosemary*
> 1 *cup dry white wine*
> 1 *cup beef broth*
> 1 *pound Great Northern beans, soaked overnight if necessary*
> 1 *medium sized onion, quartered*
> 1 *bay leaf*
> 1 *teaspoon salt*
> *Freshly ground black pepper*
> 1 *tablespoon butter*
> *Finely chopped parsley for garnish*

Make slits in the roast and insert garlic slivers. Heat the oil in a large, heavy casserole and brown the roast on all sides. Pour out the oil and add the salt, pepper, rosemary, white wine and beef broth to the pan with the lamb. Bring to a simmer, cover and cook slowly on top of the stove or in a 300° oven for 2½ to 3 hours or until tender. While the lamb is cooking, place the beans, onion, bay leaf, salt and pepper in a heavy saucepan. Cover with water, bring to a boil, cover and simmer 1½ to 2 hours or until tender. When the lamb is done, remove it from the casserole and keep warm. Skim the fat from the liquid and boil it down to concentrate the flavor. Drain the beans, stir in 2 tablespoons of the reduced liquid and transfer to an ovenproof serving dish.

Slice the lamb and arrange attractively on top of the beans. Moisten with a little of the liquid, dot with butter and place in a 400° oven for 4 minutes. Garnish with chopped parsley before serving. Pass the remaining braising liquid separately.

Navarin de mouton

Lamb stew

6 servings

> 2½ *pounds shoulder of lamb, cut into 3 inch cubes*
> 1 *tablespoon butter*
> 2 *tablespoons vegetable oil*
> 3 *onions, sliced*
> 2 *cloves garlic, crushed*
> 2 *tablespoons flour*
> 1½ *cups beef broth*
> ½ *teaspoon salt*
> *Freshly ground black pepper*
> 1 *teaspoon rosemary*
> 1 *bay leaf*
> 12 *small potatoes, peeled*
> 6 *carrots, sliced*
> ½ *turnip (optional), chopped*
> 1½ *pounds fresh peas in the pod or 1 package frozen peas*

Brown lamb in hot butter and oil. Transfer lamb to a casserole. Sauté onions and garlic in the same skillet. Stir in flour and add beef broth. Season with salt and pepper. Add rosemary and bay leaf. Add these ingredients to the lamb. Bring broth to boiling point. Lower heat, cover and simmer for 1 hour until lamb is almost tender. Add potatoes, carrots and turnip and simmer for 20 minutes. Add peas and continue simmering another 10 minutes. Serve hot.

Côtelettes de mouton Comtoise

Broiled lamb chops in onion sauce

4 servings

> 8 *loin lamb chops*
> 2 *tablespoons olive oil or vegetable oil*
> ½ *teaspoon salt*
> *Freshly ground black pepper*
> 8 *medium sized onions, sliced*
> 2 *cloves garlic, crushed*
> 2 *tablespoons butter*
> 2 *tablespoons flour*
> ⅓ *cup heavy cream*

Heat butter and simmer onions and garlic over moderate heat for 30 minutes until a soft purée is formed. Stir in flour and add cream. Simmer another 15 minutes. Brush lamb chops with oil and broil 8 minutes on each side. Season with salt and pepper. Place onion purée on a hot serving plate. Arrange lamb on the purée and serve hot.

Berliner Leber

Bratwurst

Braised sausage

4 servings

1½ *pounds link sausages*
 ¼ *cup fine dry bread crumbs*
 4 *tablespoons margarine or
     butter*
 ½ *cup chopped onion*
 1 *tablespoon flour*
 1 *cup water*
 1 *tablespoon tomato sauce*
 ¼ *teaspoon salt*
 ¼ *teaspoon thyme*

Place sausages in large skillet,
in one layer; just cover with
hot water. Simmer 1–2 minutes
until sausages are no longer
pink. (Be sure sausages are
cooked to center). Discard
water. Drain on paper towels.
Roll sausages in bread crumbs,
coating well. Heat margarine
in same skillet until quite hot.
Place sausages in skillet;
prick with a sharp-tined fork.
Brown on all sides over moderate
heat. Remove from pan and
keep warm. Cook onion in fat
remaining in pan over low
heat until onion is transparent.
Stir in flour, gradually add
water and cook over medium
heat, stirring frequently, until
thickened, about 1 minute.
Stir in tomato sauce. Season
with salt to taste. Stir in thyme
Serve gravy over sausages with
mashed potatoes.

Westfälische Hammelkeule

Westphalian leg of lamb

4–6 servings

> 1 small onion, chopped
> 1 carrot, chopped
> 1 tablespoon chopped parsley
> 2 tablespoons margarine or
>   butter
> 1 bay leaf
> 1 (8 oz.) container plain
>   yogurt or
> 1 cup buttermilk
> 1 tablespoon flour
> ½ leg of lamb (about 3½ lbs.)
> 1 teaspoon salt
> ⅛ teaspoon pepper
> 1 tablespoon cornstarch
> 2 tablespoons cold water

Sauté onion, carrot and parsley in margarine until onion is transparent. Add bay leaf and yogurt. Sprinkle flour in cooking bag large enough to contain the lamb. Place half of the yogurt mixture in the bag. Sprinkle lamb with salt and pepper. Place in bag on the yogurt mixture. Cover lamb with remaining mixture. Seal bag with twist tie. Puncture bag in 3 or 4 places with a 2-tined fork. Insert meat thermometer into the thickest part of the meat. Roast in a moderate oven (350°) until lamb registers 165° for medium or 180° for well-done. Carefully strain liquid from bag. Measure and make up to 1 cup with water, if necessary. Stir cornstarch into cold water. Add to liquid; cook over medium heat until thickened, stirring constantly. Taste, season with salt and pepper. Serve sauce with sliced lamb.

Rahmschnitzel mit Spätzle

Creamed veal cutlets with spatzle

4 servings

> 1 pound (4) veal cutlets
> ½ teaspoon salt
> ⅛ teaspoon black pepper
> 4 tablespoons margarine or
>   butter
> 2 tablespoons chopped chives
> 1 teaspoon parsley flakes
> ½ cup dry white wine
> 1 tablespoon flour
> ½ cup sour cream
> 1 recipe spatzle page 69 or
>   hot cooked noodles

Sprinkle cutlets with salt and pepper. Melt margarine in large skillet. Brown cutlets in margarine. Add chives, parsley and wine. Cover. Simmer 20–25 minutes. Remove cutlets; keep warm. Blend in flour. Cook, stirring constantly, until slightly thickened. Stir in sour cream; heat thoroughly pour over veal. Serve with spatzle or noodles.

Weimarer Ochsenzunge

Tongue with raisin sauce

8 servings

> 1 pre-cooked beef tongue
>   (3–4 lbs.)
>   Water to cover
> 1 onion, sliced
> 1 celery stalk
> 1 sprig of parsley
> 2 tablespoons margarine or
>   butter
> 2 tablespoons flour
> ½ teaspoon salt
> 2 tablespoons vinegar
> 2 tablespoons sugar
> ⅔ cup raisins

Place tongue in deep saucepan with any juices packed with tongue; add water to cover. Add onion, celery, and parsley. Heat thoroughly; remove tongue and keep warm. Strain liquid and reserve 1½ cups. Melt margarine in saucepan; stir in flour and salt; slowly add the reserved cooking fluid. Stir until smooth and thickened; stir in vinegar, sugar, and raisins. Continue to cook until well heated. Serve with sliced tongue.

Nieren Stuttgarter Art

Kidneys Stuttgart style

4 servings

> 1½ pounds beef kidneys
> 2 tablespoons flour
> 1 teaspoon salt
> ¼ teaspoon black pepper
> 2 medium onions, sliced
> ¼ cup margarine or butter
> 1 cup beef bouillon
> 2 tablespoons lemon juice
> ¼ cup chopped parsley
> ⅓ cup cream or evaporated
>   milk
> 2 tablespoons white wine
>   (optional)
> 1 teaspoon paprika
> 1 tablespoon chopped chives

Soak kidneys in lightly salted water for about 1–2 hours. Slice and remove white membranes. Dry well. Dredge with flour seasoned with salt and pepper. Melt margarine in skillet and sauté onions until golden. Remove from pan. Sauté kidney slices until lightly browned. Add onions, bouillon, lemon juice, and parsley. Stir in cream or evaporated milk, and wine. Simmer for 5 minutes. Sprinkle with paprika and chives. Serve with rice.

Berliner Leber

Liver and apples, Berlin style

4 servings

> 1 pound beef liver, cut into
> 4 slices
> ½ teaspoon salt
> ⅛ teaspoon black pepper
> ¼ cup margarine or butter
> 1 large onion, cut into thick
> slices (optional)
> 2 apples, peeled, cored and
> cut into thick slices

Sprinkle liver with salt and
pepper. Melt margarine in large
skillet. Cook liver slices in
margarine about 3 minutes
each side. Remove; keep warm.
Add onion and apple slices to
skillet; cook, turning frequently,
until onions are lightly
browned. Serve over liver.

Gefüllte Kalbsburst

Geschnetzelte Leber

Liver with mushrooms and white wine

4 servings

4 slices bacon, diced
¼ cup finely chopped onion
1 (6 oz.) package frozen
   sliced mushrooms
1 pound sliced baby beef liver,
   about 4 slices
1 tablespoon flour
½ teaspoon salt
   Dash black pepper
½ cup dry white wine
1 cup half-and-half or light
   cream
1 tablespoon chopped parsley

In large frying pan over moderate heat, fry bacon until crisp. Remove bacon pieces, drain and reserve. Add chopped onion and mushrooms to bacon fat in pan. Cook over medium heat until onions are transparent. Remove skins and tubes from liver; cut into ¼″ × ½″ × 2″ strips. Add to hot fat and toss to brown, 3–4 minutes. Sprinkle flour, salt and pepper over liver. Stir to blend. Stir in wine, then half-and-half. Heat to a boil; reduce heat and simmer 4–5 minutes. Serve garnished with parsley and reserved bacon pieces. Serve with rice or spatzle.

Gefüllte Kalbsbrust

Stuffed breast of veal

4–6 servings

1 (3 ½ lb.) breast of veal with
   pocket for stuffing
½ teaspoon salt
⅛ teaspoon black pepper
¾ cup finely chopped onion
2 tablespoons chopped parsley
4 slices day old bread, cubed
2 tablespoons half-and-half
2 tablespoons salad oil
2 eggs
½ teaspoon paprika
½ teaspoon salt
   Dash black pepper
¼ cup margarine or butter
½ cup water
1 tablespoon cornstarch
¼ cup currant jelly
1 teaspoon lemon juice

Sprinkle inside pocket and outside of veal with salt and pepper. Mix together onion, parsley, bread cubes, half-and-half, oil, eggs, paprika, salt and pepper. Fill pocket with bread mixture; skewer shut. Melt margarine in Dutch oven. Place meat in margarine; add water. Cover. Cook over medium heat until veal is tender when pierced with a fork, about 1½ hours. Turn meat once after 45 minutes. Remove veal; keep warm. Measure any liquid in pan; add water to make 1 cup. Stir in cornstarch; return to pan. Cook over medium heat, stirring and scraping up browned bits, until thickened. Add jelly and lemon juice; stir until jelly is dissolved. Serve with veal.

Schlesisches Himmelreich

Silesian pork and dried fruit

4–6 servings

> 1 tablespoon flour
> 2 pounds boneless rolled pork
> 1 cup dried apricots
> 1 cup dried pitted prunes
> ¼ cup granulated brown sugar
> ½ cup dry white wine

Dust the inside of a cooking bag with flour. Place meat and fruit in cooking bag; sprinkle with brown sugar. Pour wine over all. Tie bag securely. Puncture 4 small holes about 4″ apart in top of bag. Place bag in shallow roasting pan. Cook in a slow oven (325°) 1½ hours. Place meat on serving platter; arrange fruit around meat.

Schlesischer Schwärtelbraten

Silesian fresh ham

8 servings

1 fresh ham (5–6 lb.)
1 teaspoon salt
½ teaspoon black pepper
1 teaspoon caraway seed
1 cup boiling water
1 medium onion, sliced
1 tablespoon cornstarch
¼ cup cold water
½ cup sour cream (optional)

Rub meat with salt. pepper, and caraway seed. Place on rack in roasting pan. Pour water in bottom of roasting pan; add onions. Roast in moderate oven (350°) for 3–3½ hours or until a meat thermometer reaches 185°. Remove from pan and keep warm. Pour off all but 3 tablespoons of fat.
Remove onions. Stir to loosen drippings from pan, adding water as necessary to increase liquid to 1 cup. Mix cornstarch with cold water. Add to gravy. Cook over low heat, stirring constantly, until thickened. If desired, stir in sour cream. Slice meat and serve with gravy.

Bayerische Haxen

Bavarian veal or pork roast

6 servings

1 (4 lb.) rump of veal or
1 (3 lb.) boneless pork shoulder roll
1 teaspoon salt
½ cup boiling water
1 large onion, thinly sliced
1 carrot, chopped
3 peppercorns, crushed
½ teaspoon caraway seed

Place meat in roasting pan. Sprinkle with salt. Pour boiling water into pan. Add vegetables, peppercorns and caraway seed. Roast in a moderate oven (350°) until meat tests done on a meat thermometer, veal 170°; pork 185°, about 1 hour, 45 minutes. Baste with pan juices during roasting, adding more water if needed.

Bremer Matrosenfleisch

Rindsrouladen

Schwäbischer Schlachtbraten

There is a droll German proverb that 'the most delicous vegetable in the world is meat' ...and another that 'in times of disaster sausages are eaten even without bread'.

Meat, as we can see, means quite a lot to the German diet, particularly in the form of 'Wurst' (sausage) which is the pillar of German cooking and is found in an almost endless variety of tastes: the light 'Weisswurst' from Munich, which is delicious with beer, the dark Thüringer Blutwurst (blood sausage), the hard Bierwurst, full-flavored Mettwurst, lightly sour Sülzle, spicy Kasseler or Berliner Leberwurst. They hang in the delicatessen in an appetizing and confusing array of colors and shapes: black, white, red and brown, hard and soft, long and short, thin and thick. At the wine feasts in Dürkheim and at the October beer festival in Munich, sausages are eaten by the million. For the great wine feast in Dürkheim alone, at least 200,000 liters of wine are poured out, and some 1000 oxen and 600 pigs disappear into the sausages.

Sailors' stew

6 servings

    2 tablespoons salad oil
    1 pound beef, cut into 1" cubes
    1 pound pork, cut into 1" cubes
    2 medium onions, finely
       chopped
    2 carrots, chopped
    2 stalks celery, chopped
    1 teaspoon salt
    ⅛ teaspoon black pepper
    1 bay leaf
    1 cup dry red wine
    1 teaspoon cornstarch
    ¼ cup water
    2 teaspoons horseradish

Heat oil in large Dutch oven. Brown meat on all sides. Add vegetables, salt, pepper, bay leaf and wine. Bring to a boil. Cover. Reduce heat; simmer 45–50 minutes. Discard bay leaf. Dissolve cornstarch in water; add horseradish. Stir into beef mixture. Continue to cook, stirring constantly, until slightly thickened.

Braised stuffed beef rolls

4 servings

    8 very thin slices top beef
       round
    1 medium onion, chopped
    ¼ pound bacon, diced
    ¼ cup flour
    1 teaspoon paprika
    ½ teaspoon salt
    ½ teaspoon pepper
    2 tablespoons salad oil
    1 carrot, sliced
    1 stalk celery, sliced
    1 small onion or 1 leek,
       sliced
    ¼ cup coarsely cut parsley
    1 cup hot water
    1 tablespoon cornstarch
    2 tablespoons cold water

Pound beef slices with mallet until very thin. Divide onion and bacon among the 8 beef slices, placing them across one end. Roll up with filling in center; secure rolls with toothpicks. Sprinkle all sides of rolls with flour, paprika, salt and pepper. In large skillet, brown in oil on all sides. Add carrot, celery, onion or leek and parsley; add hot water. Cover and simmer until tender, about 1½ to 2 hours, adding more water if needed. Remove rolls, remove toothpicks carefully and keep rolls warm. Strain and measure 1 cup liquid from skillet. Stir cornstarch into cold water; add to measured meat juices. Cook over medium heat, stirring constantly, until thickened. Serve with beef rolls.

Swabian fillet of beef

6 servings

    1 (3–3½ lb.) beef tenderloin
    1 large onion, chopped
    1 stalk celery, chopped
    1 carrot, chopped
    4 tablespoons melted margarine
       or butter
    1 cup beef bouillon
    1 teaspoon flour
    2 tablespoons dry white wine

Place meat on rack in roasting pan. Arrange vegetables around meat. Brush meat with melted butter. Insert meat thermometer into center of thickest part of meat. Roast in a very hot oven (450°), basting frequently, about 45–60 minutes or to 140° on thermometer. Remove meat; keep warm. Drain off fat, leaving brown bits in pan. Add bouillon to drippings in pan; scrape and stir until all brown bits are loosened. Mash vegetables with fork. Strain into saucepan. Stir in flour and wine; heat thoroughly. Serve over meat.

Bistecca fiorentina

Bistecca fiorentina

Florentine steak

6 servings

    4 tablespoons parsley
       flakes
    1 teaspoon dried oregano
    1 teaspoon dried basil
  1/4 teaspoon dried thyme
    4 tablespoons salad oil
    1 (2″ thick) round steak
1 1/2 teaspoon salt
  1/2 teaspoon garlic salt
       Freshly ground black
       pepper
  1/2 cup dry red wine
    6 large mushrooms caps
    2 tablespoons melted
       margarine or butter
   12 rolled anchovy fillets

Combine parsley, oregano, basil
and thyme; mix well. Place steak
on large piece heavy duty foil.
Rub 2 tablespoons oil on 1 side
of steak; sprinkle with half the
salt, garlic salt and plenty of
black pepper. Sprinkle half the
herb mixture over steak; gently
pat herbs into steak. Turn steak
over; use remaining oil, salt,
garlic salt, pepper and herb
mixture. Pour wine on steak.
Close foil securely, using a drug
store wrap. Let steak marinate
in foil, 3–4 hours, turning once
or twice. If steak is to be
marinated longer than 4 hours,
refrigerate. Broil steak in foil,
3–4″ from heat, 10 minutes each
side. Remove foil. Brush
mushroom caps with melted
margarine; place on broiler pan
with steak. Continue to broil
3–4 minutes, each side of steak,
or until desired doneness. Slice
steak diagonally to serve.
Garnish with broiled mushroom
caps and rolled anchovy fillets.

Ossobucco alla milanese

Scaloppine

Ossobucco alla milanese

Veal shanks Milanese style

6 servings

  6 *veal shanks, about*
      $2^1/_2$" thick
$^1/_2$ *cup flour*
$^1/_2$ *cup salad oil*
  1 *onion, finely chopped*
  1 *carrot, grated*
  1 *stalk celery, finely*
      chopped
  2 *cloves garlic, minced*
  1 *teaspoon dried marjoram*
$^1/_2$ *cup dry white wine,*
      optional
  1 *(1 pound) can tomatoes*
  1 *cup beef bouillon*
  1 *tablespoon chopped*
      parsley
  1 *teaspoon grated lemon*
      rind

Dredge veal shanks with flour. Heat oil in large Dutch oven. Brown veal in hot oil; remove. Add onion, carrot, celery, 1 clove garlic and marjoram. Cook over medium heat, stirring constantly, about 3 minutes. Add wine, cook until wine is reduced by half. Return veal shanks; add tomatoes and bouillon. Cover. Simmer $1-1^1/_2$ hours or until veal is tender. Stir in remaining garlic, parsley and lemon rind; cook 1 minute.

Braciuolini di vitello

Veal rollettes

6–8 servings

  1 *($1^3/_4$ ounce) can*
      anchovy fillets, optional
$^1/_4$ *cup milk*
  8 *veal cutlets, $^1/_8$" thick*
  8 *slices prosciutto or ham*
  8 *slices provolone cheese*
  4 *tablespoons margarine*
      or butter
  1 *tablespoon chopped parsley*
  1 *tablespoon lemon juice*

Soak anchovies in milk, 15 minutes, to remove excess salt; rinse; dry on paper towel. On each slice of veal place 1 slice of prosciutto, 1 slice of cheese, and 2 anchovies. Roll and fasten securely with toothpicks. Melt margarine in large skillet. Brown veal rolls on all sides in margarine. Stir in parsley and lemon juice. Cook over medium heat, basting rolls frequently, until veal is cooked, about 12–15 minutes.

Bistecca con peperoni e pomodori

Steak with peppers and tomatoes

4 servings

  4 *tablespoons margarine*
    or butter
1¹/₂ *pounds sirloin steak,*
    cut into 1″ cubes
  2 *green peppers, cut*
    into strips
  2 *tomatoes, chopped*
  1 *teaspoon dried oregano*
  1 *teaspoon Worcestershire*
    sauce
¹/₂ *teaspoon salt*
¹/₈ *teaspoon black pepper*
    Italian bread, cut
    into 1″ slices

Melt margarine in large skillet over medium heat. Brown meat in margarine; remove; keep warm. Add peppers, tomatoes, oregano, Worcestershire sauce, salt and pepper. Cook 5 minutes or until peppers are softened. Return meat. Cook 2–3 minutes or until steak is of desired doneness. Serve over sliced bread.

Casseruole di manza e melanzane

Beef and eggplant casserole

8–10 servings

  2 *pounds ground beef*
  1 *medium onion, chopped*
  1 *green pepper, chopped*
  2 *(8 ounce) cans tomato*
    sauce
  1 *teaspoon salt*
¹/₂ *teaspoon dried oregano*
¹/₂ *teaspoon dried basil*
¹/₈ *teaspoon black pepper*
  2 *medium eggplants,*
    cut into 2″ cubes
¹/₂ *pound mozzarella*
    cheese, sliced

Brown meat in heavy skillet. Add onion and pepper; cook about 2 minutes, stirring frequently. Add tomato sauce, salt, oregano, basil, and pepper; stir well to blend. Cook 5–10 minutes. Place eggplant in buttered 13³/₄″ × 9¹/₂″ × 2″ baking dish. Pour meat mixture over eggplant. Bake in a moderate oven (350°) about 20–25 minutes or until hot and bubbly. Arrange cheese slices on meat. Continue to bake 5–10 minutes or until cheese melts.

Medaglione di vitello alla piemontese

Veal cutlets Piedmont style

4 servings

  4 *tablespoons margarine*
    or butter
  4 *veal cutlets,* ¹/₂″ *thick*
¹/₂ *cup dry white wine*
¹/₂ *teaspoon salt*
¹/₄ *teaspoon dried basil*
¹/₈ *teaspoon black pepper*
  4 *slices provolone*
    cheese

Melt margarine in large skillet. Brown veal cutlets in margarine. Add wine, salt, basil and pepper. Cook over low heat, basting frequently, 10–12 minutes. Place cutlets in shallow baking dish. Pour wine sauce over veal. Place 1 slice of cheese over each cutlet. Bake in a hot oven (400°) about 10 minutes or until cheese is melted.

Scaloppine di vitello al marsala

Veal scallops in Marsala wine

4 servings

12 *thin veal cutlets*
¹/₂ *teaspoon salt*
    Dash black pepper
¹/₄ *cup flour*
  4 *tablespoons margarine*
    or butter
¹/₂ *cup Marsala wine*
¹/₄ *cup beef bouillon*

Flatten veal cutlets between sheets of plastic wrap with smooth mallet. Sprinkle with salt, pepper and flour; shake off excess flour. Melt margarine in large skillet. Brown veal on both sides in margarine; remove; keep warm. Stir wine into pan juices. Mix 1 tablespoon of the flour used for dredging with the bouillon. Add to skillet; cook over medium heat until thickened, stirring constantly. Pour over cutlets. Serve with stewed tomatoes, if desired.

Pierna de cordero al estilo de Badajoz

Leg of lamb Badojoz style

6 servings

>   5 pound leg of lamb
>   3 large cloves garlic
>   3 tablespoons butter, softened
>   ¼ cup salt
>   1½ cups white wine

Pierce the lamb in several places with the point of a small sharp knife. Cut the garlic into thin slivers and insert the slivers into each cut. Coat the surface of the lamb with butter. Sprinkle salt on the bottom of a roasting pan. Pour the wine over the salt. Place the lamb on a roasting rack over the wine. Roast uncovered in a preheated 350° oven for 1 hour or until a meat thermometer reading is 145°. (If you prefer the lamb more well done increase the cooking time to 1¼ hours.) Baste the lamb every 15 minutes with salted wine. Allow the lamb to rest for 15 minutes before carving. Serve with small, whole new potatoes, fried in oil until golden brown, and a green vegetable or salad.

Cordero asado a la manchega

Roast lamb à la Manchega

4 servings

>   2½ pounds boneless leg or
>   shoulder of lamb, rolled and
>   tied
>   2 tablespoons butter
>   1 teaspoon salt
>   Freshly ground black pepper
>   1 bay leaf
>   ½ cup dry white wine
>   1 clove garlic, crushed
>   2 tablespoons finely chopped
>   parsley
>   Beef broth

Rub the surface of the lamb with butter and sprinkle with salt and pepper. Roast in a 450° oven for 10 minutes. Turn and roast 10 minutes more. Reduce the heat to 350°, add the bay leaf and wine and continue roasting 50 to 60 minutes. Place the lamb on a cutting board and let rest 15 minutes. Strain the pan juices into a small bowl. In a small saucepan, heat 1 tablespoon of the fat which will have risen to the top of the bowl. Discard any remaining fat. Sauté the garlic and parsley until brown. Add the meat juices and enough beef broth to measure 1 cup and simmer 5 minutes. Slice the lamb and arrange on a warm platter. Spoon a little of the sauce over the meat and pass the rest separately. Serve sautéed new potatoes and fried artichokes or a salad with the lamb.

Chuletas de cordero a la navarra

Lamb chops Navarra style

4 servings

>   8 loin lamb chops
>   2 tablespoons butter
>   2 tablespoons oil
>   ¼ pound boiled ham
>   1 onion, finely chopped
>   2 medium-sized tomatoes,
>   peeled, seeded and chopped
>   ½ teaspoon salt
>   1 teaspoon sugar
>   ½ pound spicy Spanish or
>   Italian sausage

Fry the lamb chops for 6 minutes on each side in hot combined butter and oil. Transfer the chops to a large casserole. Cut the ham into small pieces. Fry the ham and onion in the same butter and oil used for the lamb chops. When the onion has softened, add the tomatoes. Simmer these ingredients together for 5 minutes. Season with salt and sugar and transfer to the casserole. Cover and cook in a preheated 350° oven for 20 minutes until the chops are tender. Five minutes before serving, cut the sausage into very thin slices and add to the casserole. The sausage should be hot when the dish is served.

Cordero a la pastora

Lamb shepherd's style

4 servings

>   2 pounds leg of lamb, cut into
>   2 inch cubes
>   ¼ teaspoon salt
>   Freshly ground black pepper
>   ⅛ teaspoon crushed dried red
>   hot pepper
>   1 teaspoon pickling spices
>   1 clove garlic, crushed
>   2 tablespoons vinegar
>   ¼ cup dry white wine
>   3 tablespoons olive oil
>   ½ teaspoon thyme
>   ½ teaspoon rosemary
>   ¼ teaspoon mint
>   1 bay leaf
>   1 teaspoon flour
>   1½ cups chicken broth or water
>   8 whole small potatoes, peeled
>   1 cup milk or
>   ½ cup heavy cream
>   1 tablespoon chopped parsley

Place the lamb in a large bowl and season with salt and pepper. Combine hot pepper, pickling spices, garlic, vinegar and wine and add to lamb. Toss the lamb in the mixture. Cover and marinate the lamb in the refrigerator for at least 2 hours, and preferably for 12 hours. Heat the oil in a casserole. Add the lamb, thyme, rosemary, mint and bay leaf. Cover and cook over low heat for 30 minutes. Stir in the flour and add the chicken broth and potatoes. Cover and cook over low heat for 15 minutes and add the milk. Continue cooking for 15 minutes. Taste the sauce, adding more salt if necessary. Garnish with parsley and serve from the casserole.

Orense, where this dish originates, is in mountainous Galicia. In this region of rich pastures, lamb and mutton are especially delectable.

Pierna de carnero a la orensana

Leg of lamb à la Orensana

6 servings

    1 (4 pound) leg of lamb,
       boned, rolled and tied
    1 teaspoon salt
       Freshly ground black pepper
    1 tablespoon butter
    2 tablespoons oil
    3 carrots, peeled and quartered
    3 onions, quartered
    2 cups beef broth
    1 (16 ounce) can lima beans,
       drained

Sprinkle the lamb with salt and pepper. Brown the lamb on all sides in the hot combined butter and oil. Remove the lamb and brown the carrots and onions in the same oil. Pour off all the fat, return the lamb to the pan and add the broth. Bring to a simmer, cover and cook slowly 2 hours or until lamb is nearly tender. Add the lima beans and simmer, covered, 30 minutes more. Remove the lamb and slice it. Arrange the meat on a platter surrounded by the carrots, onions and lima beans.

Asturian bean stew

Sanabulhada

Fabada asturiana

Pork and liver stew

4 servings

  1 pound pork tenderloin
  ½ pound beef liver
  4 tablespoons butter
  1 onion, finely chopped
  1 clove garlic, crushed
  2 bay leaves
  ½ teaspoon salt
    Freshly ground black pepper
  ½ pound blood sausage
    (optional), cut into small
    pieces
  1 lemon, thinly sliced
  1 teaspoon caraway seeds

Cut the pork and liver into small cubes. Heat the butter and sauté the onion and garlic until soft. Add the pork and liver and brown quickly. Add the bay leaves, salt and pepper. Lower the heat, cover the pan and cook very slowly for 35 to 40 minutes or until the meat is tender. Add the blood sausage and continue cooking for 10 minutes. Garnish with lemon slices and caraway seeds and serve with rice.

Asturian bean stew

6 servings

  1 ham bone
  1 pig's foot (optional)
  1 pound corned beef
  2 pounds navy or lima beans,
    soaked overnight
  2 cloves garlic, crushed
  1 bay leaf
  ½ pound marcilla (spiced
    Spanish sausage)
  3 chorizo sausages or substitute
    pepperoni
    Salt if necessary

Soak the ham bone and pig's foot together overnight, changing the water once or twice. Place the ham bone, pig's foot and corned beef in a large heavy pan and add water to cover. Bring to a boil, lower the heat, cover and simmer slowly 1 hour. Cook the beans in plenty of boiling salted water for 3 minutes. Drain and add to the meats. Add the garlic and bay leaf. Cover and simmer slowly, for 1 hour. Add the sausages and salt, if needed, and continue simmering 1 hour. Slice the sausages and meat and place in a serving bowl. Place the beans in another bowl and serve the 2 dishes together.

Jamón asado

Broiled ham

4 servings

> 4 *green peppers*
> 5 *tablespoons olive oil*
> 2 *cloves garlic, crushed*
> 8 *slices cooked ham or*
>   *4 ham steaks*

Cut the peppers into halves and remove the membranes and seeds. Heat 4 tablespoons of oil in a large skillet and fry the peppers over moderately low heat for 8 minutes until tender. Sprinkle the garlic over the peppers. Brush ham with remaining oil and broil for 4 minutes on each side. Place the ham on 4 serving plates and surround with the peppers. Heat the oil in which peppers were cooked until it is very hot and pour the oil over the ham and peppers. Serve very hot.

Lomo de cerdo a la aragonesa

Loin of pork in wine sauce

4 servings

> 6 *tablespoons olive oil*
> 1 *clove garlic, crushed*
> 5 *peppercorns, crushed*
> 4 *thick slices pork tenderloin*
>   *or*
>   *4 pork chops*
> ¼ *cup flour seasoned with*
>   *½ teaspoon salt*
>   *Freshly ground black pepper*
> 1 *onion, finely chopped*
> ¼ *cup beef broth*
> ¼ *cup dry white wine*
> 1 *tablespoon red wine vinegar*

Combine 4 tablespoons olive oil, garlic and peppercorns in a shallow pan. Add the pork and turn the pieces over to coat both sides. Cover with plastic wrap and marinate overnight, turning the pork occasionally. Heat the remaining oil in a skillet or shallow casserole. Dry the pork with paper towels and dredge in seasoned flour. Fry on both sides until golden brown. Remove from the pan. Add the onions and sauté until softened. Add the beef broth, wine and vinegar and stir to scrape up the brown pieces clinging to the bottom of the pan. Return the pork to the pan and simmer slowly, uncovered, for 30 minutes, turning the pork after 15 minutes. If the sauce tends to stick, add 1 tablespoon of broth from time to time. Serve directly from the pan.

Carne de vinha

Marinated pork

4 servings

> 1½ *pounds pork tenderloin*
> ¾ *cup red wine vinegar*
> ½ *teaspoon salt*
> ¼ *teaspoon cayenne pepper*
> 2 *cloves garlic, crushed*
> 1 *bay leaf*
> ½ *teaspoon thyme*
> 1 *whole clove*
> 4 *tablespoons olive oil*
> 4 *slices dark firm textured*
>   *bread*

Place the pork in a small casserole. Combine the vinegar, salt, cayenne pepper, garlic, bay leaf, thyme and clove and pour the mixture over the pork. Cover tightly with plastic wrap and let the pork marinate in the refrigerator 48 hours. Turn the meat occasionally. Place the casserole on a burner and bring the liquid to a simmer. Lower the heat, cover and cook slowly for 30 minutes. Remove the pork from the marinade and dry thoroughly on paper towels. Heat 2 tablespoons oil in a heavy pan and brown the pork quickly on all sides. Reduce the heat and continue cooking 20 minutes, turning the pork every 5 minutes. Heat the remaining oil in a skillet until very hot. Dip the slices of bread briefly in the marinade and let the excess liquid drip off. Sauté the bread quickly on both sides, drain on paper towels and place on individual plates. Slice the pork thickly and arrange on the bread slices.

Magras con tomate

Loin of pork with tomatoes

4 servings

> 8 *tablespoons butter*
> 8 *slices ham, ¼ inch thick*
> 8 *slices French bread*
> 1 *teaspoon sugar*
> 2 *tablespoons vinegar*
> 3 *tablespoons dry white wine*
> 1 *tablespoon flour*
> ½ *cup water*
> 4 *medium-sized tomatoes,*
>   *peeled, seeded and chopped*
> ¼ *teaspoon salt*
>   *Freshly ground black pepper*

Melt 4 tablespoons butter in a skillet and sauté the ham slices 3 minutes on each side. Remove and keep warm. Sauté the slices of bread in 2 tablespoons butter until crisp and golden. Remove and keep warm. Add ½ teaspoon of the sugar, vinegar and wine to the skillet. Blend in flour and water and cook until smooth. Place the bread on a serving dish, top with ham slices and pour over the sauce. Sauté the tomatoes in the remaining 2 tablespoons butter. Season with salt, pepper and ½ teaspoon of sugar and simmer until a thick sauce is formed. Pour over the ham slices and serve hot.

Cozido Português

Portuguese meat stew

8 to 10 servings

> 2 *pounds beef marrow bones,*
>   *with meat clinging to the*
>   *bones*
> 3 *pounds boneless chuck*
>   *steak or top round of beef*
> 10 *cups water*
> 1½ *teaspoons salt*
> 1 *teaspoon peppercorns*
> 5 *large potatoes, peeled and*
>   *cut into small chunks*
> 4 *carrots, peeled and sliced*
> 1 *cup string beans*
> 1 *cup green peas*
> 2 *large turnips, peeled and*
>   *cut into small chunks*
> 3 *medium sized yellow*
>   *onions, cut into chunks*
> ½ *small cabbage, cut into*
>   *8 pieces*
> ½ *pound boiled ham, cut into*
>   *1 inch cubes*
> ½ *pound bacon, cut into small*
>   *pieces*
> 1 *pound (total) cooked*
>   *sausages, chorizo, pepperoni*
>   *and other spicy sausages,*
>   *sliced*
> 10 *slices brown bread, toasted*

Place the soup bones, beef and water in a large soup pan or casserole and bring to a boiling point slowly. Skim off the scum. Add ½ cup cold water and skim again. Cover the pot and simmer over low heat for 1½ hours. Remove chuck steak and reserve. Add salt and peppercorns to the pot and continue simmering for 3 hours. Strain the broth and discard the soup bones. Add the potatoes and carrots and simmer 10 minutes in the broth. Add the string beans and peas and simmer another 5 minutes. Cook the turnips, onions and cabbage separately in plenty of boiling salted water for 15 minutes. Drain and add to the broth. Add ham, bacon and sausages. Season with more salt and pepper if necessary. Return the reserved beef to the pot. Simmer for 10 minutes. Spoon off any fat which has risen to the surface. Place a bread slice in each serving bowl and ladle some of the broth and vegetables into each bowl. Arrange the rice (arroz de sustancia) on a large serving platter. Slice the beef and arrange the slices of beef on the rice. Add sausage slices and strained vegetables. Serve very hot on hot plates.

Though the ingredients in this traditional Portuguese meat stew may be varied slightly, the dish itself is governed by very strict rules. If the rules are broken you must change the name of the stew! For instance, even if you have a tasty piece of raw, fried or boiled goat in your refrigerator, do not be tempted to add it . . . nor can you think of adding mutton or lamb, chicken, duck, game or any winged bird. Parsley, bay leaves and cloves are quite out of the question and very little salt and pepper is used. Strongly flavored vegetables, such as turnips, cabbage, pumpkin and cauliflower must be cooked separately and added at the last moment. Peas, carrots and string beans can, happily, be cooked in the broth and all will be well.

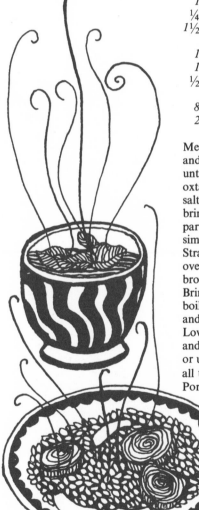

Arroz de sustancia:

8 to 10 servings

> 3 *tablespoons butter*
> 1 *large onion, chopped*
> 1 *clove garlic, peeled*
> ¼ *pound raw ham*
> 1½ *pounds oxtail, cut into*
>   *1 inch pieces*
> 1 *carrot, peeled and chopped*
> 1 *tablespoon tomato purée*
> ½ *teaspoon salt*
>   *Freshly ground black pepper*
> 8 *cups water*
> 2 *cups rice*

Melt the butter in a large pan and sauté the onion and garlic until softened. Add the ham, oxtail, carrot, tomato purée, salt, pepper and water and bring to a boil. Lower the heat, partially cover the pan and simmer at least 3 hours. Strain the broth and refrigerate overnight. Lift the fat from the broth and measure 4 cups. Bring the 4 cups of broth to a boil in a saucepan. Add the rice and stir once with a fork. Lower the heat, cover the pan and simmer about 25 minutes or until the rice has absorbed all the liquid. Serve with cozido Português.

Perdices de capellán

Mock partridge

4 servings

8 (2 ounce) slices veal cutlet
8 paper thin slices smoked ham
8 paper thin slices salami
½ cup flour seasoned with
  ½ teaspoon salt
  Freshly ground black pepper
3 tablespoons olive oil
½ cup dry white wine
1 clove garlic, crushed
¼ teaspoon thyme
¼ teaspoon oregano
¼ teaspoon basil
¼ teaspoon salt
  Freshly ground black pepper

Pound the veal slices to make them as thin as possible. Place a slice of ham and a slice of salami on each veal slice. Roll up tightly and tie with string. Dredge the rolls in seasoned flour. Heat the olive oil in a shallow casserole and brown the rolls on all sides over high heat. Add all the remaining ingredients, cover and simmer slowly for 30 minutes. Check occasionally to see if the sauce is thickening too much. Add wine, 1 tablespoon at a time, to thin. Remove the strings and place the rolls on a warm serving dish. Spread a little of the sauce over each roll and serve.

Carne de vaca à Catarina

Beef à la Catarina

4 to 6 servings

3 tablespoons olive oil
2 pounds beef (chuck steak or top round) cut into 1½ inch cubes
18 white onions
2 cloves garlic, crushed
2 green peppers, seeded and quartered
4 tomatoes, peeled, seeded and chopped
1 bay leaf
1 tablespoon finely chopped parsley
½ teaspoon salt
  Freshly ground black pepper
1¼ cups dry white wine
1 tablespoon vinegar

Heat the oil in a skillet and sauté the pieces of beef quickly until browned on all sides. Transfer beef to a casserole with a slotted spoon. Sauté the onions, and garlic in the same oil until lightly browned. Transfer the onions to the casserole. Add the peppers, tomatoes, bay leaf, parsley, salt and pepper to the skillet and cook 10 minutes, stirring occasionally. Add the wine and vinegar and bring to a boil. Pour the sauce over the beef and onions in the casserole. Cover and simmer slowly for 2½ hours or until beef is tender. Serve from the casserole with boiled new potatoes.

Guisado de vaca al estilo de vigo

Beef stew

4 servings

2 pound piece of beef, top or bottom round
2 cups water
½ teaspoon salt
1 onion, sliced
1 carrot, sliced
1 stalk celery, sliced
¼ pound bacon
2 tablespoons oil
1 onion, finely chopped
2 cloves garlic, crushed
1 tablespoon flour
1½ cups dry white wine
⅛ teaspoon nutmeg
⅛ teaspoon powdered cloves
2 tablespoons finely chopped parsley
¼ teaspoon salt

Tie the beef with string at 2 inch intervals so that it will keep its shape. Place the beef in a small casserole and cover it with water. Add salt, onion, carrot and celery. Cover and simmer over low heat for 1 hour. Cool the beef and then cut it into thick slices. Cut the bacon into small pieces and fry it in a skillet. When the fat has rendered, transfer the bacon to a clean casserole. Fry the beef slices in 1 tablespoon bacon fat and 1 tablespoon oil. Transfer beef to the casserole when it is lightly browned. Add the remaining tablespoon of oil to the skillet and fry the onion and garlic for 3 minutes until softened. Stir in the flour and add the wine, nutmeg, cloves, parsley and salt. Transfer all these ingredients to the

casserole. Cover the casserole and cook over low heat for 30 minutes.

POULTRY & GAME DISHES

Roast duck with apple stuffing

Roast duck with apple stuffing

4 servings

- 1 (4 pound) duck
- 1 tablespoon butter, softened

Dressing:
- 2 tablespoons butter
- 1 onion, finely chopped
- 3 stalks celery, finely chopped
- 1 green cooking apple, peeled, cored and sliced
- ¼ teaspoon cinnamon
- ½ teaspoon salt
  Freshly ground black pepper
  Rind of 1 lemon
- 1½ cups breadcrumbs, freshly made
- ½ cup apple cider

To prepare the dressing: melt 2 tablespoons butter in a skillet. Fry the onions, celery and apple 3 minutes until softened. Remove from the heat and stir in the remaining ingredients. Fill the dressing into the cavity of the duck and secure with poultry skewers. Prick the duck skin with a fork in several places to allow the fat to drain. Rub the duck skin with softened butter and season lightly with salt and pepper. Place the duck on a rack in a roasting tin. Roast uncovered in a 350° oven for 1½ hours until the duck is tender. Cut duck into quarters and serve hot or cold.

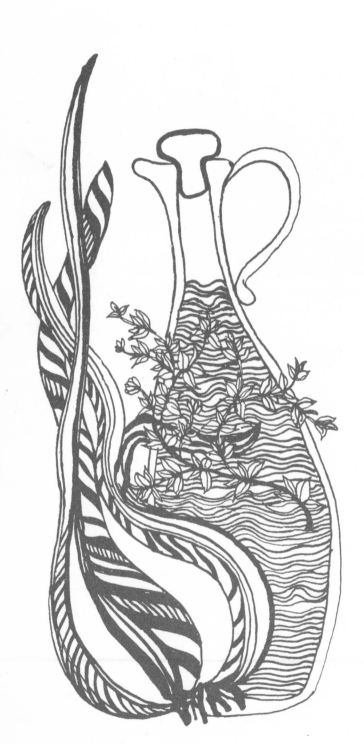

Chicken with tomatoes

6 servings

2 (2 pound) chickens, cut
    into serving pieces
2 tablespoons butter
1 tablespoon oil
1 teaspoon salt
    Freshly ground black pepper
2 medium sized onions,
    chopped
2 cloves garlic, crushed
3 medium sized tomatoes,
    peeled and seeded
1 teaspoon tomato paste
½ teaspoon basil
1½ cups chicken broth
1 tablespoon cornstarch
    dissolved in
2 tablespoons cold water
2 tablespoons finely chopped
    parsley
12 black pitted olives

Brown the chicken pieces in
hot combined butter and oil.
Remove the chicken and season
with salt and pepper. Cook the
onions and garlic in the same
oil for 3 minutes. Add 2 of
the tomatoes, cut into thin
wedges. Add tomato paste, basil
and chicken broth.
Replace the chickens. Cover
the casserole and cook in a
350° oven for 50 minutes.
Arrange the chicken pieces on a
bed of rice. Strain the pan
juices and return to a clean
saucepan. Stir in cornstarch
dissolved in cold water. Add
remaining tomato, cut into
wedges, and heat 3 minutes
until sauce is hot. Spoon the
sauce over the chicken and
garnish the plate with parsley
and black olives.

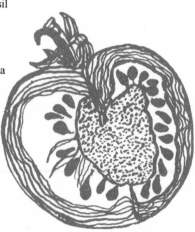

West country chicken

6 servings

2 (2½ pound) chickens, cut
　into serving pieces
2 tablespoons butter
1 tablespoon vegetable oil
2 onions, finely chopped
1 clove garlic, crushed
6 mushrooms, thinlly sliced
2 tablespoons flour
1½ cups chicken broth
½ teaspoon salt
　Freshly ground black pepper
6 slices bacon, fried until crisp
2 tomatoes, peeled, seeded and
　chopped
2 tablespoons finely chopped
　parsley

Brown the chicken in combined
hot butter and oil. Transfer
the chicken pieces to a casserole.
Fry the onions and garlic
in the same fat for 3 minutes.
Add and fry the mushrooms for
3 minutes. Lower the heat and
stir in the flour. Add the
chicken broth gradually,
stirring to form a medium
sauce. Season with salt and
freshly ground black pepper.
Transfer all these ingredients
to the casserole. Drain and
crumble the bacon. Add bacon
and tomatoes to the casserole.
Cover and cook in a 350° oven
for 50 minutes. Garnish with
parsley. Serve on a bed of rice.

Baked chicken

4 servings

2 (2 pound) frying chickens,
　cut into serving pieces
1 cup breadcrumbs, freshly
　made
1 teaspoon salt
　Freshly ground black pepper
1 teaspoon rosemary
2 tablespoons finely chopped
　parsley
2 tablespoons butter

Combine breadcrumbs, salt,
pepper, rosemary and parsley.
Roll the chicken pieces in
seasoned breadcrumbs. Place
in a buttered baking dish.
Dot the chicken with butter
and bake uncovered in a 350°
oven for 1 hour. Serve with
broiled tomato halves and
fried or boiled potatoes.

Chicken patties

4 servings

2 cups left over cooked
　chicken
4 scallions, finely chopped
3 slices boiled ham, diced
2 hard boiled eggs, finely
　chopped
1 tablespoon lemon juice
1 teaspoon mild (Dijon type)
　mustard
4 tablespoons butter
4 tablespoons flour
1 cup milk
½ teaspoon tarragon
1 tablespoon finely chopped
　chives
½ cup flour, seasoned with
1 teaspoon salt
　Freshly ground black pepper
2 eggs, lightly beaten
½ cup breadcrumbs
　Oil or shortening for deep
　frying

Shred the chicken into very
small pieces. Place in a bowl
and combine with scallions,
ham, eggs, lemon juice and
mustard. Heat the butter in a
small saucepan. Stir in the
flour and add the milk
gradually, stirring with a wire
whisk to form a very thick
"sauce". Add tarragon and
chives. Stir the sauce into the
chicken mixture. Chill the
mixture in the refrigerator for
2 hours. Form chicken into
8 patties. Dredge patties first
in flour, then in beaten egg and
finally in the breadcrumbs.
Fry the patties in deep hot
fat for 8 to 10 minutes until
hot and lightly browned.

Cumberland chicken

6 servings

2 (2½ pound) chickens, cut
　into serving pieces
2 tablespoons butter
1 tablespoon oil
6 slices bacon, fried until crisp
2 onions, finely chopped
1 clove garlic, crushed
4 mushrooms, quartered
3 tablespoons flour
2 cups chicken broth
1 tablespoon tomato paste
3 tomatoes, peeled, seeded
　and chopped
½ teaspoon salt
　Freshly ground black pepper
2 tablespoons finely chopped
　parsley

Brown the chicken pieces in a
skillet in combined hot butter
and oil. Transfer chicken to a
large casserole. Add drained
and crumbled bacon to
casserole. Fry onions and garlic
in the same oil for 3 minutes
until softened. Add mushrooms
and cook 3 minutes. Stir in the
flour and add 1 cup of the
chicken broth gradually,
stirring to form a thick sauce.
Add tomato paste and tomatoes.
Transfer all these ingredients to
the casserole. Add remaining
chicken broth and season with
salt and pepper. Cover and
cook in a 350° oven for 1 hour.
Garnish with chopped parsley.

Roast turkey with stuffing

12 servings

1 *(10 pound) turkey*
2 *tablespoons butter or*
  margarine, softened
1 *teaspoon salt*
  Freshly ground black pepper
1 *teaspoon paprika*

Dressing:

2 *pounds sausage meat*
2 *tablespoons butter*
2 *medium sized onions*
  finely chopped
2 *stalks celery, finely chopped*
1 *cup English walnuts, chopped*
  Liver from turkey, chopped
4 *tablespoons finely chopped*
  parsley
1 *teaspoon salt*
  Freshly ground black pepper
2 *cups breadcrumbs, freshly*
  made
3 *eggs, lightly beaten*

Giblet gravy:

  Giblets from turkey
2 *onions, finely chopped*
2 *stalks celery, stems and*
  leaves
1 *bay leaf*
3 *sprigs parsley*
½ *teaspoon salt*
1 *teaspoon peppercorns*
1 *cup white wine*
1½ *cups chicken broth*
3 *tablespoons butter*
3 *tablespoons flour*

To prepare the dressing: Fry
sausage meat until all the fat
has rendered. Place sausage
meat in a bowl. Heat the butter
and fry the onions, celery,
nuts and turkey liver for 5
minutes over moderate heat.
Add these ingredients to the

sausage. Stir in all the remaining
ingredients and fill into the
turkey cavity. Secure dressing
with poultry skewers.
Rub the outside skin of the
turkey with softened butter.
Season with salt, pepper and
paprika. Place the turkey on a
rack in a roasting pan.
Roast uncovered in a 325° oven
for 3½ hours. (Allow 15
minutes additional time for
each extra pound of turkey.)
Place giblets, onions, celery,
bay leaf, parsley, salt, pepper,
wine and broth in a saucepan.
Cover and simmer over very
low heat for 1½ hours. Strain
the broth. When the turkey
has cooked, skim the fat from
the juices in the roasting pan.
Pour the liquid into the broth.
Add butter to the roasting tin.
Place tin over low heat and
allow the butter to melt.
Stir in the flour. Add ½ cup
cold chicken broth and scrape
up the brown pieces clinging to
the bottom of the pan. Add
reserved strained chicken
broth. Stir to form a medium
thick gravy.

Roast chicken

4 servings

1 *(3½ pound) roasting chicken*
2 *tablespoons butter, softened*
1 *teaspoon salt*
  Freshly ground black pepper

Sage and onion dressing:

3 *onions, coarsely chopped*
1 *cup breadcrumbs, freshly*
  made
1 *tablespoon sage*
½ *teaspoon salt*
  Freshly ground black peppe
2 *tablespoons butter, melted*

Bread sauce:

2 *cups milk*
2 *onions, finely chopped*
2 *cloves*
½ *teaspoon salt*
  Dash cayenne pepper
1 *bay leaf*
1½ *cups breadcrumbs, freshly*
  made

To prepare the dressing: cook
the onions in boiling, salted
water for 15 minutes until
softened. Drain the onions.
Place in a bowl and stir in
remaining ingredients. Fill
dressing into the chicken cavity
and secure with poultry skewers.
Rub chicken with butter and
season with salt and pepper.
Place chicken on a rack in a
baking dish. Roast uncovered
in a 350° oven for 1 hour and
15 minutes.
To prepare the bread sauce:
bring the milk to simmering
point in a saucepan. Add
onions, cloves, salt, pepper and
bay leaf. Simmer 15 minutes and
strain the milk. Stir in
breadcrumbs and serve the
sauce hot.

Chicken breasts with lemon and brandy

6 servings

6 *whole chicken breasts*
  (12 single breasts), with
  skin and bones removed
½ *cup flour seasoned with salt*
  and pepper
1 *teaspoon oregano*
3 *tablespoons butter*
2 *tablespoons lemon juice*
2 *tablespoons brandy, warmed*
2 *tablespoons finely chopped*
  parsley

Combine the flour, salt, pepper
and oregano. Dredge the
chicken breasts in the seasoned
flour. Fry breasts in hot butter
6 minutes on each side until
white and tender. Do not
overcook. Add lemon juice
and brandy. Light the brandy
with a match. When the flame
have died down, serve the
chicken breasts on a bed of
boiled rice. Spoon the pan
juices over the chicken and
garnish with chopped parsley.

Chicken stewed in a pot together with vegetables can be found almost everywhere in the world, but in Rumania they vary it by adding white beans.

Pui Românese

Chicken stew

4 servings

1 (3 to 3½ pound) chicken,
  cut into serving pieces
1 teaspoon salt
  Freshly ground black pepper
3 tablespoons butter
2 carrots, finely chopped
2 kohlrabi or turnips, finely
  chopped
1 tablespoon finely chopped
  parsley
1 tablespoon sugar
2 cups chicken broth
1 cup fresh peas
2 tablespoons flour combined
  with
  1 tablespoon softened butter

Sprinkle the chicken pieces with salt and pepper. Heat the butter in a casserole and sauté the chicken a few pieces at a time over medium heat until golden brown on all sides. Remove from the casserole and keep warm. Add the carrots, kohlrabi, parsley and sugar and cook slowly, stirring until the sugar caramelizes. Return the chicken to the pan and add 1 cup broth. Bring to a boil, lower the heat and simmer, covered, 30 minutes until chicken is tender. Add the peas and cook 10 minutes more. Add the remaining broth, bring to a simmer and add the flour/butter mixture a little at a time, stirring constantly. Simmer 3 more minutes to thicken the sauce. Serve from the casserole.

Sacher Huhn

Eingemachtes Huhn

Sacher chicken

6 servings

- 1 *(3½ to 4 pound) roasting chicken*
- ½ *pound bulk sausage*
- 1 *pair sweetbreads, blanched, peeled and chopped*
- ¾ *teaspoon salt*
  Freshly ground black pepper
- 2 *tablespoons butter*
- 3 *tablespoons Madeira*

Remove the giblets from the cavity of the chicken. Chop the liver and reserve the remaining parts for another use. In a bowl, combine the chopped liver, sausage, sweetbreads, ¼ teaspoon salt and pepper. Heat the butter in a skillet and sauté the mixture about 7 minutes, stirring occasionally. Pour off the accumulated fat. Add the Madeira and simmer 2 minutes. Sprinkle the cavity of the chicken with the remaining salt and pepper and stuff with the sausage mixture. Truss the chicken securely and place on a rack in a roasting pan. Roast 10 minutes in a 400° oven. Reduce the heat to 350° and roast 1 hour more until the juices run clear when pricked with a fork. Place the chicken on a platter, remove the trussing strings and serve.

Chicken stew

4 servings

- 1 *(3 pound) chicken, cut into 4 pieces*
- 1 *teaspoon salt*
  Freshly ground black pepper
- ¼ *teaspoon marjoram*
- ½ *teaspoon paprika*
- 4 *tablespoons butter*
- 2 *tablespoons olive oil*
- 2 *onions, cut into rings*
- 2 *carrots, sliced*
- 1 *leek, cut into rings*
- 1 *pound canned lima beans, drained*
- ½ *cup chicken broth*
- 1 *teaspoon lemon juice*

Rub the chicken pieces with salt, pepper, marjoram and paprika. Heat 2 tablespoons butter and 2 tablespoons olive oil in a skillet and brown the chicken pieces on all sides for 10 minutes. Heat the remaining butter in a casserole, add the onions and fry until golden. Add carrots, leek and lima beans and cook for 15 minutes. Add chicken pieces and broth and simmer for 50 to 60 minutes until the chicken is tender. Add lemon juice before serving. Serve with a cabbage salad and sliced green peppers.

Csirke tejfolben

Chicken in sour cream

4 servings

- 3 pounds chicken breasts
- ½ cup flour
- 3 tablespoons butter
- 1 teaspoon salt
  Freshly ground black pepper
  Bouquet garni
- 1 cup chicken broth
- 2 teaspoons paprika
- 1 cup sour cream

Bouquet garni:
- 3 or 4 sprigs parsley
- ½ bay leaf
- 2 sprigs thyme
- ½ small onion
- 2 cloves
- ½ stalk celery

Tie the bouquet garni ingredients in a small piece of cheesecloth that can be removed from the broth.

Dredge the chicken pieces in flour. Heat the butter in a large skillet and fry the chicken until golden brown on both sides. Season with salt and pepper. Add the bouquet garni, chicken broth and paprika. Bring to a boil and simmer for 25 minutes. Discard the bouquet garni. Stir in the sour cream and heat without boiling.

Csirke bácska

Chicken Bacska style

4 to 6 servings

- 3 slices bacon, cut into small pieces
- 2 onions, finely chopped
- 1 tablespoon paprika
- 2 (2 pound) chickens, cut into serving pieces
- ½ teaspoon salt
- 1 cup chicken broth
- 2 tablespoons butter
- 1 cup raw rice
- 2 green peppers, seeded and cut into strips
- 4 medium sized tomatoes, peeled, seeded and sliced
- 1 cup water
- 1 tablespoon chopped parsley

Fry the bacon in a heavy skillet until the fat is rendered. Add the onions and fry 4 to 5 minutes, until the onions are golden and the bacon is crisp. Add the paprika. Sprinkle the chicken with salt and place in the skillet. Add the chicken broth and bring to a boil. Simmer for 25 minutes. Heat the butter in a saucepan, add the rice and stir for 2 to 3 minutes. Add the rice, peppers, tomatoes and 1 cup water to the chicken. Cover and cook in a preheated 375° oven for 20 to 25 minutes until the rice is tender and has absorbed the liquid. Garnish with chopped parsley.

Hühnerragout

Chicken ragout

6 servings

- 1 (3½ to 4 pound) chicken
- 1¼ teaspoons salt
  Freshly ground black pepper
- 3 tablespoons butter
- ⅓ cup finely chopped celery
- 2 carrots, peeled and finely chopped
- 1 parsnip, finely chopped
- 1 cup button mushrooms
- 2 cups chicken broth
- 1 tablespoon lemon juice
- 1 tablespoon flour combined with
  ½ tablespoon softened butter
- 2 tablespoons finely chopped parsley

Sprinkle the chicken inside and out with 1 teaspoon salt and pepper. Heat the butter in a casserole and sauté the chicken over high heat until nicely browned on all sides. Reduce the heat to the lowest possible point, cover the casserole and place an asbestos pad under it. Cook 20 minutes, turning the chicken once. Remove the chicken from the pan and set aside until it is cool enough to handle. Discard the skin and bones and cut the meat into bite sized pieces. Place in a clean casserole and add the celery, carrots, parsnip, mushrooms, ½ the broth, lemon juice, remaining salt and pepper. Bring to a boil, reduce the heat and simmer, partially covered, for 30 minutes. Stir in the remaining broth, the flour mixture and parsley and simmer 20 minutes more.

Paprikás csirke

Paprika chicken

4 servings

- 2 tablespoons olive oil
- 2 onions, finely chopped
- 1 clove garlic, crushed
- 1 tablespoon paprika
- ½ teaspoon cumin
- 1 (2½ to 3 pound) chicken, cut into serving pieces
- ½ teaspoon salt
- 2 cups chicken broth
- 2 carrots, peeled and sliced
- 2 tablespoons tomato paste

Heat the oil in a casserole and sauté the onions and garlic until golden brown. Stir in the paprika and cumin and cook 1 minute. Arrange the chicken pieces on top of the onions and sprinkle with salt. Pour in the broth and add the carrots. Bring to a simmer, cover and cook over low heat 25 minutes. Stir the tomato paste into the broth and simmer, covered, 25 minutes more until chicken is tender. Serve with macaroni or other pasta.

Braised chicken in soy sauce is slowly cooked to perfection.

Chicken and mushrooms

2 American servings
4 Chinese servings

1 whole chicken breast, skinned, boned and cut into ¼ inch cubes
½ teaspoon salt
⅛ teaspoon white pepper
2 teaspoons cornstarch
2 tablespoons oil
1 thin slice fresh ginger root, minced
1 cup small fresh button mushrooms
½ green pepper, seeded and cut into strips 1½ inches long
2 teaspoons cornstarch dissolved in
2 tablespoons chicken broth

Mix salt, pepper and cornstarch. Add chicken cubes and toss to coat. Heat the oil in a wok until very hot. Add ginger root and stir fry ½ minute. Add chicken and stir fry until all traces of pink have disappeared. Remove chicken from the pan. Add mushrooms and green pepper and stir fry 1½ minutes. Return chicken to the pan, add cornstarch mixture and stir until thickened. Serve immediately.

Braised chicken in soy sauce

4 American servings
6 Chinese servings

1 (3 to 4 pound) chicken
¾ cup soy sauce
3 tablespoons sherry
1½ cups chicken broth
½ tablespoon sugar
3 tablespoons oil
3 whole scallions, cut into 1 inch pieces
1 clove garlic, crushed and minced
2 thin slices fresh ginger root, minced

Cut chicken through the bone with a cleaver into 2 inch pieces. Combine soy sauce, sherry, chicken broth and sugar. Bring liquid to boiling point. Cover the saucepan and remove from the heat. Heat oil in a wok or flame-proof casserole. Add chicken pieces and stir fry for 3 minutes until lightly browned on all sides. Add scallions, garlic and ginger root and stir fry for 1 minute. Add hot soy sauce mixture and return to boiling point. Reduce the heat. Cover and simmer for 40 minutes. Place chicken in a serving dish. Strain sauce and add a little of the sauce to the chicken.

Stir fried cooked chicken in oyster sauce

4 American servings
8 Chinese servings

1 (3 pound) chicken, cooked
2 Chinese dried mushrooms
1 small onion
3 tablespoons oil
½ teaspoon salt
1 clove garlic
1 thin slice fresh ginger root
¼ cup chicken broth
2 tablespoons soy sauce
1 tablespoon sherry
2 tablespoons oyster sauce
1 teaspoon sugar
1 tablespoon cornstarch
2 tablespoons water

Cut cooked chicken (through the bones) into 2 inch pieces. Soak dried mushrooms in hot water for 20 minutes, then squeeze dry. Cut off the stems and cut caps in ¼ inch wide strips. Cut onion into 1 inch pieces. Heat 2 tablespoons oil in a wok or other pan. Add salt, garlic and ginger root. Stir fry until lightly browned. Remove garlic and ginger root. Add chicken and stir fry for about 2 minutes or until well browned. Remove from the pan. Add remaining oil, heat and stir fry onion for about 1 minute. Return chicken to the pan. Add mushrooms, chicken broth, soy sauce, sherry, oyster sauce and sugar, and heat through. Dissolve cornstarch in water and stir in to thicken. Serve immediately.

Stir fried shredded chicken and bamboo

2 American servings
4 Chinese servings

1 whole chicken breast
2 tablespoons oil
¼ teaspoon salt
2 scallions, minced
¾ cup shredded bamboo shoots
4 to 5 fresh mushrooms, sliced (optional)
½ cup chicken broth
1 tablespoon soy sauce
½ teaspoon sugar
1 tablespoon cornstarch dissolved in
3 tablespoons water

Remove skin and bones from chicken breast and shred meat. Heat 1 tablespoon oil in a wok or other pan. Add salt and stir fry for 30 seconds. Add chicken and stir fry until it has lost any trace of pink. Remove from pan. Add remaining oil, heat and stir fry scallions, bamboo shoots and mushrooms for 1 to 1½ minutes. Return chicken to the pan. Add chicken broth, soy sauce and sugar and simmer, covered, for another 1½ to 2 minutes. Stir in cornstarch to thicken and serve.

Chicken and nuts

2 American servings
4 Chinese servings

3 single chicken breasts
1 tablespoon cornstarch
2 tablespoons sherry
½ medium onion, finely chopped
2 slices fresh ginger root, minced
1 clove garlic, minced
3 tablespoons soy sauce
1½ tablespoons sherry
1 teaspoon sesame oil
1 teaspoon sugar
¼ cup chicken broth
3 tablespoons oil
¼ cup roasted cashew nuts
1 teaspoon cornstarch
1 tablespoon water

Remove the skin and bones from chicken breasts and cut breasts in ¾ inch cubes. Place the cubes in a small bowl and add 1 tablespoon cornstarch and 2 tablespoons sherry. Mix well. Combine the onion, ginger root and garlic. Combine soy sauce, sherry, sesame oil, sugar and chicken broth. Heat 2 tablespoons of the oil in a wok or a skillet. Add chicken and stir fry for 2 to 3 minutes until chicken is very lightly browned. Remove chicken from the pan. Add remaining 1 tablespoon of oil and heat until the oil is hot. Add onion, ginger root and garlic. Stir fry for 1 minute. Add cashew nuts and stir fry to coat with oil. Return chicken to the pan, add soy sauce mixture and stir fry to heat through. Mix remaining 1 teaspoon cornstarch with water and add to chicken. Stir 1 minute until sauce has thickened. Serve immediately.

Red simmered chicken

4 American servings
8 Chinese servings

1 (3 to 4 pound) chicken
1 to 2 thin slices fresh ginger root, minced
1 clove garlic, crushed
1 tablespoon sugar
1 to 2 cloves star anise
2 tablespoons sherry
½ cup soy sauce
1 tablespoon dark soy sauce (optional)
½ cup chicken broth or water
½ tablespoon sesame oil
6 onion brushes

Dry chicken thoroughly, inside and out, with paper towels. In a heavy casserole, combine all the remaining ingredients except the onion brushes. Bring to a boil and add the chicken. Reduce the heat, cover and simmer 1 to 1½ hours, turning the chicken every 15 minutes. Drain chicken and cut into 2 inch pieces. (You may also remove the meat from the bones and serve it moistened with a little of the sauce.) Decorate with onion brushes and serve.

In China, a chicken with its head and neck intact is used for this dish. The cavity is filled with more sherry and broth or water. The neck is tied closed and the other opening is trussed. The bird is then cooked by the same method, but for a shorter period of time.

White cooked chicken

4 American servings
8 Chinese servings

1 (4 pound) fresh chicken
   Water to cover
3 scallions
3 slices fresh ginger root
1 recipe soy-oil dip sauce or
1 recipe sherry-soy dip sauce

It is important that the chicken used for this dish is of the best quality available. As you will see, the flavor comes only from the chicken itself and not from any other ingredients. Place the whole chicken in a flame-proof casserole just large enough to hold it. Fill the casserole with enough water to cover the chicken. Remove the chicken and bring the water to boiling point. Cut scallions into pieces one inch long. Add scallions and ginger root slices to the water. Replace chicken in the casserole. When the water regains the boiling point, reduce the heat, cover the casserole and cook the chicken for 12 minutes. Turn the chicken, replace the lid and simmer another 10 minutes. Remove the casserole from the heat and allow the chicken to cool in the liquid. Cut the chicken legs and wings into 2 inch sections, cutting through the bone with a heavy cleaver. Arrange slices of breast meat in the center of a serving plate. Place the sections of wing, leg and thigh around the breast. Serve cold with soy-oil or sherry-soy dip sauce

Salt roasted chicken

3 American servings
6 Chinese servings

1 (3 pound) roasting chicken
3 thin slices fresh ginger root
1 scallion
¼ teaspoon salt
1 tablespoon sherry
   Coarse salt

Dip the chicken in boiling water and take it out at once. Wipe dry thoroughly inside and out. Cut the ginger slices in half and the scallion in 1 inch long pieces. Mix with the ¼ teaspoon salt and sherry and rub into the cavity of the chicken. Skewer or truss the chicken. In a casserole that is just big enough to hold the chicken comfortably, make a layer of salt about 1 to 1½ inches thick. Place the chicken on top and surround and top the chicken with a thick layer of salt. Remove the chicken and heat the measured salt in another heavy pan over medium heat, stirring occasionally, for about 45 minutes or until the salt is piping hot. Place a layer of hot salt in the casserole. Lay the chicken on it, breast-side down and surround and top it again with the remaining hot salt. Cover and cook over very low heat for 1 to 1¼ hours. Remove chicken and wipe off all excess salt. Remove skewers or trussing string and remove cavity seasoning. Serve hot or cold, cut into 2 inch pieces.

Deep fried chicken balls

2 American servings
4 Chinese servings

1 whole chicken breast, skinned, boned and coarsely ground
2 scallions, minced
1 tablespoon soy sauce
1 tablespoon sherry
1½ tablespoons cornstarch
¼ teaspoon salt
⅛ teaspoon sugar
1 egg, separated
   Oil for deep frying

Combine all the ingredients except the egg white and oil. Mix until thoroughly blended. Beat the egg white until stiff and fold into the chicken mixture. Chill 1 hour. Heat oil for deep frying until almost smoking. Form chicken mixture into small ovals and deep fry 4 or 5 at a time until golden brown. Remove with a slotted spoon and drain on paper towels. Serve with sweet sour sauce

Deep fried chicken

2 American servings
4 Chinese servings

1 young (2 pound) chicken
   Boiling water
2 teaspoons salt
¼ teaspoon freshly ground pepper
1 tablespoon sherry
½ teaspoon minced fresh ginger
   Oil for deep frying
8 onion brushes

Drop the chicken into boiling water and immediately lift it out. Wipe completely dry with clean towel. Mix salt, pepper, sherry and ginger and rub the chicken with this mixture inside and out. Heat the oil for deep frying until hot but not smoking (about 340 degrees on a deep frying thermometer). Lower chicken in a wire basket into the hot oil and deep fry for about 10 minutes, turning occasionally. Reduce heat to very low, lift out chicken and let cool for 6 to 8 minutes. Reheat oil, return chicken and deep fry for another 8 to 10 minutes or until golden brown and done. Lift out and drain well on paper towels. Arrange on a platter and garnish with onion brushes. Serve with a dip sauce made of 3 tablespoons sherry, 1 tablespoon soy sauce, 1 teaspoon chili sauce and ¼ teaspoon sugar, mixed until well blended.

Stir fried duck slices and bitter melon

4 *American servings*
6 *Chinese servings*

   1 *tablespoon fermented*
      black beans
   1 *clove garlic, minced*
   1 *(4 pound) duck*
   1 *teaspoon soy sauce*
   2 *teaspoons sherry*
  ½ *teaspoon salt*
  ½ *teaspoon sugar*
   2 *teaspoons cornstarch*
  ½ *pound fresh bitter melon (or*
     ½ *of a 16 ounce can bitter*
     melon) or substitute
     cucumber
   4 *to 6 tablespoons oil*
   1 *cup chicken broth*
   2 *teaspoons cornstarch*
1½ *tablespoons water*

Soak black beans in water for 30 minutes. Drain and mash the beans with the garlic. Cut the duck meat from breast and legs and reserve carcass for making stock. Cut meat across the grain in ⅛ to ¼ inch thick slices. Mix soy sauce, sherry, salt, sugar and cornstarch. Add duck slices and mix well. Leave for 20 minutes. When using fresh bitter melon, wash and drain. Remove stalks, cut bitter melon in half lengthwise and remove seedy center. Cut into ¼ inch slices. Bring plenty of salted water to a boil, add bitter melon and parboil for 4 minutes.
Rinse under cold running water until completely cooled. Drain. When using canned bitter melon, just drain off liquid, rinse under cold running water, drain and cut into slices. When cucumber is substituted follow instructions, for fresh bitter melon. Peel the cucumber but do not parboil. Heat half of the oil in a wok or other pan. Add black bean mixture and stir fry for 30 seconds. Add duck slices and stir fry for about 2 to 2½ minutes or until lightly colored. Remove from pan and keep warm. Add remaining oil, heat and stir fry the bitter melon for 1 to 1½ minutes. Add broth and bring to a boil. Return duck slices to the pan, reduce heat, cover and simmer for about 1½ to 2 minutes to heat through. Mix cornstarch with water and stir in to thicken. Serve.

Braised duck with pineapple

6 to 8 *American servings*
6 to 8 *Chinese servings*

   1 *(4 pound) duck*
   6 *slices canned pineapple*
  ½ *cup pineapple juice*
   1 *clove garlic, crushed*
   2 *thin slices fresh ginger root,*
     minced
  ¼ *teaspoon salt*
   3 *tablespoons soy sauce*
   3 *tablespoons sherry*
   1 *teaspoon sugar*
   2 *tablespoons oil*
   2 *whole scallions, cut in ½*
     inch pieces
   3 *cups boiling water*
   1 *tablespoon cornstarch*
     dissolved in
   3 *tablespoons water*

Dip a clean cloth in hot water and wring it out well. Wipe the duck with the cloth. Cut pineapple slices in half and reserve ½ cup pineapple juice. Prick the skin of the duck in several places so the fat will drain. Combine garlic, ginger root and salt and rub the duck with this mixture inside and out. Leave for 10 minutes. Mix the soy sauce with half of the sherry and 1 teaspoon sugar and brush the skin of the duck with the mixture. Let stand 10 minutes and again brush the duck with the mixture. Heat the oil in a heavy casserole just large enough to hold the duck comfortably. Add the duck and fry until nicely browned all over. Discard the accumulated fat. Add the water to the casserole. Bring to a boil, reduce heat, cover and simmer for 1 to 1¼ hours, turning every 15 minutes. Remove the duck carefully and place on a serving dish. Arrange halved pineapple slices around the duck. Stir the cornstarch mixture into the duck broth to thicken. Pour over duck and serve.

Steaming best preserves the rich, natural flavor of chicken, Chinese sausages or ham. Chinese mushrooms provide a colorful and savory contrast to the pure, white chicken meat.

Steamed chicken and sausages

3 American servings
6 Chinese servings

    1   *(2½ pound) chicken*
    2   *tablespoons sherry*
    ½   *teaspoon salt*
    2   *teaspoons cornstarch*
    2 to 3   *Chinese sausages, cut into thick diagonal slices*

With a cleaver, chop chicken into 2 inch pieces. Combine sherry, salt and cornstarch and toss chicken pieces in this mixture. Transfer chicken to a shallow dish and place sausage slices in between and on top of the chicken pieces. Place dish in a steamer and steam 45 minutes to 1 hour or until chicken is tender.

Steamed chicken and ham

3 American servings
6 Chinese servings

    2   *large chicken breasts, boned, but not skinned*
    2 to 3   *slices lean, smoked ham, cut ¼ inch thick*
    6   *large dried Chinese mushrooms*
    ½   *teaspoon salt*
    1   *tablespoon oil*
    1   *tablespoon sherry*

Cut chicken breasts crosswise into ⅓ inch thick slices with a very sharp knife. (Make sure the skin remains attached to the meat.) Cut the ham in as many slices as there are pieces of chicken and in approximately the same shape. Soak the mushrooms in hot water for 20 minutes. Squeeze dry carefully. Cut off the stalks and cut the caps in half. Sprinkle the chicken slices with salt and oil. Sprinkle the ham slices with sherry. In a shallow heatproof bowl, place rows of alternating chicken slices (skin side up) and ham slices. Surround with mushrooms halves or arrange mushrooms between chicken and ham. Steam for about 25 minutes or until tender. Serve hot.

Waterzooi van kip

Belgian chicken stew

4 servings

- *1 (3 pound) roasting chicken*
  Salt
  Freshly ground black pepper
- *3 tablespoons butter*
- *1 leek, finely chopped*
- *1 stalk celery, finely chopped*
- *1 onion, finely chopped*
- *1 carrot, peeled and finely chopped*
- *2 tablespoons finely chopped parsley*
- *¾ cup chicken broth*
- *2 egg yolks*
- *2 tablespoons finely chopped parsley for garnish*

Cut the chicken into 8 pieces and rub each piece with salt and pepper. Butter the bottom of a heavy casserole and make a layer of leek, celery, onion, carrot and parsley. Arrange the chicken pieces on top and place the pan over low heat for 10 minutes. Pour in the hot broth, cover the pan and simmer 1 hour. Remove the pieces of chicken. Beat the egg yolks lightly and add to the broth and the vegetables, stirring constantly. Place part of the mixture in shallow soup bowls. Top with the pieces of chicken and sprinkle with finely chopped parsley.

Brusselse kipgalantine

Chicken pâté

6 to 8 servings

- *4 cups water*
- *1 sprig parsley*
- *½ cup leafy celery tops*
- *½ teaspoon salt*
- *1 bay leaf*
- *¼ teaspoon thyme*
- *1 (1½ pound) chicken*
- *½ pound ground pork*
- *½ pound ground veal*
- *1 clove garlic, crushed*
- *1 small onion, finely chopped*
- *2 eggs*
- *3 tablespoons brandy*
- *¼ pound sliced bacon*

For the pastry:
- *1½ cups flour*
  Pinch of salt
- *5 tablespoons butter*
- *4 tablespoons ice water*

- *1 egg yolk*
- *1 tablespoon cream*

Place the water, parsley, celery tops, salt, bay leaf and thyme in a heavy pan and bring to a boil. Lower the heat, add the chicken and simmer slowly for 1 hour. Meanwhile, prepare the pastry; place the flour and salt in a mixing bowl. Cut the butter into the flour with a pastry blender or 2 knives until the mixture resembles coarse meal. Add the water and stir with a fork until the dough can be gathered into a ball. Wrap the dough in wax paper and refrigerate 1 hour. When the chicken is cooked, drain it and remove the skin and bones. Cut the large pieces into strips and chop the remainder finely. Combine the ground chicken with the pork, veal, garlic, onion, eggs and brandy. Line a pâté mold with the bacon strips and add the ground meat mixture. Arrange the strips of chicken on top lengthwise. Roll out the pastry and cover the pâté. Brush the top with lightly beaten egg yolk combined with 1 tablespoon cream. Make a funnel from aluminum foil and insert into the center of the pâté. Bake the pâté for 1 hour in a preheated 375° oven. Lower the oven temperature to 325°, cover the pâté with foil and bake 1 hour more. The pâté may be served warm or cold and should be sliced very thinly.

Kip met kerrie rijst

Chicken and curry rice

4 servings

- *1 (3½ pound) chicken, cut into serving pieces*
- *1 carrot, peeled and sliced*
- *1 onion, finely chopped*
- *1 sprig parsley*
- *1 bay leaf*
- *¼ teaspoon mace*
- *1 teaspoon salt*
- *4 peppercorns, crushed*
- *1 cup rice*
- *1 tablespoon curry powder*

For the sauce:
- *3 tablespoons butter*
- *4 tablespoons flour*
- *3 cups reserved chicken broth*
- *¼ cup tomato purée*

Place chicken, carrot, onion, parsley, bay leaf, mace, salt and peppercorns in a heavy pan. Add water to cover and bring to a boil. Lower heat, cover and cook for 45 minutes to 1 hour or until chicken is tender. Meanwhile, cook the rice according to package directions. Stir the curry powder into the rice halfway through the cooking time. Remove the chicken pieces and keep warm. Strain and reserve the broth. Heat the butter in a saucepan. Stir in the flour and cook 2 minutes. Add 3 cups of broth gradually, stirring constantly until sauce is thickened and smooth. Stir in tomato purée. Rinse a ring mold with cold water and pack rice into mold. Insert rice on a warm platter and arrange chicken pieces in center.

Gans met appel

Goose with apples

8 servings

- 8 *medium sized cooking apples*
- 5 *tablespoons butter*
- 2 *tablespoons brown sugar*
- 2 *teaspoons cinnamon*
- 4 *cups freshly made breadcrumbs*
- 1 *(9 to 10 pound) young goose or*
- 2 *(4 to 5 pound) ducks*
- 1 *teaspoon salt*

Peel, core and chop the apples. Heat the butter in a large skillet and sauté the apples until lightly browned. Add the sugar, cinnamon and breadcrumbs and cook, stirring, for 2 minutes. Dry the goose thoroughly inside and out and sprinkle the cavity with salt. Stuff the goose with the apple mixture and truss. Prick the skin of the goose or ducks all over with a fork to allow the fat to drain off while cooking. Place the goose on a rack in a roasting pan and roast breast side up in a preheated 400° oven for 15 minutes. Reduce the heat to 350°, turn the bird on its side and roast 50 minutes to 1 hour. Turn the bird onto the other side and roast another 50 minutes to 1 hour. Turn breast side up for the last 15 minutes roasting time. It will take 2¼ to 2½ hours total time for the goose to cook. The ducks will be done in about 1½ hours. Follow the same procedure for roasting the ducks but roast on each side 30 minutes only. Place the goose on a serving platter, remove trussing strings and let stand 10 to 15 minutes before carving.

Hazepeper

Peppered hare

6 servings

- 1 *(4 pound) hare or substitute chicken*
- 1 *cup red wine*
- ½ *cup red wine vinegar*
- 1 *carrot, peeled and sliced*
- 1 *onion, finely chopped*
- 3 *juniper berries*
- 1 *bay leaf*
- 4 *peppercorns, crushed*
  Salt
  Freshly ground black pepper
- 3 *tablespoons butter*
- ½ *medium sized onion, finely chopped*
- ½ *cup thinly sliced fresh mushrooms*
- ¼ *cup chopped smoked ham*
- 2 *cups water*
- 5 *tablespoons flour*
- 3 *to 4 tablespoons butter, softened*
- 2 *tablespoons finely chopped parsley*
- 1 *cup crisp croutons*

Cut the hare into serving pieces and place in a bowl with the wine, vinegar, carrot, onion, juniper berries, bay leaf and peppercorns. Cover the bowl with plastic wrap and let the hare marinate in the refrigerator for 1 to 2 days. Remove the hare. Strain and reserve the marinade. Wipe the pieces of hare thoroughly dry and rub them with salt and pepper. Heat the butter in a casserole and quickly brown the hare on all sides over high heat. Remove the hare from the pan. Add the onion, mushrooms and ham and sauté for about 5 minutes. Remove from the pan and set aside. Pour off all the fat from the pan. Return the pieces of hare to the pan along with the reserved marinade and the water. Bring to a simmer and cover the pan. Cook over low heat for 1¼ hours. Return the onion, mushrooms and ham to the pan and simmer 15 minutes more. Blend the flour and butter together in a small bowl. Add the mixture bit by bit to the simmering liquid, stirring until the sauce is thickened and smooth. Arrange the meat on a platter and pour the sauce over. Garnish with parsley and croutons. Serve with potatoes and applesauce or red cabbage.

Hazebout met pruimen

Hare with prunes

4 servings

    3 tablespoons butter
    2 hare legs or substitute
      turkey legs
    1 onion, finely chopped
    3 tablespoons flour
1½ cups red wine
 ½ teaspoon salt
    Freshly ground black pepper
    2 teaspoons vinegar
    1 tablespoon sugar
    1 cup dried pitted prunes

Melt the butter and sauté the hare legs over moderately high heat until nicely browned. Remove from the pan, add onion and sauté in the same butter until tender. Sprinkle on the flour and cook, stirring, for 1 minute. Add the red wine gradually, stirring to scrape up the brown bits clinging to the bottom of the pan. Return the hare legs to the pan and add salt, pepper, vinegar and sugar. Cover and simmer over low heat for 40 minutes. Add the prunes and continue cooking 30 minutes or until the hare legs are tender.

Brabants konijn

Rabbit Brabant style

4 servings

    1 young (2½ to 3 pound)
      rabbit, cut into serving
      pieces or use chicken
    1 medium sized onion,
      thinly sliced
    1 teaspoon thyme
    1 bay leaf
    1 cup red wine vinegar
 ½ cup water
 ¼ teaspoon salt
    Freshly ground black pepper
 ½ cup flour
    2 tablespoons butter
 ½ pound prunes, soaked
      overnight in water.
    1 tablespoon brown sugar
 ½ cup beer
    2 tablespoons flour

Place the rabbit pieces in a shallow pan. Combine the onion, thyme, bay leaf, vinegar and water and pour the mixture over the rabbit. Cover the pan tightly with plastic wrap or aluminum foil and allow the rabbit to marinate overnight in the refrigerator. Remove the rabbit from the marinade and dry the pieces thoroughly. Sprinkle with salt and pepper and roll in flour. Heat the butter and brown the rabbit on all sides over high heat until golden. Strain and add the marinade. Lower the heat, cover the pan and simmer slowly for 30 minutes. Add the drained prunes and brown sugar and simmer 15 minutes more. Combine the beer and flour and stir until smooth. Add the beer mixture to the rabbit, stirring constantly until the sauce is thickened. Place the rabbit and prunes on a warm serving dish and pour the sauce over.

Vlaams konijn met mosterd

Rabbit with mustard

4 servings

    1 young (2½–3 pound) rabbit
      or substitute chicken
    4 tablespoons mild (Dijon
      type) mustard
    1 teaspoon salt
      Freshly ground black pepper
    6 thin slices bacon
 ½ cup heavy cream
    1 tablespoon flour combined
      with
    2 tablespoons heavy cream

Spread 2 tablespoons of the mustard in the cavity of the rabbit. Sprinkle the outside with salt and pepper. Cover the rabbit with bacon slices and spread the bacon with the remaining mustard. Place the rabbit in a heavy casserole just large enough to hold it. Cover and cook in a 350° oven for 1 to 1½ hours or until tender. Transfer the rabbit to a heated platter. Add cream to the pan juices and bring to a simmer. Stir in the flour-cream mixture with a wire whisk and cook, stirring, 2 to 3 minutes. Cover the rabbit with a little of the sauce and pass the rest separately. This dish is equally good using chicken so don't hesitate to try it.

Stuffed drumsticks baked in wine.

Ta'am V'reah

Stuffed drumsticks baked in wine

6 servings

  6 *large chicken drumsticks*
  2 *medium sized onions, finely chopped*
  2 *tablespoons butter*
  ½ *pound chicken livers, finely chopped*
  1 *cup blanched almonds, toasted and chopped*
  ½ *teaspoon salt*
    Freshly ground black pepper
  2 *cups dry white wine*

Cut lengthwise along the inside of the thigh and leg of each drumstick. Remove the bone, taking care to preserve the shape of the leg. Sew the leg closed, leaving a small opening at the top. Sauté the onions in the butter until softened. Remove from the pan with a slotted spoon. Combine half the onions with the chicken livers, ½ cup almonds, salt and pepper. Fill the mixture into the drumsticks using a pastry bag. Sew up the opening. Arrange the drumsticks in a buttered baking pan. Let them brown in a 400°oven for 10 minutes. Reduce the oven heat to 350°. Pour the wine into the baking pan and bake the drumsticks 1 hour, basting occasionally with the wine. Arrange the drumsticks on a heated platter and sprinkle with the remaining almonds.

Shorabat khodar bidshash

Chicken with vegetable stew

4 servings

1 (2½ pound) chicken, cut in
  8 pieces
6 tablespoons butter
1¾ cups chicken broth
½ teaspoon salt
  Freshly ground black pepper
¼ teaspoon cinnamon
6 small white onions
1 small zucchini, cut in ½ inch
  thick slices
1 carrot, cut in 1 inch pieces
2 medium sized potatoes,
  peeled and cubed
3 medium sized tomatoes,
  peeled, seeded and coarsely
  chopped

Brown the chicken in 4 tablespoons of the butter in a large casserole for about 10 minutes. Add the chicken broth, salt, pepper and cinnamon. Simmer gently for 30 minutes. Sauté the vegetables in the remaining butter for 10 minutes and add to the chicken. Simmer 15 minutes more until the vegetables are tender.

Riz bidshash u banadura

Chicken with rice and tomatoes

4 servings

1½ cups raw rice
1 (3½ pound) frying chicken,
  cut in serving pieces
4 tablespoons butter
2 large tomatoes, peeled,
  seeded and chopped
1 tablespoon tomato paste
1½ cups chicken broth
1½ teaspoons salt
  Freshly ground black pepper
¼ teaspoon cinnamon

Cover the rice with hot water and let stand 30 minutes. Fry the chicken pieces in the butter over a moderately high heat for 15 minutes or until browned. Add the tomatoes, tomato paste, chicken broth, salt, pepper and cinnamon. Bring to a boil, cover, reduce the heat and simmer for 35 minutes until tender. Remove the chicken and reserve ½ cup of the sauce from the pan. If necessary, add enough water to the remaining sauce to make 3 cups. Add the rice and cook for about 20 minutes until tender. Transfer the rice to a serving dish, top with the chicken and pour on the reserved ½ cup of sauce.

Dshash mashi

Stuffed chicken

4 servings

1 (3 pound) chicken
½ pound sausage meat
½ cup rice, cooked for 10
  minutes
1 onion, finely chopped
¼ cup pine nuts, coarsely
  chopped
¼ cup almonds, coarsely
  chopped
½ teaspoon salt
  Freshly ground black pepper
  Few strands of saffron
¼ teaspoon cinnamon
1 tablespoon finely chopped
  parsley
3 tablespoons melted butter

Wash and dry the chicken. Combine the sausage meat, rice, onion, nuts, salt, pepper, saffron, cinnamon, parsley and 2 tablespoons of butter. Stuff the chicken with this mixture and truss. Brush with the remaining butter and roast in a preheated 350° oven for 1¼ hours until tender.

Kotopoulo yemisto

Stuffed chicken

4 servings

1 (3½ pound) chicken
2 slices bacon, diced
2 tablespoons butter
¾ cup finely chopped onions
¾ cup toasted breadcrumbs
½ cup ground walnuts
¼ cup ground filberts
3 tablespoons finely chopped
  parsley
¼ teaspoon salt
  Freshly ground black pepper
  Pinch of cinnamon
2 eggs
1 tablespoon softened butter

Wash and dry the chicken. Reserve the liver. Fry the bacon until crisp. Remove with a slotted spoon and drain on paper towels. Add the butter to the rendered bacon fat and sauté the liver until nicely browned. Remove, drain on paper towels and chop. Add the onions to the pan and sauté until lightly browned. In a bowl, combine the bacon, chicken liver, onions, breadcrumbs, walnuts, filberts, parsley, salt, pepper, cinnamon and eggs. Stuff the chicken with the mixture and truss. Rub the chicken with softened butter and place on a rack in a roasting pan. Roast the chicken in a 350° oven for 1½ hours, basting occasionally with the accumulated pan juices. Remove the trussing strings and place on a serving platter.

Merchavia

Stuffed turkey breast

6 servings

1¾ pounds turkey breast
1 cup pitted green olives
1 egg
½ teaspoon salt
  Freshly ground black pepper
½ teaspoon ground ginger
  Flour
2 tablespoons butter
2 tablespoons oil
¾ cup sweet white wine
1 cup orange juice
½ cup chicken broth
½ cup pitted black olives

Cut 6 slices from the turkey breast and arrange on a flat surface. Chop the remaining turkey meat with half of the green olives and place in a bowl. Add the egg, salt, pepper and ginger and combine thoroughly. Spread some of the mixture on each slice of turkey breast. Roll up each piece beginning at one long side and secure with toothpicks. Dredge each roll in flour and sauté in hot combined butter and oil until golden brown on all sides. Transfer the rolls to an ovenproof baking dish. Add the wine, orange juice and broth to the pan in which the rolls were browned. Bring to a boil and let boil 5 minutes. Chop the remaining green olives with the black olives and sprinkle over the turkey rolls. Pour on the sauce and bake in a 350° oven for 25 minutes. Slice the rolls, place on a heated serving platter and spoon a little of the sauce over the meat. Serve with boiled cauliflower in white sauce, baked eggplant or fried mushrooms.

Fesenjan

Duck in walnut and pomegranate sauce

4 servings

1 (4 pound) duck, cut into
  serving pieces
¾ teaspoon salt
  Freshly ground black pepper
1 cup fresh pomegranate juice
  or
¼ cup pomegranate syrup
4 tablespoons butter
2 medium sized onions, finely
  chopped
1 teaspoon turmeric
½ cup ground walnuts
2 cups chicken broth
  Pinch of sugar
1 tablespoon finely chopped
  parsley
8 whole walnuts

Sprinkle the pieces of duck with ½ teaspoon salt and pepper. If using fresh pomegranate juice, boil it over high heat until reduced to ¼ cup. Heat 2 tablespoons butter in a skillet and sauté the onions 2 minutes. Add the remaining salt, pepper and turmeric and sauté 5 minutes more. With a slotted spoon, transfer the onions to a casserole and add the ground walnuts and chicken broth. Cover and simmer 20 minutes. Meanwhile, heat the remaining butter in the skillet and sauté the pieces of duck over medium heat until well browned on all sides. Transfer to the casserole and cook 45 minutes. Stir in the reduced pomegranate juice or syrup and the sugar and simmer, uncovered, 10 to 15 minutes. Place the duck pieces on a serving dish and pour the sauce over. Garnish with chopped parsley and whole walnuts and serve.

Roast duck with orange sauce.

Although turkey comes from the New World, the dish received quite an enthusiastic welcome in the Old World, and particularly *in the countries around the Mediterranean. Stuffed turkey breast.*

Barvas wusach Yafo

Roast duck with orange sauce

8 servings

- 2 (4 pound) ducks
- 2 teaspoons salt
  Freshly ground black pepper
- 6 oranges
- 2 tablespoons sugar
- 4 tablespoons cornstarch
  dissolved in
  ¼ cup water

Season the cavity of the ducks with salt and pepper. Truss the ducks. Prick the skin with a fork and place on a rack in a large roasting pan. Roast uncovered in a 350° oven for 1¼ hours. Squeeze 5 oranges. Heat the sugar in a pan until melted and brown. Add the orange juice. Stir the cornstarch mixture into the sugar and orange juice and simmer 3 minutes, stirring constantly. Cut the ducks into serving pieces and arrange on a heated platter. Cover with the orange sauce and garnish with slices from the remaining orange. Serve with steamed cabbage, green peas tossed in butter and roast potatoes.

Canard aux pruneaux

Poulet aux olives

Poulet Provençal

Provençal chicken

4 servings

- 1 (2½ to 3 pound) chicken
- 1 teaspoon salt
  Freshly ground black pepper
- 1 teaspoon butter
- 2 tablespoons olive oil
- 4 cloves garlic, peeled and
  cut in half
- ¼ teaspoon rosemary
- ½ teaspoon basil
- ¼ teaspoon thyme

Season the cavity of the chicken with ½ teaspoon of the salt, the pepper and butter. In a pan just large enough to hold the chicken, pour in 1 tablespoon of the oil and add the garlic. Place the chicken in the pan and sprinkle it with the remaining salt, pepper, rosemary, basil, thyme and remaining olive oil. Roast the chicken in a 425° oven for 1 hour, basting frequently. Remove from the pan and cut in serving pieces. Serve hot or cold.

Salpicon de dinde à la Berrichonne

Turkey in red wine sauce

6 servings

- 3 cups left over roast turkey,
  cut into small pieces
- ½ pound bacon, fried until
  crisp, then crumbled
- 2 tablespoons butter
- 1 onion, finely chopped
- ½ pound mushrooms, sliced
- 1 teaspoon paprika
- 2 tablespoons flour
- 1 cup chicken broth
- 1 cup red wine
- 2 tablespoons brandy (optional)
- 1 bay leaf
- ½ teaspoon marjoram or oregano
- 1 teaspoon salt
  Freshly ground black pepper
- 2 tablespoons finely chopped
  parsley

Sauté onion in hot butter for three minutes until softened. Add mushrooms and cook over moderate heat for 2 minutes. Stir in the paprika and flour and add chicken broth, red wine and brandy. Place turkey and bacon in a buttered baking dish. Add bay leaf, marjoram, salt and pepper. Add the sauce. Cover and cook in a 400° oven for 15 minutes. Garnish with parsley.

Poulet au citron

Chicken with lemon

6 servings

2 (2 pound) chickens, cut into
   serving pieces
2 tablespoons butter
1 tablespoon olive oil or
   vegetable oil
   Grated rind and juice of
   2 lemons
1 teaspoon salt
   Freshly ground black pepper
2 tablespoons finely chopped
   parsley
2 tablespoons finely chopped
   chives
1 teaspoon marjoram
1 tablespoon paprika
2 tablespoons butter
1 cup chicken broth
¼ cup white vermouth
2 tablespoons cornstarch,
   dissolved in 3 tablespoons
   cold water
   Watercress or parsley
   for garnish

Brown chicken pieces in combined
hot butter and oil. Adjust the
heat to prevent the butter from
burning. Transfer chicken with
its cooking butter to a large
baking dish. Sprinkle with lemon
rind and juice. Season with salt
and pepper. Cover the dish
with foil and bake in a 350° oven
for 45 minutes. Remove foil and
add parsley, chives, marjoram
and paprika. Dot chicken with
butter and place under a broiler
for 5 minutes until the skin is
crisp and golden. Pour juices
out of the dish into a saucepan.
Add chicken broth and vermouth
Bring to boiling point and stir
in cornstarch dissolved in cold

water. Simmer 2 more minutes
until sauce is thickened. Serve
hot with rice. Garnish plate with
watercress or parsley clusters.

Poulet à la moutarde

Broiled chicken with mustard

4 servings

2 (1½ pound) frying chickens,
   cut into quarters
2 tablespoons butter, melted
1 tablespoon olive oil or
   vegetable oil
1 teaspoon salt
   Freshly ground black pepper
2 tablespoons scallions, finely
   chopped
2 tablespoons mild (Dijon)
   mustard
1½ tablespoons flour
1 cup chicken broth
1 teaspoon tomato paste
1 tablespoon lemon juice
¼ teaspoon thyme

Brush chickens with combined
butter and oil. Season with salt
and pepper. Place 5 inches
from the broiler and broil
chickens 20 minutes on each side.
Spoon 2 tablespoons of butter
from broiling pan into a saucepan
and sauté scallions four minutes
until tender. Stir in mustard
and flour. Add chicken broth,
tomato paste, lemon juice and
thyme. Spoon sauce over the
chicken and serve hot.

Suprèmes de volaille au fromage

Chicken breasts with ham and cheese

6 servings

6 whole (12 single breasts)
   chicken breasts
6 slices Proscuitto ham or
   thinly sliced boiled ham
6 thin slices Swiss or Gruyère
   cheese
1 cup flour seasoned with 1
   teaspoon salt
   Freshly ground black pepper
3 eggs, lightly beaten
1 cup fine breadcrumbs
2 tablespoons butter
1 tablespoon olive oil or
   vegetable oil
3 tablespoons finely chopped
   parsley

Ask the butcher to remove skin
and bones from each chicken
breast and pound them ½ inch
thick. Cut each slice of ham and
cheese in half and place on
each breast. Fold each breast in
half. Trim ham and cheese so
they fit neatly into each breast
and do not protrude from the
edges. Dip breasts first in seasoned
flour, then into the egg and
finally into the breadcrumbs.
Heat butter and oil in a large
skillet. Sauté breasts 6 minutes on
each side until white and tender.
Garnish with parsley and
serve hot.

Poulet ou oie farcie aux pommes

Stuffed chicken or goose with apples

6 servings

- *1 (5 pound) roasting chicken or goose*
- *2 tablespoons butter, melted*
- *1 pound pork sausage meat*
- *2 tablespoons butter*
- *2 onions, finely chopped*
- *2 stalks celery, chopped*
- *½ cup English walnuts, chopped*
- *2 apples, peeled, cored and thinly sliced*
- *1 teaspoon salt*
- *Freshly ground black pepper*
- *1 teaspoon sage*
- *1 egg, lightly beaten*
- *1 (1 pound) jar small unpeeled red apples, drained*
- *2 pounds fresh chestnuts, boiled and peeled or 1 pound canned chestnuts*

Cook pork sausage and drain off the accumulated fat. Heat 2 tablespoons butter in a skillet and sauté onions, celery and nuts for three minutes. Add and cook apples three minutes until slightly softened. Remove from the heat and stir in sausage meat. Season with salt, pepper and sage. Stir in the egg. Fill dressing into the chicken or goose and skewer the cavity. Brush chicken with melted butter. Place on a roasting rack and roast uncovered in a 375° oven for 2¼ hours. Simmer cooked chestnuts in boiling water for 5 minutes until they are hot. Place chicken or goose on a serving platter. Arrange apples and chestnuts around the chicken and serve hot.

Note: Though goose is generally difficult to find in the supermarket, you may be fortunate enough to come across one at Christmas time, or ask the butcher. He might know of a source and be able to order one for you.

Dinde à la Poitevine

Turkey from Poitou

6 servings

- *1 (4½ pound) turkey breast, boned, rolled and tied*
- *3 tablespoons butter*
- *2 medium onions, sliced*
- *2 cloves garlic, crushed*
- *2 slices bacon*
- *4 medium tomatoes, peeled, seeded and chopped*
- *1 teaspoon salt*
- *Freshly ground black pepper*
- *½ teaspoon thyme*
- *1 tablespoon chopped parsley*
- *2 cups dry white wine*
- *2 tablespoons olive oil*
- *1 pound small white onions*
- *1 tablespoon sugar*
- *¼ cup dry red wine*
- *¼ cup brandy*
- *1 tablespoon arrowroot or cornstarch dissolved in 3 tablespoons water*
- *Sprigs of parsley*

In a large heavy casserole, melt the butter until foaming. Brown the turkey quickly on all sides. Remove to a side dish and add the onions and garlic to the pan. Cook until softened. Strain off the butter. Return the turkey to the casserole and cover with bacon to prevent it from drying out. Add the tomatoes, salt, pepper, thyme, parsley and white wine. Bring to a simmer, cover and cook slowly for 2 hours or until the meat is tender Meanwhile, sauté the white onions in olive oil until golden. Drain off the oil and add the sugar and red wine. Cook until the liquid is syrupy. When the turkey is done, remove it from the casserole, wrap in aluminum foil and keep warm in a 200° oven. Strain the sauce and skim off the fat. Purée the onions and tomatoes in the blender or force through a sieve. Return the purée to the sauce and bring to a simmer. Add the white onions and brandy and simmer slowly 5 minutes. Thicken, with the arrowroot mixture. Slice the turkey and arrange attractively on a warmed platter. Pour the sauce over and decorate the dish with sprigs of parsley. Serve hot.

Poulet Provençal

Coq au vin blanc

Chicken in white wine

4 servings

- 1 (3½ pound) chicken, cut into serving pieces
- 2 tablespoons butter
- 1 tablespoon olive oil or vegetable oil
- 1 onion, finely chopped
- 1 clove garlic, crushed
- 3 tablespoons flour
- 1 cup white wine
- 1 cup chicken broth
- 1 tablespoon tomato paste
- 2 ripe tomatoes, peeled, seeded and chopped
- ½ teaspoon basil
- 1 bay leaf
- ¼ teaspoon salt
  Freshly ground black pepper
- 2 tablespoons parsley, finely chopped

Brown chicken in combined butter and oil. Transfer chicken pieces to a casserole. In the same skillet, sauté onion and garlic for 3 minutes until softened. Stir in flour and add wine and chicken broth gradually. Add tomato paste, tomatoes, basil, bay leaf, salt and pepper. Cover casserole and cook 45 minutes in a 350° oven. Garnish with parsley.

Berliner Hühnerfrikassee

Böhmisches Huhn

Chicken à la Bohème

3–4 servings

1 *(2–3 lb.) roasting chicken*
½ *teaspoon salt*
4 *ounces vermicelli spaghetti,*
 cooked
¼ *cup chopped parsley*
¼ *cup grated cheese*
1 *egg*
1 *tablespoon margarine or*
 butter
2 *cups chicken bouillon*

Wash and dry chicken; sprinkle
salt in cavity. Mix cooked
spaghetti, parsley, cheese, and
egg; stuff chicken with mixture.
Rub margarine on chicken.
Place in roasting pan on rack.
Roast in (350°) oven for about
1½ hours or until chicken
is done when tested. Remove
chicken from pan. Cut in half
lengthwise; place vermicelli
stuffing on platter and place
chicken halves on top. Pour
bouillon into roasting pan
and stir to combine with pan
juices; serve as gravy.

Huhn mit Gemüse und Kräuter

Chicken poached with vegetables and herbs

8 servings

2 *(2–3 lb.) frying chickens cut*
 into serving pieces
1 *tablespoon flour*
1 *teaspoon salt*
⅛ *teaspoon pepper*
¼ *pound bacon, diced*
1 *medium onion, chopped*
1 *medium carrot, chopped*
¼ *cup chopped parsley*
1 *medium sized tart apple,*
 cored and chopped or
¼ *cup canned apple slices,*
 chopped
6 *peppercorns*
1 *bay leaf*
½ *teaspoon whole dried thyme*
½ *cup dry white wine*
 Hot cooked noodles

Sprinkle flour in cooking bag
large enough to contain
chicken pieces comfortably.
Sprinkle chicken with salt and
pepper. Cook diced bacon in
large skillet until crisp. Add
chopped vegetables and apple;
cook over medium heat until
transparent. Add peppercorns,
bay leaf and thyme. Spread
mixture in cooking bag in pan
with 2″ sides. Place chicken
pieces on vegetables; add wine.
Close bag with twist tie;
puncture bag with sharp-tined
fork 3 or 4 times. Place pan
with bag in moderately slow
oven (325°) until chicken is
tender and slightly browned,
about 1 hour. Serve with hot
buttered noodles.

Hähnchen Berliner Art

Rock-Cornish hens, Berlin style

4 servings

4 *(1¼ lb.) frozen Rock-*
 Cornish hens, thawed
1 *(6 oz.) package rice and*
 wild rice, prepared
 according to package
 directions
1 *small onion, chopped*
1 *stalk celery, finely chopped*
½ *cup seedless grapes, halved*
½ *cup slivered almonds*
½ *teaspoon salt*
½ *teaspoon thyme*
¼ *cup melted margarine or*
 butter

Wash and dry hens. Combine
rice, onion, celery, grapes,
almonds, salt and thyme; mix
well. Fill neck and body
cavities lightly with stuffing;
skewer openings shut. Place
hens in large shallow roasting
pan; brush with melted
margarine. Roast hens in a hot
oven (400°) about 1 hour or
until well browned and
drumstick twists easily out of
thigh joint, basting several
times with margarine.

Gebratene Hähnchen

Roast Rock-Cornish hens

4 servings

4 *(1–lb.) frozen Rock-Cornish*
 hens, thawed
1 *teaspoon salt*
¼ *teaspoon black pepper*
4 *slices bacon, diced*
2 *slices day-old bread*
⅓ *cup milk*
1 *tablespoon chopped parsley*
5 *tablespoons margarine or*
 butter
1 *cup beef bouillon*
1 *tablespoon flour*
½ *cup sour cream*

Wash and dry hens. Rub inside
cavities with salt and pepper.
In a skillet, cook bacon until
crisp. Brown the livers of the
hens; chop into small pieces.
Soften bread in milk and
squeeze out. Add bacon,
chopped livers, and parsley.
Stuff hens with mixture. Melt
margarine in roasting pan
and brown each hen. Roast in
moderate oven (350°) for 1–1½
hours or until hens are
cooked. Remove hens and keep
warm. Pour bouillon into
roasting pan and stir over direct
heat to loosen drippings. Stir
in flour. Cook until slightly
thickened. Stir in sour cream.
Serve gravy with roast hens.

Berliner Hühnerfrikassee

Festlicher Putenbraten

Berlin style chicken fricassee

6 servings

2 *(8 oz.) cans chicken gravy*
4 *tablespoons dry white wine*
1 *tablespoon lemon juice*
2 *cups cubed, cooked chicken*
1 *cup diced ham*
6 *sausages, cooked and sliced*
1 *(3 oz.) can sliced mushrooms, drained*
1 *tablespoon capers*
1 *(8½ oz.) can asparagus pieces, drained*
½ *cup sour cream*
Hot cooked rice

Combine gravy, wine and lemon juice in saucepan; blend well. Stir in chicken, ham, sausages and mushrooms. Heat, stirring constantly. Add capers and asparagus spears; heat. Stir in sour cream until well blended. Serve over rice.

Roast stuffed turkey

8–10 servings

1 *tablespoon margarine or butter*
1 *large onion, chopped*
1 *apple, peeled, cored and chopped*
1 *pound ground pork*
½ *pound sausage meat*
8 *dried apricots, halved*
8 *prunes, pitted and halved*
1 *(8 oz.) package stuffing mix*
1 *cup apple juice or water*
1 *(10–12 lb.) turkey*
1 *onion, quartered*
1 *stalk celery, chopped*
2 *teaspoons salt*
4 *tablespoons flour*

Melt margarine in large skillet; sauté onion and apple in margarine until onion is transparent. Add meat; cook until lightly browned, stirring constantly. Add fruit, stuffing mix and juice; blend lightly. Remove giblets from turkey; place in 1 quart saucepan with onion, celery and 1 teaspoon salt. Cover with water. Simmer, covered, about 1–1½ hours. Strain; reserve stock. Rub neck and body cavities of turkey lightly with remaining teaspoon salt. Stuff neck and body cavities lightly with stuffing; skewer openings shut. Place turkey, breast side up, on rack in shallow roasting pan. Insert meat thermometer in thigh muscle. Place a loose tent of foil over bird (remove last 30 minutes). Roast in a slow oven (325°) about 2½–3 hours or until thermometer reads 185°.

Move drumstick up and down; if it moves easily, bird is done. Place bird on warm platter. Drain off fat. Stir flour into 2 cups stock; add to drippings. Cook over medium heat, stirring constantly, until thickened.

Thüringer Gans

Thuringian roast goose

4–6 servings

  1 (8–9 lb.) goose, fresh or frozen
  1 tablespoon salt
  1 teaspoon dried marjoram
  2 medium onions, peeled
  1 stalk celery, broken into 3–4 pieces
  Salt
  Pepper
  6 cloves
  2 apples, well washed
  1 cup chicken or goose stock or water
  1 cup orange juice
  2 tablespoons cornstarch
  ¼ cup cold water

Thaw goose, if frozen. Remove giblets; place in 1-qt. saucepan with one of the onions, celery pieces, salt and pepper. Cover with water. Simmer, partially covered, for about 1–1½ hours. Strain; reserve stock. Meanwhile, wash and dry goose; sprinkle inside and out with salt. Sprinkle marjoram inside, stick cloves in second onion and place in cavity with the apples. Skewer openings together. Place goose on a rack in a large roasting pan, breast side down. Roast in a hot oven (400°) for 45 minutes. Drain fat from roasting pan. Reduce oven temperature to 325° and roast until tender when pierced with a fork and juices are light yellow, not pink, about 1 hour. Drain fat from pan. Turn goose breast side up on rack; brown in oven until golden, about 30 minutes. Remove to a warm platter. Skim off remaining fat. Add stock or water and orange juice to pan juices. Mix cornstarch and cold water, add to pan. Cook over medium heat, stirring constantly, until gravy is thickened.

Vierländer Mastente

Roast duckling with apples

4–6 servings

  1 (4–5 lb.) frozen duckling thawed
  1 teaspoon salt
  ¼ teaspoon black pepper
  4 apples, thinly sliced and peeled
  2–3 slices day-old bread, cubed
  ½ teaspoon poultry seasoning
  ¼ cup blackberry brandy (or orange juice)
  1 onion, sliced

Thoroughly wash duck. Sprinkle inside cavity with salt and pepper. Mix apple slices, bread cubes, poultry seasoning and brandy. Stuff duck with mixture. Place on rack in roasting pan. Prick breast with fork. Place onion in pan around duck. Roast, uncovered, at (325°) for 2½–3 hours. Pour off fat as it accumulates. Baste occasionally with pan drippings. Serve with baked stuffed apples, if desired.

Ente, Berliner Art

Berlin style duckling

4 servings

  1 frozen duckling (about 5 pounds), thawed
  1½ teaspoons salt
  ¼ teaspoon black pepper
  ½ teaspoon powdered marjoram
  4 tart apples, peeled, cored and quartered
  ¾ cup hot water
  1 tablespoon cornstarch
  2 tablespoons cold water

Wash and dry thawed duckling. Sprinkle inside and out with salt and pepper. Sprinkle marjoram inside, place apples in cavity and skewer shut. Pour water into roasting pan. Place duckling breast side down in pan. Roast in moderate oven (350°) for about 40 minutes. Pour off fat. Baste frequently with pan juices. Turn duck over, cook another 50–60 minutes or until thigh is tender when pierced with a fork and juices are yellow, not pink. Remove duck to a warm platter. Pour off fat. Measure drippings, make up to 1 cup with water or stock. Stir cornstarch into cold water, add to pan juices. Cook over medium heat, stirring constantly, until thickened. Serve with carved duckling.

Pollo alla cacciatora

Pollo alla cacciatora

Chicken hunters' style

4 servings

  4 tablespoons salad oil
  1 (3 pound) chicken, cut
     into 8 pieces
  2 thick slices bacon, diced
  2 medium onions, chopped
  1 ($4^1/_2$ ounce) can sliced
     mushrooms, drained
  1 tablespoon chopped parsley
  1 teaspoon dried basil
  1 teaspoon salt
$^1/_8$ teaspoon black pepper
$^1/_4$ cup dry white wine
  1 (1 pound) can tomatoes,
     drained
  1 (10 ounce) package frozen
     peas, cooked

Heat oil in large skillet; brown chicken; remove. Add bacon; cook about 1 minute over medium heat. Add onions and mushrooms; cook until onions are transparent. Return chicken to skillet; sprinkle with parsley, basil, salt and pepper. Add wine and tomatoes. Cover. Simmer, turning once, until tender about 25–30 minutes. Remove chicken to heated platter; pour sauce over chicken. Arrange peas around chicken. Serve at once.

Anitra brasata con lenticchie

Braised duck with lentils

4 servings

1¹/₂ cups dry lentils
    Water
1 (5 pound) duck
3 tablespoons salad oil
4 slices bacon, diced
1 medium onion, chopped
1 medium carrot, chopped
1 large stalk celery,
    chopped
1 tablespoon chopped
    parsley
¹/₂ teaspoon dried thyme
1 bay leaf, if desired
1 cup dry white wine
1 teaspoon salt
¹/₈ teaspoon black pepper
¹/₂ cup chicken bouillon
    or water

Wash lentils; place in 2-quart
bowl. Cover lentils with water;
let soak 2 hours. Prick skin of
duck all over with fork. Heat oil
in large roasting pan; brown
duck in hot oil; remove. Discard
fat. Fry out bacon; add onion,
carrot, celery, parsley, thyme
and bay leaf. Cook over medium
heat until onion is transparent;
add ¹/₂ cup wine. Return duck
to pan. Cover. Roast in a
moderate oven (350°) about 1
hour. Meanwhile, drain lentils.
Place in large saucepot; cover
with water; add salt and pepper.
Bring to a boil; reduce heat;
simmer until tender, about 15
minutes. Drain well. Pour lentils
around duck. Add remaining
wine and bouillon. Cover.

Simmer on top of range, over
low heat, about 30 minutes or
until duck is tender, or no pink
juice appears when duck is
pricked with fork. Serve hot
with the lentils.

Anitra brasata con olive verdi

Duck with olives

4 servings

1 (5 pound) duck
¹/₄ cup olive oil
3 tablespoons brandy
1 bay leaf
3 sprigs parsley
1 stalk celery, chopped
¹/₂ teaspoon dried rosemary
¹/₂ teaspoon dried thyme
¹/₂ cup dry white wine
1 cup pitted green
    olives, chopped

Wash and dry duck. Pour olive
oil into heavy roasting pan;
heat. Brown duck on all sides,
pricking with fork in several
places. Remove from heat.
Warm brandy; pour over duck;
light with a match. When flames
subside, add bay leaf, parsley,
celery, rosemary, thyme, and
wine to roasting pan. Cover;
bake in a slow oven (325°) until
duck is tender, about 2–2¹/₂
hours. Remove duck from pan;
keep warm. Discard bay leaf,
parsley and celery; skim off
excess fat. Cook until liquid is
reduced to 1 cup; stir in olives.
Serve over duck.

Spezzatino di pollo alla trasteverina

Trastevere chicken

6 servings

- *1 (2¹/₂–3 pound) chicken, cut into 8 pieces*
- *1 teaspoon salt*
- */₄ teaspoon black pepper*
- *¹/₃ cup flour*
- *5 tablespoons olive oil*
- *¹/₄ pound ham, cubed*
- *2 cloves garlic, minced*
- *¹/₂ cup dry white wine*
- *2 green peppers, cut into rings*
- *1 cup sliced mushrooms*
- *2 medium onions, chopped*
- *1 (¹/₂ pound) zucchini, sliced*
- *¹/₂ teaspoon dried marjoram*
- *1 tablespoon chopped parsley*
- *1 (1 pound) can tomatoes*

Sprinkle chicken with salt, pepper and flour. Heat oil in a large skillet; brown chicken in oil. Cook until tender, about 15–20 minutes. Remove; keep warm. Brown ham; remove; drain. Stir in garlic and wine; cook until wine is reduced by half. Add remaining ingredients; simmer 8–10 minutes. Add chicken and ham; stir to blend. Cook until heated throughout, about 10–15 minutes.

Pollo farcito lessato con salsa di capperi

Chicken with caper sauce

4 servings

- *³/₄ cup margarine or butter*
- *¹/₄ pound chicken livers, chopped*
- *1 (4 ounce) can sliced mushrooms*
- *2¹/₂ cups bread crumbs*
- *¹/₂ cup milk*
- *1 tablespoon parsley*
- *¹/₄ teaspoon dried oregano*
- *¹/₄ teaspoon nutmeg*
- *1 (4–5 pound) roasting chicken*
- *2 cups water*
- *1 medium onion, sliced*
- *1 stalk celery, chopped*
- *1 carrot, chopped*
- *¹/₄ teaspoon dried thyme*
- *1 bay leaf*
- *2 tablespoons capers*
- *4 anchovy fillets*

Melt 4 tablespoons margarine in large skillet. Brown chicken livers in margarine; add mushrooms; cook 1 minute. Soak bread crumbs in milk; drain. Add bread crumbs, parsley, oregano, and nutmeg; mix lightly. Stuff body and neck cavities of chicken lightly; truss. Place chicken in Dutch oven; add water, onion, celery, carrot, thyme and bay leaf. Cover. Cook over low heat until chicken is tender, about 1¹/₂ hours. Chop capers and anchovies together. Melt remaining margarine in small saucepan; add capers and anchovies. Serve over chicken.

Pollo oreganato

Chicken oregano

4 servings

- *1 (2¹/₂–3 pound) chicken, quartered*
- *1 teaspoon salt*
- *¹/₈ teaspoon black pepper*
- *¹/₃ cup olive or salad oil*
- *4 tablespoons lemon juice*
- *1 clove garlic, minced*
- *1 teaspoon finely chopped parsley*
- *2 teaspoons dried oregano*

Place chicken skin side up, on broiler pan. Sprinkle with half the salt and pepper. Combine remaining ingredients; blend well; brush on chicken. Broil under medium heat, 3″ from heat, basting frequently, about 10–12 minutes. Turn chicken with tongs, sprinkle with salt and pepper; baste well. Continue to cook, basting frequently, until chicken is done. or no pink juice appears when chicken is pricked with a fork.

Filetti di pollo alla piemontese

Piedmontese breast of chicken

4 servings

- *4 chicken breasts, skinned and boned*
- *¹/₃ cup flour*
- *1 teaspoon salt*
- *¹/₄ teaspoon black pepper*
- *4 tablespoons margarine or butter*
- *1 chicken bouillon cube*
- *³/₄ cup hot water*
- *¹/₂ cup dry white wine*
- *¹/₃ cup grated Parmesan cheese*
- *1 tablespoon chopped parsley*

Place chicken breasts between 2 sheets waxed paper; pound to flatten. Place flour, salt and pepper in large brown paper bag. Drop several pieces of chicken into bag at a time; shake to coat each piece with the flour mixture. Melt margarine in large skillet; brown chicken in margarine. Cook until done, about 5–8 minutes. Remove chicken from pan; keep warm. Dissolve bouillon cube in water. Stir bouillon and wine into skillet; blend with drippings; cook until liquid is reduced by half. Place chicken pieces on a heatproof platter; pour sauce over chicken. Sprinkle with grated Parmesan cheese. Heat under broiler until cheese browns, about 3–5 minutes. Garnish with chopped parsley.

Pollo imbottito arrostito

Pollo imbottito arrostito

Roast chicken with ham stuffing

6 servings

> 1 *(4–5 pound) roasting*
>   *chicken*
> 3 *tablespoons olive oil*
> 4 *bread slices, cubed*
> 1 *egg*
> 4 *ounces prosciutto or*
>   *smoked ham, chopped*
> 1 *tablespoon chopped parsley*
> 1 *clove garlic, minced*
> $^1/_2$ *teaspoon salt*
> $^1/_4$ *teaspoon dried marjoram*
> $^1/_8$ *teaspoon black pepper*
> $^1/_4$ –$^1/_2$ *cup chicken bouillon*

Rub chicken with olive oil inside
and out. Combine remaining
ingredients; mix lightly. Stuff
body and neck cavities of
chicken lightly; truss. Place
chicken on rack in roasting pan.
Roast in a slow oven (325°)
$1^1/_2$–2 hours or until chicken is
tender and well browned.
Remove chicken from oven.
Place on serving platter.
Remove stuffing from chicken;
arrange around chicken.
Garnish with quartered tomato.

Filetti di pollo alla bolognese

Bolognese breast of chicken

4 servings

> 2 *whole boned chicken*
>   *breasts*
> $^1/_2$ *teaspoon salt*
>   *Dash black pepper*
> 2 *tablespoons flour*
> 2 *eggs, slightly beaten*
> $^1/_3$ *cup dry fine bread crumbs*
> 4 *tablespoons margarine or*
>   *butter*
> 4 *slices boiled ham*
> 4 *slices fontina or*
>   *provolone cheese*
> $^1/_4$ *cup dry white wine*
> 1 *(10^{1}2 ounce) can chicken*
>   *gravy*

Separate each chicken breast
into two portions. Place chicken
breasts between two pieces
waxed paper; pound to flatten.
Sprinkle with salt, pepper and
flour; shake off excess flour.
Dip into beaten egg, then into
bread crumbs. Melt margarine
in large skillet over medium
heat. Sauté chicken breasts until
golden brown, about 3–4
minutes each side. Place in
$11^3/_4'' \times 7^1/_2'' \times 1^3/_4''$ baking
dish. Place ham slice on each
chicken breast; top with slice of
cheese. Bake in hot oven (450°),
about 10 minutes or until cheese
is melted. Brown under broiler,
if desired. Combine wine and
chicken gravy in small saucepan.
Heat, stirring constantly until
hot. Serve with chicken breasts.

Christmas turkey Menorca style

Duck Ribadeo style

Pavo de Navidad a la menorquina

Christmas turkey Menorca style

6 to 8 servings

  1 *(8 pound) turkey*
  4 *cups breadcrumbs, freshly made*
  4 *tablespoons butter, melted*
  2 *tablespoons honey*
½ *cup raisins*
½ *cup boiling water*
    Grated rind 1 lemon
½ *teaspoon cinnamon*
  2 *eggs, lightly beaten*
½ *teaspoon salt*
    Freshly ground black pepper
  4 *tablespoons solid shortening*
  2 *teaspoons paprika*

To prepare the stuffing, place the breadcrumbs in a bowl. Add the butter and honey. Soak the raisins in boiling water for 5 minutes. Drain and add raisins to breadcrumbs. Stir in the lemon rind, cinnamon, eggs, salt and pepper. Fill the stuffing into the turkey cavity and secure with poultry lacers or truss with string. Rub the outer skin with shortening and sprinkle with paprika. Roast the turkey uncovered in a preheated 350° oven for 2½ to 3 hours. Cover the turkey with foil and allow it to stand 20 minutes before carving.

Frango na púcara

Chicken in the pot

4 servings

- 1 *(3 pound) chicken, cut into serving pieces*
- 1 *tablespoon oil*
- 2 *tablespoons mild prepared mustard*
- ¼ *pound boiled ham, diced*
- 10 *small white onions, peeled*
- 2 *tomatoes, peeled, seeded and cut into wedges*
- ½ *cup Port wine*
- ¼ *cup brandy*
- 1 *cup dry white wine*
- ½ *teaspoon salt*
  Freshly ground black pepper
- 2 *tablespoons butter*
- 1 *tablespoon cornstarch dissolved in 2 tablespoons cold water*

Brown the chicken pieces in hot combined butter and oil. Remove the chicken and brush with mustard. Arrange the chicken in a baking dish. Place ham over the chicken and add onions and tomatoes to the dish. Add Port wine, brandy and white wine. Season with salt and pepper and dot with butter. Cover and cook in a preheated 350° oven for 1 hour until tender. Stir the cornstarch paste into the juices and cook for 2 minutes until thickened.

Pato a la moda de Ribadeo

Duck Ribadeo style

6 servings

- 1 *(4 pound) duck*
- ½ *teaspoon salt*
  Freshly ground black pepper
- ½ *pound bacon, cut into small pieces*
- 3 *tablespoons butter*
- 1 *small turnip, peeled and cut into wedges*
- 18 *small white onions, peeled*
- 4 *carrots, peeled and cut into 2 inch pieces*
- 1 *bay leaf*
- 1 *clove garlic, crushed*
- ½ *teaspoon thyme*
- ½ *teaspoon marjoram*
- 3 *sprigs parsley*
- ½ *cup white wine*
- 3 *tablespoons anisette liqueur (optional)*
- 24 *roasted chestnuts or 1 (1 pound) can whole chestnuts*

Wash and dry the duck thoroughly. Season cavity and the skin with salt and pepper. Truss the duck or lace with poultry skewers. Fry the bacon in a large casserole or baking dish until all the fat has rendered. Remove the bacon and add the butter. Brown the duck, breast side first, in combined hot bacon fat and butter. When the duck has browned on all sides, leave it breast side up in the dish. Add the turnip wedges, onions, carrots, bay leaf, garlic, thyme, marjoram and parsley. Cover with a lid or aluminum foil and cook in a preheated 350° oven for 1 hour. Pour off the fat from the dish and add the wine and anisette. Cover and continue cooking for 20 minutes. Add the chestnuts and cook for 10 minutes longer until the chestnuts are hot. Serve the duck whole or cut into serving pieces. Surround the duck with the vegetables. Strain the pan juices and spoon over the duck.

Pastelão de aves

Poultry pie

6 servings
Preheat oven to 350°

- 6 *tablespoons olive oil*
- 1 *(2½ pound) chicken, cut into 8 pieces*
- 1 *medium sized carrot, sliced*
- 2 *cloves garlic, crushed*
- 1 *tablespoon chopped parsley*
- 1 *teaspoon salt*
  Freshly ground black pepper
- 1 *onion, finely chopped*
- ¼ *pound chicken livers, washed and dried*
- ½ *cup slivered ham*
- 4 *large mushrooms, sliced*
- 2 *tablespoons flour*
- 2 *tablespoons Port wine*
- 1 *prebaked pie crust*

Heat 4 tablespoons olive oil in a casserole and brown the chicken pieces on all sides. Pour off fat and add carrot, garlic, parsley, salt, pepper and enough water to just cover the chicken. Cover the pan and simmer 45 minutes or until chicken is tender. Strain broth and reserve 1 cup. Remove skin from chicken and chop meat into small pieces. Heat remaining oil in a large skillet. Add onion and sauté over high heat until softened. Fold in chicken livers, ham and mushrooms and sauté over high heat, stirring constantly, until chicken livers are browned. Sprinkle on flour and cook, stirring, 1 minute. Add reserved broth and Port and stir until sauce is thickened. Add reserved chicken meat. Fill pie crust with the mixture and bake in a 350° over for 15 minutes.

Pato com arroz à Portuguesa

Duck with rice Portuguese style

6 servings

- 5 ounces ham steak
- 1 (4 to 5 pound) duck
- 1 onion, chopped
- 1 teaspoon salt
- 6 peppercorns, crushed
- 4 strips bacon
- 1 medium-sized carrot, sliced
- 4 cups water
- 1 tablespoon flour

For the rice:
- 5 tablespoons butter
- 1 onion, finely chopped
- 1 teaspoon salt
  Freshly ground black pepper
- 1 cup raw rice
- ½ pound chorizo sausage, or other spicy sausage

Cut ham into 1 inch pieces. Add ham, duck giblets, onion, salt, peppercorns, 1 strip bacon and carrot to 4 cups water and simmer 1 hour. Strain broth, remove the ham and reserve the liquid. Sprinkle the cavity of the duck with salt and pepper, place on a rack in a roasting pan and roast in a preheated 350° oven for 1½ hours until crisp and brown. Allow to stand for 15 minutes, carve the meat from the bone and cut into 2 inch pieces. Make a sauce by adding 1 tablespoon flour to 1 tablespoon of the hot drippings. Stir in ¾ cup of the broth from the giblets. Cook until smooth and add the ham and duck meat. To prepare the rice, heat 3 tablespoons of the butter in a saucepan and sauté the onion until golden brown. Add the salt, pepper and rice and cook until rice is lightly browned. Add 2 cups of the strained broth and the remaining butter and cook over low heat until the liquid is absorbed and the rice is cooked (about 30 minutes). Arrange the duck meat and ham over the rice in a buttered ovenproof casserole. Cover with the thinly sliced sausage and remaining chopped bacon and bake in the preheated 350° oven for 20 minutes. Serve hot.

Conejo con arroz

Rabbit with rice

4 servings

- 2 artichokes
- 2 tablespoons olive oil
- 1½ pounds skinless rabbit or chicken meat, cut into large pieces
- 1 medium sized onion, finely chopped
- 2 medium sized tomatoes, peeled, seeded and chopped
- ½ cup fresh or frozen green peas
- 2 cups chicken broth
- ½ teaspoon salt
  Freshly ground black pepper
- 1 cup converted rice
  Large pinch saffron combined with
- 1 clove garlic, crushed

Remove the tough outer leaves from the artichokes and cut off the tips of the leaves. Slice each into 8 wedges, remove the spiny inner core and cook the artichokes in plenty of boiling salted water for 10 minutes. Drain and pat dry. Heat the oil in a casserole. Add the rabbit and sauté 3 minutes. Add the onion and sauté until lightly browned. Add the tomatoes, peas and artichokes and continue cooking 5 minutes. Add 1 cup of the broth and simmer, covered, 15 minutes. Add the remaining broth, rice and saffron mixture. Stir with a fork and bring to a boil. Reduce the heat and simmer slowly 20 minutes or until the rice has absorbed all the liquid. Let rest for 5 minutes and serve from the casserole.

Liebre estofada

Stewed hare

4 servings

- 1 (4 to 5 pound) hare or substitute chicken
- 2 medium sized onions, finely chopped
- 2 cloves garlic, crushed
- 1 bay leaf
- ½ teaspoon thyme
- 2 tablespoons finely chopped parsley
- ½ teaspoon salt
  Freshly ground black pepper
- ½ cup dry white wine
- 2 tablespoons vinegar
- ¼ cup water
- 1 (16 ounce) can Great Northern or navy beans, drained
- 1 small canned hot chili, finely chopped

Cut the hare into serving pieces and place in a heavy casserole with the onions, garlic, bay leaf, thyme, parsley, salt, pepper, wine, vinegar and water. Bring to a simmer and cover with a sheet of aluminum foil, then the lid. Lower the heat and simmer slowly 1 hour. Add the beans and the chili, cover and simmer 20 minutes more. Serve from the casserole.

Turkey was unknown in Europe until after the discovery of the New World. The French Jesuit Fathers who went to North America sent back the first

turkeys. Since then flocks of turkeys have become a common sight in Europe, and turkey is a favorite holiday dish in Spain.

Stewed hare

Pavo asado a la madrileña

Roast turkey Madrid style

6 servings

> 1 (6 pound) turkey
> 4 tablespoons butter
> 1 teaspoon salt
>   Freshly ground black pepper
> 4 slices fat bacon
> 2 cups dry white wine
> 1 bunch watercress

Rub the cavity of the turkey with 2 tablespoons butter and season with ½ teaspoon salt and pepper. Truss the turkey. Rub the outside of the turkey with the remaining butter, sprinkle with salt and pepper and arrange the bacon slices over the turkey breast. Place on a rack in a roasting pan and roast in a 300° oven for 1 hour. Add the wine to the roasting pan and roast 1 hour more. Baste the turkey with the pan juices every 20 minutes during the roasting period. Remove the bacon from the breast the last 30 minutes of cooking time. When the turkey is done, remove the trussing strings or skewers, place on a platter and let rest 20 minutes. Strain the pan juices, skim off the fat and pour into a sauce dish. Decorate the turkey platter with watercress and serve with fried potatoes.

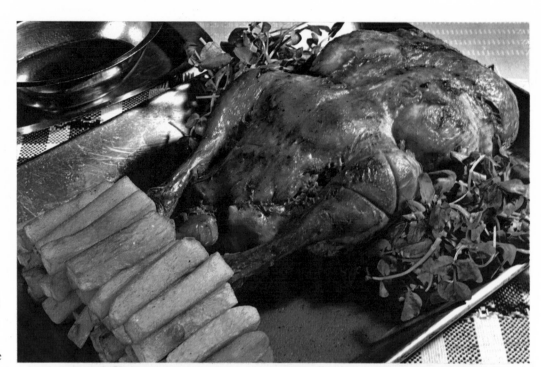

Chicken Beira style

Chicken Campurian style

Frango assado à moda da Beira

Chicken Beira style

4 servings

- 1 (3 pound) chicken
- 8 slices Canadian bacon
- 1 cup cottage cheese
- ½ teaspoon salt
  Freshly ground black pepper
- 2 tablespoons butter
- 2 tablespoons olive oil
- 8 small whole potatoes or 4 medium sized potatoes, cut into cubes
- 2 strips bacon

Beginning at the neck of the chicken, run your finger beneath the skin to lift it from the chicken meat. Slip a slice of Canadian bacon beneath the skin. Use 4 slices of bacon for the breast, making sure each slice is flat and smooth. Arrange remaining slices beneath the legs and back skin of the chicken. Fill the cottage cheese into the cavity and truss the chicken or secure with poultry skewers. Season the chicken with salt and pepper. Place the chicken, breast side up in a baking dish. Add the butter, oil and potatoes. Cover the breast with bacon strips. Roast in a 350° oven for 1 hour until the chicken is tender. The cottage cheese and bacon are an extremely good combination and the chicken will be moist and full of flavor.

Pollo campurriano

Chicken Campurian style

4 servings

  1 *(2½ pound) chicken, cut
    into serving pieces*
  ½ *pound bacon*
  4 *tablespoons butter*
  ¼ *teaspoon salt*
    Freshly ground black pepper
  1 *large onion, chopped*
  1 *teaspoon flour*
  1 *cup wine*
  1 *bay leaf*
  ½ *cup chicken broth*
  3 *green peppers*
  1 *teaspoon paprika*
  1 *cup rice*
  2 *cups boiling chicken broth
    or water*

Fry the bacon in a deep
casserole. When all the fat has
rendered, remove the bacon and
pour off all except 1 tablespoon
fat. Add 2 tablespoons butter to
the casserole and brown the
chicken pieces evenly on all
sides. Remove the chicken and
season it with salt and pepper.
Add half of the onion to the
same fat and fry 3 minutes until
softened. Stir in the flour and
add the wine and bay leaf. Cook
over high heat until only ½ cup
of wine remains. Replace the
chicken and bacon in the
casserole. Add the chicken broth.
Cover the casserole and cook in
a preheated 350° oven for 50
minutes until tender. Heat the
remaining 2 tablespoons of
butter in a skillet. Remove the
membranes and seeds from the
green peppers and cut them into
1 inch squares. Add the peppers
and remaining onion to the

butter and fry over moderate
heat for 5 minutes. Stir in the
paprika and rice. Fry the rice
3 minutes stirring constantly.
Transfer these ingredients to a
saucepan. Add the boiling
chicken broth or water. Cover
and simmer for 20 minutes.
Discard the bay leaf and serve
the chicken from the casserole.
Serve the rice separately.

Pollo en escabeche

Marinated chicken

4 servings

  1 *(3 pound) chicken*
  4 *tablespoons olive oil*
  2 *cups dry white wine*
  2 *tablespoons lemon juice*
  2 *tablespoons vinegar*
  2 *bay leaves*
  2 *cloves garlic*
  8 *peppercorns*
  4 *juniper berries*
  ½ *teaspoon salt*
  1 *orange or 1 lemon, sliced*

Brown the chicken on all sides in
hot oil. Place the chicken in a
deep casserole. Pour the wine
into a saucepan. Add lemon
juice, vinegar, bay leaves, garlic,
peppercorns, juniper berries and
salt. Bring all these ingredients
to simmering point and pour
over the chicken in the casserole.
Cover and cook in a preheated
350° oven for 1 hour until the
chicken in tender. Allow the
chicken to cool in the marinade.
Chill for one day before serving.
Serve cold garnished with orange
or lemon slices.

Frango estufado à Portuguesa

Chicken Portuguese style

4 servings

  1 *(3½ pound) chicken, cut
    into serving pieces*
  ½ *cup butter*
  ½ *cup dry white wine*
  2 *small onions, finely chopped*
  1 *teaspoon salt*
    Freshly ground black pepper
  1 *chicken liver*
  4 *eggs*

In a casserole, place the chicken,
4 tablespoons butter, wine,
onions, salt and pepper. Cover
and simmer over low heat about
45 minutes or until the chicken
is tender. Remove the chicken
from the pan and keep warm.
Rub the chicken liver through a
sieve into the cooking liquid.*
Heat, stirring, without allowing
the liquid to boil. Return the
chicken pieces to the casserole.
Fry the eggs in the remaining
butter and serve with the
chicken. Serve boiled rice
separately.
*Alternatively, you may add
2 tablespoons tomato purée to
the liquid and simmer 10
minutes. To thicken the sauce in
this case, combine 2 egg yolks
and 2 tablespoons cream. Add
to the liquid and heat until the
sauce thickens. Do not allow it
to boil.

VEGETABLE DISHES

Pease pudding is a traditional English dish. Children in England skip rope to the old rhyme of:

*'Pease pudding hot
Pease pudding cold
Pease pudding in the pot
Five days old…'*

Cauliflower cheese

4 servings

- 1 medium sized cauliflower divided into flowerets
- 1 teaspoon salt
- 2 tablespoons butter
- 3 tablespoons flour
- 1½ cups milk
- 1 cup Cheddar cheese, grated
- Dash cayenne pepper
- 4 tablespoons bread crumbs

Boil the cauliflower in salted water 10 minutes until almost tender. Drain cauliflower and place in a small buttered casserole. To prepare the sauce, melt the butter in a saucepan. Stir in the flour and add the milk gradually. Stir in ¾ cup grated cheese and cayenne pepper. Cook 2 minutes until the sauce has thickened. Pour the sauce over the cauliflower. Sprinkle with remaining cheese and breadcrumbs. Place in a 400° oven for 5 minutes and then under the broiler for 3 minutes to brown the cheese and bread crumbs.

Pease pudding

Pea purée

6 servings

- 1 pound (2 cups) dried split green peas
- 3 cups water
- 1 teaspoon salt
- 1 teaspoon sugar
- 1 tablespoon lemon juice
- 3 tablespoons butter
- Freshly ground black pepper

Wash peas thoroughly. Add salt to the water and bring water to boiling point. Add peas, sugar and lemon juice. Cover and simmer over low heat for 1½ hours until peas are tender. Drain the peas and force them through a sieve. Melt the butter in a skillet. Add peas and cook over low heat until the peas are hot, about 5 minutes. Season with freshly ground pepper and serve with boiled beef.

Apple chutney

Makes 3 (1 pint) jars

- 6 cups green cooking apples, peeled, cored and chopped
- 3 onions, roughly chopped
- 2½ cups seedless white raisins
- 2¼ cups brown sugar
- 2 cups cider vinegar
- 1 teaspoon salt
- 1 tablespoon mustard seeds, crushed
- Dash cayenne pepper
- 2 red peppers, seeded and chopped (opt.)
- 1 tablespoon ginger root, grated or 1 teaspoon ground ginger
- 1 teaspoon pickling spice

Place all the ingredients in a large heavy pot. Simmer, uncovered, over low heat for 2½ hours until all the liquid has evaporated and the mixture has thickened. Stir occasionally to prevent sticking. Fill into sterilized jars and seal.

Boxty is a traditional dish from Donegal, eaten on the eve of 'All Saints' Day.

Cauliflower cheese

Boxty

Potato pancake

6 servings

    4 cups peeled and grated
       potatoes (about 2 pounds)
1⅓ cups flour
    2 teaspoons salt
    6 tablespoons milk
    2 tablespoons butter
 ¼ cup brown sugar
    4 tablespoons melted butter

Squeeze grated potatoes as dry as possible in a linen or terrycloth tea towel. In a bowl, combine the potatoes, flour and salt. Stir in the milk gradually, using just enough to make the mixture hold together. Let the mixture stand 1 hour. Heat a 9 to 10 inch heavy skillet until very hot. Drop in the butter and let it melt. Pat the potato mixture into the skillet with a spatula, distributing it evenly. Cook over medium heat until the underside is set and golden brown. Slide the pancake out onto a plate and invert it back into the skillet. Let the other side brown. Serve the pancake straight from the pan with brown sugar and melted butter.

Paprika Tomaten Gemüse

Peppers and tomatoes

4 servings

½ pound bacon, diced
2 onions, cut into rings
1 clove garlic, crushed
4 green and/or red peppers,
   seeded and cut into strips
1 pound tomatoes, peeled,
   seeded and cut into wedges
¼ teaspoon salt
   Freshly ground black pepper
¼ teaspoon thyme
½ cup dry white wine
1 cup diced soft cheese,
   such as Port Salut

Fry the bacon in a casserole
until the fat is rendered. Pour
off all but 2 tablespoons of the
accumulated fat. Add the onions
and garlic and cook 5 minutes.
Add the peppers and tomatoes
and cook over low heat 20
minutes, stirring occasionally.
Add salt, pepper, thyme and
wine and simmer 5 minutes
more. Add the cheese and
remove from the heat when the
cheese is just melted. Serve
from the casserole with
dark bread.

Karfiol Wiener Art

Papet Vaudois

Spinat Pizokel

Viennese cauliflower

4 to 6 servings

> 1 pound sweetbreads
> 5 anchovies
> 1 medium sized whole
>   cauliflower
> 2½ tablespoons butter
> ½ teaspoon salt
>   Freshly ground black pepper
> 1 tablespoon flour
> 4 tablespoons milk
> 2 egg yolks, lightly beaten
> 4 tablespoons cream
> 1½ tablespoons finely chopped
>   parsley
> 2 tablespoons grated
>   Parmesan cheese
> 3 tablespoons breadcrumbs

Cover the sweetbreads with boiling water and allow them to stand for 5 minutes. Rinse under cold water, drain, peel and cut into small cubes. Rinse the anchovies to remove excess salt. Drain and chop the anchovies. Cook the cauliflower in boiling, salted water for 15 minutes until tender. Drain and keep warm. Heat 1½ tablespoons butter in a skillet, add the sweetbreads and fry gently for 4 minutes. Season with salt and pepper and remove from heat. Heat 1 tablespoon butter in a saucepan and stir in the flour until blended. Add the milk gradually, stirring to form a thick sauce. Remove sauce from heat and add the beaten egg yolks and cream. Return to the heat for 3 minutes, stirring constantly. Do not allow the sauce to boil. Add sweetbreads and anchovies. Place the cauliflower in a buttered casserole and cover with the sauce. Combine the parsley, Parmesan cheese and breadcrumbs and sprinkle over the cauliflower. Dot with butter and bake in a preheated 400° oven for 10 minutes or until lightly browned. Serve hot.

Leek dish from Vaud

4 servings

> 4 large potatoes, peeled and
>   sliced
> 4 large leeks, cut into rings
> 1 cup beef broth
> 1 tablespoon flour
> 2 tablespoons milk
> 1 teaspoon salt
>   Freshly ground black pepper
> ¼ teaspoon dried basil
> ¼ teaspoon dried thyme
> ⅛ teaspoon ground nutmeg
> ½ pound bacon, cut into slices
> ½ pound bratwurst sausage,
>   in one piece

Place layers of potatoes and leeks in a casserole. Add the beef broth, cover and simmer over a low heat 40 to 45 minutes. Stir together the flour and milk and add to the casserole. Season with salt, pepper, basil, thyme and nutmeg. Simmer the bacon and sausage in boiling water for 10 minutes. Cover the leek dish with slices of bacon and place the sausage on top. Cover and simmer gently over low heat for 10 minutes. Slice the sausage and arrange in the center of the dish for serving.

Spinach dumplings

> 2½ cups flour
> 1½ teaspoons salt
>   Freshly ground black pepper
> 1 cup milk
> 1 cup water
> 6 eggs
> ½ cup butter
> 2½ cups fine dry breadcrumbs
> 1 tablespoon finely chopped
>   parsley
> 1 tablespoon finely chopped
>   chives
> 2 packages frozen chopped
>   spinach, cooked
> ½ cup grated Parmesan cheese

Place the flour, salt and pepper in a bowl. Add the milk and water and beat until smooth. Add the eggs, 1 at a time, beating well after each addition. Heat ½ the butter in a skillet and sauté the breadcrumbs, stirring constantly until golden brown. Add the breadcrumbs, parsley and chives to the batter. Drain the spinach in a colander, pressing out as much liquid as possible. Add the spinach to the batter. Cover and set aside at least 1 hour. Bring plenty of salted water to a simmer. Form small dumplings using a tablespoon and slip them into the simmering water a few at a time. Remove them with a slotted spoon when they rise to the surface and keep warm while the remaining dumplings are cooking. Arrange on a heated serving dish and sprinkle with cheese. Serve a tomato sauce separately.

Asparagus salad

4 American servings
4 Chinese servings

1 pound asparagus
2 tablespoons soy sauce
1 teaspoon sugar
¼ teaspoon sesame oil
1 teaspoon minced preserved red ginger

Wash asparagus, cut off tough ends and cut in a rolling cut, diagonally, into 1½ inch long pieces. Parboil tender tops for 30 seconds and the stems for 2 minutes. Drain thoroughly and place in a bowl. Mix soy sauce, sugar and sesame oil and pour over asparagus. Chill in the refrigerator 10 to 15 minutes before serving. Transfer to a serving dish, garnish with red ginger and serve.

Mushrooms in cream sauce

2 to 4 American servings
4 Chinese servings

12 large, uniformly sized fresh mushrooms
1 to 1½ tablespoons oil
½ teaspoon salt
½ cup chicken broth
½ cup heavy cream
1 tablespoon cornstarch
2 tablespoons water
1 tablespoon ham garnish

3 sprigs Chinese parsley

Remove lower part of stems from the mushrooms, but leave the caps whole. Rinse mushrooms quickly under cold running water. In a wok or other pan, heat the oil over medium heat. Add the mushrooms and salt and stir fry gently for about 2 minutes. Add chicken broth and cook for about 4 minutes. Add cream and heat to boiling point. Dissolve cornstarch in water and stir in to thicken. Transfer mushrooms to a shallow dish and cover with the sauce. Garnish with shredded ham and parsley leaves and serve hot.

Stir fried sweet and sour vegetables

2 American servings
4 Chinese servings

1 small green pepper (or ½ a large one)
1 medium onion
2 stalks celery
2 carrots
3 tablespoons vinegar
2 tablespoons sugar
1 tablespoon sherry
2 tablespoons chicken broth or water
2 tablespoons oil
1 clove garlic, crushed
2 thin slices fresh ginger root, minced
½ cup shredded canned bamboo shoots
¼ teaspoon white pepper
1 tablespoon cornstarch dissolved in
2 tablespoons water

Remove membrane and seeds from pepper and cut into 2 inch long diamond shapes. Peel the onion, halve lengthwise and cut each half into ½ inch wide strips lengthwise. Cut celery in 2 inch pieces diagonally. Cut carrots in a rolling cut, diagonally, into 1½ inch pieces. Heat vinegar. Remove from heat and add sugar, sherry and broth. Cover to keep warm. Heat oil in a wok or other pan until quite hot. Add garlic, ginger root and carrots and stir fry for 1 minute. Add all other ingredients and stir fry over high heat for about 2 minutes. Add vinegar mixture and stir fry for another 2 minutes. Stir in cornstarch mixture to thicken and serve.

Radish and cucumber salad

4 to 6 American servings
4 to 6 Chinese servings

About 16 to 20 radishes
½ cucumber
1 tablespoon salt
4 tablespoons vinegar
2 teaspoons sugar
½ teaspoon salt
2 tablespoons soy sauce
¼ teaspoon sesame oil

Remove ends of the cucumber and then quarter lengthwise. Scoop out seedy center to leave about ½ to ¾ inch thickness. Cut into 2 inch long pieces and then into slices ⅛ inch thick. Sprinkle radishes and cucumber with salt and leave for about 10 minutes. Rinse under cold running water. Drain thoroughly. Meanwhile, bring vinegar to a boil in a small enamelled saucepan. Stir in sugar and salt until dissolved. Cool the liquid and stir in soy sauce and sesame oil. Pour over radishes and cucumber and place in the refrigerator for about ½ hour. Pour off excess liquid and carefully spread cucumber into a fanlike design on a serving plate. Decorate the plate with radish roses. This salad may be served as a side dish or with appetizers.

Stir fried bean sprouts

2 American servings
4 Chinese servings

¾ *pound bean sprouts*
½ *teaspoon salt*
 1 *thin slice fresh ginger root,*
    minced
½ *green pepper, shredded*
½ *medium sized onion, shredded*
 3 *to 4 whole scallions, shredded*
 2 *thin slices boiled ham,*
    shredded
 2 *tablespoons chicken broth*
    combined with
½ *tablespoon sherry*
 2 *tablespoons oil*

Pour boiling water over bean
sprouts and let stand 20 seconds.
Wash in cold running water,
drain and dry on tea towels.
Arrange the ingredients on a
plate in the order in which
they are to be cooked. Heat the
oil in a wok. Add salt and
ginger root and stir fry ½
minute. Add green pepper,
onion and scallions and stir
fry 1½ minutes. Add bean
sprouts and ham and stir fry
½ minute. Add combined broth
and sherry and bring to a boil.
Remove from the heat and
serve immediately.

Stir fried cauliflower

4 American servings
8 Chinese servings

 2 *cups cauliflower, flowerets*
    only
 2 *tablespoons oil*
 2 *thin slices fresh ginger root*
 2 *scallions, minced*
 4 *water chestnuts, thinly sliced*
½ *cup chicken broth*
 1 *tablespoon sherry*
 1 *tablespoon soy sauce*
 1 *teaspoon oyster sauce*
½ *cup boiled shrimp, peeled*
 2 *teaspoons cornstarch*
 1 *tablespoon water*

Wash cauliflower and parboil
in rapidly boiling salted water
for 2 to 3 minutes. Cool at
once under cold running water
and drain. Heat the oil in a
wok or other pan, add ginger
root and stir fry for 30 seconds.
Add scallions and water
chestnuts and stir fry for
another 30 seconds. Add
cauliflower, stir fry for a few
seconds (just long enough to
coat the vegetable with oil)
and then add chicken broth,
sherry, soy sauce and oyster
sauce. Bring quickly to a boil
and reduce heat. Add shrimp,
cover and simmer for about
2 minutes. Meanwhile dissolve
cornstarch in water and stir in
to thicken. Serve immediately.

Celery and dried shrimp

2 American servings
4 Chinese servings

 6 *large stalks celery*
12 *dried shrimp*
½ *red pepper*
 2 *cakes bean curd*
 3 *tablespoons oil*
½ *cup chicken broth*
 3 *tablespoons soy sauce*
½ *teaspoon sugar*
⅛ *teaspoon white pepper*
 1 *teaspoon cornstarch*
    dissolved in
 1 *tablespoon water*

Remove leaves from celery and
cut stalks in 1½ inch long
pieces diagonally. Soak shrimp
in hot water for 30 minutes.
Drain. Remove membrane and
seeds from pepper and cut into
2 inch long and ½ inch wide
strips. Cut bean curd cakes into
1 inch squares. Heat the oil
in a wok or other pan until
quite hot, add the celery and
stir fry for 45 seconds.
Add the pepper and stir fry for
another ½ minute over high
heat. Add shrimp, bean curd,
chicken broth, soy sauce, sugar
and pepper. Bring to a boil
over high heat. Reduce heat,
cover and simmer for 15 to
20 minutes. Stir in the cornstarch
to thicken and serve immediately.

Stir fried cabbage

3 American servings
6 Chinese servings

 2 *dried Chinese mushrooms*
 1 *thin slice fresh ginger*
    root, minced
½ *cup chicken broth*
¼ *teaspoon sugar*
 1 *tablespoon soy sauce*
 2 *tablespoons oil*
 1 *thin slice fresh ginger*
    root, minced
 1 *pound Chinese cabbage,*
    shredded
 1 *teaspoon cornstarch*
    dissolved in
 1 *tablespoon water*

Soak dried mushrooms in warm
water for 20 minutes. Squeeze
dry. Remove and discard stems
and shred caps. Combine
chicken broth, sugar and soy
sauce in a small bowl. Heat the
oil in a wok, add the ginger
root and stir fry ½ minute.
Add mushrooms and cabbage
and stir fry 1 minute. Add the
chicken broth mixture, bring
to a boil and cook 2 minutes.
Stir in the cornstarch mixture
to thicken. Serve immediately.

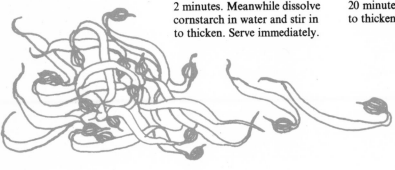

Vegetable stew

Sebze bastısı

Vegetable stew

4 servings

    1 medium sized (1 pound)
      eggplant
    1 teaspoon salt
    4 tablespoons butter or oil
    2 onions, sliced
    2 green peppers, seeded and
      cut into strips
    2 zucchini, sliced ¼ inch thick
    1 cup string beans, cut into 1½
      inch pieces
    2 cloves garlic, crushed
    2 tablespoons chopped parsley
    ½ teaspoon sugar
      Freshly ground black pepper
    1 cup beef broth
    2 tablespoons chopped parsley
      for garnish

Cut the eggplant into ¼ inch slices, sprinkle with salt and set aside for 15 minutes. Wash off salt, drain and pat dry with paper towels. Heat 2 tablespoons butter in a skillet. Add the eggplant slices and fry until lightly browned on both sides. Transfer to a baking dish. Fry the onions and peppers in the remaining butter 3 minutes. Add the zucchini and beans and fry for 2 more minutes, stirring frequently. Place the vegetables on top of the eggplant. Add garlic, parsley, sugar, pepper and beef broth. Cover and place in a preheated 350° oven for 1 hour. Garnish with parsley and serve hot.

The people of the Eastern Mediterranean are very fond of vegetables, especially of the so-called 'fruit vegetables', such as eggplants, zucchini and cucumbers. Most popular of all is the cucumber. In the old quarters of Istanbul and of other Eastern cities, stalls along the sidewalks sell cucumbers as a cheap and refreshing treat during the hot, humid days of summer. Cucumber salad is also a favorite during the summer months, especially if it is served with yoghurt.
Eggplant is another vegetable very much appreciated. Eggplants have been grown throughout the Middle East since ancient times, but they probably originated in Persia. The original Persian word for 'eggplant' was 'badindjan'. The Arabs added an article in front of it to make 'al-badindjan', and the word entered most European languages as 'aubergine'. During the summer, stacks of shiny, dark-purple eggplants are highlights of markets from Athens to Tel Aviv. Eggplants are fried, baked, stewed, stuffed or eaten in salads; they can also be roasted, pickled or finely crushed. The eggplant is in fact a universal vegetable, and with its subtle flavor it can be combined with a variety of other tastes.
In Greece, zucchinis, the oblong, yellow-green vegetables so loved in ancient Rome, are still especially popular. There is a great deal to be said on a hot day for a Greek salad made of slices of zucchini in olive oil with a lot of lemon juice and pepper.

Karnı yarık

Stuffed eggplant

6 servings

  6 *very small eggplants*
1½ *teaspoons salt*
  6 *tablespoons olive oil*
  3 *large onions, thinly sliced*
  4 *ripe tomatoes, peeled, seeded and chopped*
  2 *cloves garlic, crushed*
1½ *tablespoons chopped parsley*
  ½ *teaspoon sugar*
      Freshly ground black pepper
      Juice of 1 lemon
  1 *cup beef broth*

Wash the eggplants and make a deep incision lengthwise without cutting through the underside or both ends. Sprinkle with 1 teaspoon salt and set aside for 5 minutes. Heat 2 tablespoons oil in a skillet and fry the onions until soft and lightly browned. Remove from the heat, add the tomatoes, garlic, ½ the parsley, sugar, ¼ teaspoon salt and pepper and combine thoroughly. Wash the eggplants to remove the salt and pat dry. Heat 2 tablespoons oil in a pan and fry the eggplants over medium heat for 10 minutes or until softened. Transfer the eggplants to a baking dish. Spread them open and stuff with the tomato-onion mixture. Sprinkle with the remaining oil, salt, pepper and lemon juice. Add the beef broth and bake in a preheated 350° oven for 45 minutes. Remove from the oven. Allow to cool completely. Garnish with remaining parsley and serve cold.

Pirincli ispanak

Spinach with rice

4 servings

  2 *pounds spinach*
  1 *cup raw rice*
  4 *tablespoons butter*
  1 *onion, thinly sliced*
  ½ *cup tomato purée*
  4 *medium sized tomatoes, peeled, seeded and chopped*
1¼ *cup water*
  1 *teaspoon salt*
      Freshly ground black pepper

Wash and drain the spinach and chop finely. Soak the rice in hot water for 10 minutes and drain. Heat the butter and fry the onion about 3 minutes until soft and golden. Remove from heat and place onion in a heatproof casserole. Cover with the chopped spinach and then an even layer of rice. Mix the tomato purée, tomatoes, water, salt and pepper and pour over the rice. Place over moderate heat and cook until all the liquid has been absorbed. Cover, place an asbestos pad under the casserole and steam over the lowest possible heat until the rice is tender and fluffy.

Domatesli fasulye

Kidney beans with tomatoes

4 servings

  ½ *pound kidney beans, soaked overnight*
  3 *cups cold water*
  1 *teaspoon salt*
  2 *tablespoons olive oil*
  2 *onions chopped*
  6 *medium sized tomatoes, peeled, seeded and chopped*
  2 *cloves garlic, crushed*
  ½ *teaspoon salt*
      Dash cayenne pepper
  ½ *tablespoon chopped fresh basil or*
      ½ teaspoon dried basil
  1 *bay leaf*
  ¼ *teaspoon paprika*
  2 *tablespoons chopped parsley*

Place the beans in a saucepan and add water and salt. Bring to boiling point and simmer for about 2 hours until tender and soft. Drain the beans. Heat the oil in a skillet. Add the onions and fry until soft and golden. Add the tomatoes, garlic and salt and cook, stirring occasionally, until mixture is reduced to a smooth purée. Add the pepper, basil, bay leaf and paprika. Place the beans in a casserole, add the tomato sauce, cover and simmer for 20 minutes. Remove the bay leaf, sprinkle with parsley and serve either hot or cold.

Pancar salatası

Beet salad

4 servings

1½ *tablespoons olive oil*
  1 *tablespoon lemon juice*
1¼ *cups yogurt*
  1 *clove garlic, crushed*
  ¼ *teaspoon salt*
  ⅛ *teaspoon white pepper*
  ½ *pound cooked beets, diced*
  2 *tablespoons finely chopped parsley*

In a bowl, beat the olive oil and lemon juice together with a wire whisk. Add the yogurt, garlic, salt and pepper and stir until thoroughly blended. Fold in the diced beets and transfer to a serving bowl. Sprinkle with parsley and serve.

Chou au marrons

Braised cabbage with chestnuts

6 servings

  1 *medium sized head white cabbage*
  1 *cup chicken broth*
  1 *cup dry white wine*
  ½ *teaspoon salt*
  4 *thin slices cooked ham, diced*
  10 *canned chestnuts, drained and chopped*

Wash and shred the cabbage. Plunge it into boiling salted water and cook for 2 minutes. Drain and transfer to a heavy saucepan. Add broth, white wine and salt. Bring the liquid to a boil, lower the heat, cover and cook slowly 30 to 45 minutes. Before serving, stir in the ham and chestnuts.

Ratatouille

Vegetable stew

8 servings

  1 *medium sized eggplant*
  1 *tablespoon salt*
  ¼ *cup olive oil or vegetable oil*
  2 *large onions, cut into rings*
  3 *cloves garlic, crushed*
  2 *green peppers, cut into strips*
  4 *medium sized zucchini, cut into bite-sized pieces*
  2 *medium sized ripe tomatoes, cut into wedges*
  ¼ *teaspoon salt*
     Freshly ground black pepper
  ½ *teaspoon thyme*
  1 *bay leaf*
  2 *tablespoons parsley, finely chopped*

Cut eggplant into thick slices and then into small pieces. Sprinkle with salt. Allow eggplant to stand for 30 minutes, then rinse and pat dry on paper towels. Heat the oil in a large skillet. Sauté onions and garlic for two minutes. Add green pepper and cook for two minutes. Add eggplant and cook over high heat for three minutes, stirring constantly. Add zucchini and continue stirring for three minutes. Add tomatoes, salt, pepper, thyme and bay leaf. Simmer uncovered for 40 minutes until all the vegetables are tender. Remove bay leaf.*
Garnish with parsley and serve hot.
* Can be prepared in advance to this point.
Ratatouille can also be served cold as an appetizer.

Ratatouille

Champignons Cévenols

Mushrooms provençale

4 servings

  1 *pound mushrooms*
  ½ *cup olive oil*
  ¼ *teaspoon salt*
  1 *small clove garlic, crushed*
  1 *tablespoon finely chopped*
     parsley
  4 *tablespoons fresh breadcrumbs*

Wash the mushrooms. Separate the stems from the caps. Chop the stems finely. In a heavy skillet, heat the oil. Add the caps, cover with a circle of wax paper and cook over low heat 10 minutes. With a slotted spoon, transfer them to a plate or shallow bowl. Add the stems to the skillet, raise the heat and sauté 3 to 4 minutes. With the slotted spoon, remove the stems to a small mixing bowl and mix in the salt, garlic and parsley. Place the mixture on top of the caps. Add the breadcrumbs to the skillet and sauté until golden. Sprinkle over the mushrooms. Cover the plate and let the mushrooms stand 1 day before serving.

Cèpes sautés paysanne

Sautéed mushrooms country style

4–6 servings

  6 *slices bacon*
  2 *pounds cépes or mushrooms*
  1 *teaspoon lemon juice*
  1 *small onion, finely chopped*
  1 *clove garlic, crushed*
  2 *tablespoons fine dry*
     breadcrumbs
  ½ *teaspoon salt*
     Freshly ground black pepper
  1 *tablespoon finely chopped*
     parsley

In a large skillet, cook the bacon over low heat until crisp. Drain and crumble. In the pan in which the bacon was cooked, sauté the mushrooms for 3 minutes in the remaining fat. Adding a little butter if necessary. Sprinkle with lemon juice. Add the onion, garlic and breadcrumbs, and sauté over high heat, stirring constantly, for 3 minutes. Add the bacon, salt, pepper and parsley and mix well. Serve hot.
Note: Cépes are one of the many types of mushrooms found in France, Italy and Germany. They are available here both dried and in cans. If you are unable to find any, use fresh mushrooms for this dish. Serve with roast beef.

Large brown cèpes (a kind of mushroom) grow in the extensive pinewood forest located near the city of Bordeaux. On Sundays whole families leave Bordeaux with baskets and pick their way among the trees to look for them.

Cèpes sautés paysanne

Asperges au jambon

Asparagus with ham

6 servings

2 pounds fresh asparagus
½ teaspoon salt
2 tablespoons lemon juice
6 thin slices boiled ham
   Hollandaise sauce

Peel lower third of asparagus spears with a potato peeler. Place asparagus in a large skillet. Cover with cold water. Add salt and lemon juice. Simmer uncovered 10 minutes until tender. Place a piece of ham on each individual serving dish. Cover with drained asparagus and spoon Hollandaise sauce over asparagus. Serve immediately.

The large orange pumpkin ripens at the same time as the grapes and always grows along the edges of the vineyard. Soup made from this pumpkin is a traditional dish served to grape-pickers.

Carrotes Vichy

Potiron au gratin

Endives au lard gratinées

Champignons à la Bordelaise

Glazed carrots

6 servings

12 carrots, sliced
½ teaspoon salt
1 tablespoon butter
1 teaspoon sugar
3 tablespoons white vermouth
2 tablespoons finely chopped parsley

Cover carrots with salted boiling water in a skillet. Cover and simmer 15 minutes until almost tender. Drain carrots and return them to the skillet. Add butter, sugar and vermouth. Cook uncovered for 5 minutes until the wine has evaporated and the carrots are glazed and shiny. Garnish with parsley. Serve hot.

Pumpkin au gratin

4 to 6 servings

1 can (1 pound) pumpkin
½ teaspoon salt
Freshly ground black pepper
Dash of nutmeg
¼ teaspoon ground cloves
2 tablespoons melted butter
1 egg
½ cup heavy cream
2 tablespoons grated Parmesan cheese

Thoroughly combine the pumpkin, salt, pepper, nutmeg, cloves and butter. Place in a small, lightly buttered casserole. Beat the egg lightly and mix in the cream and Parmesan cheese. Pour over the pumpkin. Bake in a 400° oven 30 minutes or until the top is puffed and lightly browned. Serve warm.

Endives au gratin

4 servings

8 endives
4 slices bacon
1 tablespoon butter
2 cups Béchamel sauce

½ cup Parmesan cheese, grated

Cut a V shaped notch in the base of each endive and wash carefully. Simmer whole endives in salted water for 20 minutes. Fry bacon until almost crisp and all the fat has rendered. Cut each bacon slice in half across the width. Wrap each endive in bacon. Place in a buttered baking dish.* Spoon sauce over the endives. Top with cheese and bake in a 375° oven for 15 minutes until lightly browned. Serve hot with roast lamb or chicken.
*Can be prepared in advance to this point.

Stuffed mushrooms

4 servings

1 pound fresh mushrooms
2 tablespoons butter
2 tablespoons olive oil or vegetable oil
4 scallions, finely chopped
2 cloves garlic, crushed
3 tablespoons parsley, finely chopped
¼ teaspoon salt
Freshly ground black pepper
2 tablespoons lemon juice
¼ cup heavy cream
¼ cup fine breadcrumbs

Wash mushrooms quickly under cold running water and pat them dry on paper towels. Remove the stems from the caps. Sauté mushroom caps in hot butter for two minutes on each side until lightly browned. Place caps in a buttered baking dish, hollow side up. Add oil to the skillet. Chop mushroom stems finely. Combine with scallions, garlic and parsley. Season with salt and pepper. Sauté mushroom mixture in hot oil and butter for five minutes.
Add lemon juice and cream. Simmer five more minutes.
Fill this mixture into mushroom caps and top with breadcrumbs. Bake 5 minutes in a 400° oven just before serving. Serve hot on freshly made toast.

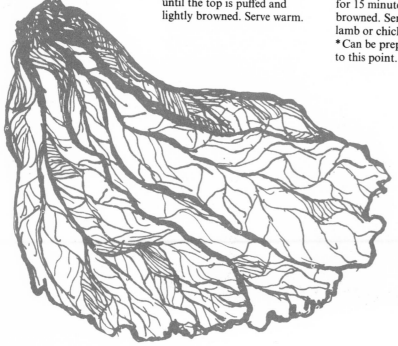

Sauerkraut

Braised sauerkraut

4 servings

¼ cup margarine or butter
1 medium onion, chopped
3 cups sauerkraut, drained
2 cups beef bouillon
2 apples, sliced
2 slices bacon
1 potato, grated

Melt margarine in large skillet. Sauté onion until golden brown. Stir in sauerkraut and apple slices. Pour in bouillon and place bacon slices on top. Cover; simmer for 30–40 minutes. Add grated potato and continue to simmer until mixture thickens, stirring constantly. Remove bacon and serve hot.

Schwäbische Spätzle

Tiny dumplings

4–6 servings

2 eggs, slightly beaten
1 cup water
1 teaspoon salt
3 cups flour

Combine eggs, water, salt, and flour. Beat until dough is thick and smooth. Add more flour if necessary. In a large saucepan, bring 2–3 quarts of salted water to a boil. Place ⅓ of the dough on a small, wet chopping board. With a sharp knife, cut thin strips (¾″ × 2½″) one at a time, slipping off board directly into boiling water. Repeat until all dough is used. Do not crowd in boiling water. Dumplings are done when they float. Remove from boiling water; rinse with hot water and keep warm. Serve with meat and gravy.

Lappenpickert

Potato cake

6–8 servings

4 cups firmly packed, peeled, grated and drained potatoes (about 2 lbs.)
2 eggs, slightly beaten
3 tablespoons flour
1 teaspoon salt
⅓ cup sour cream
¼ cup salad oil

Put grated potatoes into mixing bowl. Add eggs, flour, salt and sour cream. Beat with mixing spoon until well blended. Heat 2 tablespoons of the oil in each of 2 large skillets until very hot. Carefully spread half the potato mixture in each skillet, about ½″ thick. Cook over moderately high heat until browned on bottom. Carefully turn over. (If necessary, cut into quarters and turn each quarter separately.) Add more oil, if needed. Cook until browned. Serve immediately. If desired, wrap cooled potato sections in waxed paper. May be reheated in a little oil over moderate heat. Serve either as a meat accompaniment or with jelly or syrup.

Stangenspargel

Buttered asparagus

4 servings

2 pounds fresh green or white asparagus
1½ teaspoons salt
1 teaspoon sugar
¼ cup melted margarine or butter
1 hard cooked egg, finely chopped, optional

Arrange asparagus in 2 layers in 9″ or 10″ skillet. Sprinkle with salt and sugar. Pour on 1″ boiling water. Boil, uncovered, 5 minutes; cover and cook 7–10 minutes longer, or until just tender crisp when tested with a fork. Carefully lift out asparagus; arrange on serving dish. Pour melted margarine over asparagus. Garnish with chopped egg if desired.

Hannoversches Gurkengemüse

Hannoversches Gurkengemüse

Braised cucumbers

4 servings

¼ cup margarine or butter
1 tablespoon sugar
½ teaspoon salt
2 large cucumbers, peeled and
   cut into 2″ pieces
1 medium onion, chopped
2 tomatoes, quartered
¼ cup water
1 teaspoon lemon juice
¼ teaspoon dill weed
½ cup sour cream

Melt margarine in large
saucepan. Add sugar and salt;
cook until lightly browned.
Add cucumbers and onion.
Cook, stirring constantly, until
onions are transparent. Add
tomatoes, water, lemon juice,
and dill weed. Cook 10–12
minutes. Stir in sour cream.
Serve immediately.

Finocchio al gratin

Finoccho al gratin

Fennel au gratin

8 servings

    4 *fennel bulbs*
    3 *tablespoons margarine*
      or butter
    3 *tablespoons flour*
$^1/_2$ *teaspoon salt*
$^1/_8$ *teaspoon black pepper*
      Dash nutmeg
    2 *cups milk*
    2 *eggs, slightly beaten*
    4 *tablespoons grated*
      Parmesan cheese

Wash and quarter fennel bulbs. Cook fennel in boiling salted water, 6–8 minutes; drain. Melt margarine in saucepan; blend in flour, salt, pepper and nutmeg. Add milk. Cook over medium heat, stirring constantly, until mixture thickens and bubbles. Stir a small amount of sauce into beaten eggs; blend well. Stir egg mixture into hot sauce until well blended. Remove from heat. Stir in 2 tablespoons Parmesan cheese. Place fennel in buttered 8″ square baking dish. Pour sauce over fennel. Sprinkle remaining Parmesan over top. Bake in a hot oven (400°), 10–15 minutes or until golden brown.

Carciofi bolliti

Artichokes

Break stems off artichokes; cut off top third of vegetable. Wash under cold running water. Rub cut portions of artichokes with lemon juice. Drop artichokes into 7–8 quarts boiling salted water. (Do not use aluminum or iron pot). Boil, uncovered, 30–35 minutes. Artichokes are done when leaves pull out easily. Remove; drain upside down. Spread leaves; pull out tender center cone of leaves in one piece. Scrape off and scoop out 'fussy, prickly' portions. Serve hot with melted margarine or butter. Artichokes may also be stuffed and baked. Allow one artichoke per serving.

Carciofi imbottiti

Stuffed artichokes

4 servings

   4 artichokes
   1 (8 ounce) can crabmeat, flaked or
   1 cup cooked chopped shrimp
$^1/_2$ *cup grated provolone or gruyere cheese*
$^1/_2$ *cup mayonnaise*
   1 tablespoon grated onion
$^1/_2$ *teaspoon salt*
   5 teaspoons lemon juice
   1 tablespoon salad oil

Prepare artichokes according to previous recipe. Combine crabmeat, cheese, mayonnaise, onion, salt and 2 teaspoons lemon juice. Spoon crab mixture into center of each artichoke. Arrange artichoke in a shallow baking dish just large enough to hold them, standing upright. Pour boiling water into baking dish to a depth of 1″; add 3 teaspoons lemon juice. Brush artichokes with salad oil. Bake in a moderate oven (350°), about 30 minutes. Serve hot or cold.

Broccoli alla romana

Braised broccoli

4 servings

   2 pounds broccoli or
   2 (10 ounce) packages frozen broccoli
   4 tablespoons margarine or butter
$^1/_2$ *cup chopped celery*
$^1/_4$ *cup chopped pimento*
   2 tablespoons lemon juice
$^1/_4$ *teaspoon salt*
$^1/_8$ *teaspoon black pepper*

Wash and trim broccoli; cook in boiling salted water 15–20 minutes, or cook frozen broccoli according to package directions. Melt margarine in small skillet; sauté celery 1 minute. Stir in remaining ingredients. Drain broccoli well. Pour margarine mixture over broccoli.

Carote all'anice

Carrots with anise

4 servings

   1 pound carrots
   2 tablespoons margarine or butter
$^1/_2$ *teaspoon anise seed, crushed*
$^1/_4$ *cup orange juice*

Peel carrots; cut diagonally into $^1/_2$″ slices. Cook carrots in 1″ boiling salted water about 10–12 minutes or until tender. Drain well; return to pot. Add margarine and anise seed; cook 1 minute. Stir in orange juice; cook 1–2 minutes or until heated throughout.

Piselli alla menta

Minted peas

3 servings

> *1 (10 ounce) package*
> *frozen peas*
> *1 tablespoon margarine*
> *or butter*
> *1 tablespoon mint jelly*
> *¹/₄ teaspoon dried oregano*

Cook peas according to package directions; drain well; return to saucepan. Add margarine, jelly and oregano. Cook over low heat, stirring constantly just until jelly melts. Serve immediately.

Fagiolini verdi con pancetta

String beans

6 servings

> *2 slices bacon, diced*
> *1 small onion, chopped*
> *2 (10 ounce) packages*
> *frozen string beans*
> *¹/₄ cup water*
> *¹/₂ teaspoon salt*
> *¹/₄ teaspoon dried oregano*
> *Dash black pepper*
> *Grated Parmesan cheese*

Fry out bacon in large skillet. Add onion; cook 1 minute. Drain off excess fat. Add stringbeans, water, salt, oregano and pepper; mix well. Cover. Cook over medium heat 5–8 minutes or until stringbeans are tender. Sprinkle with grated Parmesan cheese before serving.

Insalata dei tre fagioli

Three bean salad

6–8 servings

> *1 (17 ounce) can lima*
> *beans, drained*
> *1 (15¹/₂ ounce) can*
> *garbanzo beans, drained*
> *1 (15¹/₂ ounce) can*
> *kidney beans, drained*
> *1 green pepper, chopped*
> *2 pimentos, diced*
> *3 scallions, chopped*
> *1 teaspoon salt*
> *¹/₈ teaspoon black pepper*
> *2 cloves garlic, minced*
> *1 (8 ounce) bottle Italian*
> *salad dressing*

Combine beans, pepper, pimento, scallions, salt and pepper; mix well. Add garlic to salad dressing; pour over beans. Let salad marinate at least 4 hours in refrigerator.

Asparagi con le erbe

Asparagus with herb sauce

4 servings

> *2 (10 ounce) packages*
> *frozen asparagus spears*
> *4 tablespoons margarine*
> *or butter*
> *1 clove garlic, cut in half*
> *1 teaspoon chopped chives*
> *1 teaspoon parsley flakes*
> *1 teaspoon lemon juice*
> *¹/₄ teaspoon salt*

Cook asparagus according to package directions. Melt margarine in small skillet over medium heat. Sauté garlic in margarine; remove. Stir in remaining ingredients. Drain asparagus. Pour sauce over asparagus.

Bagna cauda

Asparagi

Bagna cauda

Vegetable fondue

8 servings

Vegetables:
- 4 stalks celery, cut into 2″ pieces
- 1 green pepper, cut into 1″ strips
- 2 carrots, cut into 2″ strips
- 1 bunch scallions, trimmed
- 8 cherry tomatoes
- 1 small head cauliflower, broken into flowerets
- 8 asparagus spears, trimmed
- $^1/_4$ pound small whole mushrooms

Dip:
- $^1/_2$ cup margarine or butter
- $^1/_2$ cup salad oil
- 4 cloves garlic, minced
- 1 ($1^3/_4$ ounce) can anchovy fillets, chopped

  Bread sticks

Crisp vegetables except mushrooms in a bowl of water and ice for 1 hour; drain; dry on paper towel. Wipe mushrooms with damp cloth. Arrange vegetables on serving tray; cover tightly with plastic wrap; refrigerate until ready to serve. Combine margarine, oil, garlic and anchovies in flameproof casserole or fondue pan. Heat over medium heat. *Do not boil.* Serve immediately with vegetables and bread sticks. Keep sauce warm over candle or on electric hot tray.

The Finns have learned to pre-pare their simple fare with great imagination. They can turn the unpretentious turnip into a delect-able dish.

Stuvade grönsaker

Swedish creamed vegetables

6 to 8 servings

¼ cup water
½ teaspoon salt
1 (10 ounce) package frozen succotash
1 (10 ounce) package frozen peas and onions
1 (9 ounce) package frozen Italian green beans
4 tablespoons flour
½ teaspoon salt
¼ teaspoon ground white pepper
1½ cups milk
3 tablespoons margarine or butter
2 tablespoons chopped parsley

Bring water to a boil in 2-quart saucepan, add salt. Add succotash, cover and simmer for 7 minutes. Add peas and onions, cover, return to simmer and cook 4 minutes. Add beans, cover, return to simmer and cook 2 to 4 minutes or until all vegetables are tender, *Do not overcook.* Pour off liquid, measure; make up to 1 cup with water; add to vegetables. Stir flour, salt and pepper into cold milk; add to vegetables. Bring to a boil, stirring constantly; reduce heat and simmer until thickened, about 1 to 2 minutes. Stir in margarine. Sprinkle with parsley.

Kermaanmuhennetut porkkanat

Finnish creamed carrots

4 servings

2 tablespoons margarine or butter
3 tablespoons flour
1 tablespoon sugar
Dash of ground white pepper
1 cup milk
½ cup half-and-half
1 (1 pound) can sliced carrots, drained
Chopped parsley

Melt margarine; add flour, sugar and pepper. Stir until well-blended. Remove from heat, slowly add milk and half-and-half; return to heat. Simmer, stirring constantly, until thickened. Add drained carrots; heat. Garnish with chopped parsley.

Lanttulaatikko

Finnish turnip pie

6 servings

2 pounds yellow turnip, peeled and cut into ½" cubes
½ teaspoon salt
1½ cups fine dry bread crumbs
1 cup half-and-half
1 tablespoon sugar
Dash ground white pepper
⅛ teaspoon ground nutmeg
2 eggs, lightly beaten
2 tablespoons margarine or butter

Cook turnip in just enough salted water to cover until tender, about 30 minutes. Drain and mash. Stir in 1 cup of the bread crumbs, half-and-half, sugar, pepper and nutmeg. Taste and add salt, if needed. Stir in beaten eggs. Use part of the margarine to grease a 9" round cake tin, about 2" deep. Coat with 1 to 2 tablespoons of remaining crumbs. Spread turnip mixture in pan, sprinkle with remaining crumbs and dot with remaining margarine. Bake in a slow oven (325°) 1 hour or until lightly browned.

Punajuuripihvit

Finnish beet steaks

4 servings

1 (1 pound) can sliced beets, drained
1 egg, lightly beaten
½ cup fine dry bread crumbs
2 tablespoons margarine or butter
1 tablespoon lemon juice
1 tablespoon chopped parsley

Dip beets in beaten egg. Sprinkle half of bread crumbs on paper towels; place beet slices on crumbs and sprinkle with remaining crumbs. Melt margarine in skillet. Sauté beet slices, turning to brown each side. Place on platter, sprinkle with lemon juice and parsley.

Lanttu

Finnish turnip

4 to 6 servings

- 2 tablespoons margarine or butter
- 2 pounds yellow turnip, peeled and cut into ½″ cubes
- 2 teaspoons salt
- 2 beef bouillon cubes
- 2 cups boiling water
  Parsley sprigs

Melt margarine in 2-quart saucepan. Sauté turnip cubes over medium heat, turning occasionally to brown lightly on all sides. Sprinkle with salt; add bouillon cubes and water. Bring to a boil; cover, reduce heat and simmer until tender about 25 minutes. Garnish with parsley.

Rotmos

Mashed Swedes

4 to 6 servings

- 1 pound yellow turnips, peeled and cut into ½″ cubes
- 2 beef bouillon cubes
- 2 cups boiling water
- ½ teaspoon salt
- ⅛ teaspoon ground white pepper
- ⅛ teaspoon ground allspice
- 1½ pounds potatoes, peeled and cut into ½″ cubes

Place turnip cubes into 2-quart saucepan. Add bouillon cubes, water, salt, pepper and allspice. Boil about 15 minutes or until half-cooked; add potatoe cubes; cook 15 minutes more or until tender. Drain and mash vegetables; if needed, add a little of the drained liquid.

Raggmunkar

Danish fried potato cakes

4 servings

- 1 egg
- 1 cup flour
- 2 cups milk
- 1½ teaspoons salt
- 6 medium potatoes, peeled, cut into 1″ cubes
- ¼ cup salad oil

In blender jar, combine egg, flour, milk and salt; blend ½ minute. Add a few pieces of potato at a time until all are blended into batter. Heat a thin layer of oil on a griddle or frying pan; use about 1 tablespoon batter for small cakes or 2 to 3 tablespoons for large crepe-type cake, spreading thinly. Fry on both sides until crisp and brown. Serve with a fruit preserve, maple syrup, or plain with meat.

Syltede agurker

Danish pickled cucumbers

6 to 8 servings

   3 *medium cucumbers*
 ½ *cup vinegar*
 ½ *cup water*
   2 *tablespoons sugar*
   1 *teaspoon salt*
 ¼ *teaspoon ground white
      pepper
      Chopped parsley*

Peel cucumbers, if desired;
slice very thinly into serving
bowl. Combine remaining
ingredients; beat with fork.
Pour over cucumbers. Cover;
chill at least one hour before
serving. Sprinkle with chopped
parsley before serving.

Halländsk långkål

Halländsk kale

4 to 6 servings

   2 *(10 ounce) packages frozen
      chopped kale*
   2 *cups water*
 ½ *teaspoon salt*
 ½ *cup diced cooked salt pork*
   2 *tablespoons cornstarch*
 ½ *teaspoon ground ginger*
   1 *cup milk*
   2 *tablespoons maple syrup
      Dash ground white pepper
      Salt, if needed*

Place kale, water, salt and diced
pork in 2-quart saucepan.
Cover, bring to a boil; reduce
heat and simmer until kale is
tender, about 15 to 20 minutes.
Drain. Blend cornstarch and
ginger with milk; stir into kale
with syrup and pepper. Cook
over medium heat, stirring
constantly, until mixture has
thickened. Taste, add salt, if
needed.

Stekt lök

Norwegian fried onions

4 servings

   2 *tablespoons margarine or
      butter*
   4 *medium onions, peeled and
      thinly sliced*
   1 *teaspoon salt*
   1 *teaspoon Worcestershire
      sauce*
   1 *tablespoon chopped parsley*

In large frying pan, melt
margarine, add onions and salt;
saute over medium heat,
stirring occasionally, until
transparent and golden brown
Stir in Worcestershire sauce.
Sprinkle with parsley before
serving.

Rödkål

Braised cabbage

6 servings

   4 *tablespoons margarine or
      butter*
   2 *pounds white cabbage,
      shredded*
   1 *beef bouillon cube*
   1 *cup boiling water*
   2 *tablespoons maple or dark
      corn syrup*
 ⅓ *cup vinegar*
 ½ *teaspoon salt*

In a large heavy saucepan, melt
margarine. Lightly brown
cabbage over moderately high
heat, turning frequently, about
5 minutes. Dissolve bouillon
cube in water. Add to cabbage
with syrup, vinegar, and salt;
toss with fork to blend. Cover;
cook over medium heat about
45 minutes or until cabbage is
tender. Remove cover during
last 10 minutes to allow any
excess liquid to evaporate. Serve
with Christmas ham or cooked
pork sausages.

Finnish hasselback potatoes

Smalandsk potato cakes

Småländska raggmunkar

Smalandsk potato cakes

4 servings

2½ pounds potatoes, peeled, and
    cut into large cubes
1½ teaspoons salt
    Water, if needed
½ cup oil

Start blender on high speed.
Add potato cubes a few at a
time until finely chopped. Add
salt, and if mixture is very thick,
add a drop or two of water.
Heat large, heavy skillet; cover
surface with thin layer of oil.
For each cake, pour 2 to 3
tablespoons of potato mixture
onto hot pan; spread thinly.
Brown well on each side over
moderate heat until cakes are
very crisp. Drain on paper
towels. Serve immediately.

Hasselbackspotatis

Finnish hasselback potatoes

4 servings

12 oval-shaped potatoes, peeled
 1 teaspoon salt
 3 tablespoons margarine or
    butter
 4 tablespoons grated Parmesan
    cheese
 2 tablespoons bread crumbs

Cut potatoes into thin slices,
but not quite through to the
lower edge, so that the slices
hold together. Place potatoes,
with slices upward, into a
well-buttered casserole. Sprinkle
with salt and dot with bits of
margarine. Bake in a very
hot oven (450°) 20 minutes;
basting occasionally. Sprinkle
with cheese and bread crumbs
and bake another 25 minutes
without basting.

Coliflor al ajo arriero

Cauliflower in hot vinegar

4 servings

> 1 small cauliflower
> 2 tablespoons olive oil
> 2 cloves garlic
> 1 teaspoon paprika
> 2 tablespoons wine vinegar
> 2 tablespoons cooking liquid
>   from the cauliflower

Wash the cauliflower and cut into flowerets. Simmer the cauliflower in plenty of boiling salted water for 10 minutes until nearly tender. Drain the cauliflower and reserve 2 tablespoons of the cooking liquid. In the meantime, heat the oil in a small saucepan. Fry the garlic cloves until lightly browned. Discard the garlic. Remove the saucepan from the heat and stir in the paprika, wine vinegar and cooking liquid. Place the cauliflower in a casserole. Pour the sauce over the cauliflower. Cover and simmer over very low heat for 5 to 10 minutes.

Patatas en salsa verde

Batatas estufadas à portuguesa

Couve lombarda recheada

A vegetable market anywhere around the Mediterranean is a festive array of colors: deep red tomatoes, green, yellow and red peppers, shining as if they were varnished, purple eggplants, gray-green artichokes, yellow-green zucchini, cauliflower, cabbages, carrots, and so on. There are long strings of silver garlic bulbs, onions and leeks, and in the corner of the market entrance sits the country woman behind her fragrant stall of garden herbs: dried bunches of oregano and rosemary, basil and thyme, marjoram and lavender. There are also tiny packets of orange-yellow saffron, a spice worth more than its weight in gold. Exotic Eastern spices abound, as well as bunches of such fresh herbs as parsley, tarragon and chervil. And as fiery balls of color, there hang long reeds of hot Spanish peppers.

Potatoes in green sauce

4 servings

- 3 tablespoons olive oil
- 2 cloves garlic, crushed
- 6 potatoes, peeled and thinly sliced
- ½ teaspoon crumbled dried mint leaves
- ½ cup frozen green peas
- 1 teaspoon salt
  Freshly ground black pepper
- 4 tablespoons finely chopped parsley

Heat the olive oil in a casserole. Add the garlic and sauté until lightly browned. Add the potato slices in an even layer and sprinkle with the mint. Cook 1 minute then add 3 tablespoons of water, shaking the casserole to distribute the water evenly. Continue cooking and shake the casserole occasionally. Every few minutes add a few more tablespoons of water. Continue in this manner until the potatoes are just covered with liquid. Add the peas, salt and pepper and shake the casserole. Cover and cook over low heat for about 25 minutes or until the potatoes are tender. Shake the casserole occasionally to prevent sticking. When done, sprinkle the potatoes with parsley and serve from the casserole.

Potatoes Portuguese style

4 to 6 servings

- 5 medium-sized potatoes, unpeeled
- 4 tablespoons butter
- 1 onion, finely chopped
- 2 medium-sized tomatoes, peeled, seeded and sliced
- 6 tablespoons grated Swiss cheese
- ½ teaspoon salt
  Freshly ground black pepper

Cook the potatoes in boiling salted water for 15 to 20 minutes. Drain, peel the potatoes and cut into cubes. Heat the butter in a saucepan and sauté the onion until lightly browned. Add the tomatoes and simmer for 15 minutes. Put the cubed potatoes in a buttered fireproof dish, sprinkle with grated cheese, salt and pepper and cover with the tomato sauce. Place in a preheated 350° oven for 10 minutes and serve hot. These potatoes are delicious with any fish dish.

Stuffed cabbage

4 servings

- 4 to 8 white cabbage leaves, depending on size
- 1 cup left over roast meat (pork, lamb, beef or veal)
- ¼ cup chopped ham
- 6 tablespoons grated Parmesan cheese
  Juice of ½ lemon
- 2 tablespoons finely chopped black olives
- 1 tablespoon finely chopped parsley
- ¼ teaspoon salt
  Freshly ground black pepper
- 1½ cups Portuguese tomato sauce
- 2 tablespoons butter

Cook the cabbage leaves in plenty of boiling salted water until just tender. Rinse under cold running water and drain. In a bowl, combine the leftover meat, ham, 2 tablespoons cheese, lemon juice, olives, parsley, salt and pepper. Divide the filling into as many portions as there are leaves and place 1 portion in the center of each leaf. Fold the sides of the leaf to the center, fold the stem end over and roll the leaf. Place the stuffed leaves in a buttered shallow casserole just large enough to hold them and pour over the tomato sauce. Sprinkle with the remaining cheese and dot with butter. Bake in a 375° oven for 15 minutes or until the cheese is brown.

SAUCES

Oyster sauce

If bottled oyster sauce is not available, a fair substitute can be made following this recipe. Do not use smoked oysters or any other flavored preparation.

1 (8 ounce) can oysters
1 tablespoon water
1 teaspoon salt
Soy sauce
½ tablespoon dark soy sauce

Drain the oysters and reserve the liquid. Mince the oysters and place them in a saucepan. Add water and reserved oyster liquid and bring to a boil over low heat. Reduce heat, cover and simmer for about 10 minutes. Remove from the heat, add salt and let cool completely. Force the mixture through a fine sieve into a heavy saucepan and discard the minced oysters. Measure the liquid, adding 2 tablespoons soy sauce to each ½ cup of oyster liquid. Add the dark soy sauce and bring to a boil. Reduce heat and simmer over low heat for about 7 minutes. Let cool to room temperature and pour into a clear jar. Seal and store in the refrigerator. This sauce can be kept for several weeks.

Plum sauce

1 cup fresh plums, pitted and finely chopped
¼ cup dried apricots, soaked in warm water 1 hour and finely chopped
⅛ teaspoon cayenne pepper
1 teaspoon salt
1 to 2 tablespoons water
½ to ¾ cup sugar
½ cup vinegar

Place the plums and apricots in a heavy saucepan. Add cayenne pepper, salt and about 1 tablespoon water. Bring to a boil over low heat and simmer 15 minutes. Add a little more water if the mixture becomes too dry. Stir in sugar and vinegar and simmer 20 to 30 minutes or until the sauce reaches a chutney-like consistency. Place the sauce in a covered jar and refrigerate when cool. The sauce will keep several months.

Pepper and salt mix

3 tablespoons salt
2 tablespoons Szechuan peppercorns or crushed black peppercorns

Heat a heavy skillet until very hot. Place salt and peppercorns in the skillet. Reduce the heat and stir the mixture 5 to 6 minutes or until the salt is light brown. Remove from the pan and crush the peppercorns in a mortar. Sift the mixture through a sieve. Store the pepper and salt mix in a tightly covered jar.

Dip sauces

Soy-oil dip sauce

2 tablespoons oil
1 teaspoon finely minced scallions, white part only
½ teaspoon ginger root, finely minced
4 tablespoons soy sauce

Heat the oil in a small saucepan until hot. Add scallions and ginger root. Stir fry 20 to 30 seconds. Add soy sauce. Remove from heat and stir to mix well. Serve with white cooked chicken.

Sherry-soy dip sauce

2 tablespoons sherry
2 tablespoons soy sauce
¼ teaspoon sugar

Stir the above ingredients together until the sugar has dissolved. Serve as a dip for white cooked or deep fried chicken.

Sweet sour sauce

½ cup sugar
½ cup vinegar
4 to 5 tablespoons light
   soy sauce
1 tablespoon dark soy
   sauce (optional)
2 tablespoons sherry
1½ tablespoons cornstarch
   dissolved in
½ cup water

Place sugar, vinegar, light soy
sauce, dark soy sauce and
sherry in a heavy saucepan.
Bring to a boil and stir in the
cornstarch mixture to thicken.
Use as directed in recipes.

Sweet sour sauce

¼ inch thick slice fresh ginger
   root, chopped
½ cup sugar
½ cup vinegar
6 tablespoons water or
   pineapple juice
1 tablespoon sherry
1½ tablespoons cornstarch
   dissolved in
4 tablespoons water

Using a garlic press, squeeze
the ginger juice into a heavy
saucepan. Add the sugar,
vinegar, water or pineapple
juice and sherry. Bring the
sauce to a boil and stir in the
cornstarch mixture to thicken.
Use as directed in recipes.

Sauce for foo young eggs

¾ cup chicken broth
½ teaspoon salt
1 tablespoon soy sauce
2 teaspoons sherry
3 teaspoons tomato catsup
¼ teaspoon sugar
2 teaspoons cornstarch
1½ tablespoons water

Bring chicken broth to boiling
point. Add salt, soy sauce,
sherry, catsup and sugar.
Stir to blend. Dissolve cornstarch
in water and stir to thicken.
Note: Oyster sauce may be
substituted for tomato catsup
in this recipe.

Master sauce

This is a sauce which can go on
for ever and ever and, like a
good wine, improves with age.
However, it is worth the trouble
only if you like red simmered
dishes and intend to make them
regularly. To make this sauce,
prepare any of the red simmered
dishes in this book. Eat the meat
and reserve the sauce. Strain it
through a layer of cheesecloth.
Skim off the fat, pour it into a
jar and refrigerate. The next
time you prepare a red
simmered dish, cook the meat
in this sauce instead of using
the liquid ingredients mentioned
in the specific recipe. Not only
will the meat taste better, but
the sauce will improve with the
addition of the new meat juices.
In each subsequent preparation,
the meat or chicken as well as
the sauce will become richer
in taste and flavor, especially
when you add some soy sauce,
sherry, sugar, scallion, ginger
root and salt every third time
you use the sauce. After using
the sauce 6 or 8 times, you may
add a little star anise, cinnamon
or a pinch of five spice powder.
A few tablespoons of fresh
meat broth may be added from
time to time to rejuvenate
the sauce. If the sauce has not
been used for a week, it is
necessary to bring it to a boil
again. Cool it to room
temperature and refrigerate.
This will keep the sauce from
becoming sour. The sauce may
very well outlive you and be
inherited by your children as it
was and still is in some
Chinese families!

The garlic sauce 'aioli' was originally served to accompany the fish cooked in the bouillabaisse. Today this lively *garlic sauce is also used as a dip with raw vegetables, shellfish and the like.*

Aioli

Garlic mayonnaise

Makes 2 cups

¼ cup breadcrumbs
3 teaspoons tarragon or
   wine vinegar
6 cloves garlic, crushed
¼ teaspoon salt
3 egg yolks
1½ cups olive oil or salad oil
3 tablespoons boiling
   bottled clam juice
3 tablespoons lemon juice

Place breadcrumbs in the blender. Add vinegar, garlic and salt: Add egg yolks. Turn on the motor and add oil in a steady continuous drizzle of drops. (Do not add the oil too quickly or the sauce will not thicken.) Add boiling clam juice and lemon juice. Serve with fish or vegetables.

Bouillon blanc de veau

White beef broth

1–2 pounds veal bones with meat attached, the same herbs, vegetables and liquid used for white chicken broth. Follow the directions given for white chicken broth

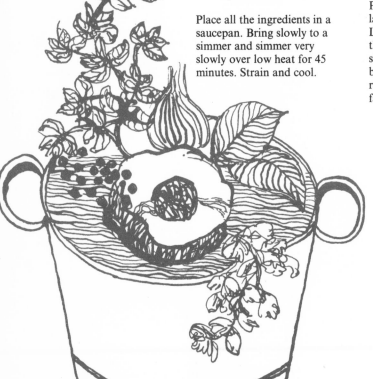

Bouillon de poisson

Fish broth

1 pound fish trimmings
(heads, bones, fins, etc.)
1 slice lemon
3 parsley stems
1 small onion, thinly
sliced
1 small carrot, chopped
¼ teaspoon salt
5 peppercorns
4 fresh mushroom stems,
chopped (optional)
½ cup dry white wine or
dry vermouth
3 cups cold water

Place all the ingredients in a saucepan. Bring slowly to a simmer and simmer very slowly over low heat for 45 minutes. Strain and cool.

Bouillon blanc de volaille

White chicken broth

1–2 pounds chicken backs,
necks, wings, hearts,
gizzards
1 large onion, washed but
unskinned, and quartered
1 carrot, roughly cut
2 stalks celery, roughly cut
1 tomato quartered
2 bay leaves
½ teaspoon thyme
10 peppercorns
3 parsley stalks
2 quarts water

Place all the ingredients in a large pot and bring to a boil. Lower the heat, partially cover the pot and let simmer very slowly for 3 hours. Strain the broth. Chill it in the refrigerator and lift off the fat before using the broth.

Bouillon brun

Brown broth

1–2 pounds beef or veal
(or both) bones with
meat attached
1 large onion, washed but
unskinned, and quartered
1 carrot, roughly cut
2 stalks celery, roughly cut
1 tomato, quartered
2 bay leaves
½ teaspoon thyme
10 peppercorns
3 parsley stalks
2 quarts water

Place the bones with meat in a roasting pan and brown for 15 minutes in a 400° oven. Add the vegetables and continue browning for 10 minutes. Transfer the bones, meat and vegetables to a large pot, add the herbs and water and bring to a boil. Reduce the heat, partially cover the pot and simmer very slowly for 4 to 5 hours. Only an occasional bubble should break the surface. Strain the broth, chill it in the refrigerator and lift off the fat before using the broth.

Sauce vinaigrette

French dressing

¼ teaspoon salt
   Freshly ground black pepper
1 teaspoon mild (Dijon)
   mustard
2 scallions, finely chopped or
1 teaspoon onion, finely
   chopped
1 tablespoon parsley, finely
   chopped
2 tablespoons wine vinegar
6 tablespoons olive oil or
   salad oil

Combine salt, pepper, mustard,
scallions, onion, parsley and
vinegar in a bowl. Add oil
and stir until well blended.
French dressing may be used
not only for tossed green
salads but also to marinate
cold cooked vegetables such
as asparagus, broccoli,
cauliflower and peas.
It is also very good with
cold meats and fish.

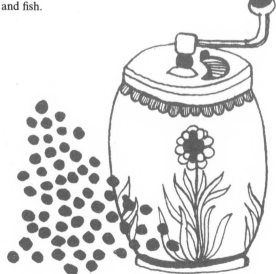

Sauce Béarnaise

Béarnaise sauce

¼ cup white wine
¼ cup tarragon or wine
   vinegar
1 teaspoon dried tarragon
2 tablespoons scallions,
   finely chopped
⅔ cup butter
3 egg yolks
⅛ teaspoon salt
   Freshly ground black pepper
½ teaspoon dried tarragon

Place wine, wine vinegar,
tarragon and scallions in a
saucepan. Boil uncovered
until the liquid is reduced
to 2 tablespoons. Strain and
reserve liquid. Reserve 2
tablespoons of butter. Heat
the remaining butter until
very hot. Remove butter from
the heat. Beat egg yolks in a
small saucepan until slightly
thickened. Add strained wine
and vinegar. Place pan over
moderate heat. Add one
tablespoon cold reserved butter
and cook until butter has
melted, stirring constantly.
Add second tablespoon of
reserved butter and continue
stirring until butter has melted.
Remove the pan from the heat.
Add hot butter a little at a
time, stirring rapidly. Season
sauce with salt, pepper and
tarragon. Béarnaise sauce is
served with broiled steaks
and fish.

Sauce velouté

Velouté sauce

2 tablespoons butter
4 level tablespoons flour
1½ cups chicken broth
1 egg yolk
1 teaspoon lemon juice
⅛ teaspoon salt
   Freshly ground black pepper

Melt the butter and stir in
the flour. Cook over low heat
for one minute. Add chicken
broth gradually, stirring with
a whisk. Simmer one minute
until the sauce has thickened.
Add egg yolk, lemon juice
salt and pepper. Velouté sauce
may also be made with fish
stock, (or ¾ cup clam broth
combined with ¾ water) if
the sauce is to be served with
fish. Beef broth can be
substituted for chicken broth
for beef dishes.

Sauce Hollandaise

Hollandaise sauce

- ²⁄₃ cup butter
- 3 egg yolks
- ⅛ teaspoon salt
  Freshly ground black pepper
- 2 tablespoons lemon juice

Reserve 2 tablespoons butter.
Heat the remaining butter
until very hot. Remove butter
from the heat. Beat egg yolks,
salt, pepper and 1 tablespoon
lemon juice in a small saucepan
until slightly thickened. Place
pan over moderate heat.
Add one tablespoon cold
reserved butter and cook until
butter has melted, stirring
constantly. Add second
tablespoon of reserved butter
and continue stirring until
butter has melted. Remove
the pan from the heat. Add
hot butter a little at a time,
stirring rapidly. Add remaining
tablespoon of lemon juice.

Sauce ravigotte

Ravigotte sauce

- 1 cup oil
- ¼ cup red wine vinegar
- ¼ teaspoon salt
  Freshly ground black pepper
- 2 teaspoons mild (Dijon)
  mustard
- 1 tablespoon capers
- 1 shallot or scallion, finely
  chopped
- 2 tablespoons combined
  finely chopped fresh herbs
  (parsley, chives, tarragon,
  chervil) or 1 tablespoon
  dried herbs
- 1 clove garlic, crushed
- 1 hard-boiled egg, finely
  chopped (opt.)

In a small bowl, combine the
oil, vinegar, salt, pepper and
mustard and beat with a wire
whisk or fork until well
blended. Add the remaining
ingredients and beat until well
combined.

Sauce Béchamel

Béchamel sauce

- 4 tablespoons butter
- 4 level tablespoons flour
- 1½ cups milk or light cream
- ⅛ teaspoon salt
  Dash nutmeg

Melt the butter and stir in the
flour. Cook over low heat for
one minute. Add milk gradually
stirring constantly. Continue
cooking over moderate heat
for two minutes until the sauce
has thickened. Season with
salt and nutmeg. White sauce
is served with vegetables
(e.g. cauliflower, squash,
broccoli and endives).

Sauce Mornay

Mornay sauce

To prepare Mornay sauce, follow the directions for Béchamel sauce in the previous recipe and add ½ cup grated Swiss cheese. Mornay sauce is served with eggs, vegetables and pasta such as macaroni.

Sauce mousseline

Mousseline sauce

To prepare mousseline sauce, follow the directions for Hollandaise sauce in the previous recipe and add ½ cup heavy cream. Mousseline sauce is served with poached fish.

Sauce Espagnole

Classic brown sauce

2⅓ cups brown broth,
or 3 beef bouillon
cubes dissolved in 2⅓ cups
boiling water
⅔ cup dry red wine
3 tablespoons butter
3 tablespoons flour
1 teaspoon tomato paste

Place the broth and wine in a saucepan and boil until reduced to 1½ cups. In another heavy saucepan, melt the butter and add the flour. Stir with a wire whisk and cook for 3 to 4 minutes or until the flour is light brown. Add the bouillon/wine mixture gradually, beating with a wire whisk. Return the sauce to the simmer and cook until thick. Beat in the tomato paste. Brown sauce is used to accompany braised meats, game and steaks.

Sauce Madère

Madeira sauce

Prepare Sauce Espagnole and add 2 tablespoons Madeira. Just before serving, beat in 1 tablespoon butter.

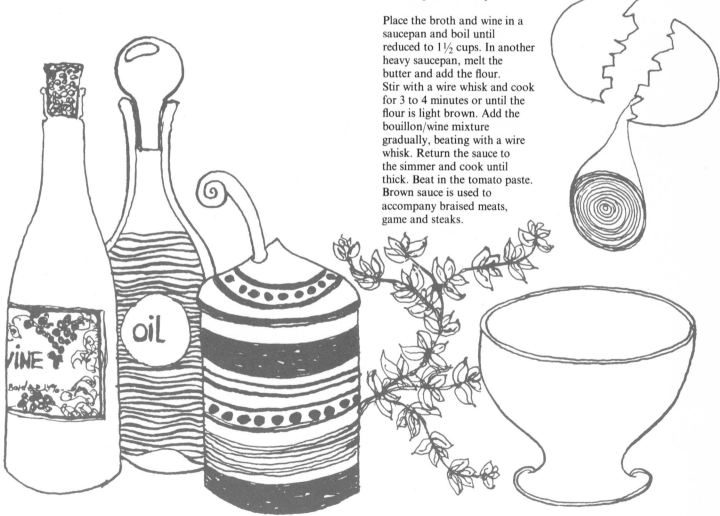

Mayonaise

Sauce verte

Mayonnaise

3 egg yolks
¼ teaspoon dry mustard
   powder
½ teaspoon salt
   Freshly ground black pepper
3 tablespoons lemon juice
   or red wine vinegar or a
   combination of the two
1½ cups olive oil or salad oil

Place the egg yolks in a bowl.
Using a hand or standard
electric mixer or a wire whisk,
beat the yolks until they are
thick and creamy. Beat in the
mustard powder, salt, pepper
and 1 tablespoon lemon juice
or vinegar. Add the oil in a
slow, steady, continuous
stream of drops, beating
constantly, until all the oil is
used and the mayonnaise is
thick. Be sure not to add the
oil too quickly or the
mayonnaise may curdle. Beat
in the remaining lemon juice
or vinegar. If the mixture
curdles, beat an egg yolk in
another bowl until it is thick
and creamy. Add the curdled
mayonnaise by droplets,
beating continuously. Continue
until you have beaten all the
curdled mayonnaise into the
fresh egg yolk.

Green mayonnaise

Prepare mayonnaise as
directed. Beat in 3 to 4
tablespoons finely chopped
combined green herbs such as
parsley, chives, chervil,
tarragon, basil, oregano or
boiled spinach.

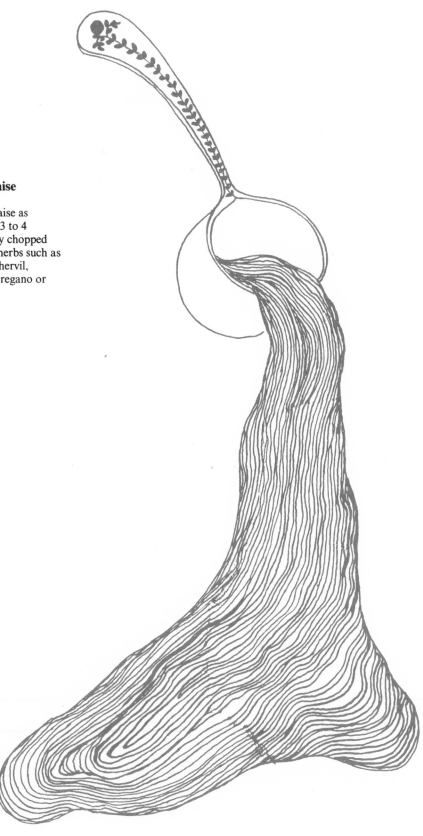

Semmelkren

Horseradish and bread sauce

Makes 2 cups

  2 *cups beef bouillon*
  ½ *cup prepared horseradish*
  2 *slices white bread, crusts removed and cubed*
  1 *tablespoon cornstarch*
  2 *tablespoons water*
  ½ *cup light cream*
  ½ *cup sour cream*

Combine bouillon, horseradish and bread in saucepan; bring to a boil. Reduce heat; simmer 5–8 minutes or until bread dissolves. Mix cornstarch and water; stir into bouillon mixture. Cook, stirring constantly, until thickened. Stir in cream and sour cream; heat.

Kalte Schnittlauchsauce

Cold chive sauce

Makes 1 cup

  2 *(3 oz.) packages cream cheese and chives*
  2 *teaspoons chives*
  ¼ *teaspoon salt*
     Dash black pepper
  ¼ *cup milk*

Cream together cheese, chives, salt and pepper. Gradually stir in milk; blend until smooth.

Frankfurter grüne Sauce

Herb sauce

Makes 1 cup

  1 *(8 oz.) package plain yogurt, chilled*
  ¼ *cup mayonnaise*
  ½ *teaspoon dill weed*
  ½ *teaspoon dried chervil*
  ½ *teaspoon parsley flakes*
  ½ *teaspoon chives*
  ¼ *teaspoon salt*
  ⅛ *teaspoon black pepper*
  2 *hard cooked eggs, chopped*

Combine yogurt, mayonnaise and seasonings; blend well. Stir in chopped egg.

Süddeutscher Salat

South German salad dressing

Makes ½ cup

  1 *small onion, quartered*
  2 *tablespoons chopped parsley*
  2 *tablespoons chopped chives*
  2 *tablespoons boiling water*
  2 *tablespoons vinegar*
  4 *tablespoons salad oil*
  1 *teaspoon prepared mustard*
  ½ *teaspoon salt*
  ¼ *teaspoon black pepper*

Combine all ingredients in blender jar; blend smooth.

Senfsauce

Specksauce

Mustard is so important to German cooking that many sauces use it as a base. Mustard is the best friend of pork, and given the immense popularity of pork products in Germany, the mustard pot is almost always on the table.

Mustard is an ancient herb. The Roman legions took it with them throughout Europe. Under the primitive conditions of Europe's Dark Ages, where many of the arts of civilization had been lost, mustard was very popular for preserving the freshness of meat and fish.

Basically, mustard consists of seeds from the mustard plant, which are ground to a fine powder (in the old days with a large stone crusher) and mixed with vinegar and spices. Mustard used to be prepared with sour grape juice, hence the name 'most', meaning unfermented grapejuice.

There are many different varieties of mustard in Germany, some stronger than others, some prepared with wine vinegar, some with beer vinegar and some with fresh green herbs. For fish the Germans use a very light mustard, made from white mustard seeds, and a somewhat darker mustard is used to accompany beer sausages.

Mustard is also used in German cooking to give certain sauces more body and in the preparation of braised meat and game. Meat that has been rubbed with mustard becomes deliciously

tender when braised: the sharp flavor of the mustard disappears and only the aroma remains.

Medium mustard sauce

Makes 2 cups

> 4 tablespoons margarine or
>   butter
> 4 tablespoons flour
> 1–2 tablespoons dry mustard
> 1 teaspoon sugar
> 2 cups beef bouillon

Melt margarine in saucepan over low heat. Add flour, mustard and sugar; stir until blended smooth. Slowly add bouillon, stirring constantly to avoid lumps. Cook, stirring until smooth and thickened. For thick sauce increase flour to ½ cup.

Bacon sauce

Makes 2 cups

> ½ pound lean bacon, diced
> 1 medium onion, chopped
> 5 tablespoons flour
> 2 cups beef bouillon
> 1 teaspoon vinegar

Fry out bacon in heavy saucepan. Add onion; cook until onion is transparent. Drain off fat; return 2 tablespoons to saucepan. Add flour; stir until blended smooth. Slowly add bouillon and vinegar, stirring constantly to avoid lumps. Cook, stirring until smooth and thickened.

Pasta sauces

Salsa con carne e funghi

Meat and mushroom sauce

4 cups sauce

> 1 pound lean ground beef
> 1 clove garlic, minced
> 2 (4 ounce) cans chopped
>   mushrooms
> $^1/_2$ teaspoon dried basil
> 2 cups (28 ounce cans)
>   tomato sauce
> 1 (6 ounce) can tomato paste
> $^1/_2$ teaspoon sugar

Brown meat in heavy saucepan. Add remaining ingredients, stir well. Simmer uncovered, over medium heat, 30–35 minutes.

Salsa mayonesa

Mayonnaise

3 egg yolks
½ teaspoon salt
  Freshly ground black pepper
2 tablespoons lemon juice or
  vinegar
2 cups olive oil
2 tablespoons boiling water

Place the egg yolks, salt, pepper and 1 tablespoon lemon juice or vinegar in a bowl. Beat with a wire whisk or an electric mixer until the yolks are thick and creamy. Add the oil in a very slow steady stream of drops, beating continuously until all the oil is added. Beat in the remaining lemon juice or vinegar. Finally, add the boiling water to make the mayonnaise smooth.

All-i-oli

Garlic mayonnaise

1 cup

2 tablespoons white
  breadcrumbs
½ teaspoon lemon juice
6 cloves garlic, crushed
½ teaspoon salt
2 egg yolks
1 cup olive oil or salad oil

Place breadcrumbs in the blender. Add the lemon juice, garlic, salt and egg yolks. Add the oil slowly, drop by drop, as mixture is blending. (Do not add the oil too quickly or mixture will not thicken.)

Salsa de colorada

Red sauce

1½ cups

 3 unpeeled tomatoes
 6 cloves garlic
 2 yolks from hard boiled eggs
12 toasted blanched almonds
 ¾ cup olive oil
 ¼ cup red wine vinegar
 ¼ teaspoon salt
   Dash of cayenne pepper

Bake tomatoes and garlic in a 350° oven for 10 to 15 minutes or until tomatoes are soft. Peel the tomatoes and garlic and purée in the blender. Add the egg yolks and almonds and continue blending. Turn the blender to the lowest speed and add the oil and vinegar alternately drop by drop until it is all incorporated. Transfer to a bowl and stir in the salt and cayenne pepper. This sauce is a good accompaniment for cold meats and fish.

Salsa Romesco

Romesco sauce

4 servings

1 ripe tomato, peeled, seeded
  and chopped
1 small dried hot chili pepper
3 cloves garlic, crushed
2 tablespoons ground almonds
¾ cup olive oil
2 tablespoons wine vinegar
2 tablespoons sherry
¼ teaspoon salt

Pound the tomatoes, chili pepper, garlic and almonds into a smooth paste with a mortar and pestle. Combine the oil, wine vinegar and sherry. Add the mixture, drop by drop into the paste, stirring constantly in the same direction. Season with salt to taste.

Note: This sauce can be made in a blender but the result is not quite as good.

DESSERTS

Lemon custard

Syllabub

6 servings

- 4 tablespoons butter
- 1 cup sugar
  Juice and rind of 1 large lemon
- 2 egg yolks
- 1 cup milk
- 3 tablespoons sifted flour
- 2 egg whites, stiffly beaten

Cream butter until light. Beat in sugar, lemon juice and rind, egg yolks, milk and flour. Fold in egg whites. Pour into a buttered 1½ quart oven-proof dish and bake in a 350° oven 30 minutes. Chill 3 hours before serving.

Note: A creamy custard will form on the bottom of the dish with a cake like texture on top.

4 servings

- Grated rind and juice of 1 lemon
- ½ cup sugar
- 3 tablespoons sherry
- 2 tablespoons brandy
- ½ teaspoon vanilla extract
- 1¼ cups heavy cream

Place the lemon rind and juice in a mixer bowl. Stir in the sugar, sherry, brandy and vanilla. Stir until the sugar dissolves. Add the cream and beat until the cream is thick. Pour into 4 wine glasses or parfait glasses. Chill 4 hours. Serve with ladyfingers, macaroons or sugar cookies.

Dundee cake

Dundee cake

¾ cup butter
¾ cup sugar
 4 eggs
 2 cups all purpose flour
1¼ teaspoons baking powder
 2 tablespoons ground almonds
1¼ cup currants
 1 cup golden raisins
¼ cup candied cherry halves
⅓ cup chopped mixed candied
    orange and lemon peel
    Grated rind of 1 lemon
    Split blanched almonds

Cream the butter and sugar
together until light and fluffy.
Add 2 eggs, 1 at a time beating
well after each addition. Sift
together the flour and baking
powder. Beat in ½ cup of the
flour. Add the remaining eggs,
1 at a time, and beat well. Add
the remaining flour gradually.
Fold in all the other ingredients
except the split almonds. Butter
and flour an 8″ spring form or
other deep cake tin and place a
circle of buttered wax paper on
the bottom. Transfer the batter
to the prepared tin distributing it
evenly. Arrange the split
almonds in circles over the top
of the cake. Bake in a 350°
oven for 1½ hours or until a
cake tester comes out clean.
Cool 5 minutes in the pan
before transferring to a wire
rack.

Rice girdle cakes

Rice girdle cakes

Rice griddle cakes

4 servings

1¼ *cups all purpose flour*
 ½ *teaspoon salt*
1½ *teaspoons baking powder*
1¼ *cups milk*
1¼ *cups cooked rice*
1½ *tablespoons melted butter*
 1 *egg, beaten*

Sift the flour, salt and baking powder together into a bowl. Add the milk and stir to moisten the flour. Add the remaining ingredients and stir until just combined. Drop tablespoons of the batter on a very hot oiled griddle or frying pan. Cook until holes appear on the surface of the cakes and they are brown. Turn and brown the other side. Serve immediately with melted butter and warm syrup.

Note: What we call a "griddle" the English refer to as a "girdle". Hence the English title.

Richmond maids of honor

Makes 16

Recipe for short crust pastry

⅔ cup ground almonds
½ cup sugar
3 tablespoons flour
5 tablespoons heavy cream
1 egg, beaten
Grated rind of 1 lemon
1 tablespoon rosewater
(optional)

Line 16 1 inch deep tartlet tins with the pastry. In a small bowl, mix the almonds, sugar and flour. Add the cream, egg, lemon rind and optional rosewater and beat well. Fill the mixture into the pastry shells. Bake the tarts in a 350° oven for 35 minutes or until golden brown.

Drop scones

Makes 20

1 cup all purpose flour
½ teaspoon baking soda
1 teaspoon baking powder
¼ teaspoon cream of tartar
2 tablespoons sugar
2 tablespoons butter
1 egg
1 tablespoon golden syrup or corn syrup
5 tablespoons milk

In a bowl, sift together the flour baking soda, baking powder, cream of tartar and sugar. Cut the butter into the flour using a pastry blender or 2 knives. Beat the egg lightly and add the syrup and milk. Stir the liquid ingredients into the flour mixture. The batter should just drop from a spoon. Let batter stand 15 minutes. Drop the batter from a teaspoon onto a very hot oiled griddle or frying pan. Cook about 3 minutes or until golden brown and turn to brown the other side. Wrap the scones in a clean cloth to keep them soft.

Seed cake

¾ cup butter
¾ cup sugar
3 eggs
1 teaspoon orange flower water (optional)
1½ cups flour
1½ teaspoons baking powder
¼ teaspoon salt
2 tablespoons caraway seeds
Grated rind of 1 orange

Cream the butter with the sugar until light and fluffy. Beat in the eggs 1 at a time. Beat in the optional orange flower water. Sift the flour with the baking powder and salt. Add the flour to the butter mixture gradually, beating well after each addition. Fold in the caraway seeds and orange rind. Butter and flour an 8 inch spring form pan or other cake pan with sides at least 1½ inch high. Place a buttered circle of wax paper on the bottom of the pan. Spread the batter evenly in the pan. The batter will be quite thick. Bake the cake in a 350° oven for 45 to 55 minutes or until a cake tester inserted in the center comes out clean. Cool the cake in the pan 5 minutes then turn out on a wire rack to cool completely.

Oatcakes

Makes 16

1½ cups Irish oatmeal
½ teaspoon salt
½ teaspoon baking soda
2 tablespoons melted butter
¼ to ⅓ cup hot water
Oatmeal for dusting

Grind the oatmeal, ½ cup at a time, in a blender until fine. Place in a bowl and add the salt and soda. Stir in the butter. Add the water gradually until the dough just sticks together. Sprinkle a board with unground oatmeal and roll out the dough ⅛ inch thick. Cut into 2 inch rounds and place on a baking sheet that has been dusted with oatmeal. Bake in a 350° oven 20 minutes. Leave the cakes in the turned off oven with the door open for 5 minutes. Serve immediately with butter and cheese.

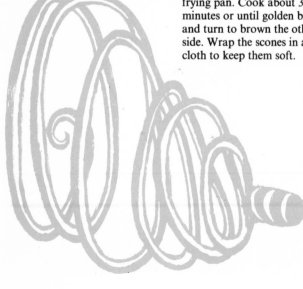

Madeira cake

½ cup butter
½ cup sugar
4 eggs
2 cups self-rising flour
Grated rind of 1 lemon
2 tablespoons superfine sugar
3 inch piece of candied
lemon peel

Cream the butter with the
sugar until light and fluffy. Add
2 eggs, 1 at a time, beating
well after each addition. Add ½
cup of flour and beat thoroughly.
Add the remaining eggs, then
the flour and lemon rind.
Combine thoroughly. Place the
batter in a buttered and floured
loaf tin. Bake in a 350° oven
for 30 minutes. Sprinkle the
sugar on top of the loaf and
place the strip of lemon peel in
the center. Continue to bake
30 minutes more. This is called
Madeira cake because
traditionally, it is served with a
glass of Madeira.

Irish soda bread

Makes 1 loaf

2 cups all purpose flour
2 tablespoons sugar
1½ teaspoons baking powder
½ teaspoon baking soda
½ teaspoon salt
2 tablespoons butter
¾ cup plus 2 tablespoons
buttermilk
½ cup currants

In a bowl, combine the flour,
sugar, baking powder, baking
soda and salt. Cut the butter
into the flour mixture with a
pastry blender or 2 knives. Add
the buttermilk and mix
thoroughly into a soft dough.
Add the currants. Knead the
dough on a lightly floured
board about 3 minutes or until
smooth. Form the dough into a
7 inch flat round, and place in
a lightly oiled cake tin. Cut a
cross about ½ inch deep in the
center of the round. Bake in a
375° oven 40 minutes. Cool
on a wire rack.

Gingerbread

2 eggs
¾ cup dark brown sugar
¾ cup dark molasses
½ cup butter
1 cup boiling water
2½ cups flour
½ teaspoon baking powder
2 teaspoons baking soda
2 teaspoons ground ginger
1½ teaspoons cinnamon
½ teaspoon nutmeg
½ teaspoon ground cloves
½ cup diced candied ginger

Beat the eggs and sugar
together until very thick. Beat
in the molasses. Cut the butter
into small pieces and let it melt
in the water. Sift together the
remaining ingredients except
the candied ginger. Add the
sifted ingredients to the egg
mixture alternately with the
liquid. Combine thoroughly.
Fold in the candied ginger. Pour
the batter into a square cake
pan and bake in a 400° oven
40 minutes.

In the Swiss canton of Thurgau, the apple slices are arranged to stand up in the tart.

Thurgauer Apfeltorte

Apple cake from Thurgau

½ cup butter
⅔ cup sugar
2 eggs, separated
  Juice of ½ lemon
2 cups sifted flour
2 teaspoons baking powder
¼ teaspoon salt
4 tart apples, peeled, cored
  and halved
2 tablespoons sugar

In a bowl, beat the butter until creamy. Add the sugar and continue beating until the mixture is light and fluffy. Add the egg yolks 1 at a time, beating well after each addition. Beat in the lemon juice. Beat the egg whites until stiff. Sift together the sifted flour, baking powder and salt. Add the egg whites and flour mixture alternately, mixing only enough to combine the ingredients. Spread the batter in a buttered and floured 9 inch spring form cake pan. Slice the apple halves crosswise into fan-like shapes, leaving the slices attached at the bottom. Arrange the "fans" on top of the batter, pressing them into the dough. Sprinkle the cake with sugar and bake in a 350° oven about 50 minutes or until it tests done. Let cool 10 minutes before slicing. This makes an excellent coffee cake.

St. Galler Klostertorte

Monastery pie from St. Gallen

6 to 8 servings

2 cups flour
1 teaspoon baking powder
8 tablespoons butter, cut into
  small pieces
½ cup ground almonds
1 teaspoon cinnamon
½ cup sugar
2 to 3 tablespoons milk
1 cup blackberry preserves
1 egg yolk, beaten

Combine the flour, baking powder, butter, almonds, cinnamon and sugar with a pastry blender or the finger tips. Add the milk and stir with a fork to form a smooth dough. Refrigerate for 1 hour. Roll out ¾ of the dough and fit into a buttered and floured 8 inch spring form tart tin. Cut the remainder of the pastry into long strips. Lay one strip in a circle around the sides of the pastry. Fill the shell with preserves and lay a criss cross pattern of pastry strips on top. Brush with egg yolk and bake in a preheated 350° oven for 40 minutes. Cool and serve.

Tarte aux poires à la Genevoise

Pie with pears from Geneva

6 to 8 servings

1 9 inch unbaked pie shell
  (use 1 package frozen patty
  shells, thawed and rolled into
  a circle)
1 tablespoon flour
2 tablespoons sugar
1 teaspoon cinnamon
6 ripe pears
½ teaspoon grated lemon rind
½ teaspoon grated orange rind
¼ cup raisins
2 to 3 tablespoons dry white
  wine
2 tablespoons oil
2 to 3 tablespoons sugar
½ cup heavy cream

Line a 9 inch pie plate with the pastry and prick with a fork. Combine the flour, sugar and cinnamon and sprinkle on top of the pastry. Peal the pears and cut each pear in half. Remove the cores and arrange the pears cut side down on the pastry. Cut the pears into slices, cutting almost all the way through but keeping the slices still joined together. Sprinkle the pears with lemon rind, orange rind and raisins. Combine the wine and oil and pour over the pears. Top with sugar and cream. Place in a preheated 400° oven and bake for 10 minutes. Reduce the heat to 350° and bake for another 25 minutes.

Weintorte

Wine cake

Cake:

7 eggs, separated
1⅓ cups sugar
  Grated rind of 1 lemon
2 tablespoons rum
1 cup plus 2 tablespoons ground
  almonds
1 cup plus 2 tablespoons fine
  dry breadcrumbs
  Pinch of salt

Topping:

1 cup red wine
½ cup sugar
¼ teaspoon cinnamon
¼ teaspoon ground cloves

Butter a 9 inch spring form cake pan and dust with fine dry breadcrumbs. Beat the egg yolks with the sugar until very thick. Do not underbeat. Gradually add the lemon rind, rum, almonds and breadcrumbs, beating just until the dry ingredients are incorporated. Beat the egg whites with a pinch of salt until stiff peaks form. Stir ⅓ of the whites into the batter, making sure the ingredients are thoroughly combined. Carefully fold in the remaining whites and transfer the batter to the prepared cake pan. Bake in a 275° oven 1 to 1¼ hours, until a cake tester comes out clean. Meanwhile, place the wine, sugar, cinnamon and cloves in a saucepan and stir over low heat until the sugar dissolves. When the cake is done, pour the wine mixture over it. Remove from the pan and serve warm or cold.

Peking dust

Eight precious pudding

6 American servings
8 Chinese servings

  2 pounds chestnuts or 1
    (1 pound) can unsweetened
    chestnut purée
¼ *cup sugar*
  2 cups heavy cream
  3 tablespoons powdered sugar
  1 teaspoon vanilla extract
  1 tablespoon brown sugar,
    sifted
¼ *cup water*
½ *cup sugar*
¼ *cup canned Mandarin*
    oranges
¼ *cup pitted cherries or*
    blanched almonds

Score chestnuts crosswise on
their flat side. Place them on
a baking sheet and heat them
in a 400° oven for about
15 minutes or until slightly
opened. Skin them when they
are cool enough to handle.
Place the chestnuts in a pan
and cover with water. Bring to
a boil and cook for about 35
minutes or until just tender.
Force the chestnuts through a
sieve and combine with the
¼ cup sugar. If canned
chestnut purée is used, simply
combine it with the sugar.
Whip the cream until slightly
thickened. Beat in the powdered
sugar and vanilla and continue
beating until very stiff. Divide
the cream into 2 equal portions.
Fold the brown sugar and the
chestnut purée into 1 portion
of the cream until well blended.
Lightly oil a bowl just large
enough to hold the chestnut
mixture. Place it in the bowl
and press down firmly. Invert

the chestnut cream onto a
plate and top with the remaining
cream. Bring the water to a
boil. Add the sugar and boil
until syrupy. Dip the fruits
and nuts, if used, into the
syrup. Let them cool and
harden on a greased surface.
Decorate the Peking Dust with
the glacéed fruits in a beautiful
pattern.

8 American servings
8 Chinese servings

  2 cups long grain rice
  1 to 1½ cups assorted fruits
    and nuts*
  4 cups water
¼ *cup sugar*
  6 tablespoons lard
  8 tablespoons canned red
    bean paste or homemade
    red bean paste
  1 cup water
  8 tablespoons sugar
  1 teaspoon almond essence
  1 tablespoon cornstarch
  3 tablespoons cold water

Wash the rice and drain.
Prepare fruits and nuts. (See
note at the end of the recipe.)
Place the rice in a heavy pan,
add 4 cups water and bring to a
boil. Reduce heat, cover and
cook over low heat for about
25 minutes or until dry and
fluffy. Let rice cool slightly and
then mix in ¼ cup sugar and
4 tablespoons lard until well
blended. Brush the inside of a
rather shallow, heatproof bowl
or dish with the remaining
melted lard, let cool and allow
to set slightly. Place fruits and
nuts in a beautiful pattern on
the bottom and sides of the dish,
pressing them lightly so they
will be embedded in the lard.
Carefully fill the dish with half
of the rice, pressing down
gently without damaging the
fruit and nut design. Cover with
a layer of bean paste, keeping
the paste within 1 to 1½ inches
from the sides. Add the
remaining rice and press down
gently so the pudding will hold

its shape when it is unmolded.
Cover with a clean cloth or foil
and steam for 1 hour. Take the
bowl out of the steaming pan
and cover with a flat serving
plate just large enough to hold
the pudding. Invert the pudding
onto the plate. Heat 1 cup
water to boiling point. Stir in
the sugar and almond essence.
Continue cooking until the
sugar has dissolved. Dissolve
the cornstarch in the water.
Add cornstarch paste to boiling
syrup and stir until thickened.
Pour sauce over pudding and
serve hot or cold.
* The original Chinese recipe
prescribes all sorts of dried or
preserved fruits and nuts which
are not obtainable in this
country. They can be substituted,
however, by your own choice of
fresh or preserved fruits and
nuts, such as, plums, raisins,
dates, candied cherries, orange
peel and other candied or
preserved fruits and nuts such
as almonds, walnuts, lotus seeds,
melon seeds etc. It is good to
have at least 8 different items
to justify the name of the
pudding. Nuts should be
blanched and halved evenly.
The fruits should be pitted
and halved or quartered, if
large. Though the lard may be
substituted by oil, lard is
preferable because the fruits
and nuts have to be arranged on
the bottom of the dish and will
stick to the surface better.
Fruits, especially candied fruits,
can be cut into half moon or
other patterns to make a
beautiful decoration.

It is often a great disappointment for people to discover that the Chinese have only a very limited range of desserts and sweets. And out of this limited range, most desserts are not even served with

family meals, but reserved for banquets and formal dinners. Even in the bakery section there are only very few sweet foods, and the cakes are steamed rather than baked in the oven. But even

though there are so few desserts, the lack is one of quantity rather than quality. The recipes in this section are all fine creations which can stand comparison with desserts from all over the world.

Almond cookies

30 to 40 cookies

  1 cup sugar
  1 cup lard
  1 egg
  2 teaspoons almond extract
  3 cups all purpose flour
1½ teaspoons baking powder
  ¼ teaspoon salt
  ¾ cup blanched, slivered almonds
    Whole blanched almonds for decoration

Cream the sugar and lard together until light and fluffy. Beat in the egg and almond extract. Sift together the flour, baking powder and salt. Add 1 cup of the flour mixture and all of the slivered almonds and combine thoroughly. Add the rest of the flour, ½ cup at a time. (You may have to knead in the last bit.) Knead the dough until it is firm and pliable. Roll it out to a ¼ to ½ inch thickness on a floured board. Cut the cookies with a 1½ to 2 inch round cookie cutter. Transfer to a lightly oiled cookie sheet. Place a whole blanched almond in the center of each cookie. Bake in a preheated 350° oven for 20 minutes or until light brown. Cool on wire racks.

Almond float

6 American servings
6 Chinese servings

For the gelatin:
  1 cup blanched slivered almonds, finely ground
  3 cups water
  ¼ cup sugar
1½ packages unflavored gelatin

For the fruit:
  3 cups water
  ¾ cup sugar
  2 cups drained canned Mandarin oranges, pitted cherries, lychees or a combination of all 3

Place the almonds, 2½ cups water and ¼ cup sugar in a saucepan. Bring to a boil stirring constantly. Reduce heat and simmer, stirring occasionally, for 15 minutes. Meanwhile, sprinkle gelatin over ½ cup cold water. Strain the almond mixture pressing as much liquid as possible out of the almonds. Add the gelatin to the hot liquid, stirring to dissolve. Pour into an 8 × 8 × 2 inch pan and refrigerate until set. Bring the remaining 3 cups water to a boil. Add the sugar and stir until dissolved. Cool the liquid to room temperature, add the fruit and chill. When ready to serve, cut the almond gelatin into diamond shapes. Place the fruit and syrup in a serving bowl. "Float" the diamonds in the syrup and serve.

Steamed sponge cake

  4 eggs, separated
  1 cup sugar
  ½ teaspoon vanilla extract
  1 cup flour
  ½ teaspoon baking powder

Beat the egg whites until stiff. Beat the egg yolks separately with the sugar and vanilla extract until creamy. Fold in egg whites. Sift flour and baking powder together and stir into egg mixture until well blended. Oil a square 8 inch cake pan very lightly and pour in the batter. Place in a steamer and steam for about 25 minutes. Test with a tooth pick. If it comes out clean, the cake is done. Remove from pan and let cool for 10 minutes. Invert cake onto a platter and cut into 2 inch squares. May be served hot or cold.

4 to 6 American servings
4 to 6 Chinese servings

  4 firm apples
  1 egg
  1 egg white
  2 tablespoons flour
  2 tablespoons cornstarch
    Oil for deep frying
  ¼ cup oil
  ¼ cup sugar
  ¼ cup honey
1½ tablespoons white sesame seeds (optional)
  1 bowl of ice water

Peel and core the apples and cut each apple in 6 to 8 wedges. Beat egg and egg white until well blended and beat in the flour and cornstarch. Heat the oil for deep frying until hot. Dip apple wedges in the batter and deep fry until golden. Remove and drain on paper towels. In a saucepan, heat ¼ cup oil, add the sugar and heat, stirring constantly, until the sugar has dissolved. Stir in the honey. Coat apple fritters with the syrup. Transfer fritters and syrup to a bowl and sprinkle with sesame seeds. Bring to the table while still piping hot. Let each guest dip the apple fritters into the ice water. This will cause the syrup coating to harden so that the fritters will be crisp and crackling on the outside.

There are only a few Chinese desserts but this simple Almond cookie and the scooped out and decorated watermelon filled with lychees and other fruits, make up for the absence of a wide choice.

Watermelon and lychees

8 American servings
12 Chinese servings

> *1 watermelon*
> *1 (16 ounce) can lychees in syrup*
> *1 (16 ounce) can pitted cherries, Mandarin oranges or other fruit (or a combination of several), drained*

Cut away the top of the watermelon about ¼ of the way down to form a boat. Scoop out the fruit with a melon ball scoop, making neat round balls. Combine the watermelon balls, lychees with their syrup and cherries. Scoop out the ridges in the watermelon boat, making sure to leave a 1 inch thickness of rind. The edges of the rind may be decorated with a vegetable notcher. Place the combined fruits in the watermelon boat and chill 1 hour before serving.

Pie from Limburg. The best known speciality of Limburg is the 'vlaai,' a pie filled with fruit. Businessmen from the North of Holland who have to go on business trips to Limburg always bring back a 'vlaai' for their wife and children.

Dumkes

Small thumbs

2½ cups sifted all purpose flour
1½ cups sugar
⅓ cup finely chopped hazelnuts
   (filbert nuts)
1 teaspoon cinnamon
1 teaspoon powdered anise
3 eggs, lightly beaten

In a bowl, combine the flour, sugar, hazelnuts, cinnamon and anise. Add the beaten eggs and mix until all the ingredients are thoroughly blended. Pinch off pieces of dough and form cookies the shape of your thumb. Place on a buttered cookie sheet and bake in a preheated 375° oven for 20 to 25 minutes or until golden brown. Cool the cookies on wire racks. In the Dutch province of Friesland, "dumkes" are served with tea.

Appelbollen

Apple balls

8 servings

2 cups sifted all purpose flour
½ teaspoon salt
10 tablespoons butter
4 to 5 tablespoons cold water
8 sweet apples, peeled and
   cored
2 tablespoons sugar
2 teaspoons cinnamon
¼ cup raisins
2 tablespoons butter
1 egg, lightly beaten

Combine the flour and salt in a bowl. Cut the butter into the flour with a pastry blender or 2 knives until the mixture resembles coarse meal. Stir the water in with a fork. Add only as much as is necessary to make the dough stick together. Wrap the dough in waxed paper and refrigerate for 1 hour. Roll the dough into a rectangle on a floured board. Cut into 8 squares each large enough to enclose an apple. Center an apple on each square of pastry. Combine the sugar, cinnamon and raisins and stuff each apple with a little of the mixture. Dot the top with butter and gather the pastry up around the apple. Pinch the edges together to seal. Brush each apple ball with beaten egg. Place on a buttered baking sheet and bake in a preheated 375° oven for 25 minutes or until golden brown.

Weesper moppen

Almond cookies

40 to 45 cookies

1½ cups finely ground almonds
1¼ cups sugar
2 eggs
   Grated rind of 1 lemon

In a bowl, blend all the ingredients together thoroughly. Chill the dough in the refrigerator for about 2 hours. Shape the dough into a cylinder 1½ inches in diameter and cut into ¼ inch thick slices. Butter a cookie tin and cover with baking paper. Butter the paper very generously. Place the cookies well apart on the baking paper. Let them stand 1 hour so the dough will dry out a little. Bake the cookies in a preheated 350° oven for 20 minutes or until golden brown. Carefully remove them from the baking paper and cool on wire racks.

Limburgse vlaai

Pie from Limburg

1 package dry yeast
½ cup lukewarm milk
2½ cups flour
¼ teaspoon salt
3 tablespoons melted butter
1 egg, lightly beaten
¼ cup sugar

Sprinkle the yeast over the lukewarm milk and stir to dissolve. Combine the flour and salt in a bowl and make a well in the center. Add the yeast mixture, melted butter, egg and sugar and knead into a smooth and elastic dough. Place the dough in an oiled bowl, cover with a damp cloth and let rise in a warm spot for 1 hour. Punch the dough down, cover and let rise another 30 minutes. Roll the dough out to a ¼ inch thickness. Line the bottom and sides of a buttered pie tin with the dough and prick with a fork. Cover with a damp cloth and let rise 30 minutes. Bake in a preheated 400° oven for 15 to 20 minutes or until golden brown. Remove the pastry from the pan and cool on a wire rack. Fill the pie with apricots, cherries or stewed fruits.

Boules Ardennaises

Ardenne balls

> 1 package dry yeast
> ¼ cup lukewarm water
> 1 (8 ounce) package cream
> cheese, softened
> 13 tablespoons butter, softened
> 2½ cups sifted all purpose flour
> 3 eggs, separated
> Oil for deep frying
> Powdered sugar

Sprinkle the yeast over the
water and stir to dissolve. In the
bowl of an electric mixer, beat
the cream cheese and butter
until smooth and fluffy. Add the
flour and egg yolks alternately
to make a thick batter. Beat the
egg whites until stiff. Add the
yeast mixture and ¼ of the egg
whites to the flour mixture and
combine thoroughly. Carefully
fold in the remaining egg
whites. Let the batter rise in a
warm place for 30 minutes. Heat
the oil for deep frying. Drop the
batter by spoonfuls into the hot
oil and fry 4 or 5 minutes or
until the balls are puffy and
brown. Drain on paper towels.
Sprinkle with powdered sugar
and serve.

Gateau Ardennais

Ardenne potato cake

> ½ pound potatoes
> 3 tablespoons flour
> 1 cup confectioners' sugar
> 3 eggs, separated

Boil the potatoes until tender.
Drain and mash. Blend in the
rice flour, confectioners' sugar
and egg yolks until the
ingredients are thoroughly
combined. Beat the egg whites
until stiff and carefully fold
them into the potato mixture.
Shape the mixture into a cone
and place on a buttered baking
sheet. Bake in a preheated 400°
oven for 45 minutes to 1 hour.
Serve cold with applesauce.

Kempense
pruimetaartjes

Prune tarts from the Campine

2 tarts

For the pastry:
> 2 packages dry yeast
> 1 cup lukewarm milk
> 5 cups flour
> ½ teaspoon salt
> 6 tablespoons melted butter
> ½ cup sugar
> ½ teaspoon cinnamon
> 2 eggs, lightly beaten

For the filling:
> ½ pound dried pitted prunes,
> soaked overnight in water
> to cover
> ½ cup brown sugar
> 1 teaspoon cinnamon
> 1 egg, lightly beaten
> 2 tablespoons sugar

Prepare the pastry as described
in the recipe for Pie from
Limburg adding the
cinnamon when the butter is
added. Let the dough rise as
directed there. Cook the prunes,
covered, in their soaking water
with the brown sugar and
cinnamon for 30 minutes or
until tender. Drain and force the
prunes through a sieve. Divide
the pastry in half and roll each
half out to a ¼ inch thickness.
Line the bottom and sides of
2 buttered pie tins with the
pastry and prick with a fork.
Brush each tart with beaten egg
and let stand 30 minutes. Spread
the cakes with the prune mixture
and sprinkle with sugar. Bake in
a preheated 400° oven for
25 minutes. Cool the tarts on
wire racks.

Hazelnut cake

Hazelnoottaart

Hazelnut cake

      4 eggs, separated
    ¾ cup sugar
    1½ cups ground hazelnuts
      1 cup self-rising flour
    ⅔ cup confectioners' sugar
      1 tablespoon water
    ½ teaspoon vanilla
    ½ cup hazelnuts
            (filbert nuts)

Beat the egg yolks with ½ cup sugar until the mixture is very thick. Fold in the ground hazelnuts and flour. Beat the egg whites until soft peaks form. Add the remaining ¼ cup sugar and beat until stiff. Mix ⅓ of the egg whites into the batter until thoroughly combined. Fold in the remainder carefully. Place the batter, which will be quite stiff, in a well buttered and floured 8 inch spring form cake tin or other cake pan with 1½ inch sides. Bake in a preheated 350° oven for 40 to 45 minutes or until the cake tests done. Cool 5 minutes in the pan then remove to a wire rack. Mix together the confectioners' sugar, water and vanilla until smooth. Ice the top of the cake with the sugar mixture and decorate with hazelnuts.

Pistachios are light apple-green colored nuts in a beige-brown shell which bursts open when roasted. Most pistachios come from Syria. They are used unsalted for ice cream and pastry; when lightly salted they are served as appetizers with the aperitif.

Date rolls stuffed with nuts.

Glida fistoor halabi

Ice cream with pistachio nuts

10 servings

6 *eggs, separated*
¾ *cup sugar*
 Pinch of salt
2 *cups shelled pistachios*
2 *cups heavy cream*
 Few drops green food coloring
 Shelled pistachios for garnish (optional)

Beat the egg yolks with 6 tablespoons sugar and a pinch of salt until very thick and lemon colored. Do not underbeat. Fold in the pistachio nuts. Beat the egg whites until soft peaks form. Add 2 tablespoons sugar and continue beating until stiff. Stir ⅓ of the egg whites into the yolk mixture and carefully fold in the remainder. Beat the cream until it thickens slightly. Add the remaining ¼ cup sugar and beat until stiff. Fold the cream and food coloring into the egg mixture gently but very thoroughly. Spoon into individual serving dishes, garnish with pistachios and freeze 6 hours before serving. Alternatively, you may transfer the mixture to a large plastic container. Cover tightly and freeze overnight until firm.

Mishlahat Haneger

Date rolls stuffed with nuts

40 servings

2 *egg yolks*
2 *tablespoons whipping cream*
1 *cup milk*
5 *tablespoons sugar*
1 *tablespoon almond essence*
 Green food coloring
7 *tablespoons butter*
5 *tablespoons flour*
1 *cup ground roasted almonds*
80 *dates*
2 *pounds filbert nuts*
80 *half almonds*

Beat the egg yolks lightly with the cream and leave to one side. Pour the milk into a saucepan. Add the sugar, almond essence and a few drops of food coloring. The mixture should be light green in color. Bring to boiling point. In the meantime, heat the butter and stir in the flour. Cook over low heat for 1 minute but do not allow the flour to turn brown. Add the boiling milk mixture gradually, stirring constantly to form a smooth sauce. Add the egg yolks and cream. Stir in the ground almonds. Place the mixture in the refrigerator for 4 hours. It will become a firm dough. Remove the pits from the dates and stuff each date with 2 or 3 whole filberts. Roll the dough into a rectangle and cut into 80 strips 2½ inches long and ½ inch wide. Wrap the strips lengthwise around the stuffed dates. Decorate each date with ½ almond. Serve in portions of two for dessert or with Turkish coffee or liqueurs.

Sholleh zard

Yellow rice

8 servings

9 *cups water*
2 *cups rice*
2 *drops yellow food coloring*
2 *tablespoons butter*
1 *cup rosewater*
2 *cups sugar*
 Pinch of saffron soaked in 1 teaspoon water
1 *teaspoon cinnamon*
½ *teaspoon cardamom*
¼ *cup slivered almonds*

Bring 6 cups water to a boil. Add rice and stir once with a fork. Lower the heat, cover and simmer 30 minutes until the rice has absorbed most of the liquid. Heat the remaining water and add to the rice. Stir in the food coloring and butter and simmer 2 hours, stirring frequently. Add rosewater, sugar, saffron, cinnamon and cardamom and simmer 5 more minutes. Stir in the almonds and remove from the heat. Pour into a serving dish and let cool to room temperature before serving.

Ugat pereg

Pastry with poppy seeds

8 to 10 servings

Pastry:
1 *package dry yeast*
¼ *cup lukewarm water*
1 *tablespoon sugar*
1 *teaspoon salt*
3 *cups flour*
2 *eggs, lightly beaten*
¾ *cup butter, melted*

Filling:
¾ *cup poppy seeds*
⅓ *cup water*
⅓ *cup sugar*
1 *teaspoon vanilla*
2 *tablespoons fruit preserves*

Pastry: Dissolve the yeast in water and add the sugar and salt. Place the flour in a bowl and add the eggs, butter and yeast mixture. Knead to form a smooth elastic dough and set in a warm place until doubled in bulk.
Filling: Place the poppy seeds, water and sugar in a pan and cook over medium heat until the mixture has thickened slightly. Add the vanilla and preserves. Roll the pastry into a rectangle ¼ inch thick. Spread with the filling and roll up. Bake in a preheated 350° oven for 45 minutes.

Rizogalo

Rice pudding

4 servings

2½ *cups milk*
  1 *teaspoon grated lemon rind*
½ *cup raw rice*
½ *cup sugar*
  2 *egg yolks*
  1 *tablespoon milk*

Heat 2½ cups milk in a
saucepan. Add the lemon rind
and bring to a boil. Stir in the
rice and cook for 5 minutes,
stirring frequently. Add the
sugar and stir until dissolved.
Cook over a very low heat until
the rice is tender. Remove from
heat. Beat the egg yolks with the
remaining milk and stir into the
rice mixture. Return to the heat
and cook 2 minutes without
letting it boil. Pour into a
heatproof serving dish. Let cool
to room temperature and then
chill in the refrigerator.

Loukoumades

Honey puffs

2½ *cups flour*
½ *teaspoon salt*
½ *package dry yeast*
  1 *cup lukewarm water*
    Oil for deep frying
½ *cup honey*
¾ *cup sugar*
1¾ *cups water*
  2 *teaspoons lemon juice*
  2 *teaspoons cinnamon*

Sift the flour and salt together
into a bowl. Sprinkle the yeast
over the lukewarm water and
stir to dissolve. Add the yeast
mixture to the flour and beat or
knead 5 minutes until the dough
is smooth and elastic. Cover the
bowl with a damp cloth and let
rise 1 hour or until the dough
has doubled in bulk. Heat the
oil for deep frying. Pinch off
small pieces of dough and fry in
the hot oil for about 3 minutes
until golden brown. Drain on
paper towels and keep warm. In
a saucepan, combine the honey,
sugar, water and lemon juice and
bring to a boil. Cook, stirring,
until the sugar dissolves and the
mixture is syrupy. Pour over the
hot puffs and sprinkle with
cinnamon.

Kourabiedes

Almond cakes

  1 *cup butter*
½ *cup sugar*
  1 *egg yolk*
  2 *cups flour*
  1 *teaspoon baking powder*
    Pinch of salt
  1 *cup finely ground almonds*
½ *teaspoon almond extract*
    Orange flower water or rose
    water (optional)
    Powdered sugar

Beat the butter until creamy.
Add the sugar and continue
beating until the mixture is light
and fluffy. Beat in the egg yolk.
Sift together the flour, baking
powder and salt. Gradually beat
the flour mixture, almonds and
almond extract into the butter
mixture. Unless you have a very
strong mixer, you will probably
have to beat in the last of the
flour and almonds by hand.
Knead the dough 5 minutes.
Roll pieces of the dough into
small egg shaped balls and place
on buttered baking sheets. Bake
in a 350° oven 25 minutes.
Remove to a wire rack and let
cool a few minutes. Sprinkle
with orange flower water or
rosewater if desired and roll in
powdered sugar.

Gâteau aux raisins

Gâteau aux raisins

Grape cake

8 servings

 2 cups water
 8 tablespoons butter cut into
    small pieces
 ½ teaspoon salt
 2 tablespoons sugar
 2 cups all purpose flour
 8 eggs

Filling:
 1 cup sugar
 5 egg yolks
 ¾ cup flour
 1 cup milk, simmering
 1 cup heavy cream, simmering
 1 teaspoon vanilla extract
 1 small bunch white grapes
 1 small bunch black grapes

Place water, butter, salt and
sugar in a heavy saucepan.
Adjust the heat so that the butter
has completely melted when the
water boils. Remove the pan
from the heat as soon as the
water boils. Add the flour all
at once and stir vigorously.
Return the pan to a moderate
heat for two minutes until the
dough can be formed into a ball.
Remove the pan from the heat
and add the eggs one at a time.
Beat each egg well into the
mixture before adding the next
egg. Butter and flour three
cookie sheets and draw three
9 inch circles in the flour using
a plate as a guide. Spread the
mixture within the circles as
smoothly as possible. Bake 20
minutes in a 350 degree oven.
Turn the oven off and leave
the layers in the oven for another
five minutes. Remove and allow

Kougelhopf

the layers to cool. In the meantime, prepare the custard. Beat the sugar and eggs together until thick and lemon colored. Beat in the flour. Stir in the combined simmering milk and cream. Place in a saucepan over moderate heat and stir continuously with a wire whisk to form a thick custard. Add the vanilla and cool the custard.

To assemble the cake, place one third of the firm, cool custard on the bottom layer and cover with a layer of white and black grapes. Continue with the second layer and arrange the grapes attractively on the top layer. Allow the cake to stand for 1 hour before cutting.

Kougelhopf

Raisin cake

10 to 12 servings

1 cup butter
5 eggs
2⅓ cups all purpose flour, sifted
½ teaspoon salt
2 tablespoons sugar
2 tablespoons lukewarm water
1 package dry yeast
1 teaspoon vanilla
1 teaspoon lemon extract
1 cup raisins
½ cup slivered almonds
2 tablespoons powdered sugar

Beat the butter in a bowl until light and fluffy. Add the eggs one at a time and beat well. Add the flour, salt and sugar beating constantly. Dissolve the yeast in the water and beat into the dough along with the vanilla and lemon extract. Stir in the raisins. Butter a 10″ tube pan and sprinkle the bottom with the almonds. Turn the dough into the pan, distributing it evenly. Cover and let rise until the dough almost reaches the top of the pan. Bake in a 350° oven for 45 minutes. Let the kougelhof cool in the pan for 20 minutes. Turn it out and sprinkle the top with powdered sugar. Cool thoroughly before slicing.

Gâteau Saint-Honoré

Gateau Saint-Honoré

8 servings

Cream puff base:
1 cup water
¼ teaspoon salt
3 tablespoons sugar
4 tablespoons butter
1 cup sifted all purpose flour
4 eggs

Filling:
1½ cups heavy cream
2 tablespoons sugar
1 teaspoon vanilla
½ cup apricot preserves, heated and strained
½ cup sliced almonds

Decoration:
3 tablespoons confectioners' sugar

Prepare the cream puff base following the directions in the recipe for Gougère.
Using two spoons, form the mixture into a 9 inch circle. Bake on a buttered and floured baking sheet in a 375° oven for 30 minutes. Remove from the oven. Cool and cut in half horizontally. Whip the cream until it is slightly thickened. Add the sugar and vanilla. Sandwich cream between the 2 layers of the gateau. Spread the almonds on a baking sheet. Toast almonds in a 350° oven for 8 minutes. Cool the almonds. Brush the top layer of the gateau with clear warm liquid from the strained apricot preserves. Sprinkle with toasted almonds. Dust with sifted confectioners sugar.

Tourte au fromage

Cheese cake

6 to 8 servings

2 egg yolks
1½ cups sugar
1 package (8 ounce) Philadelphia cream cheese, softened
½ cup butter, softened Grated rind of one lemon
1 teaspoon vanilla
1 cup sifted self-rising flour
3 egg whites, stiffly beaten
1 pint strawberries
1 tablespoon Grand Marnier or other orange liqueur

Beat the egg yolks until they thicken slightly. Add ½ cup of sugar and beat until thick and lemon colored. Add the cream cheese and butter alternately with the remaining sugar, beating constantly. Beat in the lemon rind and vanilla. Fold in the flour carefully until just combined. Stir in ⅓ of the egg whites and fold in the remainder. Place the batter in a well buttered and floured 8 inch spring form cake pan. Tap the pan on the counter a few times to settle the batter. Bake in a 350° oven for 1 hour or until the cake tests done. Let cool in the pan 15 minutes before removing to cool further on a wire rack. Slice the strawberries and sprinkle with Grand Marnier. When ready to serve, place the cake upside down on a serving platter and top with the strawberries.

Millar

Corn cake

6 servings

1 teaspoon butter
1 tablespoon flour
1¼ cups sugar
5 egg yolks
¾ cup sifted all purpose flour
2 cups milk, simmering
1 (12 ounce) can golden corn Rind from 1 orange, finely grated
Rind from 1 lemon, finely grated
1 teaspoon vanilla
5 egg whites

Butter and flour a 1½ quart soufflé dish or 9 inch cake tin. Beat 1¼ cups sugar and the egg yolks until very thick. Beat in the flour. Stir in simmering milk. Place in saucepan and heat until thickened into a custard. Add corn and grated orange rind, lemon rind and vanilla. Beat egg whites until they stand in soft peaks. Fold custard into egg whites. Place in the prepared dish and bake in a 375° oven for 25 minutes. Serve immediately.

Cerises à l'eau de vie

Cherries in brandy

3 pounds slightly unripe cherries
4 cups (1 quart) brandy
2 cups sugar
¼ cup water

Remove the stems from the
cherries. Put the cherries in glass
jars. Pour in the brandy. Put the
lids on the jars and leave for
6 weeks in a warm, preferably
sunny, place. Pour the brandy
from the cherries into a jug.
Combine sugar and water and
boil uncovered for 5 minutes.
Cool the syrup and add to the
brandy. Pour back over the
cherries. Close the jars again
and place in a warm place for
14 days before serving. Serve
with ice cream.

Moka parfait

Bavarian coffee-cream

4 servings

1¼ cups milk
*½ cup whole dark roast coffee
beans or 1½ teaspoons
instant coffee*
3 egg yolks
⅓ cup sugar
⅓ cup water
1 package unflavored gelatin
1 teaspoon sugar
*1 tablespoon Kahlua or other
coffee liquer*
*1 cup heavy cream, partially
whipped*
Grated sweet chocolate

Scald the milk with the coffee
beans. Beat the egg yolks with
the sugar until very thick and
mousse-like. Strain the milk
and beat into the egg yolks.
Return the mixture to the pan
and cook, stirring constantly,
over low heat until the mixture
thickens. Allow the mixture to
cool for 10 minutes. Sprinkle the
gelatin over the water to soften.
Add 1 teaspoon sugar and place
over gentle heat, stirring to
melt the gelatin. Add the gelatin
and Kahlua to the cooled egg
mixture. Fold in the cream.
Pour into small individual molds
and refrigerate at least 3 hours.
Decorate with grated sweet
chocolate before serving.

Riz à l'impératrice

Empress rice

8 servings

¾ cup diced candied fruits
4 tablespoons Kirsch
2 cups milk
*1 vanilla bean, split or 1
teaspoon vanilla extract*
½ cup uncooked rice
½ cup sugar
*½ cup dried apricots, cooked
for 30 minutes then drained*
1 package unflavored gelatin
¼ cup water
1 teaspoon sugar
½ cup red currant jelly
*1¼ cups heavy cream, partially
whipped*

Combine the candied fruits and
Kirsch in a small bowl and let
stand while preparing the rice.
In a large saucepan, bring the
milk to a simmer with the vanilla
bean. Add the rice, stir and
simmer slowly until the rice is
tender. Remove from the heat,
discard the vanilla bean or add
vanilla extract if bean was not
used. Stir in the sugar. Add the
marinated fruits. Purée the
apricots in a blender and force
through a sieve to remove the
skins. Add to the rice. Sprinkle
the gelatin over the water to
soften. Add the 1 teaspoon sugar
and place over gentle heat,
stirring to melt the gelatin. Add it
to the rice and mix well. Set in
the refrigerator to cool, stirring
every 15 minutes to suspend the
fruits in the mixture. Oil a 1½
quart mold and place a circle
of wax paper on the bottom.
Melt the red currant jelly and
pour into the mold. Place in the
freezer a few minutes to set the
jelly. When the rice mixture has
started to set slightly, fold in
the cream and turn the mixture
into the mold. Cover with a
circle of oiled wax paper and
refrigerate overnight. Run a knife
around the edge of the mold
and invert the rice on a serving
plate.

Bayerischer Apfelstrudel

Bayerischer Apfelstrudel

Bavarian apple strudel

18 servings

  1 tablespoon oil
  1 egg
  ⅓ cup warm water
  ¼ teaspoon salt
1½ cups sifted flour
  ⅓ cup melted margarine or
    butter
  6 tablespoons fine dry bread
    crumbs
  8 cups thinly sliced, peeled and
    cored tart apples
  2 tablespoons dark rum
  3 tablespoons sugar
  ½ teaspoon cinnamon
  ¼ cup finely chopped almonds
  ¼ cup seedless raisins
    Confectioners' sugar or
    whipped cream, optional

Beat together oil, egg, water and salt; add flour while beating, until a firm dough which pulls away from bowl is formed. Knead several times until smooth and elastic. Cover; let stand 30 minutes. Cut with sharp knife into two equal parts. Roll out each piece on floured cloth to a 12″ × 18″ rectangle. Brush with melted margarine. Sprinkle evenly with bread crumbs. Spread 4 cups of the apples on each portion, lengthwise down the center of the dough. Sprinkle each with 1 tablespoon rum, 1½ tablespoons sugar, ¼ teaspoon cinnamon, 2 tablespoons almonds and 2 tablespoons raisins. Fold dough over apples on one side, then the other. Slide rolls onto greased baking sheet. Brush

Schwarzwälder Kirschtorte

Zwetschgendatschi

Zwetschgendatschi

with melted margarine. Bake in a
hot oven (400°) 45 minutes.
Cut each roll into 2″ slices.
Serve warm or cold sprinkled
with confectioners' sugar or with
whipped cream, if desired.

Fresh plum cake

One 9″ × 13″ cake

  2 *pounds fresh blue plums*
  1 *package dry yeast*
  1 *cup milk, lukewarm*
3½ *cups flour*
  1 *teaspoon salt*
  1 *cup sugar*
 ¼ *cup margarine or butter*
  1 *egg, slightly beaten*
  2 *tablespoons margarine or*
    butter

Wash and gently cut plums in
half, removing the pits. Sprinkle
yeast into ¼ cup of the milk.
Let stand until dissolved.
Mix flour, salt, and ⅓ cup of
the sugar in a large bowl. Stir
dissolved yeast, margarine, egg,
and remaining milk into flour.
Knead into a soft dough.
Let rise for 30–40 minutes in a
warm place. Punch down and
roll on a lightly floured board
into an oblong about 9″ × 13″.
Fit into a greased pan of that
size. Pinch edges to make a
slight edge around all sides.
Let rise for 20 minutes. Place
plums on top with cut side up.
Sprinkle with remaining sugar;
dot with margarine. Bake in a
moderate oven (350°) for
35–40 minutes. Slice and
serve warm.

Schwarzwälder Kirschtorte

Black forest cherry cake

One 8″ layer cake

½ cup margarine or butter
½ cup sugar
3 eggs
½ cup almonds, finely chopped in blender
1 (6 oz.) package semi-sweet chocolate pieces, chopped fine in blender
1 teaspoon vanilla
¾ cup sifted cake flour
1 teaspoon baking powder
½ teaspoon salt
1 cup heavy cream
2 tablespoons honey
½ cup Kirschwasser or ½ cup cherry brandy
2 (1 lb.) cans sour pitted cherries, well-drained
  Maraschino cherries

Cream together margarine and sugar until light and fluffy; add eggs one at a time, beating well after each addition. Beat in almonds, ¾ cup of the chopped chocolate, and vanilla. Sift together flour, baking powder and salt. Stir into butter mixture. Divide evenly between three greased, waxed-paper-lined and re-greased 8″ layer cake pans. Bake in a moderately hot oven (375°) about 20 minutes, or until edges start to pull away from sides of pan. Cool on cake rack about 10 minutes. Turn out; remove waxed paper. Cool cake layers on cake rack. Whip cream with honey until stiff. Place one cake layer on serving plate; sprinkle with one-third of the liquer; spread with one-third of the whipped cream; cover evenly with one-half of the sour cherries. Place second layer on top, pressing down slightly. Repeat as for first layer. Top with third layer, press down slightly, sprinkle with liquer, cover with whipped cream. Decorate top and sides with reserved ¼ cup chopped chocolate and Maraschino cherries. Chill well before serving.

Streuselkuchen

Streusel coffee cake

One 13″ × 9″ cake

1 package hot roll mix
¼ cup margarine or butter, melted
1 cup flour
1 cup sugar
2 teaspoons cinnamon
1 teaspoon grated lemon rind
½ cup margarine or butter

Prepare hot roll mix according to package directions. After first rising, knead and roll into large rectangle 13″ × 9″. Fit into a buttered pan of equal size. Brush top with melted margarine. Put in warm place until dough rises to double original size. Combine flour, sugar, cinnamon, and lemon rind. Cut in margarine with pastry blender or two knives. Spread over surface of buttered dough. Bake in moderate oven (350°) for 40–45 minutes or until browned.

Feiner Sahnekuchen

Delicate sour cream cake

One 9″ × 13″ × 2″ cake

1 (13¾ oz.) package hot roll mix
2 tablespoons soft margarine or butter
½ cup sugar
1 pint sour cream
4 tablespoons sugar
1 teaspoon vanilla

Prepare hot roll mix according to package directions, adding margarine and ½ cup sugar when adding the egg called for in package directions. Cover; allow to rise in a warm place until doubled in size, about 30–45 minutes. Knead lightly on a floured surface several times until dough is no longer sticky. Roll or press out with fingers to fit a buttered 9″ × 13″ × 2″ pan. Place in pan. Mix together sour cream, sugar and vanilla. Spread over surface of dough. Let rise in warm place until doubled, about 30–45 minutes. Bake in a moderate oven (350°) about 35–45 minutes or until edges are browned. Allow to cool at least 30 minutes before cutting into squares.

Bienenstich

"Bee sting" cake

One 15″ × 10″ × 1″ cake

> 1 package hot roll mix
> 1 cup margarine or butter
> 1 cup sugar
> 1 (6 oz.) package slivered
> almonds

Prepare hot roll mix according to package directions. After first rising, knead and roll into a large rectangle about 15″ × 10″. Place in a buttered pan of equal size. Put dough in a warm place and allow the dough to double in volume, about 20–30 minutes. Melt margarine. Pour ¼ cup over the surface of the dough. Add sugar to the rest of the margarine and beat until the sugar is dissolved. Mix in almonds. Spread mixture on top of buttered dough. Bake in a moderate oven (350°) for 35–40 minutes or until the top is lightly browned. Cool and cut in squares.

Prinzregententorte

Chocolate layer cake

One 8″ cake

> 1 (17-oz.) package pound
> cake mix
> ½ cup softened margarine or
> butter
> 1 (6-oz.) package semi-sweet
> chocolate pieces, melted
> 2 eggs, separated
> 1 cup sifted confectioners'
> sugar
> 3 squares unsweetened
> chocolate, melted

Prepare cake mix according to package directions. Bake as follows: Grease and line with waxed paper, grease again, two 8″ round cake pans. Pour ¾ cup (¹/₅ of the batter) into each pan, spreading evenly. Bake in moderate oven (350°) until golden brown and edges pull away from sides of pan, about 30 minutes. Remove from pan and carefully peel off paper. Cool on rack. Bake three more layers in this way.

Filling: Beat margarine into melted semi-sweet chocolate. Add egg yolks; beat until mixture is glossy and of spreading consistency. Spread filling between layers; press each layer down firmly. Cool until well set before frosting cake.

Frosting: Beat egg whites until foamy; beat in confectioners' sugar gradually, until well blended. Stir in melted unsweetened chocolate. Spread over top and sides of cake. Cool.

Berliner Pfannkuchen

Berliner Pfannkuchen

Berlin style jelly doughnuts

Makes 18–20

3½ cups flour
¼ cup sugar
1 teaspoon salt
1 package yeast
1 cup milk, lukewarm
2 tablespoons salad oil
1 egg, slightly beaten
2 teaspoons rum
1 egg white, slightly beaten
   Marmalade
   Oil or fat for deep frying
1 cup confectioners' sugar

Sift flour, sugar and salt. Soften yeast in ¼ cup of the warm milk. Stir in ¾ of flour mixture. Add oil, egg, and rum. Add remaining flour mixture. Work into soft dough. Cover and let rise in a warm place for 45 minutes to 1 hour. Punch down and roll out on floured board into ½″ thickness. Cut into 3″ rounds. Place 1 teaspoon of marmalade in center of each round. Brush edges with egg white. Pinch edges together to seal completely. Place balls on floured surface, smooth side up; let rise 20 minutes. Heat oil to 360°; fry doughnuts a few at a time until browned on one side then turn over (about 3–4 minutes on each side). Remove from oil with slotted spoon and drain on paper towels. Sprinkle with confectioners' sugar.

Granita di caffè con panna montata

Granita di caffè con panna montata

Coffee granita sundae

4 servings

$^1/_2$ *cup sugar*
$^1/_2$ *cup water*
   3 *tablespoons instant coffee*
$1^1/_2$ *cups ice and water*
$^1/_2$ *cup chocolate syrup*
$^1/_2$ *cup heavy cream, whipped*
$^1/_4$ *cup chopped nuts*
   4 *crisp sugar cookies*

Combine sugar and $^1/_2$ cup water in heavy 1-quart saucepan; bring to a boil over medium heat, stirring constantly. Stir in instant coffee. Add ice and water; stir until ice is melted. Pour into metal freezer tray. Place in freezer or freezing compartment. Freeze until almost solid, about 45 minutes. Break up mixture; place in large mixer bowl. Beat at low speed on electric mixer, until consistency of applesauce. Return to tray. Freeze one hour. Break up; beat again. Return to tray. Freeze until firm, about 1 hour. Scoop coffee granita into 4 sherbet glasses. Pour chocolate sauce over granita; top with whipped cream; sprinkle with nuts. Serve with sugar cookie.

Gelato di mandorla

Almond ice cream

2 quarts

> 1 *recipe vanilla ice*
>   *cream*
> 1 *cup almonds*
> $^1/_4$ *cup sugar*
> 1 *tablespoon almond extract*
> $^1/_2$ *teaspoon vanilla extract*

Prepare recipe for vanilla ice cream; freeze until firm but not hard. Toast almonds in a moderate oven (375°) until light golden brown. Remove from oven; cool. Chop almonds in blender until very fine. Combine ground almonds, sugar, almond extract, and vanilla extract; blend well. Break up vanilla mixture; place in large mixer bowl. Beat with electric mixer on high speed until double in volume. Return to trays; freeze until firm but not hard. Break up; beat again; freeze until firm but not hard. Break up; beat again. Stir in almond mixture; blend well. Freeze until firm.

Granita di limone

Lemon granita

1 quart

> 2 *cups sugar*
> 1 *cup water*
> 1 *cup lemon juice*
> 1 *cup ice and water*
> 1 *tablespoon finely*
>   *grated lemon rind*

Combine sugar and water in heavy 1-quart saucepan; bring to a boil over medium heat, stirring constantly. Cool to room temperature. Add lemon juice, ice and water, and lemon rind; stir until all ice is melted. Pour into two metal freezer trays; place in freezer or freezing compartment. Freeze until almost completely solid. Break up mixture; place in large mixer bowl. Beat at low speed on electric mixer until the consistency of applesauce. Return to trays; freeze one hour. Break up; beat again. Return to trays; freeze until firm, about 1 hour. Serve immediately as a meat or salad accompaniment, or as a dessert.

Gelato alla vaniglia

The Chinese were probably the first people to invent ices. It was not ice cream, but a kind of sherbet made of fruit mixed with snow. In order to be able to enjoy this refreshing delight in the Summer, they preserved Winter snow in air-tight isolated storage areas. No one can be sure of the exact date of the invention, but it was certainly thousands of years ago. The Greek writer Xenophon writes that 'ices' were eaten in Persia more than 400 years before Christ. When Alexander the Great rode into India more than 300 years before Christ, he saw snow from the mountains isolated and preserved in canals covered with oak tree branches and leaves.

The Romans brought ice from the mountains and packed it in straw and wool because the Emperor Nero liked his fruit juice ice-cold and filtered through snow. But the true art of freezing fruit juice in snow should not to be credited to the Romans but to the Chinese, Indians and Persians. The Arabians and later the Turks, who conquered the Middle East, acquired the art of ice-making from the Persians. In 1191 when the English king and crusader, Richard the Lion Heart, met the Turkish Sultan, Soliman, he was offered fruit sherbet. It seems that King Richard talked about this delicacy for the rest of his life. Italians learned to make ices in the Middle Ages from the Arabs.

Renaissance noblemen enjoyed the refreshing taste of fruit sherbet after the heavy meals at court. Ices were first introduced to France in 1533 by the Italian Bountalenti, one of the cook's assisting at the wedding of Caterina de Medici to the French dauphin. Almost one hundred years later the English tasted ices prepared by Mirra, the Italian cook of King Charles I. Thanks to the Sicilian Procopio, the common man could partake of the pleasure brought by ices. He opened the first ice parlour in Paris in 1670. It was an immediate success and within 6 years there were over 250 cafés in operation in Paris for the sale of Italian ices. The ices were still sorbets prepared according to the Arab-Persian-Chinese recipes: ice, fruit, and water. But Tortoni, owner of one of the Parisian ice parlours, created 'ice cream' in the last half of the 18th century. The Italian, Giovanni Bosio, was the first to sell ice cream in the United States. This began in the last half of the 19th century. Italian ices and ice cream are still considered to be the best in the world; and it makes no difference whether it be the creamy ice cream, or delicious sorbets, or even the heavenly 'granita', half frozen, crushed ice mixed with either coffee or lemon juice. Ice cream is eaten all over Italy but there are two places where the best ice cream in the world can be found: the restaurant

Pappagallo in Bologna (strawberry ice cream such as nowhere else!) and the restaurant Tito del Mole in Viareggio (all kinds of fruit are used: apples, pears, bananas, peaches, melon, etc.). At Tito del Mole, the center of the fruit is used to make ice cream, the ice cream is used to stuff the fruit, and then it is all frozen. The conception of fruit filled with ice cream piled up together with fruit leaves and blossoms and placed in a basket provides a cool sweet delight of which the Chinese, Persians, and Arabs never dreamed!

Vanilla ice cream

2 quarts

6 egg yolks
2 cups whole milk
2 cups heavy cream
1 cup sugar
1 teaspoon vanilla extract

Beat egg yolks until foamy. Combine milk, cream, and sugar in top of double boiler; heat until small bubbles form around sides of pan. Add small amount of cream mixture to egg yolks; then stir yolks into cream mixture in top of double boiler. Cook over simmering water, stirring constantly, until mixture thickens enough to lightly coat a metal spoon. Add vanilla. Strain; cool thoroughly. Pour into two deep metal freezer trays; cover with foil. Freeze until firm but not hard. Chill bowl and beater. Beat with electric mixer on high speed until double in volume. Return to trays; freeze until firm but not hard. Break up; beat again; freeze until firm but not hard. Repeat; freeze until firm about 2 hours.

Savoiardi

Ladyfingers

3 dozen

 4 *eggs, separated*
$^1/_8$ *teaspoon salt*
10 *tablespoons sugar*
$^1/_2$ *teaspoon vanilla*
$^1/_3$ *cup sifted flour*

Cut brown paper to fit two cookie sheets. Beat egg whites and salt until foamy. Add 2 tablespoons sugar; beat until soft peaks form; set aside. Beat egg yolks until thickened; gradually beat in remaining sugar and vanilla; beat until very thick and light lemon yellow in color. Sprinkle flour over egg yolk mixture; fold in flour carefully. Fold egg yolk mixture into egg whites. Pipe 3″ long 'finger' shapes on brown paper with pastry tube or spoon, 2″ apart. Bake in moderate oven (350°) 15 minutes or until deep golden brown. Slide paper from cookie sheet. Cool 2–3 minutes. Carefully remove ladyfingers from paper with sharp knife. Cool. Store in airtight container when dry.

Pane di spagna

Sponge cake

2–9″ layers

 6 *eggs, separated*
$^1/_2$ *teaspoon salt*
 1 *cup sugar*
 1 *tablespoon water*
 1 *cup sifted cake flour*
$1^1/_2$ *teaspoons baking powder*
 1 *teaspoon lemon rind*

Combine egg whites and salt; beat until they stand in soft peaks. Gradually beat in $^1/_4$ cup sugar. In another bowl, beat egg yolks until thick and foamy; slowly beat in remaining sugar and water. Sift together flour and baking powder; slowly add yolk mixture; stir in lemon rind. Fold egg whites into egg yolk mixture until well blended. Pour into 2 (9″) cake pans lined with lightly floured waxed paper. Bake in moderate oven (350°) 25–30 minutes or until cake springs back when lightly touched with finger. Allow to cool; then remove from pans and peel off waxed paper.

Cannoli alla siciliana

Sicilian rolls

10 rolls

Filling:
$1^1/_2$ *cups Ricotta cheese*
$^1/_4$ *cup chopped candied fruit*
 3 *tablespoons chopped pistachio nuts or almonds*
2–3 *tablespoons chopped semi-sweet chocolate morsels*
 3 *tablespoons sugar*
$^1/_4$ *teaspoon almond extract*

Rolls:
 1 *cup sifted flour*
$^2/_3$ *cup sugar*
$^1/_4$ *teaspoon salt*
$^1/_4$ *cup Marsala wine Salad oil*
 4 *Cannoli tubes or clean, unpainted broomstick pieces, 6″ long*

Combine Ricotta cheese, candied fruit, nuts, 2 tablespoons of the chocolate, sugar and almond extract; stir well. Chill. Sift together flour, sugar and salt. Stir in wine, kneading until firm and elastic. Add a drop or two of wine, if needed; do not allow to become sticky. Continue to knead on floured surface until dough becomes elastic. Place in lightly floured bowl; cover with a damp towel; let stand 2 hours. Roll out on lightly floured board to a rectangle, $22^1/_2$″ × 9″ × $^1/_8$″. Cut into 10 ($4^1/_2$″) squares. Wrap each square diagonally around a cannoli tube or broomstick piece. Moisten surfaces of points which will overlap with a drop of water; press gently to seal. Fry in deep hot fat (350°), 3 or 4 at a time, until golden brown. Drain on paper towel for about $^1/_2$ minute. Using tongs, carefully slip the tubes out of the rolls. Cool. Just before serving, fill with Ricotta filling. Garnish ends with chocolate.

'Light and airy like a summer's cloud' – Swedish whipped farina is a popular dessert, especially with youngsters.

Norwegian rice porridge

Klappgröt

Swedish whipped farina

6 servings

2½ cups water
  1 (6 ounce) can frozen
       concentrate for punch
  4 tablespoons farina

In a saucepan, combine water and punch concentrate; bring to a boil. Sprinkle farina into boiling mixture; stir vigorously. Simmer over low heat until farina is cooked, about 5 minutes. Pour mixture into 1½-quart bowl. Beat with an egg beater or hand electric mixer for about 1 minute at a time, at intervals of about 5 minutes, until pudding is fluffy and cool. Chill. Serve with milk or cream if desired.

Risgrynsgröt

Norwegian rice porridge

4 to 6 servings

  3 *cups cooked rice*
4½ *cups milk*
  1 *tablespoon margarine or*
     butter
⅛ *teaspoon salt*
2–3 *tablespoons sugar*

In a large heavy saucepan, combine well drained rice with milk. Cook, covered, over low heat until milk is absorbed; stir occasionally. Stir in margarine, salt and sugar. Chill. Serve with cream or apple compote.

Bärkräm

Swedish berry cream

6 to 8 servings

  1 *pint fresh strawberries,*
     raspberries, blueberries or
     gooseberries (mixture)
2½ *cups water*
  2 *tablespoons sugar*
  3 *tablespoons cornstarch*
  3 *tablespoons water*

Rinse berries. In a large saucepan, combine berries and water; simmer over medium heat 2 to 3 minutes. Stir in sugar. Blend cornstarch and water into a smooth paste. Add cornstarch to berries, stirring constantly. Bring mixture to a boil; cook 3 minutes. Chill.

Rödgröd med flöde

Norwegian fruit jelly with cream

4 servings

  1 *pint red currants*
  1 *pint raspberries*
  2 *cups water*
½ *cup sugar*
  1 *tablespoon cornstarch*
  2 *tablespoons water*
  1 *teaspoon vanilla extract*

In a large saucepan, rinse fruit. Combine fruit and water; simmer over medium heat about 10 minutes. Drain; stir in sugar. Blend cornstarch and water into a smooth paste. Add cornstarch to fruit, stirring constantly. Bring mixture to a boil; cook 3 minutes. Remove from heat and stir in vanilla. Sieve mixture, if desired. Chill. Serve with cream and decorate with blanched almonds, if desired.

Rabarberkräm

Swedish rhubarb cream

4 to 6 servings

  4 *cups rhubarb, peeled and cut*
     into 1½" pieces
  2 *cups water*
¼ *cup sugar*
  3 *tablespoons cornstarch*
  3 *tablespoons water*

In a large saucepan, combine rhubarb and water; cook over medium heat until tender. Stir in ¼ cup sugar and taste; add more sugar if desired. Blend cornstarch and water into a smooth paste. Add cornstarch to fruit, stirring constantly. Bring mixture to a boil; cook 3 minutes; cool. Chill well before serving.

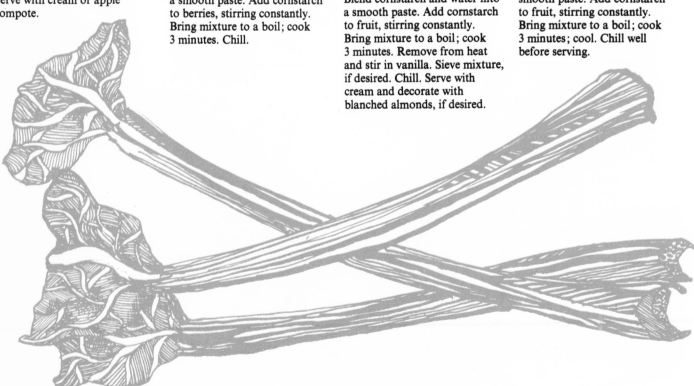

Karamellpudding

Norwegian caramelcream

6 to 8 servings

- *2 cups sugar*
- *3 tablespoons boiling water*
- *3 egg yolks*
- *2 tablespoons sugar*
- *1 cup milk*
- *1 teaspoon vanilla extract*
- *½ cup heavy cream*
- *3 cups applesauce*

In cast-iron skillet or heavy saucepan, melt sugar over very low heat; stir until completely melted and golden brown. Remove from heat. Carefully add boiling water to melted sugar; stir mixture until well blended. Combine egg yolks and 2 tablespoons of sugar, milk and vanilla in top of double-boiler. With wire-whip, beat mixture until foamy; cook until hot. Beating constantly, (do not use electric mixer) add melted sugar, now cooled to "soft-ball" stage to custard mixture. Continue to beat until mixture cooks. Remove from heat and continue beating until mixture has cooled completely. Beat cream and fold into cooled custard mixture. Chill. Serve cold over applesauce.

Aeblegröd

Danish applesauce

6 to 8 servings

- *2 pounds apples, peeled, cored and cubed*
- *¼ cup water*
- *2 tablespoons white wine*
- *1 tablespoon sugar*

In a large saucepan, cook apples with water until just tender; stir in wine. Mash, do not sieve. Add sugar and taste; add more sugar if desired. Chill.

Kan ikke lade vaere

Danish lemon delight

12 servings

- *10 eggs, separated*
- *1 cup sugar*
- *1 envelope unflavored gelatin*
- *½ cup water*
- *½ cup lemon juice*

Beat egg yolks and sugar together with electric mixer until well blended. Sprinkle gelatin over water in small saucepan. Place saucepan over low heat. Cook until gelatin is melted about 2 to 3 minutes. Let cool slightly, then beat gradually into egg yolk mixture. Beat in the lemon juice. In a large bowl, beat egg whites until stiff; fold into yolk mixture. Pour into a glass bowl. Chill until set.

Vaniljsås

Swedish custard

4 to 6 servings

- *3 egg yolks*
- *¼ cup sugar*
- *1½ cups heavy cream*
- *1 teaspoon vanilla extract*

In top of double boiler over boiling water, beat egg yolks, sugar, 1 cup heavy cream and vanilla. Cook until thick, beating constantly. Remove from heat; stir vigorously until the custard is cool. Whip remaining half cup of cream; fold into custard. Chill.

*The pancake is a Swedish spe-
cialty, the perfect dessert on a
chilling winter's day.*

Swedish crisp pancakes

Ugnspannkaka

Swedish baked pancake

8 to 10 servings

2	eggs
2½	cups milk
½	teaspoon salt
2	teaspoons sugar
1½	cups sifted flour

In a medium bowl, beat eggs
with 1 cup of the milk until well
blended. Stir in salt, sugar and
flour to make a smooth batter.
Stir in remainder of milk; blend
until smooth. Set batter aside
for 10 minutes. Butter a
12″ × 8″ × 2″ baking dish. Stir
batter and pour into prepared
pan. Bake in a hot oven (400°)
for 30 minutes or until pancake
is golden brown and puffy.
Serve immediately with jam or
fruit purée.

March 19th is the feast of St.Joseph, celebrated especially in Valencia with fireworks and sweet treats. St. Joseph is a very popular saint *with Spanish housewives. They honor him as the self-denying, careful, and faithful spouse.*

Flan

Crema de San José

Vanilla custard

6 servings

1⅔ cups sugar
4 cups milk
   Grated rind of 1 orange
1 teaspoon vanilla
4 eggs, lightly beaten

Melt ⅔ cup of sugar in a small saucepan and cook until it is a rich brown color. Move the pan constantly and watch carefully so that the sugar does not burn. Immediately pour the caramel into 6 individual 1 cup molds. In a large saucepan, bring the milk to simmering point. Add the remaining sugar and orange rind and simmer 5 minutes. Remove from the heat and stir in the vanilla. Let the milk cool several minutes then beat it into the eggs. Fill the caramelized molds with the custard and place in a larger pan of cold water. Bake in a preheated 350° oven for 35 to 40 minutes or until the custard is set and lightly browned on top. Chill 4 hours in the refrigerator. Unmold the custard on individual serving plates when ready to serve.

St. Joseph's custard

6 servings

4 egg yolks
½ cup sugar
3 tablespoons cornstarch
4 cups milk
1 cinnamon stick
   Peel of 1 lemon
¼ cup sugar

Beat the egg yolks and sugar together in a deep bowl. Dissolve the cornstarch in ½ cup cold milk. Add the cinnamon stick and lemon peel to the remaining milk and bring to simmering point. Strain the hot milk into the bowl with the egg yolks and sugar. Add the cold milk mixture immediately and stir to combine well. Return the mixture to the saucepan and place over low heat. Stir the custard constantly until it almost comes to a boil. Do not let it boil or it will separate. Remove from the heat and pour into a 9 or 10 inch pie plate. Chill for 4 hours until firm. Sprinkle remaining ¼ cup sugar to form a thin layer on top of the custard. Place under a preheated broiler for 5 minutes. The sugar layer will caramalize and harden Allow the custard to stand 5 minutes before serving. In Spain, this delicious dessert is sometimes served with whipped cream and ladyfingers or small cookies.

Pudim de amêndoas e ovos

Almond and egg cake

2 cups freshly ground almonds
1½ cups sugar
8 egg yolks
2 tablespoons all purpose flour
4 egg whites
⅛ teaspoon salt
Powdered sugar
Cinnamon for topping

Butter and flour two 9-inch cake tins. Combine almonds and sugar. Stir in egg yolks and flour. Beat the egg whites with the salt until stiff and fold evenly into the mixture. Turn the mixture into the cake tins and bake for 30 to 45 minutes until the cake shrinks from the sides of the pans. Cool cake in the pans for at least 15 minutes. Turn out of the pans and sprinkle with powdered sugar and cinnamon. This is good served as a coffee cake or iced with a lemon icing and served as a dessert.

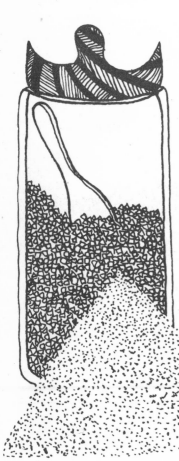

Crema de naranja

Orange cream

4 servings

2 cups milk
⅔ cup sugar
2 egg yolks
Grated rind of 1 orange
6 egg whites

Place the milk, sugar, egg yolks and grated orange rind in a saucepan. Heat the mixture, stirring constantly, until it has thickened slightly. Beat the egg whites and fold very carefully into the yolk mixture. Return to the heat and stir gently with a wooden spoon until bubbling. Let cool completely and serve in individual glass serving dishes.

Crema o leche frita

Fried custard squares

6 servings

½ cup butter
1¾ cups flour
2 cups milk
1 cup sugar
1 teaspoon cinnamon
1 teaspoon grated lemon or orange rind
4 eggs, separated
1 cup fine dry breadcrumbs
Oil for deep frying

Melt the butter in a saucepan, add 1¼ cups of the sifted flour and blend until smooth. Stir in the milk, ½ cup of the sugar, cinnamon, and lemon rind. Cook over low heat, stirring constantly until the mixture forms a very thick paste and leaves the sides of the pan. Add the egg yolks to the hot mixture one at a time, beating well after each addition. Spread the mixture in a 9 inch square pan which has been lined with wax paper. Chill in the refrigerator for 1 hour. When cold, turn out onto a floured board, remove the wax paper and cut into 1½ inch squares with a wet knife. Dip the squares in the remaining flour, then in the beaten egg whites and finally in the breadcrumbs. Fry for 2 to 3 minutes in hot oil. Drain on paper towels. Dip in remaining ½ cup sugar and serve hot. May be served freshly fried without dipping in sugar, accompanied by a thin sauce made by melting apricot or other preserves.

Bolo de amêndoras

Almond cake

½ pound ground almonds
1 cup sugar
1 cup butter, softened
1 egg, lightly beaten
2 cups flour
   Grated rind of 1 lemon
1 teaspoon cinnamon
1 teaspoon butter
1 teaspoon flour
1 egg, lightly beaten,
   for glazing
¼ cup sifted powdered sugar

Place the almonds, sugar,
butter, egg, flour, lemon rind
and cinnamon in a large bowl.
Knead the ingredients to form
a soft dough. Butter a round
9 inch cake tin and sprinkle
with flour. Place the dough in
the cake tin and brush the top
with beaten egg. Bake in a
375° oven for 30 minutes.
When it tests done, remove the
cake from the pan and allow
it to cool on a wire rack.
Sprinkle with powdered sugar
before serving.

Morgado de figo

Almond and fig cakes

1 cup water
2 ounces (2 squares)
   unsweetened baking
   chocolate
2 cups sugar
1 tablespoon cinnamon
1 teaspoon ground anise
   Grated rind of 1 lemon
1 pound dried figs, finely
   chopped
1 pound blanched almonds,
   toasted and finely chopped

Combine the water, chocolate,
sugar, cinnamon, anise and
lemon rind in a large pan Bring
to a boil, stirring constantly.
Add the figs and almonds and
simmer 5 minutes, stirring
frequently. Remove from the
heat and refrigerate until the
mixture is cold. Oil a baking
sheet very generously. Form
rounded tablespoons of the
mixture into cakes about ⅛ inch
thick and place on the baking
sheet. Bake in a 450° oven about
5 minutes or until the cakes
begin to brown. Let cool 5
minutes then remove from the
baking sheet with a metal
spatula.

Lérias de Amarante

Almond cakes from Amarante

6 servings

3 cups shelled and blanched
   almonds, ground
2 cups sugar
¾ cup flour
6 tablespoons water
   Powdered sugar

Blend together the almonds,
sugar and flour. Add the water
and knead to form a smooth
dough. Roll out ¼ inch thick
and cut into 2½ inch cookies.
Place on a very well-oiled
cookie sheet. Bake in a
preheated 350° oven for 10 to 12
minutes until lightly browned.
Remove from the cookie sheet
immediately and sprinkle with
powdered sugar while still hot.
Cool before serving.

Torta de almendras

Almond cake

6 servings

1 teaspoon butter
1 tablespoon flour
½ cup sugar
½ cup ground almonds
¼ teaspoon cinnamon
1½ tablespoons flour
4 eggs, separated
1 tablespoon brandy
2 tablespoons chopped glacéed
   cherries

Butter and flour an 8 or 9 inch
cake tin. Stir together the sugar,
almonds, cinnamon and flour.
Add egg yolks, brandy and
chopped cherries. Combine well.
Beat the egg whites until stiff
and fold them into the yolk
mixture. Transfer to the
prepared cake tin. Bake in a
preheated 325° oven for 30
minutes until the cake tests done.
Let the cake cool in the tin for
15 minutes before unmolding.
It will sink slightly as it cools.
This is a very light, excellent
cake which is best eaten on the
day it is made.

Fritters Ampurdán style

Buñuelos del Ampurdán

Fritters Ampurdán style

 1 *package dry yeast*
 ¼ *cup lukewarm milk*
 3 *cups flour*
 3 *eggs*
 ¾ *cup sugar*
    Grated rind of 1 lemon
 2 *teaspoons ground anise*
 2 *teaspoons ground coriander*
 1 *teaspoon ground cinnamon*
 ½ *teaspoon salt*
 3 *tablespoons melted butter*
    Oil for deep frying
    Powdered sugar

Sprinkle the yeast over the lukewarm milk and stir to dissolve. Beat in ½ cup of the flour and knead until smooth. Cover with a cloth and let rise in a warm place for 1 hour or until the mixture doubles in bulk. Beat the eggs in the bowl of an electric mixer and add the sugar, lemon rind, anise, coriander, cinnamon, salt and melted butter. Add the yeast mixture and beat until smooth. Sprinkle in the remaining flour, ½ cup at a time and beat well after each addition. Turn the dough out on a well floured board and knead until smooth and elastic. Place in an oiled bowl, cover tightly with plastic wrap and set aside in a warm place for 8 hours. Heat the oil for deep frying. Roll the dough out ⅜ inch thick on a floured board. Cut rounds using a doughnut cutter and deep fry 3 to 4 minutes until golden brown. Drain on paper towels and roll in powdered sugar. Serve warm.

Index by Type of Dish

309

Alphabetical Index